PANEL DATA ECONOMETRICS: FUTURE DIRECTIONS

Papers in Honour of Professor Pietro Balestra

CONTRIBUTIONS
TO
ECONOMIC ANALYSIS

244

ELSEVIER
Amsterdam – Lausanne – New York – Oxford – Shannon – Singapore – Tokyo

PANEL DATA ECONOMETRICS: FUTURE DIRECTIONS

PAPERS IN HONOUR OF PROFESSOR PIETRO BALESTRA

Edited by

Jaya KRISHNAKUMAR
Elvezio RONCHETTI
University of Geneva, Geneva, Switzerland

ELSEVIER
Amsterdam – Lausanne – New York – Oxford – Shannon – Singapore – Tokyo

ELSEVIER B.V.
Sara Burgerhartstraat 25
P.O. Box 211, 1000 AE Amsterdam, The Netherlands

First edition 2000
Second impression 2003

Library of Congress Cataloging in Publication Data
A catalog record from the Library of Congress has been applied for.

British Library Cataloguing in Publication Data
A catalogue record from the British Library has been applied for.

ISBN: 0 444 50237 8

♾ The paper used in this publication meets the requirements of ANSI/NISO Z39.48-1992 (Permanence of Paper).
Printed in The Netherlands.

INTRODUCTION TO THE SERIES

This series consists of a number of hitherto unpublished studies, which are introduced by the editors in the belief that they represent fresh contributions to economic science.

The term 'economic analysis' as used in the title of the series has been adopted because it covers both the activities of the theoretical economist and the research worker.

Although the analytical methods used by the various contributors are not the same, they are nevertheless conditioned by the common origin of their studies, namely theoretical problems encountered in practical research. Since for this reason, business cycle research and national accounting, research work on behalf of economic policy, and problems of planning are the main sources of the subjects dealt with, they necessarily determine the manner of approach adopted by the authors. Their methods tend to be 'practical' in the sense of not being too far remote from application to actual economic conditions. In addition they are quantitative.

It is the hope of the editors that the publication of these studies will help to stimulate the exchange of scientific information and to reinforce international cooperation in the field of economics.

The Editors

Preface

We are proud to present this book honouring the distinguished career of Professor Pietro Balestra, on behalf of all his friends, colleagues and students. As it is going to the press, we feel happy that it has turned out to be not only a valuable collection of papers at par with the level of achievement of Pietro Balestra but also a work that unfolds directions for future research in panel data econometrics. We hope that this volume would serve as a reference book for researchers, practitioners and decision makers who are involved with panel data analysis in one way or the other.

The contributions of this book have been made by several leading experts working in the field of panel data and cover a wide range of topics, both theoretical and applied. Areas of application of panel data modelling have only been increasing over the past years and there is no doubt that the range is going to expand further. We have divided the applied papers of this book into different fields thus showing their variety and opening up the horizon for researchers in these and other fields. The reader will notice that they all have a substantial methodological content which is indispensable for their analysis of the economic, social or other phenomena under consideration. We have such diversified areas of study as macroeconomics (Nerlove; Maddala, Wu and Liu; Haque, Pesaran and Sharma), social economics (Abul Naga and Krishnakumar; Antille and Silber), insurance/finance (Gourieroux and Jasiak; Sevestre), and energy economics (Carlevaro and Bertholet).

As a second part, we present papers that deal more with theoretical issues such as specification problems (Hsiao and Sun), unit root tests and aggregation of individual series (Hornok and Mátyás), heteroscedasticity tests for panel data models (Holly and Gardiol) and non-parametric techniques (Gourieroux, Monfort and Tenreiro).

The final part contains papers that are directly related to and elaborate on Balestra's work (Baltagi; Baranzini; Pasinetti).

At the end of such a venture, there are always important people to thank without whose help we would not have been able to complete the book successfully. First of all, we thank all the authors for readily accepting to contribute to this volume and for complying with our requirements of producing papers fitting into a unique theme. Furthermore, we owe it to them to have kept the matter confidential until the release of the book so that the intended effect of surprise to Pietro is full!

Our sincere thanks also go to the Director of our Department, Professor Fabrizio Carlevaro who kindly accepted that we make use of the Department infrastructure for the editing of the book. The typing of the book was carried out by Caroline Schneeberger along with the precious help of Andi Kabili for the competent processing and standardization of all the different input files. We are very grateful to both of them for their patience and hard work. A special word of appreciation goes to Andi for agreeing to assist us in this project in spite of his own research deadlines. We also benefitted from the able supervision of Professor Manfred Gilli regarding the handling of the software. Support from Fabrizio Quirighetti and Eva Cantoni in the initial stage of the typing process is also gratefully acknowledged. Simona Cain of the University of Southern Switzerland has been particularly helpful in putting together biographical information. Last but not the least, we would like to thank Sabine Plantevin of Elsevier Science for her kind collaboration on the editing.

It is hard for us to end the editors' note without expressing our strong emotions as we think about Pietro leaving our Department. His presence as a teacher, as a colleague and as a friend has always been a comforting feeling all along our careers and we will cherish these fond memories for ever. We would like to take this opportunity to wish him all the very best in the future and hope that he will be as proud of this product as we are.

Geneva, November 1999

Jaya Krishnakumar
Elvezio Ronchetti

List of Contributors

Ramses ABUL NAGA, Department of Econometrics and Economics (DEEP), University of Lausanne, Switzerland.

Gabrielle ANTILLE, Department of Econometrics and Laboratory of Applied Economics, University of Geneva, Switzerland.

Badi H. BALTAGI, Department of Economics, Texas A&M University, U.S.A.

Mauro L. BARANZINI, Università della Svizzera Italiana, Lugano, Switzerland and City of Cambridge, U.K.

Jean-Luc BERTHOLET, University Center for the Study of Energy Problems (CUEPE), Geneva, Switzerland.

Fabrizio CARLEVARO, Department of Econometrics and Center for the Study of Energy Problems (CUEPE), University of Geneva, Switzerland.

Lucien GARDIOL, Department of Econometrics and Economics (DEEP), University of Lausanne, Switzerland.

Christian GOURIEROUX, Centre de Recherche en Economie et Statistique (CREST) and Centre d'Etudes Prospectives d'Economie Mathématique Appliquées à la Planification (CEPREMAP), Paris, France.

Nadeem U. HAQUE, International Monetary Fund, Washington D.C., U.S.A.

Alberto HOLLY, Department of Econometrics and Economics (DEEP), University of Lausanne, Switzerland.

Attila HORNOK, Budapest University of Economics, Hungary.

Cheng HSIAO, Department of Economics, University of Southern California, Los Angeles, U.S.A. and Institute of Economics, Taipei, Taiwan.

Joanna JASIAK, York University, Toronto, Canada.

Jaya KRISHNAKUMAR, Department of Econometrics, University of Geneva, Switzerland.

Peter C. LIU, University of Miami, U.S.A.

G.S. MADDALA, Ohio State University, U.S.A.

László MÁTYÁS, Budapest University of Economics, Hungary and ERUDITE, University of Paris XII, France.

Alain MONFORT, Centre de Recherche en Economie et Statistique (CREST), Paris, France.

Marc NERLOVE, Department of Agricultural Resource Economics, University of Maryland.

Luigi L. PASINETTI, Università Cattolica S.C., Milano, Italy and Università della Svizzera Italiana, Lugano, Switzerland.

M. Hashem PESARAN, Trinity College, Cambridge, U.K.

Patrick SEVESTRE, University of Paris XII, France and Research Center, Bank of France.

Sunil SHARMA, International Monetary Fund, Washington D.C., U.S.A.

Jacques SILBER, Department of Economics, Bar-Ilan University, Ramat-Gan, Israel.

Baohong SUN, Graduate School of Industrial Administration, Carnegie-Mellon University, U.S.A.

Carlos TENREIRO, Coïmbra University, Portugal.

Shaowen WU, State University of New York at Buffalo, U.S.A.

Table of Contents

Source: Ely Riva

Pietro Balestra

Born in Lugano in the Canton of Ticino, Switzerland on April 2, 1935, Pietro Balestra received his Bachelors' Degree in Economics from the University of Fribourg, Switzerland, in 1956. He went on to do his M.A. in Economics at the University of Kansas and later moved to Stanford University for a Masters in Statistics and a Ph.D. in Economics with a minor in Statistics, obtained in January 1965 under the guidance of Marc Nerlove.

Pietro Balestra returned to Switzerland in 1965 as Professor of Economics and Econometrics at the University of Fribourg. He also started serving as Associate Professor of Econometrics at the University of Dijon in 1979. In 1980, he was called for a Professorship in Econometrics at the University of Geneva, from which he will be retiring in September 2000. However, he will continue to teach at the University of Southern Switzerland in Lugano where he holds the position of the first Dean of the Economics Faculty since the creation of the institution in 1996.

Pietro has travelled widely during his career and has been a visiting Professor in several universities in Europe, USA and elsewhere, in particular at CORE (Louvaine, Belgium), University of Lausanne, University of Zurich, Northwestern University, University of Florence, University of Southern California (Los Angeles), University of Bujumbura (Burundi), University Nova (Lisbon, Portugal). His participation in various scientific activities is extensive having been the Associate Editor of the Journal of Econometrics (1972-1984), the Treasurer and a founding fellow of the European Economic Association (1986-1990), President of the Swiss Economic Association (1981-1984) and President of the Commission for Economic Research, Canton of Ticino, Switzerland.

He is a Fellow of the Econometric Society and the Journal of Econometrics. His scientific contribution is well known through his publications in several leading international journals and collections. The range of topics that he has covered is very varied including not only the state-of-the-art research in econometrics but also general discussions on the aims and objectives of economics or even such focussed topics as the use of matrix calculus in economics.

Jaya Krishnakumar had the privilege of being part of the very first group of students that he taught at the University of Geneva. She was beginning her postgraduate degree in econometrics when Pietro Balestra was appointed as a Professor. All her classmates and the subsequent groups of students will no doubt agree that one of the most important qualities of Pietro that immediately strikes a student, is his exceptional pedagogical talent. His teaching is so effective that even complicated matters become simple when he teaches them and the message gets across smoothly. He has the ability to present complex mathematical derivations in such a flowing manner that the result seems to follow automatically. At the same time, the student is also trained to go beyond the technical aspect and see the real implication of the result obtained and even find an intuitive explanation to it. As a research supervisor, Pietro is extremely generous in devoting his time to discussions, not hesitating to spend long hours clearing the doubts of students and helping them sufficiently so that they can continue their research confidently.

His style of teaching is a great inspiration for all juniors wishing to make a career in educating others. It has encouraged large numbers of students to take up econometrics as their specialisation and many among them to pursue a doctoral degree in this subject. Jaya would not have chosen this field but for the strong motivation provided by his communication skills and clarity of presentation. She is doubly happy that in addition to editing the book, she could also undertake and complete a research project for this volume in his honour.

In research problems Pietro always finds an ingenious way to tackle complex issues through simple examples without sacrificing the big picture. This style is also reflected in his writing. For him a research article should also be as transparent as possible so that an informed reader can follow it relatively easily. This can be seen from the way his papers, lecture notes, and reports are written taking extreme care about the structure and clarity of the text. In these days when many writers may feel that the complexity of presentation of a paper reflects its quality, Pietro is a fine example that illustrates the contrary. This is also observed in his (re)search for simpler solutions without compromising on rigour as in his paper on the efficiency of Ordinary Least Squares in situations where *a priori* Generalised Least Squares is the appropriate method.

His administrative activity in Fribourg, Geneva, and presently in Lugano shows that he can provide personal and academic leadership around a project. The Faculty of Economics at the newly born University of Southern Switzerland in his hometown Lugano is benefitting greatly from his enthusiasm and leadership.

Any researcher in panel data econometrics would have referred to, at one point or the other, the pioneering work on the formulation and estimation of a dynamic error component model by Pietro Balestra and Marc Nerlove. Just as this paper was the beginning of a new field of research in econometrics, the editors hope that this collection of papers in his honour could contribute to the beginning of a new widening of the field to various conventional and non-conventional domains.

Publications of Pietro Balestra

Basic Economic Projections, United States Population 1965-1980, Stanford Research Institute, Menlo Park, California, 1964 (with N. Koteswara Rao).

The Demand for Natural Gas in the United States, A Dynamic Approach for the Residential and Commercial Market, North-Holland Publishing Company, Amsterdam 1967.

Calcul Matriciel pour Economistes, Edition Castella, Albeuve, Switzerland, 1972 (Second Edition 1977).

La Dérivation Matricielle, Collection de l'Institut de mathématiques économiques (Dijon), No. 12, Sirey, Paris, 1976.

"Pooling Cross-Section and Time Series Data in the Estimation of Dynamic Models : The Demand for Natural Gas", (with Marc Nerlove), *Econometrica*, July 1966.

"Fonctions de consommation et multiplicateurs dynamiques : l'exemple de la Suisse" (with W. Wittmann), *Revue Suisse d'Economie Politique et de Statistique*, 1, 1967.

"Empirische Investitionfunktionen für die Schweiz 1948-65", (with W. Wittmann), *Schweizerische Zeitschrift für Volkswirtschaft und Statistik*, 4, 1967.

"Formes de concurrence et progrès technique", *Revue Suisse d'Economie Politique et de Statistique*, 3, 1968.

"Rational Behavior and Gasoline Price Wars", (with D.B. Schendel), *Applied Economics*, May 1969.

"On the Efficiency of Ordinary Least Squares in Regression Models", *Journal of the American Statistical Association*, Sept. 1970.

"Some Optimal Aspects in a Two Class Growth Model with a Differentiated Interest Rate", (with M. Baranzini), *Kyklos*, 2, 1971.

"Best Quadratic Unbiased Estimators of the Variance-Covariance Matrix in Normal Regression", *Journal of Econometrics*, March 1973.

"Determinant and Inverse of a Sum of Matrices with Applications in Economics and Statistics", Document de travail de l'IME (Dijon), 1978.

"La méthode d'estimation MINQUE", in *Lectures de Mathématiques économiques*, Collection de l'IME (Dijon), No. 22, I. Aime Dixans, Sirey, 1979.

"Modèles de régression avec variables muettes explicatives", Document de travail de l'IME (Dijon), No. 39, 1980.

"I fattori regionali nelle stime econometriche", in *Saggi di Economia regionale*, Ed. Casagrande, Bellinzona, Ticino 1980.

"A Note on the Exact Transformation Associated with the First Order Moving Average Process", *Journal of Econometrics*, December 1980.

"Dummy Variables in Regression Analysis", in *Advances in Economic Theory*, Edited by Mauro Baranzini, Basil Blackwell, Oxford, 1982, 273-92.

"Dynamic Misspecification and Serial Correlation", in *Qualitative and Quantitative Mathematical Economics, Advanced Studies in Theoretical and Applied Econometrics*, Vol. 1, edited by J.H.P. Paelinck, Martinus Nijhoff Publishers, The Hague, 1982, 115-145.

"A Note on Amemiya's Partially Generalized Least Squares", *Journal of Econometrics*, 23, 1983.

"Autoregressive Model with Varying Coefficients : An Application to the Generation of Monthly Synthetic Streamflows", Cahiers du Département d'Econométrie, No. 1, 1984, with M.S. Matoussi.

"Modèles dynamiques à coefficients aléatoires pour les variables exogènes", Cahiers du Département d'Econométrie, No. 8, 1985, with F. Kria.

"The Indirect Least Square Approach to Structural Parameter Estimation", Cahiers du Département d'Econométrie, No. 9, 1985.

"Commentaire à la conférence du Professeur Luigi Pasinetti : Technical Progress and the Wealth of Nations", in F. Fleck, *Technologischer Wandel in Wirtschaft und Gesellschaft*, H. Bortis and L. Bosshart editors, Universitätsverlag Freiburg, 1985, 67-74.

"Full Information Estimation of a System of Simultaneous Equations with Error Component Structure", with J. Varadharajan-Krishnakumar, *Econometric Theory*, No. 3, 1987, 223-46.

"Missing Measurements in a Regression Problem with No Auxiliary Relations", with Jan Kmenta, in *Advances in Econometrics, Innovations in Quantitative Economics : Essays in Honor of Robert L. Basmann*, Vol. 5, 1986, 289-300.

"Dummy Variables" and "Seasonal Adjustement", in *The New Palgrave*, 1987.

"Equality Between Ordinary and Generalized Procedures in Econometrics", Cahiers du Département d'Econométrie, No. 1, 1988.

"Naturally Constrained Reduced Form and Structural Parameters Estimation", Document de travail de l'IME, No 101, Dijon, 1988.

"Optimal Experimental Design for Error Components Models", with Dennis J. Aigner, *Econometrica*, Vol. 56, No. 4, 1988, 955-971.

"La science économique des années nonante", *Revue Suisse d'Economie Politique et de Statistique*, 1989, No. 3, 239-48.

"Solutions : The Limit Distribution of the Generalized Inverse of a Singular Covariance Matrix Estimate", *Econometric Theory*, 1990, No. 6, 494-5.

"A General Kronecker Formula for the Moments of the Multivariate Normal Distribution", with A. Holly, Cahiers de Recherches Economiques, No. 90002, Lausanne.

"A Random Coefficient Simultaneous Equation System with an Application to Direct Foreign Investment by French Firms", with S. Negassi, *Empirical Economics*, 1992, 17, 205-220.

"Formulation and Estimation of Econometric Models for Panel Data", with Marc Nerlove, in *The Econometrics of Panel Data*, L. Mátyás and P. Sevestre Eds., Kluwer Academic Publishers, 1992 and 1996, 3-18.

"Introduction to Linear Models for Panel Data", in *The Econometrics of Panel Data*, L. Mátyás and P. Sevestre Eds., Kluwer Academic Publishers, 1992 and 1996, 21-29.

"Fixed Effect Models and Fixed Coefficient Models", in *The Econometrics of Panel Data*, L. Mátyás and P. Sevestre Eds., Kluwer Academic Publishers, 1992 and 1996, 30-45.

"Efficient (and parsimonious) Estimation of Structural Dynamic Error Component Models", Quaderno 98-01, Faculty of Economics, University of Southern Switzerland, 1998.

PART I

Panel Data Methodology in Various Fields

A. Macroeconomics

Panel Data Econometrics: Future Directions
J. Krishnakumar and E. Ronchetti (Editors)

CHAPTER 1

GROWTH RATE CONVERGENCE, FACT OR ARTIFACT ?
An Essay on Panel Data Econometrics*

Marc NERLOVE

Abstract

The sensitivity of the convergence rate, or the test for no convergence in the standard Barro-Baumol sense, to the econometric method employed is investigated. Two basic models are investigated: The first is the standard model with individual-specific effects for each country; the second is a model in which individual countries have different individual-specific trends in output per capita. All of the results reported support the growth convergence hypothesis conditional on savings and population growth rates in the usual sense but illustrate the rather different estimates of the rates of convergence obtained when different estimation techniques are used. In particular, I show that the use of fixed-effects panel models biases the results towards finding relatively rapid convergence and that, when more appropriate maximum-likelihood estimates, unconditional on the initial observations, are employed, very slow convergence is implied (to within 90% of equilibrium only in excess of 50 years). Biases in the estimates of the coefficient of the "state" variable for all of the usual methods of panel data analysis imply biased estimates of the coefficients of any other variables included if these are correlated with the "state" variable, which is typically the case. Thus, the significance and possibly the sign of any other determinants of growth may be seriously affected. Alternative maximum likelihood methods are developed which utilize the information contained in the initial observations for each country that reflect the operation of the growth process prior to the time at which we began to observe them.

*This paper is based on an earlier paper of similar title presented at the Sixth Conference on Panel Data Econometrics, Amsterdam, 28-29 June 1996 and also presented as the 1998 Havlicek Lecture in Applied Econometrics at Ohio State University, April 16, 1998.

My interest in the question of how the econometric approach might have influenced recent findings with respect to the convergence hypothesis was stimulated by reading Islam (1995). But there is now a vast literature utilizing the data from the Penn World Tables, which I also use here. I do not attempt a

1. INTRODUCTION

One of the most important implications of the classic papers of Solow (1956) and Swan (1956) is that the lower the starting level of real per capita GDP, relative to the long run or steady state position, the faster is the growth rate. The Solow-Swan model assumes a constant-returns-to-scale production function with two inputs, capital and labor, and substitution between inputs, a constant savings rate, and constant rate of growth of population and neutral technical change, all exogenously given. Convergence of economies starting out at different levels of per capita income to the same steady-state rate of growth reflects the diminishing returns to capital implied by the production function assumed: economies starting out with lower levels of real per capita GDP relative to the long run or steady state position have less capital per worker and therefore higher rates of return to capital. I will refer to this as the standard Barro-Baumol (BB) sense of the meaning of convergence[1]. Because the steady states of the Solow-Swan model depend on the savings rate, the rate of growth of population, and the rate of technical progress, some authors have argued that these factors need to be held constant in attempting to test the hypothesis of growth rate convergence. Convergence is, in this sense, conditional. (When population growth is endogenously determined, this implication of the neoclassical model of economic growth does not necessarily follow; see Nerlove and Raut, 1996.)

The problem of BB-convergence in the standard neoclassical model is treated both theoretically and empirically in the recent text by Barro and Sala-i-Martin (1995) and empirically in a recent paper by Islam (1995). Bernard and Durlauf (1996) provide a useful framework for understanding the time-series and cross-sectional tests of the BB-convergence hypothesis and its relation to alternative definitions. Quah (1996) discusses the problem of convergence in more general form and distinguishes several different varieties. He argues that "Simply because panel data techniques happen to apply to data with extensive cross-section and time-series variation does not mean they are at once similarly appropriate for analyzing convergence". While I do not fault Quah's conclusion, current discussions do emphasize panel data and methods and derive strong conclusions regarding BB-convergence and the significance of other determinants of growth from such data. It is therefore appropriate to consider how these conclusions, within the context of BB-convergence, are affected by the econometric methods employed.

---

comprehensive survey of this literature in this paper.

I thank Hashem Pesaran for helpful discussions, and Robert Barro, Michael Binder, William Greene, G. S. Maddala, and C. Spohr for useful comments. Special thanks are due to Anke Meyer, with whom I discussed every aspect of this work.

I am also indebted to Jinkyo Suh and Timothy Thomas for computational counsel and their assistance in straightening out the GAUSS programs which I wrote to obtain my earlier results . Suh also checked and double checked all derivations and verified that my programs accurately reflected the formulae derived.

[1]There is a good deal of current discussion regarding the appropriate definition of "convergence". Bernard and Durlauf (1995) give a nice discussion emphasizing the restrictiveness of the approach adopted here (see also Quah, 1996), which is the most prevalent, going back to the earlier work of Barro (1991) And Baumol (1986). Since my main concern is to show that the econometrics matters, I will adopt the basic Solow/Swan model in what follows. However, the general point that inconsistency in the estimation of the coefficient of the state variable implies inconsistency in the estimation of the effects of other factors is valid in this context and in general.

Perhaps even more important than the problem of convergence is the question of the determinants of growth. The World Bank Project on Economic Growth lists more than thirty published and working papers almost all of which involve dynamic panel data analysis or cross-section analysis with a state variable or initial condition[2]. Although the focus of these papers is not convergence but the effects of the other variables included, if the coefficient of the state variable in the statistical analysis is inconsistently estimated, in this sense "biased", then the coefficient of any variable correlated with the state variable will also be biased. Hence, quite misleading conclusions may be drawn concerning the significance, sign and relative magnitude of other factors included in the analysis.

In section 2, I derive a discrete form of the BB-convergence equation, also derived in a different way by Mankiw *et al.* (1992), and show that the usual equation for testing the convergence hypothesis can be obtained from it by a simple partial adjustment model rather than the approximation about equilibrium usually employed. In general, no essential restrictions are neglected in this simpler derivation, although in certain contexts the specification may neglect certain cross-equation parameter restrictions. It is the classic Solow/Swan model that, for good or for ill, underlies all recent studies of the determinants of growth and provides the justification for including a lagged value of the dependent variable, initial condition, or other state variable,

Section 3 examines recent empirical investigations of BB-convergence and the rate of convergence and argues that most are flawed by failure to allow for the inconsistencies of single cross-section or panel studies in a dynamic context[3]. In a dynamic context, a single cross-section is best viewed as a panel with time dimension 1. I do not attempt here a general review of the effects of the methods used in more general studies of the determinants of growth, but I do examine the effects on the estimated coefficients of the savings rate and the rate of growth of population.

In this section, I look at the problem of implementing the convergence hypothesis in the context of cross-country data over time, and, in particular whether the model ought to be recast so that individual countries are subject to individual specific trends[4].

In section 4, I discuss five existing methods of estimating the rate of convergence (and thus testing for convergence), show that four standard methods yield estimates which

[2]See http//www.worldbank.org/html/prdmg/grthweb.

[3]A recent study by Lee, *et al* (1996) arrives at similar conclusions but proposes a number of alternatives different from those investigated here. In particular, I do not agree that their formulation of the unconditional likelihood function is equivalent to the one I present below.

[4]Of course, the existence of conditioning country-specific trends is hardly convergence in any meaningful sense. No matter. My concern here and in Nerlove (1997) is to show the effect of the econometrics on the assessment of the effects of the initial conditions in the basic Solow/Swan model. Because the maximum likelihood methods implemented in the paper require stationarity, I argue that the data should be differenced in order to implement this modification of the basic model. I refer to the two forms as the "levels" model and the "first-differenced" model, respectively. As it turns out, the results for the first-differenced model are a great deal more reasonable than those for the levels model. I suggest that this means that much of the recent convergence debate has focused on the wrong thing, namely convergence, rather than the effects of other factors on economic growth. Country-specific trends are a clear indication of important left-out variables.

satisfy an inequality derived by Trognon and Sevestre (1996), and devise a new method of maximum-likelihood estimation based on the density of the observations *unconditional on the initial or starting values of the dependent variable.* I further show that under a mildly restrictive assumption this unconditional maximum likelihood method tends to maximum likelihood conditional on the initial observations as the cross-section dimension of the panel increases. The "biases" in conventional panel methods are reflected in the estimates of the effects of other variables included in differing ways illustrated here.

Finally, in section 5, I apply all six methods to several panel data sets drawn from the Penn World Tables. The results show clearly how misleading the standard estimates can be in assessing growth rate convergence and in the estimation of the significance and magnitude of other variables included. The contrast between the conditional and the unconditional ML estimates for a small cross-section dimension and their similarity for a large cross-section dimension is illustrated. I argue that the usual procedures for doing feasible GLS or for obtaining starting values for ML are seriously flawed and likely to yield negative estimates of the random time persistent cross-sectional effects. Results not presented here show that biases in the estimate of the coefficient of the lagged value of the dependent variable are transmitted to the estimates of other coefficients in the model such as the stock of human capital, making inferences about the determinants of growth problematic unless appropriate econometric methods are used.

Section 6 concludes.

2. THE NEOCLASSICAL THEORY OF GROWTH CONVERGENCE

The Solow/Swan model of economic growth is the starting point for all recent empirical analyses of growth convergence and the determinants of growth. In this section, I review briefly the model and dynamize it in a particularly simple approximate way.

a. The Solow/Swan Model

Consider the standard Solow/Swan (Solow, 1956; Swan, 1956) model with exogenous population growth in discrete form: Let Y_t = output, K_t = capital stock, N_t = labor force assumed to be the same as population, S_t = savings, I_t = investment, s = the savings rate, δ = depreciation rate, and $\overline{n}$ = the exogenous rate of growth of population and labor force. Production can be represented by a constant returns to scale function:

$$Y_t = F(K_t, N_t) \tag{1}$$

or

$$y_t = f(k_t),$$

where $y_t = Y_t/N_t, k_t = K_t/N_t$, and $f(k) = F(k,1)$. Solow/Swan assume that savings equals gross investment and is a constant fraction s of output:

$$I_t = S_t = sY_t \tag{2}$$

The change in the capital stock equals gross investment minus depreciation:

$$K_{t+1} = (1-\delta)K_t + I_t = sF(K_t, N_t) + (1-\delta)K_t \tag{3}$$

Population grows exogenously at a rate :

$$N_{t+1} = (1+\overline{n})N_t \tag{4}$$

Thus

$$k_{t+1} = sf(k_1) + (1-\delta)k_t\overline{1} + n = g(k_t), k_0 \text{ given} \tag{5}$$

The dynamics of the Solow/Swan model is entirely described by the path of k_t, the capital-labor ratio, since population grows exogenously, capital depreciates at a fixed rate, and gross investment is proportional to output.

The existence of stationary solutions to (5), i.e. k^* for which

$$k^* = g(k^*), \tag{6}$$

and the local stability of such solutions depends on the shape of the function g. The conditions which yield a non-negative globally stable steady state solution are the following:

$$g'(0) > 1, g(0) = 0,$$
$$g'(k) < 1, \text{for some } k > 0, \text{ and } g \text{ is concave.}$$

These properties follow if the production function satisfies:

$$f(0) = 0$$
$$f'(0) > \frac{\delta + \overline{n}}{s}$$
$$f'(k) < \frac{\delta + \overline{n}}{s}$$

and f is concave.

A stationary solution k^* is locally stable if $|g'(k^*)| < 1$. Clearly $k^* - 0$ is unstable. Under concavity of f, whenever (6) holds for some $k^* > 0$, then there can be no other $k^* > 0$ for which (6) holds and at that point $|g'(k^*)| < 1$, so the solution is necessarily unique.

b. Growth Convergence in the Neoclassical Model with Exogenous Population Growth and Savings

If $f(k_t)$ is Cobb-Douglas, we can solve explicitly for the time path of y_t:
For $y_t = A_t k_t^a$, so that

$$k_t = \left(\frac{y_t}{A_t}\right)^{1/a} \tag{7}$$

and, hence, from (5)

$$y_t = \frac{n+1}{s}k_{t+1} - \frac{1-\delta}{s}k_t = \frac{n+1}{s}\left(\frac{y_{t+1}}{A_{t+1}}\right)^{1/\alpha} - \frac{1-\delta}{s}\left(\frac{y_t}{A_t}\right)^{1/\alpha} \tag{8}$$

α is the elasticity of output with respect to capital stock; if capital is fully employed and paid its marginal product, it is the implied share of capital in total output. A_t is any function of time which may affect the productivity of capital and labor, for example neutral technical change or, more explicitly, investment in human capital or in infrastructure. In the "stationary state"

$$y_t^* = \left(\frac{n+\delta}{s}\right)^{-\alpha/(1-\alpha)} A_t^{1/(1-\alpha)} \tag{9}$$

Taking logs

$$\log y_t^* = \frac{-\alpha}{1-\alpha}\log(\frac{n+\delta}{s}) + \frac{1}{1-\alpha}\log A_t \tag{10}$$

Although (8) shows that the rate of convergence to equilibrium is not constant, an approximation is given by a partial adjustment model

$$\log y_t - \log y_{t-1} = (1-\gamma)[\log y_t^* - \log y_{t-1}] \tag{11}$$

This yields the approximate relation to be estimated and the equation employed in recent studies:

$$\log y_t = \frac{\alpha(1-\gamma)}{1-\alpha}[\log s - \log(n+\delta)] + \frac{1-\gamma}{1-\alpha}\log A_t + \gamma \log y_{t-1} \tag{12}$$

The speed of convergence to equilibrium is inversely proportional to γ. With growth convergence $0 < \gamma < 1$. In equilibrium, per capita GDP depends only on the parameters n, s, and the time path of A. In an empirical context, these differ from time to time and country to country. Clearly the extent of convergence is conditional on s, n, δ and the time path of A_t. In empirical investigations, changing n and s and sometimes a measure of changing A have been introduced. In what follows, I take account of differing s and n over time and cross-sectionally, in some additional analyses I take account of other factors by including country-specific trends, but not other variables explicitly such as infrastructure investment, which might arguably affect A[5]. Including a simple linear trend, with coefficient τ, in place of the entire term $\frac{1-\gamma}{1-\alpha}\log A_t$ gives rise to quite a different model, particularly if one argues that the trends ought to be different for different countries[6]. I

[5] As pointed out in a recent paper by Binder and Pesaran (1996), it makes a good deal of difference to the question of convergence at just what point one includes the stochastic disturbance. In this paper I follow the usual practice of taking it on the end of the equation to be estimated.

[6] In some further investigations not reported here, I have included A_t represented by the stock of human capital over time as measured by Barro and Lee (1993) raised to the power φ, $A_t = H_{it}^{\varphi}$, so that the coefficient of $\log H_{it}$ in the implied regression equation is $\frac{(1-\gamma)\varphi}{1-\alpha}$. The human capital variable constructed by Barro and Lee (1993) is available only for a subsample of countries by quinquennial for the period 1965-1985. Essentially the stock of human capital in the population is measured by Barro and Lee as the average schooling in the population as a whole over 25. In the results obtained, this variable is often the wrong sign and never significant.

will refer to (12) where A may differ from country to country but is assumed to be constant over time as the "levels" model. When the term $\frac{1-\gamma}{1-\alpha}\log A_t$, is replaced by a linear trend with slope which may differ from country to country but is assumed to be constant over time, (12) is replaced by

$$\triangle \log y_t = \frac{\alpha(1-\gamma)}{1-\alpha}\triangle[\log s - \log(n+\delta)] + v + \gamma\triangle \log y_{t-1} \qquad (12')$$

where v is the slope of the trend and may differ from country to country. I refer to this model as the "first-difference" model[7]. This approach is implemented in Nerlove (1997) and the results obtained there are reported in Table 3 below.

3. EMPIRICAL INVESTIGATIONS OF CONVERGENCE AND THE RATE OF CONVERGENCE

Equation (12) is widely used to examine the hypothesis of growth convergence (Mankiw *et al* , 1992, p.410; Barro and Sala-i-Martin, 1995, Chapter 12; Islam, 1995, p.1133; Lee *et al.* 1996). In empirical work, y_t is replaced by real per capita GDP; when varying s and n are taken into account, s is replaced by an average savings rate over the period $t-1$ to t, and n is replaced by the growth rate of population over the period $t-1$ to t. It is usual to use rates averaged over several years; following Islam (1995), I have used quinquennial averages. The restriction on the coefficients of $ln(s)$ and $ln(n+\delta)$, which arises from the constant-returns-to-scale assumption implies that $ln(s)$ and $ln(n+\delta)$ can be collapsed into a single variable. Testing the growth convergence hypothesis, in this context, revolves largely around the coefficient γ of the initial level of per capita real GDP. If this is positive but much less than one, the implication is that on average countries with low initial values are growing faster than those with high initial values and is therefore evidence of convergence. Whereas if this coefficient is close to one, perhaps even slightly larger than one, the implication is that initial values have little or no effect or even a perverse one on subsequent growth; such a finding is therefore evidence against the neoclassical theory which implies convergence. For example, if $\gamma = 0.9$, convergence to within 90% of final equilibrium occurs only in 22 periods, which, given quinquennial data, implies 110 years! Similarly, 0.8 requires 53 years, 0.7 32 years, while 0.2 requires only 7 years and 0.1 is within 90% in 5 years.

The estimates of γ presented below using cross-country quinquennial data and based on the levels model are generally in excess of 0.7 no matter what econometric procedure is employed, but vary over a wide range depending on the method, 0.7 to 0.98. It is apparent that, for all practical purposes, coefficients in excess of 0.7 represent negligible convergence, since, with unchanging s, n, and A, it would take more than a generation to achieve 90% of equilibrium real per capita GDP. Most recent work attempts to test whether $\gamma = 1$; however, this is a test for unit root in log y_{it}. Even under the best of circumstances testing for a unit root is problematic (see Diebold and Nerlove, 1990). Here the problems are compounded by the short time dimension of the typical panel. Basing

[7]Differencing the model to achieve stationarity creates some interesting problems with respect to the disturbance term which are discussed below. See especially footnote 13.

a test on the size of γ rather than equality with 1 finesses a host of problems of the sort discussed extensively in Diebold and Nerlove[8].

Tests based on a single cross-section (which can be viewed as a panel of time dimension 1) or on pooled cross-section time series (panel) data generally have yielded contradictory results: Pooled panel data studies tend to reject the hypothesis of BB-convergence (relatively high $\gamma's$), even after controlling for population growth rates, savings rates and other variables. Dynamic fixed-effects models are of course not possible for a single cross-section, but recent work (Islam, 1995) using a dynamic fixed-effects panel model yields results supporting convergence. There are serious problems with tests such as these which rely on the estimated coefficients of the initial, or lagged value, of the dependent variable in dynamic panel models, or in the special case of a single cross-section, which arise from two sources of bias. In this paper, I show that these findings are probably statistical artifacts arising from biases in the econometric methods employed to test the growth convergence hypothesis in the BB sense. This does not mean that this sense is the correct one to employ in the more general context of convergence, as emphasized by Quah(1996), but demonstrates the sensitivity of the conclusions drawn about γ to the econometric method employed, irrespective of the validity of the relationship of such conclusions to more general notions of convergence.

The first source of bias are omitted variables, especially infrastructure and investments over time in infrastructure, and the natural resource base available to each country in cross-sectional or panel studies. Systematic differences in these across countries or regions will systematically bias the conclusions. To the extent that these effects are approximated by differing trends for each country omitting such variables may account for the differences between the first-difference model and the levels model. Because such omitted variables are likely to be correlated with savings or investment rates in conventional or in human capital and with population growth rates it is not altogether clear what the net effect of omitting them on the coefficient of the initial value will be in a single cross-section. But in a pooled model it is clear that, to the extent such differences are persistent, they will be highly correlated with the initial value and therefore omitting them will bias the coefficient of that variable upwards towards one and thus towards rejecting convergence. This source of bias has been well-known since the early paper by Balestra and Nerlove (1966) and is well-supported by the Monte Carlo studies reported in Nerlove (1971). In this light, it is not surprising that pooled panel data, or single cross-sections, which are a special case of panels with $T = 1$, even with inclusion of additional variables, often reject convergence.

Second, since there are likely to be many sources of cross-country or cross-region differ-

[8]Barnard and Durlauf (1995) use cointegration techniques on rather longer time series for 15 OECD countries to test alternative time-series definitions of convergence and contrast the results with the standard BB-formulation. Using long annual time series (1865-1994) for 16 OECD countries, Michelacci and Zaffaroni (1997) extend the Solow-Swan model to allow for cross-sectional heterogeneity in the pace of convergence and conclude that the uniform 2% rate of convergence found in much of the empirical literature is a consequence of fractionally integrated nonstationarity with underlying parameter strictly between 0.5 and 1.0. My first-difference formulation (1997) is equivalent to assuming a unit root, an hypothesis which is rejected by Micellacci and Zaffaroni.

ences, many of which cannot be observed or directly accounted for, it is natural to try to represent these by fixed effects in a panel context. But, as is well-known from the Monte Carlo investigations reported in Nerlove (1971) and demonstrated analytically by Nickell (1981), inclusion of fixed effects in a dynamic model biases the coefficient of the initial value of the dependent variable included as an explanatory variable downwards, towards zero and therefore towards support for the convergence hypothesis. This may account for Islam's (1995) recent findings.

Alternative estimates based on more appropriate random-effects models, such as two-stage feasible Generalized Least Squares or maximum likelihood conditional on the initial observations are also biased in small samples and inconsistent in large, or in the case of Instrumental Variable estimates have poor sampling properties or are difficult to implement. Results for the alternative method of unconditional maximum likelihood suggested in Nerlove and Balestra (1996) are presented here[9].

Even if one has little interest in the question of convergence, or its rate, *per se*, the question of whether the coefficient of the state variable, lagged dependent or initial value, is biased in the sense of being inconsistent is an important one since biases in this coefficient will affect the estimates of the coefficients of other variables correlated with it and their levels of significance. To the extent such estimates are important in the formulation of policies to promote growth, the matter is indeed a serious one.

In the remainder of this paper, I investigate the sensitivity of the convergence rate, or the test of no convergence, in the levels model to the econometric method employed, as well as the sensitivity of the estimates of the coefficients of other variables included. All of the results reported, except those for pooled panel data, support the growth convergence hypothesis conditional on savings and population growth rates but illustrate the rather different estimates of the rates of convergence. In additional research not presented here I also show that the coefficients of other explanatory variables vary considerably when different estimation techniques are used. In addition, a technique for examining the shape of sections of a high dimensional likelihood function is developed which reveals interesting and somewhat unexpected relationships among the various estimates.

4. ALTERNATIVE METHODS FOR ESTIMATING RATES OF CONVERGENCE [10]

A good summary of the current state of knowledge about the properties of various estimators in dynamic panel models is contained in Sevestre and Trognon (1992, 2nd. ed. 1996). Trognon (1978) was the first to show the inconsistency of maximum likelihood conditional on the initial individual observations. Nickell (1981) shows the inconsistency

[9]See also Nerlove (1997). Lee *et al.* (1996) also estimate what they term is an unconditional likelihood function, but inasmuch as they do not transform to stationarity (their relationship includes both a constant and a linear trend), I do not think their formulation of the likelihood function based on what they refer to as the unconditional density of the dependent variable is equivalent to mine.

[10]I rely extensively in this section on the excellent discussion of Sevestre and Trognon, Chapter 7 in Mátyás and Sevestre (1996, pp. 120-144). Additional alternatives, more appropriate when longer time series are available, are treated by Lee *et al.* (1996), and are not discussed or implemented here.

of the estimates of the fixed-effects in a dynamic panel model. Kiviet (1995) derives exact results for the bias of leading estimators. In this section, following Sevestre and Trognon, I review the leading estimators and their properties for dynamic panel models.

For simplicity, in this section I restrict attention to the simple model containing one exogenous variable x_{it} and one lagged value of the dependent variable y_{it-1} as explanatory. Extension to the case in which more than one exogenous explanatory variable is included presents no serious difficulty.

$$y_{it} = \alpha + \beta x_{it} + \gamma y_{it-1} + \mu_i + \varepsilon_{it}, i = 1, \ldots N, t = 1, \ldots T \tag{13}$$

Taking deviations from overall means eliminates the constant α. The usual assumptions are made about the properties of the μ_i and the ε_{it}:

(i) $E(\mu_i) = E(\varepsilon_{it}) = 0$, all i and t,

(ii) $E(\mu_i \varepsilon_{jt}) = 0$, all i, j and t,

(iii) $E\mu_i\mu_j) = \begin{cases} \sigma_\mu^2 & i = j \\ 0 & i \neq j, \end{cases}$

(iv) $E(\varepsilon_{it}\varepsilon_{js}) = \begin{cases} \sigma_\varepsilon^2 & t = s, i = j \\ 0 & \textit{otherwise} \end{cases}$

Both μ_i and ε_{it} are assumed to be uncorrelated with x_{it} for all i and t. Clearly, however, y_{it-1} cannot be assumed to be uncorrelated with μ_i. It is clear, therefore, that OLS applied to (13) ignoring the component nature of the disturbances $\nu_{it} = \mu_i + \varepsilon_{it}$, which I call the *pooled regression*, will yield inconsistent estimates. In particular, if $\gamma > 0$, γ_{pooled} is "biased" upwards. So, just as in the case of ordinary serial correlation, β_{pooled} is also "biased" and the OLS residuals understate the amount of serial correlation, which in this case is measured by the intraclass correlation coefficient ρ. This parameter measures the extent of unobserved or latent time-invariant, individual-specific, variation relative to the total unobserved variation in the sample, $\frac{\sigma_\mu^2}{(\sigma_\mu^2+\sigma_\varepsilon^2)}$. It is extremely important in understanding the nature of the variation, both observed and unobserved, in the panel.

(a) Inconsistency of the pooled-sample OLS estimates of the dynamic error-components model.

Since the panel has two dimensions, it is possible to consider asymptotic behavior as $N \longrightarrow \infty$, $T \longrightarrow \infty$, or both. Generally speaking it is easier to increase the cross-section dimension of a panel, so the most relevant asymptotics are as $N \longrightarrow \infty$. This is called *semi-asymptotics* in the panel data literature. It is not necessary to assume $|\gamma| < 1$ as long as T is fixed, but the way in which the initial values of the dependent variable, y_{i0}, are assumed to be generated is crucial. To see why, write (13) as

$$y_{it} = \gamma^t y_{i0} + \sum_{j=0}^{t-1} \gamma^j \beta x_{it-j} + \frac{1-\gamma^t}{1-\gamma}\mu_i + \nu_{it}, \text{ where } \nu_{it} = \sum_{j=0}^{t-1} \gamma^j \varepsilon_{it-j} \tag{14}$$

Equation (14) expresses y_{it} as the sum of four terms: the first, $\gamma^t y_{i0}$, depends on the initial values; the second on lagged values of the exogenous variable; the third on the individual, time-invariant, component of residual variance; and the fourth on lagged values of the remaining component. This last term is an autoregressive process with initial values $\nu_{i0} = 0$ and $\nu_{it} = \gamma\nu_{it-1} + \varepsilon_{it}$. It need not be assumed to be stationary as long as T is fixed. It does not make sense in this context to assume that the y_{i0} are uncorrelated with either the μ_i or the lagged values of the x_{it}'s. On the other hand, ε_{i0} is a random variable with mean 0 and variance σ_ε^2 independently and identically distributed for all i. Thus, the initial observation can be written as a function of lagged x's, the μ_i and ε_{i0}:

$$y_{i0} = f(x_{i0}, x_{i-1}, \ldots, \mu_i, \varepsilon_{i0}) \tag{15}$$

Clearly, if the individual effects μ_i are assumed to be fixed and the lagged x's to be given, the y_{i0} are also fixed and uncorrelated with the disturbances in (15), ν_{it}, $t = 1, \ldots, T$. But, if the individual effects are considered to be random, as Nerlove and Balestra (1996) have argued they should be, the initial observations are not exogenous since they are correlated with them, as they are part of the disturbance term, namely the third and fourth terms of (13).

It is common in the literature on panel data to assume that the y_{i0} are i.i.d. random variables which are characterized by their second moments and correlations with the individual effects and not necessarily generated by the same process which generates the rest of the y_{it}'s. The properties of various estimators depend on the process generating them. One possibility is to try to model and estimate this process together with the dynamic panel model (13).

(b) Inconsistency of the OLS Estimators of the Dummy Variable, or Fixed-Effects, Model.

The ordinary least squares estimates of both the coefficient of the lagged dependent variable and the exogenous variable are inconsistent in the fixed effects model. As is well-known, the fixed effects model is equivalent to taking deviations from individual (country) means and then estimating an ordinary OLS regression:

$$\begin{aligned} y_{it} - \overline{y}_i &= \beta(x_{it} - \overline{x}_i) + \gamma(y_{it-1} - \overline{y}_{i-1}) + \nu_{it} \text{ where} \\ \nu_{it} &= \varepsilon_{it} - \overline{\varepsilon}_i \end{aligned} \tag{16}$$

Although $\sigma_{x\varepsilon}^2 = 0$,

$$\begin{aligned} \sigma_{y(-1)\varepsilon}^2 &= \text{plim } \frac{1}{T}\sum_t (y_{it-1} - \overline{y}_{i-1})(\varepsilon_{it} - \overline{\varepsilon}_{i-1}) \\ &= -\frac{1}{T^2}\frac{T - 1 - T\gamma + \gamma^T}{(1-\gamma)^2}\sigma_\varepsilon^2 \neq 0 \end{aligned} \tag{17}$$

Thus, the OLS estimates of both β and γ in the fixed effects model are inconsistent, although as $T \longrightarrow \infty$, the inconsistency disappears. But for finite, typically small T, it remains. (See Nickell, 1981, p.1424). For $T = 10$ and $\gamma = 0.5$, for example, the "bias" of the OLS estimate of γ, say c, is proportional to -0.16, the factor of proportionality being the OLS estimate of the variance of c from the within regression. It is always negative, implying that the bias of the OLS estimate of β, say b, is therefore upward. This conclusion holds regardless of whether one assumes the true model is fixed- or random-effects.

Although the inconsistency will be small when T is moderate to large, small values of T are typically the case. Nonetheless, Nerlove (1971) suggested using the fixed effects model to estimate ρ for FGLS, in contrast to the earlier suggestion of Balestra and Nerlove (1966), hereinafter BN, of a consistent instrumental variable approach. BN also suggested but did not implement a method based on estimating ρ from the pooled and fixed-effects regressions. Rejection of instrumental variables by Nerlove (1971) was based on the instability of the results in Monte Carlo trials. Since the OLS estimates of the parameters from pooled or fixed-effects regressions are inconsistent, the estimates of ρ based on this regression will not be either; hence, the FGLS estimates computed using them will not generally be consistent. In the results reported here, an estimate of ρ is derived from the estimates of residual variance from both the fixed-effects and the pooled regressions, as suggested by B and N (1966), and is not consistent.

(c) Country Means Regression and the Estimation of ρ.

Many authors (e.g., Greene, 1993, pp. 475-477, Judge *et al.*, pp. 484-488), hereinafter GJ, suggest basing an estimate of ρ on the cross-section regression of the overall means and either the pooled or fixed-effects regression. This suggestion, unfortunately, often leads to negative estimates of ρ and unwarranted rejection of the model. These estimates are also inconsistent. The GJ suggestion is, unfortunately, utilized in many computer packages for implementing FGLS for panel data or for obtaining starting values for ML, and often leads to the adoption of badly biased fixed-effects OLS when a negative estimate of ρ is obtained.

The GJ suggestion is to regress the group means of the independent variable on the group means of the dependent variables:

$$\overline{y}_{i.} = \alpha + \beta\overline{x}_{i.} + w_i, \text{ where } w_i = \mu_i + \overline{\varepsilon}_{i.} \tag{18}$$

The variance of w_i is $\sigma_\mu^2 + \frac{\sigma_\varepsilon^2}{T}$. The purely cross-sectional variation of the individual means gives us information on both the slope and the overall constant in the regression. This is often called the **between groups** regression. In many panel data problems purely cross-sectional variation may dominate, but this variation may not give us much information about the true value of the slope of the independent variable if the regression also contains a lagged value of the dependent variable. The residual SS/N = RSSB/N from this regression estimates $\sigma_\mu^2 + \frac{\sigma_\varepsilon^2}{T}$. But it will not be a very good estimate if the regression is estimated by OLS, since (18) will tend to fit too well if cross-section variation dominates the data[11].

[11]For example, when a lagged value of the dependent variable is included as one of the explanatory

σ_μ^2 is then estimated as $\sigma_w^2 - \frac{\sigma_\varepsilon^2}{T}$, where an estimate of σ_ε^2 can be obtained from the fixed-effects regression. If T is large, the estimated value of σ_μ^2 is not likely to be negative no matter how well the between groups regression fits. But if T is small, and particularly if the regression contains a lagged value of the dependent variable on the right-hand side, the chances of obtaining a negative, and therefore unacceptable, estimate of ρ are high irrespective of the validity of the model.

(d) Generalized Least Squares and Feasible GLS.

The means or between regression and the fixed-effects regression both contain information about the parameters of the model: The means regression reflects purely cross-sectional variation; whereas the fixed-effects regression reflects the individual variation over time. GLS combines these two types of information with weights which depend on the characteristic roots of $Euu' = \sigma^2\Omega$. The individual means themselves are weighted by the reciprocal of the square root of $\xi = 1 - \rho + T\rho$, while the deviations from these means are weighted by the reciprocal of the square root of $\eta = 1 - \rho$. A representative transformed observation is

$$y_{it}^* = \xi^{-1/2}\overline{y}_{i.} + \eta^{-1/2}(y_{it} - \overline{y}_{i.}), \quad i = 1, \ldots, N, \quad t = 1, \ldots, T$$

---

variables, its mean may be very close to the mean of the unlagged variable; then the fit of (18) may be nearly perfect. The estimated residual variance may be close to zero in this case. In general, if there is a lot of associated cross-sectional variation, the residual of this relationship may be very small. If combined with the estimate of σ_ε^2 obtained from the within regression, the implied estimate of σ_μ^2 may well turn out to be negative (see Greene, pp. 474-476). But this does not imply that the model is mis-specified. Balestra and Nerlove (1966, p. 607) suggest estimating σ_μ^2 from the fixed-effects model as the "variance" of the implied constant terms: $\sigma_\mu^2 = \frac{1}{N}\sum_i \left(\overline{y}_{i.} - \overline{y}_{..} - \hat{\beta}(\overline{x}_{i.} - \overline{y}_{..})\right)^2$, where $\hat{\beta}$ is the OLS estimate of β in that regression. This suggestion is the one implemented in Nerlove (1971) and used to obtain FGL estimates below. Alternatively, if a regression with dummy variables for each individual, overall constant suppressed, has been estimated, it suffices to compute the variance, sum of squared deviations from the mean value divided by N, to estimate σ_μ^2.
In the following Table, I present the three estimates of ρ discussed above as possible candidates for the transformation involved in FGLS for the 94-country sample and the model in levels. The Greene-Judge estimate is sharply biased downwards and prone to be negative; similarly, the argument Nickell gives with reference to the downward bias in the coefficient of the lagged dependent variable in a fixed-effects regression suggests that the other coefficients will be biased upwards, including the variance of the estimated fixed effects, Coupled with a downward bias in the estimate of the residual variance in the fixed-effects regression, this provides an explanation of the extremely high estimates obtained by the Nerlove (1971) method. It is interesting to note that the Balestra-Nerlove estimate, while substantially higher than the GJ estimate (it can never be negative) is, nonetheless, not too far out of line with the estimates of ρ obtained from the conditional likelihood function for the OECD countries and for both the conditional and unconditional likelihood functions for the 94-country sample.

Alternative Estimates of ρ, Levels Model :

Method	94-countries	22-countries
Balestra-Nerlove (1996)	0.2678	0.4027
Nerlove (1971)	0.7790	0.7038
G-J (1983/88)	0.0983	0.0804
Conditional ML	0.1133	0.4796
Unconditional ML	0.1288	0.7700

Thus y^*_{it} is a *weighted* combination (weighted by the reciprocals of the square roots of the characteristic roots of Ω) of individual means of the original observations $\overline{y}_{i.}$ and deviations from individual means $(y_{it} - \overline{y}_{i.})$. The other variables are similarly transformed to x^*_{it} and y^*_{it-1}. GLS then amounts to running the OLS regression:

$$y^*_{it} = a + \beta x^*_{it} + \gamma y^*_{it-1} + \nu_{it} \tag{19}$$

Let $\theta^2 = \eta/\xi = (\xi^{-1/2}/\eta^{-1/2})^2$ be the relative weight of the between variation to the within variation. Note that this weight tends to 0 from above as $T \longrightarrow \infty$, i.e., the within information dominates. For T small, $\theta^2 < 1$, so that the between variation is allowed to play a greater role. When the intraclass correlation, ρ, is close to one, the unobserved, residual cross-section variation is large relative to the unobserved individual variation. $\theta^2 = 1/\left(1 + T\frac{\rho}{1-\rho}\right) = 1/\left(1 + T\frac{\sigma^2_\mu}{\sigma^2_\varepsilon}\right)$ is smaller for fixed T than when ρ is small. Between information gets a lower relative weight when ρ is large than when ρ is small, which corresponds to the usual weighting of data from sources with varying degrees of error.

To obtain an estimate of ρ for use in a feasible GLS, I prefer to obtain both an estimate of σ^2_ε from a fixed-effects model and then an estimate of σ^2 from the pooled regression, as indicated above. Although this estimate is not consistent, it is never negative and, empirically it gives, at least the appearance of, a tighter upper bound to the true value of γ than the pooled regression does and a closer approximation to the ML estimate.

(e) Bounds for the Coefficient of the Lagged Dependent Variable.

As Maddala (1971) has pointed out, the GLS estimates with $\lambda = 1/\theta^2$ can be considered members of a more general class of estimators obtained through different choices of λ. Let $\hat{\gamma}(\lambda)$ be the estimator of γ obtained by solving the GLS normal equations for an arbitrary value of λ. Sevestre and Trognon (1996, pp. 130-133) show that for the case in which $\beta = 0$, the purely autoregressive case, the following inequality holds:

$$\underset{\text{fixed - effects}}{\text{plim } \hat{\gamma}(0)} < \gamma < \underset{\text{GLS}}{\text{plim } \hat{\gamma}(\lambda)} < \underset{\text{OLS pooled}}{\text{plim } \hat{\gamma}(1)} < \underset{\text{means}}{\text{plim } \hat{\gamma}(\infty)} \tag{20}$$

Remarkably, the GLS estimate is inconsistent even when a consistent estimate of ρ is used to compute FGLS estimates. The problem is that the lagged dependent variable is correlated even with the transformed disturbance.

Since plim $\hat{\gamma}(\lambda)$ is a continuous function of λ, there exists a value λ^* in the interval $[0, 1/\theta^2]$ for which $p\lim \hat{\gamma}(\lambda) = \gamma$. Sevestre and Trognon (1983) show that this value is

$$\lambda^* = K(1-\rho)/\frac{(1-\gamma^T)E(y_{i0}\mu_i)}{(1-\gamma)\sigma^2} + K\xi, \tag{21}$$

where $K = \dfrac{T - 1 - T\gamma + \gamma^T}{T(1-\gamma)^2}$, and ρ, ξ, and σ^2 are as before.

They also show that when $\beta \neq 0$, the estimate $\hat{\gamma}(\lambda)$ behaves almost the same as in the purely autoregressive case. Since the λ^* estimate is consistent when there are no exogenous variables, it remains so when there are. The trick is to obtain a consistent estimate of λ^* which can be accomplished by finding an appropriate instrumental variable for y_{-1}. Even in this case the results depend heavily on the distribution of the estimate of λ^*.

In the dynamic error-components model, not only are the OLS pooled regression estimates, the fixed-effect or within estimates, and the between estimates inconsistent, but so are the GLS estimates using the true value of ρ. However, the method of instrumental variables may be used to obtain a feasible member of the λ-class of estimates which is consistent. (See Sevestre and Trognon, 1996.) Unfortunately, this estimate may have a very large variance, as demonstrated in Nerlove (1971).

Nonetheless, the fixed-effects and the pooled regressions may be used to bound the true value of γ even when exogenous regressors are also included. Empirically, I have found that FGLS appears to provide an even tighter bound, although since FGLS is also based on an inconsistent estimate of ρ, there is no guarantee that this is in fact an upper bound.

(f) Maximum Likelihood Conditional on the Initial Value of the Lagged Dependent Variable.

When the likelihood function for the model (13) with $u_{it} = \mu_i \sim N(0, \sigma^2\Omega)$ is derived in the usual way from the product of the densities of y_{it} conditional on x_{it} and y_{it-1}, the joint density is conditional on y_{i0}. This likelihood function can be written in terms of the earlier notation introduced as

$$\begin{aligned}\log L(\alpha,\beta,\gamma,\sigma_\mu^2,\sigma_\varepsilon^2 \mid y_{11},\ldots,y_{NT};x_{NT};y_{10},\ldots,Y_{N0}) \\ = -\frac{NT}{2}\log 2\pi - \frac{NT}{2}\log\sigma^2 - \frac{N}{2}\log\xi - \frac{N(T-1)}{2}\log\eta \\ -\frac{1}{2\sigma^2}\sum_{i=1}^{N}\sum_{t=1}^{T}\left(y_{it}^* - \alpha\xi^{-1/2} - \beta x_{it}^* - \gamma y_{it-1}^*\right)^2\end{aligned} \tag{22}$$

where y^*, x^* and y_{-1}^* are the transformed variables. Since $\xi = \dfrac{T}{1+\lambda(T-1)}$ and $\eta = \dfrac{\lambda T}{1+\lambda(T-1)}$, $\log L$ can be expressed as a function solely of $\lambda, \sigma^2, \alpha, \beta$ and γ. Trognon (1978) shows that, when the exogenous variable x is generated by a first-order autoregression with white noise input, $w \sim wn(0, \sigma_w^2 I)$, also assumed in the Monte Carlo experiments reported in Nerlove (1971),

$$x = \delta x_{-1} + w \tag{23}$$

maximization of the conditional likelihood function (22) yields boundary solutions $\hat{\rho} = 0$, which, unlike interior maximum likelihood solutions, are inconsistent, for a considerable, and indeed likely, range of parameter values. In particular, there is a value of γ in (13),

$$\gamma^* = \frac{(T-3)^2 - 8}{(T+1)^2}$$

such that when $\gamma < \gamma^*$ there exists an interior maximum of (22) which yields consistent ML estimates, but that when $\gamma \geq \gamma^*$ there are values of ρ for which the conditional likelihood function (13) is maximized at the boundary $\rho = 0$, i.e., for the OLS estimates of the pooled regression, which we know to be inconsistent. The problem is that when T is small the permissible range of γ, the coefficient of the lagged dependent variable is implausible (e.g., negative or very small). For example, for $T = 5$, $\gamma^* = -0.11$, while for $T = 10$, $\gamma^* = 0.34$. When $\gamma \geq \gamma^*$, whether or not an interior maximum with consistent ML estimates occurs depends on the value of ρ : For $\rho < \rho^*$ boundary maxima occur where

$$\rho^* = \left(\frac{T-1}{T+1}\right)^2 \frac{\beta^2\sigma_w^2}{\sigma^2} \frac{1-\gamma}{(\gamma-\gamma^*)(1-\gamma\delta)^2}$$

For example, when $T = 5$, $\beta = 1.0$, $\gamma = 0.75$, $\delta = 0.5$, and $\frac{\sigma^2}{\sigma^2} = 1.0$, $\gamma^* = -0.11$ and the critical value of ρ is $\rho^* = 0.31$. That means that any true value of the intraclass correlation less than 0.31 is liable to produce a boundary solution to (22) $\rho = 0$ and inconsistent estimate of all the parameters. Using these results, Trognon (1978) is able to replicate the Monte Carlo results reported in Nerlove (1971)[12].

Even though ML may yield inconsistent estimates when the nonnegligible probability of a boundary solution is taken into account, it is nonetheless true that the likelihood function summarizes the information contained in the data about the parameters. (Birnbaum, 1962; Barnard, Jenkins and Winsten, 1962.) For this reason, sections of some of the multidimensional likelihood functions are also presented in the next section. When first differences are taken to eliminate a linear deterministic trend, the differenced model, the individual-specific time invariant effects become differences in the trend slopes. This makes the interpretation of the model in first-difference form different than that in levels. Moreover, the time- and individual varying disturbance is now likely to be serially correlated, a fact which needs to be taken into account in the formulation of the unconditional likelihood function[13]. The differenced model is implemented in Nerlove (1997).

[12]Maddala (1971, pp. 346 - 347) gives a condition for the gradient of the concentrated likelihood function to be positive at a boundary $\rho = 0$ (OLS on the pooled data) for the conditional likelihood function. So if ρ is constrained to the interval [0,1] this implies a local maximum at the boundary 0. Breusch (1987) shows that this condition can be easily checked at the start of his iterative GLS procedure by beginning with the pooled OLS estimates and $\rho = 0$. Unfortunately these results apply only to the likelihood function when no lagged value of the dependent variable is included or when those initial values are conditioned upon. I have not been able to derive a similar result for the unconditional likelihood function below.

[13]Adding a trend, t, to (13)

$$y_{it} = \alpha + \beta x_{it} + \gamma y_{it-1} + \tau_i t + \mu_i + \varepsilon_{it}, i = 1, \ldots N, t = 1, \ldots T, \text{ and differencing,} \tag{13'}$$

$$\Delta y_{it} = \beta \Delta x_{it} + \gamma \Delta y_{it-1} + \tau_i + \Delta\varepsilon_{it}, i = 1, \ldots N, t = 1, \ldots T, \tag{13''}$$

where Δ denotes the first-difference operator and τ_i is the individual-specific trend coefficient, assumed to have mean zero (enforced by eliminating any overall constant in the differences by deducting the sample means). Thus, not only is the meaning of ρ altered, but if ε_{it} did not contain a unit root to start with it will now; in particular, if ε_{it} is not serially correlated to start with, it will follow a first-order moving

(g) Unconditional Maximum Likelihood.

While it is not guaranteed that no boundary solution to the likelihood equations is obtained, yielding inconsistent estimates, it is apparent that in panels with a short time dimension the initial values provide important information about the parameters of the model, and to condition on them is to neglect this information.

It is not, in fact difficult to obtain the unconditional likelihood function once the marginal distribution of the initial values is specified. The problem is a correct specification of this distribution. If $|\gamma| \geq 1$ or the processes generating the x_{it} are not stationary, it will not, in general be possible to specify the marginal distribution of the initial observations. I will assume that, possibly after some differencing, both the y_{it} and the x_{it} are stationary. The difficulties associated with the formulation of the unconditional likelihood function in the case in which deterministic or stochastic trends are included are discussed in footnote 13 above.

Under this assumption, the dynamic relationship to be estimated is stationary and $|\gamma| < 1$. Consider equation (14)[14] with the intercept eliminated, for y_{i0} and the infinite past:

$$y_{i0} = \sum_{j=1}^{\infty} \gamma^j \beta x_{i,-j} + \frac{1}{1-\gamma}\mu_i + \nu_{i0}, \text{ where } \nu_{it} = \gamma \nu_{it-1} + \varepsilon_{it}{}^{15} \qquad (23')$$

If $\beta = 0$, so that the relationship to be estimated is a pure autoregression for each y_{it}, the vector of initial values $y_0 = (y_{10}, \ldots y_{N0})'$ has a joint normal distribution with means 0 and variance-covariance matrix $\left(\frac{\sigma_\mu^2}{(1-\gamma)^2} + \sigma_\nu^2\right) I_N = \left(\frac{\sigma_\mu^2}{(1-\gamma)^2} + \frac{\sigma_\varepsilon^2}{1-\gamma^2}\right) I_N$. The

average process with unit root. The variance-covariance matrix of the new disturbances $\tau_i + \Delta\varepsilon_{it}$ is now block diagonal with blocks:

$$A = \sigma^2 \begin{bmatrix} 1 & a & b & ...b \\ a & 1 & a & b... \\ b & a & 1 & a... \\ \vdots & \vdots & \vdots & ...1 \end{bmatrix} \quad \text{where } \sigma^2 = \sigma_\tau^2 + \sigma_\varepsilon^2, a = \frac{\sigma_\tau^2 - \sigma_\varepsilon^2}{\sigma^2}, \text{ and } b = \frac{\sigma_\tau^2}{\sigma^2}$$

The characteristic roots of A give the necessary transform and Jacobian. This should be taken into account in the formulation of both the conditional and the unconditional likelihood functions. As indicated, however, differencing is unnecessary when the initial values are conditioning, but then a trend variable must be included as explanatory with as many different slopes as countries. See Nerlove (1997, section 2.2) for an extended discussion of the transformation required to render the time-varying part of the disturbances serially uncorrelated.

[14]For a particular time period T and the infinite past $y_{iT} = \gamma^\infty y_{i-\infty} + \sum_{j=0}^{\infty} \gamma^j \beta x_{iT-j} + \frac{1-\gamma^\infty}{1-\gamma}\mu_i + \nu_{iT}$, where $\nu_{iT} = \sum_{j=0}^{\infty} \gamma^j \varepsilon_{iT-j}$ is the MA form of a first-order autoregression with white noise input, equation (24) follows.

[15]If all variables are expressed as deviations of from their overall means, there is no need to include an intercept; if not, μ_i should be replaced by $\alpha + \mu_i$.

unconditional likelihood is therefore

$$\begin{aligned}
\log L(\gamma, \rho, \sigma_\mu^2, \sigma_\varepsilon^2 \mid y_{11}, \ldots, y_{NT}; \ldots; y_{10}, \ldots, y_{N0}) \\
= -\frac{NT}{2}\log 2\pi - \frac{NT}{2}\log\sigma^2 - \frac{N}{2}\log\xi - \frac{N(T-1)}{2}\log\eta \\
- \frac{1}{2\sigma^2}\sum_{i=1}^{N}\sum_{t=1}^{T}(y_{it}^* - \gamma y_{it-1}^*)^2 \\
- \frac{N}{2}\log\left(\frac{\sigma_\mu^2}{(1-\gamma)^2} + \frac{\sigma_\varepsilon^2}{1-\gamma^2}\right) - \left[\frac{1}{2\left(\frac{\sigma_\mu^2}{(1-\gamma)^2} + \frac{\sigma_\varepsilon^2}{1-\gamma^2}\right)}\right]\sum_{i=1}^{N} y_{i0}^2 \qquad (24)
\end{aligned}$$

This likelihood function can easily be concentrated: To maximize, express $\sigma_\mu^2, \sigma_\varepsilon^2, \xi$ and η in terms of ρ and γ. For given ρ and γ in the interval [0,1), concentrate the likelihood function with respect to σ^2. It follows that

$$\hat{\sigma}^2(\gamma, \rho) = \frac{RSS^*(\gamma, \rho)}{N(T+1)}$$

where $RSS^*(\gamma, \rho) = \sum_{i=1}^{N}\sum_{t=1}^{T}(y_{it}^* - \gamma y_{it-1}^*)^2 + \sum_{i=1}^{N} y_{i0}^2 / \left[\frac{\rho}{(1-\gamma)^2} + \frac{1-\rho}{1-\gamma^2}\right]$.

Thus, the concentrated LF is

$$\begin{aligned}
\log L^*(\gamma, \rho) = -\frac{N(T+1)}{2}\log 2\pi - \frac{N}{2}\log\xi - \frac{N(T-1)}{2}\log\nu \\
- \frac{N(T-1)}{2}\log\left\{\frac{RSS^*(\gamma, \rho)}{N(T-1)}\right\} - \frac{N}{2}\left\{\frac{\rho}{(1-\gamma)^2} + \frac{1-\rho}{1-\gamma^2}\right\} \\
- \left({}^1/_{2RSS^*/N(T+1)}\right)\sum_{i=1}^{N}\sum_{t=1}^{T}(y_{it}^* - \gamma y_{it-1.}^*)^2 \\
- \sum_{i=1}^{N} y_{i0}^2 / \{(2/N(T+1))\left[\frac{\rho}{(1-\gamma)^2} + \frac{1-\rho}{1-\gamma^2}\right] RSS^*\}
\end{aligned}$$

This is quite a bit more complicated than the usual minimization of the sum of squares in the penultimate term because RSS^*, in that term, depends on $\sum_{i=1}^{n} y_{i0}^2$, as well as on ρ and γ, which enter the final terms as well.

When $\beta \neq 0$, things are more complicated still. Various alternative specifications considered in the literature are reported and analyzed in Sevestre and Trognon (1996, pp. 136-138)[16]. Considerable simplification, however, can be obtained if, following Nerlove

[16]One interesting possibility discussed by Trognon and Sevestre (1996, p. 136-138) is to choose y_{i0} a linear function of some *observed* individual-specific disturbances μ_i and a remainder. The first-order equations for maximizing the likelihood then take on a simple recursive form when $\beta = 0$, and permit other simplifications when $\beta \neq 0$. But if we knew some individual-specific time-invariant observed variables influenced behavior, why not incorporate them directly in (13), the equation to be estimated ?

(1971), we are willing to assume that x_{it} follows a well-specified common stationary time-series model for all individuals i. The first term in (23') is $\varphi_{i0} = \beta \sum_{j=0}^{\infty} \gamma^j x_{i,-j}$. Hence, for any stationary process x_{it}, which may be serially correlated,

$$\frac{\varphi_{it}}{\beta} = \gamma \frac{\varphi_{it-1}}{\beta} + x_{it}$$

with variances

$$\sigma^2_{\varphi_i} = \frac{\beta^2 \sigma^2_{x_i}}{1-\gamma^2} \tag{25}$$

If we suppose that the variance of the x_{it} is the same for all i, then the random variable

$$\phi_{it} = \sum_{j=0}^{\infty} \gamma^j \beta x_{it-j}$$

has a well defined variance which is the same for all i and a function of β, γ, and σ^2_x. This then enters the final term in the unconditional likelihood (25), which now becomes:

$$\begin{aligned}
\log L(\beta, \gamma, \sigma^2_\mu, \sigma^2_\varepsilon\ & |y_{11}, \ldots, y_{NT}; x_{11}, \ldots x_{NT}; y_{10}, \ldots, y_{N0}) \\
&= -\frac{N(T+1)}{2}\log 2\pi - \frac{NT}{2}\log\sigma^2 - \frac{N}{2}\log\xi - \frac{N(T-1)}{2}\log\nu \\
&\quad - \frac{1}{2\sigma^2}\sum_{i=1}^{N}\sum_{t=1}^{T}\left(y^*_{it} - \beta x^*_{it} - \gamma y^*_{it-1}\right)^2 \\
&\quad - \frac{N}{2}\log\left(\frac{\sigma^2_\mu}{(1-\gamma)^2} + \frac{\sigma^2_\varepsilon}{1-\gamma^2}\right) - \left[\frac{1}{2\left(\frac{\sigma^2_\mu}{(1-\gamma)^2} + \frac{\sigma^2_\varepsilon}{1-\gamma^2}\right)}\right]\sum_{i=1}^{n} y^2_{i0}
\end{aligned} \tag{26}$$

Concentrating the likelihood function to permit a one- or two-dimensional grid search is no longer possible. If gradient procedures yield an interior maximum, the ML estimates obtained are consistent as long as the random variables $\phi_{it} = \sum_{j=0}^{\infty} \gamma^j \beta x_{i,t-j}$ have well-defined variances and covariances, which they will if the x_{it} are generated by a stationary process. It doesn't really matter what this process is as long as it is stationary. Besides, since the x_{it} are assumed to be exogenous, we really have no basis on which to model their determination and are likely to misspecify this part of the model. In this sense we ought to prefer this kind of "almost full-information" maximum likelihood. Still we have to assume something about the variance of the x process in order to proceed. I suggest estimating σ^2_x from the sample data.

To generalize these results to the case in which there are several explanatory variables in addition to the lagged value of the dependent variable, assume that X_{it} follows a stationary VAR process and replace βx^*_{it} by $X^*_{it}\beta$ and $\beta^2\sigma^2_x$ by $\beta' \sum_{XX} \beta$ in the above formula.

5. EMPIRICAL EVIDENCE ON GROWTH RATE CONVERGENCE AND THE COMPARATIVE PERFORMANCE OF DIFFERENT PANEL DATA METHODS

(a) Numerical Results.

In order to examine the effects of the econometric methods employed on the finding of growth rate convergence or the lack of it, I initially used data on 94 countries for the period 1960 - 1985, and a subsample of 22 OECD countries, from the Penn World Tables 5.6, publicly available from the NBER web site at ftp://nber.harvard.edu/pub/. The countries are listed in the Appendix. Following Islam (1995), s and n were computed as quinquennial means over the preceding 5-year span for the 5 years 1965, 1970, 1975, 1980, 1985; y was taken as the value reported in that year and in 1960 for the lagged value applicable to 1965. Characteristics of the sample are reported in Table 1. The results of the six methods applied to these data or to their first differences are reported in Tables 2 and 3. In the case of the latter, an appropriate transformation of the original data is made to eliminate the serial correlation introduced in the time-varying part of the disturbance by the first-difference transformation, as worked out in Nerlove (1997). I have listed the regression methods in the order in which the corresponding estimates of γ appear in the inequality of Trognon and Sevestre (equation (20) above). These estimates are followed by the maximum likelihood estimates conditional on the initial values y_{i0} and the ML estimates unconditional on the initial values, assuming stationarity of both the processes generating the exogenous variable and real GDP per capita. In a substantive study of growth rate convergence, it would clearly be important to include additional explanatory variables such as, for example, the stock of human capital, also available at the NBER internet site, infrastructure investment, and so forth. However, for my purpose here, omission of relevant variables simply increases the unexplained disturbance variance and thus heightens the contrast among alternative estimators.

Table 1
Comparative Descriptive Statistics for the Two Samples

Item	**94-country sample**	**22-country sample**	**Ratio 22/94 values**
Variance initial y	0.799	0.256	0.320
Variance final y	0.899	0.222	0.247
Correlation between y_0 and y_5	0.988	0.090	0.092
Variances about overall means:			
y	1.058	0.204	0.193
z	0.698	0.040	0.058
Pooled variances about country means:			
y	0.045	0.040	0.897
z	0.083	0.007	0.084

Turning now to the regression estimates presented in Tables 2 and 3:

Consider the first four methods applied to the levels model. The estimates of γ for the 94-country sample range from a low of 0.72 (fixed-effects regression) to a high of 0.98 (country means regression) with pooled OLS and FGLS falling in between. For the OECD countries the range is 0.76 to 0.93. The implied speed of convergence thus ranges from 90% in 35 years to 90% in 570 years. None could be characterized as evidence of reasonably rapid convergence. All of the estimates of γ satisfy the Trognon-Sevestre inequality, although the regressions contain an exogenous explanatory variable in contrast to the case considered by Trognon and Sevestre. Pooled OLS and FGLS also stand in the order predicted by the Trognon-Sevestre results. While it is tempting to infer that FGLS provides a tighter upper bound to the true value of γ than the pooled OLS regression estimate, the temptation should be resisted. The FGLS estimates are doubly inconsistent: they are based on an inconsistent estimate of ρ reflecting the inconsistency of the estimates of the residual variance and the fixed effects depending on which regressions they are derived from. Not only is the estimated value of β sensitive to the method of estimation but the estimate of the elasticity of output with respect to capital stock in the production function is extremely so, reflecting the dependence of the estimated value on the coefficient of the lagged dependent variable, γ. This parameter should estimate approximately (1 - the share of labor in the real GDP). It is clear that all of the estimates of capital's share are wide of the mark. If therefore one were to infer policy implications from this parameter, it could be seriously misleading.

The most interesting estimates are those for conditional and unconditional maximum likelihood presented as methods 5 and 6 in Table 2. In the case of the 22 country OECD sample, these estimates differ quite a bit from one another, although unconditional ML is not far from the fixed-effects OLS regression, while conditional ML yields results close to FGLS using the Balestra-Nerlove (1966) first-round estimate of ρ. The contrast with the 94-country sample is striking: The conditional and the unconditional ML estimates differ little from one another. They are close to the pooled OLS regression estimates (a consequence of the fact that the estimated value of ρ is small although significantly different from zero), but are both quite different than any of the inconsistent regression estimates. As found earlier, the estimates of β are quite insensitive to the method used, but the estimates of γ are not very different either; consequently the implied estimates of capital's share are similar, albeit different for the two samples[17].

Turning now to the parameter estimates for the first-difference model presented in Table 3.

[17]What accounts for these remarkable differences between the two samples and for the similarity of the unconditional and conditional ML estimates for the 94-country sample ? Consider the log of the ratio of the unconditional to the conditional likelihood, i.e. the marginal density of y_{i0}:

log{ unconditional / conditional likelihood } =

$$-\frac{N}{2}\log 2\pi - \frac{N}{2}\log(\frac{\beta^2\sigma_x^2}{1-\gamma^2} + \frac{\rho\sigma^2}{(1-\gamma)^2} + \frac{(1-\rho)\sigma^2}{1-\gamma^2}) - \left[\frac{1}{2\left(\frac{\beta^2\sigma_x^2}{1-\gamma^2} + \frac{\rho\sigma^2}{(1-\gamma)^2} + \frac{(1-\rho)\sigma^2}{1-\gamma^2}\right)}\right]\sum_{i=1}^{n} y_{i0}^2$$

Table 2

Parameter Estimates for the Model in Levels Alternative Econometric Analyses

METHOD OF ANALYSIS	94-COUNTRY SAMPLE	22-COUNTRY SAMPLE
1. Fixed Effects OLS		
γ	0.7204 (0.0211)	0.7645 (0.0166)
β	0.1656 (0.0172)	0.1634 (0.0510)
Implied Capital Share	0.3719 (0.0278)	0.4096 (0.0783)
Residual Variance	0.0113	0.0020
2. Feasible GLS		
Estimate of ρ used*	0.2675	0.4027
γ	0.9130 (0.0119)	0.8282 (0.0156)
β	0.1520 (0.0135)	0.1913 (0.0422)
Implied Capital Share	0.6362 (0.0247)	0.5269 (0.0579)
Residual Variance	0.0213	0.0047
3. Pooled OLS		
γ	0.9487 (0.0090)	0.8857 (0.0125)
β	0.1244 (0.0108)	0.1764 (0.0308)
Implied Capital Share	0.7080 (0.0271)	0.6067 (0.0452)
Residual Variance	0.0193	0.0041
4. Country Means OLS		
γ	0.9817 (0.0112)	0.9320 (0.0148)
δ	0.0919 (0.0138)	0.1493 (0.0343)
Implied Capital Share	0.8339 (0.0704)	0.6870 (0.0593)
Residual Variance	0.0047	0.0580
5. Conditional ML		
ρ	0.1133 (0.0497)	0.4796 (0.1584)
γ	0.9339 (0.0122)	0.8189 (0.0245)
β	0.1370 (0.0131)	0.1908 (0.0438)
Implied Capital Share	0.6744 (0.0289)	0.5131 (0.0664)
Residual Variance	0.0194 (0.0013)	0.0052 (0.0012)
6. Unconditional ML		
Estimates of σ_x^2 used	0.0826	0.0069
ρ	0.1288 (0.0456)	0.7700 (0.0731)
γ	0.9385 (0.0105)	0.8085 (0.0228)
β	0.1334 (0.0124)	0.1815 (0.0521)
Implied Capital Share	0.6846 (0.0277)	0.4865 (0.0791)
Residual Variance	0.0197 (0.0013)	0.0113 (0.0028)

Figures in parentheses are standard errors.

*Estimated by the method suggested in Balestra and Nerlove (1966).

Table 3

Parameter Estimates for the Model in First Differences, Alternative Econometric Analyses

METHOD OF ANALYSIS	94-COUNTRY SAMPLE	22-COUNTRY SAMPLE
1. Fixed Effects OLS		
γ	0.4007 (0.0375)	0.4544 (0.0611)
β	0.1199 (0.0187)	- 0.0126 (0.0637)
Implied Capital Share	0.1667 (0.0246)	- 0.0237 (0.1209)
Residual Variance	0.0077	0.0014
2. Feasible GLS		
Estimate of used*	0.4866	0.3628
γ	0.4227 (0.0406)	0.5833 (0.0531)
β	0.1520 (0.0135)	0.1913 (0.0422)
Implied Capital Share	0.1864 (0.0259)	0.1322 (0.1218)
Residual Variance	0.0213	0.0047
3. Pooled OLS		
γ	0.7031 (0.0328)	0.6237 (0.0453)
β	0.1632 (0.0195)	0.0845 (0.0586)
Implied Capital Share	0.3548 (0.0373)	0.1834 (0.1121)
Residual Variance	0.0141	0.0022
4. Country Means OLS		
γ	0.9178 (0.0471)	0.7215 (0.0572)
β	0.1719 (0.0339)	0.1174 (0.0978)
Implied Capital Share	0.6763 (0.1263)	0.2965 (0.1873)
Residual Variance	0.0041	0.0005
5. Conditional ML		
ρ	0.2267 (0.0664)	0.0126 (0.0405)
γ	0.4540 (0.0651)	0.6187 (0.0490)
β	0.1368 (0.0208)	0.0815 (0.0601)
Implied Capital Share	0.2004 (0.0358)	0.1762 (0.1159)
Residual Variance	0.0122 (0.0009)	0.0021 (0.0003)
6. Unconditional ML		
Estimate of σ_x^2 used	0.0597	0.0058
ρ	0.2335 (0.0632)	0.0936 (0.0696)
γ	0.4364 (0.0578)	0.7254 (0.0512)
β	0.1340 (0.0201)	0.1478 (0.0727)
Implied Capital Share	0.1921 (0.0317)	0.3500 (0.1326)
Residual Variance	0.0120 (0.0008)	0.0027 (0.0004)

Figures in parentheses are standard errors.

* Estimated by the method suggested in Balestra and Nerlove (1966).

The contrast with the levels model is remarkable; at least in terms of reasonableness, at last we seem to be in the right "ball park". Consider the first four methods applied to the levels model. The estimates of γ for the 94-country sample range from a low of 0.40 (fixed-effects regression) to a high of 0.92 (country means regression) with pooled OLS and FGLS falling in between. For the OECD countries the range is 0.36 to 0.72. The implied speed of convergence thus much more reasonable that obtained for the levels model, although none could be characterized as evidence of reasonably rapid convergence[18]. The estimates of γ still satisfy the Sevestre-Trognon inequality. As was the case for the levels model, the estimated value of β is sensitive to the method of estimation, although generally less so, and the estimate of the elasticity of output with respect to capital stock in the production function is more so, reflecting the dependence of the estimated value on the coefficient of the lagged dependent variable, γ. This parameter should estimate approximately (1 - the share of labor in the real GDP). It is clear that these estimates bring us much closer to what could be considered a reasonable figure.

The most plausible estimates are those for conditional and unconditional maximum likelihood presented as methods 5 and 6 in Table 3. In the case of the 22 country OECD sample only, the estimates differ from one another. Implied speeds of convergence are still, however, quite slow for the OECD countries, but much, much faster for the larger group of 94 countries. Perhaps one can conclude that if differing country-specific trends are taken into account, so-called "beta convergence" obtains at a reasonably rapid rate for a group of diverse countries, but when the relatively homogeneous group of OECD countries is considered, convergence is much more problematic.

Let the sample variance of y_{i0} be var y_0 and let

$$\varphi^2 = (\frac{\beta^2\sigma_x^2}{1-\gamma^2} + \frac{\rho\sigma^2}{(1-\gamma)^2} + \frac{(1-\rho)\sigma^2}{1-\gamma^2})$$

Then

$$\log\{\text{unconditional / conditional likelihood}\} = -\frac{N}{2}\log 2\pi - \frac{N}{2}\log(\varphi^2) - \left[\frac{N \text{ var } y_0}{2\varphi^2}\right]$$

This function is clearly decreasing in N and var y_0. Its behavior with respect to φ^2 depends on the relation between var y_0 and φ^2. When var $y_0 > \varphi^2$, it is increasing; but when var $y_0 > \varphi^2$, it is decreasing. Thus for a given var y_0 the log of the ratio of the unconditional to the conditional density tends to zero, i.e. the ratio tends to one, as N increases and as φ^2 increases. In other words the unconditional becomes more and more like the conditional likelihood. For $\beta = 0.15$, $\gamma = 0.85$, $\sigma_x^2 = 0.08$, $\rho = 0.8$ and $\sigma^2 = 0.02$, $\varphi^2 = 0.73$. Table 1 above presents some descriptive statistics for the two samples. Typically, var y_0 is much less than 0.73, for example, 0.256 for the 22-country sample. On the other hand it is about that value for the 94-country sample. Thus the principle explanation for the similarity of the conditional ML and the unconditional ML estimates for the 94-country sample is the size of the cross-section dimension; similarly, the small sample in the OECD case accounts for the lack of similarity.

[18]See footnote 4 above concerning the issue of whether it is reasonable to characterize convergence conditional on country-specific trends as convergence at all.

(b) Graphical Results.

Further insight into the support for the convergence hypothesis, as modified in this paper, which is given by the likelihood functions for the two samples can be obtained graphically. Since the first-difference model gives by far the most plausible results, I present only graphs for this case. Bear in mind, however, that the convergence concept considered is "beta" convergence with a vengeance. Not only are the results conditioned on differing savings and population growth rates, but I am allowing for differing linear trends among countries. The model is reduced to stationarity by first-differencing the quinquennial averages. The explanatory variables, in this case first differences of savings rates and population growth rates are assumed to be exogenous and to be determined by some sort of stationary process. Having eliminated the constant term by taking deviations from the overall means of all variables, we are left with four parameters: ρ, γ, β and σ^2. Although there are $\binom{4}{2} = 6$ possible pairs to consider, I focus on the crucial pairs: ρ *vs.* γ and β *vs.* σ^2. It is important that the likelihood functions as formulated reflect the operation of the process which generated the data before we began to observe them; the appearance of the unconditional likelihood functions is rather different even though the ML estimates are quite close to those given by the unconditional likelihood functions.

Figures 1 and 2 give one-parameter slices and 2-parameter 3-D plots of the likelihood for the pairs $\rho - \gamma$ and $\beta - \sigma^2$ for the 94- and 22-country samples, respectively. Each figure consists of eight plots each. The figures are at the end of the paper. The main finding is that the difference between the estimates for the two samples is not great except for a much slower speed of convergence (larger γ) for the more diverse 94-country sample and is well-supported by the shape of the likelihood functions in the two cases.

The likelihood reaches a unique maximum in every case. Except for σ^2, the functions are well-behaved in the vicinity of the maximizing parameter values. Since the value of σ^2 is bounded from below by zero, the graph has the typical shape found in regression problems: a sharp rise from near zero followed by a long slow decline. I find no evidence of double maxima or a boundary maximum of the likelihood function with respect to ρ. There is clearly considerable "trade-off" between ρ and γ for the 94-country sample and to a lesser degree for the 22-country sample.

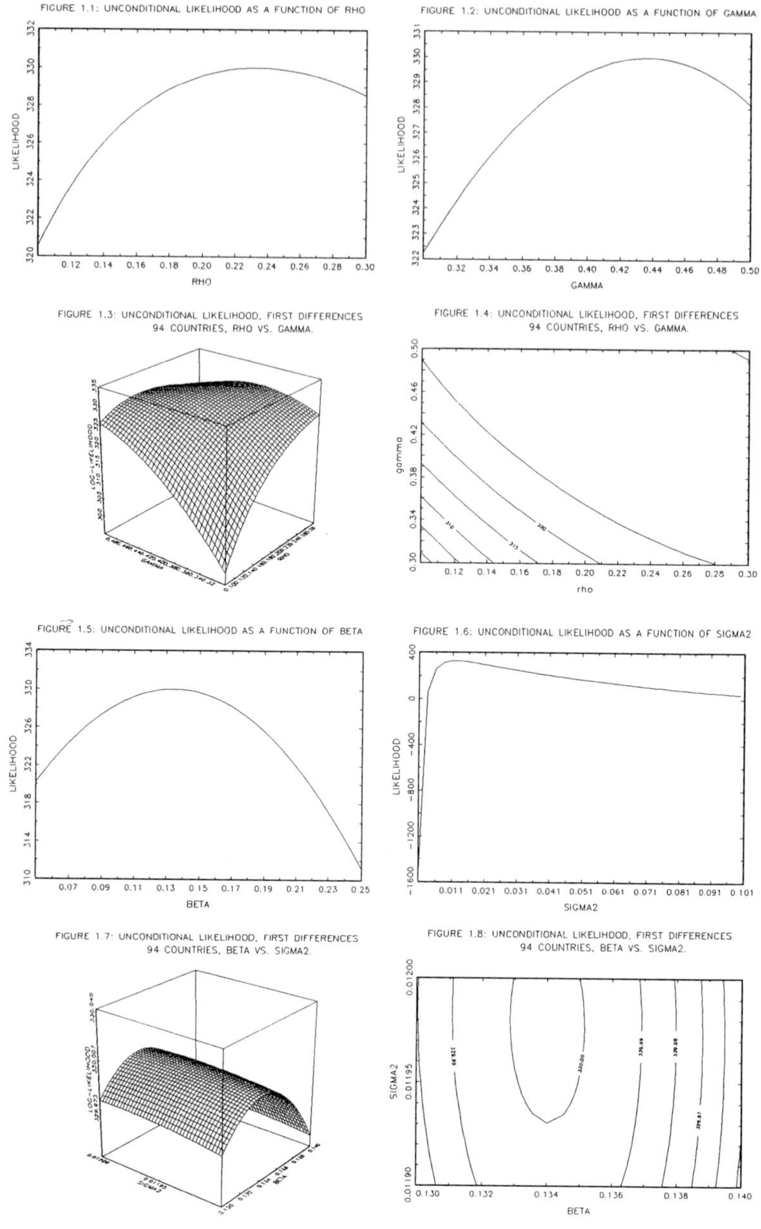
FIGURE 1.1: UNCONDITIONAL LIKELIHOOD AS A FUNCTION OF RHO
LIKELIHOOD
320 322 324 326 328 330 332
0.12 0.14 0.16 0.18 0.20 0.22 0.24 0.26 0.28 0.30
RHO
FIGURE 1.2: UNCONDITIONAL LIKELIHOOD AS A FUNCTION OF GAMMA
LIKELIHOOD
322 323 324 325 326 327 328 329 330 331
0.32 0.34 0.36 0.38 0.40 0.42 0.44 0.46 0.48 0.50
GAMMA
FIGURE 1.3: UNCONDITIONAL LIKELIHOOD, FIRST DIFFERENCES
94 COUNTRIES, RHO VS. GAMMA.
LOG-LIKELIHOOD
GAMMA
FIGURE 1.4: UNCONDITIONAL LIKELIHOOD, FIRST DIFFERENCES
94 COUNTRIES, RHO VS. GAMMA.
gamma
0.30 0.34 0.38 0.42 0.46 0.50
0.12 0.14 0.16 0.18 0.20 0.22 0.24 0.26 0.28 0.30
rho
FIGURE 1.5: UNCONDITIONAL LIKELIHOOD AS A FUNCTION OF BETA
LIKELIHOOD
310 314 318 322 326 330 334
0.07 0.09 0.11 0.13 0.15 0.17 0.19 0.21 0.23 0.25
BETA
FIGURE 1.6: UNCONDITIONAL LIKELIHOOD AS A FUNCTION OF SIGMA2
LIKELIHOOD
−1600 −1200 −800 −400 0 400
0.011 0.021 0.031 0.041 0.051 0.061 0.071 0.081 0.091 0.101
SIGMA2
FIGURE 1.7: UNCONDITIONAL LIKELIHOOD, FIRST DIFFERENCES
94 COUNTRIES, BETA VS. SIGMA2.
LOG-LIKELIHOOD
SIGMA2
BETA
FIGURE 1.8: UNCONDITIONAL LIKELIHOOD, FIRST DIFFERENCES
94 COUNTRIES, BETA VS. SIGMA2.
SIGMA2
0.01190 0.01195 0.01200
0.130 0.132 0.134 0.136 0.138 0.140
BETA

Figure 1.

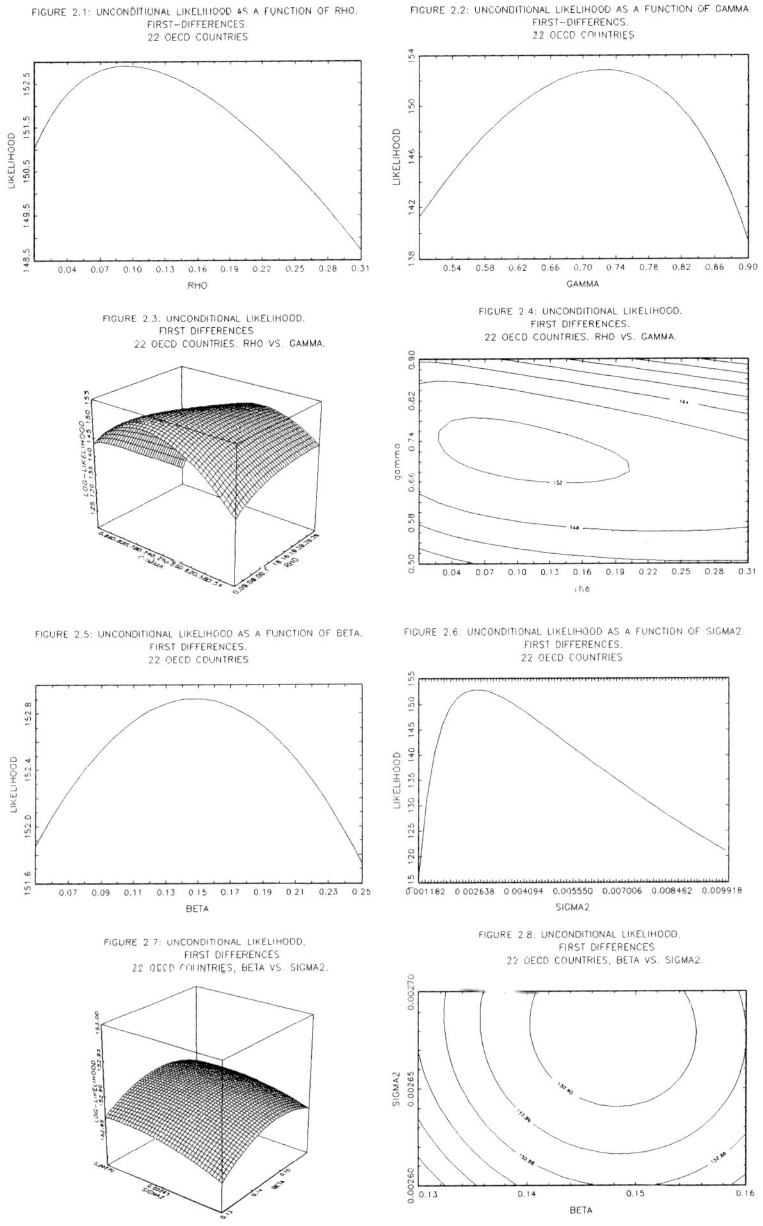
FIGURE 2.1: UNCONDITIONAL LIKELIHOOD AS A FUNCTION OF RHO.
FIRST-DIFFERENCES.
22 OECD COUNTRIES
LIKELIHOOD
148.5 149.5 150.5 151.5 152.5
0.04 0.07 0.10 0.13 0.16 0.19 0.22 0.25 0.28 0.31
RHO
FIGURE 2.2: UNCONDITIONAL LIKELIHOOD AS A FUNCTION OF GAMMA.
FIRST-DIFFERENCS.
22 OECD COUNTRIES
LIKELIHOOD
138 142 146 150 154
0.54 0.58 0.62 0.66 0.70 0.74 0.78 0.82 0.86 0.90
GAMMA
FIGURE 2.3: UNCONDITIONAL LIKELIHOOD.
FIRST DIFFERENCES
22 OECD COUNTRIES. RHO VS. GAMMA.
LOG-LIKELIHOOD
GAMMA
FIGURE 2.4: UNCONDITIONAL LIKELIHOOD.
FIRST DIFFERENCES.
22 OECD COUNTRIES. RHO VS. GAMMA.
gamma
0.50 0.58 0.66 0.74 0.82 0.90
0.04 0.07 0.10 0.13 0.16 0.19 0.22 0.25 0.28 0.31
rho
FIGURE 2.5: UNCONDITIONAL LIKELIHOOD AS A FUNCTION OF BETA.
FIRST DIFFERENCES.
22 OECD COUNTRIES
LIKELIHOOD
151.6 152.0 152.4 152.8
0.07 0.09 0.11 0.13 0.15 0.17 0.19 0.21 0.23 0.25
BETA
FIGURE 2.6: UNCONDITIONAL LIKELIHOOD AS A FUNCTION OF SIGMA2.
FIRST DIFFERENCES.
22 OECD COUNTRIES
LIKELIHOOD
115 120 125 130 135 140 145 150 155
0.001182 0.002638 0.004094 0.005550 0.007006 0.008462 0.009918
SIGMA2
FIGURE 2.7: UNCONDITIONAL LIKELIHOOD.
FIRST DIFFERENCES
22 OECD COUNTRIES, BETA VS. SIGMA2.
LOG-LIKELIHOOD
SIGMA2
BETA
FIGURE 2.8: UNCONDITIONAL LIKELIHOOD.
FIRST DIFFERENCES
22 OECD COUNTRIES, BETA VS. SIGMA2.
SIGMA2
0.00260 0.00265 0.00270
0.13 0.14 0.15 0.16
BETA

Figure 2.

6. CONCLUSIONS

The principal conclusion that can be drawn from this analysis is that, in panel data econometrics, method matters – a lot. Although, using a highly simplified Solow/Swan model without human capital stocks or infrastructure, I have found estimates of the adjustment parameter significantly different than one in every case, indicating convergence. All of the estimates based on analyses of levels, however, are so close to one, always greater than 0.7, that convergence to within 90% of equilibrium in less than one generation is effectively ruled out. This can hardly be called "convergence" in any relevant sense. Moreover, the estimates range from 0.72 to 0.98, suggesting a convergence range of from 33 to over 500 years, with most clustering around 0.8, underscoring the importance of choice of econometric method. Much of the variation in estimates of the speed of convergence appears to be due to trade-offs between the crucial parameter ρ, which measures the importance of *unobserved* cross-sectional variation relative to total residual variation, and γ, which measures the speed of adjustment. For this reason, it is especially important to introduce other relevant variables, such as infrastructure investment and human capital stock, in order to reduce the importance of unobserved cross-sectional variation. When differing country-specific trends are taken into account and when likelihood methods are employed which take into account the operation of the growth process prior to the point at which the data sample begins, however, the results are dramatically different: convergence to paths conditioned on differing savings and population growth rates and country specific trends is quite rapid for the relatively homogeneous 22-country sample, although it is still very slow for the more heterogeneous 94-country sample.

A second important finding is that the Sevestre-Trognon inequality, proved only for the case $\beta = 0$, and then only asymptotically, holds for all the examples presented except for one reversal in the case of the first-difference model. Indeed, fixed-effects OLS always yields estimates of the adjustment parameter at the extreme low end of the range of estimates obtained. The "bias" of fixed-effects models in the estimation of dynamic panel models is apparent. In this context, the use of such methods biases a test for convergence, or more appropriately rapid convergence, towards finding it. Fixed-effects models, however, are widely used, in part because they are the basis for two-round FGLS estimators, and because computer packages for panel data analysis incorporate an extremely misguided suggestion for estimating ρ, guaranteed to yield extremely low or even negative values of this parameter. These packages should be avoided, and, if they are used and do yield a negative estimate, it should not be concluded that the model is misspecified or that fixed-effects are a preferable alternative. Fixed-effects OLS remains badly biased in a dynamic context irrespective of whether the packaged routines fail.

I do find, however, that FGLS, using the Balestra-Nerlove (1966) estimate of ρ, which can never be negative, always lie between the fixed-effects OLS estimates and the pooled OLS estimates, which are known to yield upwardly biased estimates of γ. It is not appropriate to conclude that these FGLS estimates, however, represent a tighter upper bound to the true value of γ, since they are doubly inconsistent estimates and may lie below the true value. This is underscored by the finding that both conditional and unconditional ML yield different estimates of ρ and γ, sometimes higher and sometimes lower than FGLS. The interaction between ρ and γ is crucial in this regard.

Finally, maximum likelihood, unconditional on the initial observations, assuming them to be stationary and generated by the same dynamic process we are trying to estimate and assuming the exogenous variables also to be stationary, is feasible and indeed a viable alternative to conventional regression methods or conditional ML. Use of such methods will, however, generally involve removal of the overall means of all variables prior to analysis and omission of a constant term and may also involve differencing to remove deterministic or stochastic trends. Formulation of the unconditional likelihood function is somewhat more complicated in the case of differenced variables but has been carried out here without significant trauma.

Appendix

Data on 94 countries for the period 1960 - 1985 from the Penn World Tables 5.6, publicly available from the NBER web site at ftp://nber.harvard.edu/pub/.

22-Country Sample	94-country Sample = 22-Country Sample + the following:		
Japan	Algeria	Mexico	Singapore
Austria	Botswana	Nicaragua	Sri Lanka
Belgium	Cameroon	Panama	Syria
Denmark	Ethiopia	Trinidad & Tobago	Thailand
Finland	Ivory Coast	Argentina	Angola
France	Kenya	Bolivia	Benin
Germany (FRG)	Madagascar	Brazil	Burundi
Greece	Malawi	Chile	Central African Republic
Ireland	Mali	Colombia	Chad
Italy	Morocco	Ecuador	Congo
Netherlands	Nigeria	Paraguay	Egypt
Norway	Senegal	Peru	Ghana
Portugal	South Africa	Uruguay	Liberia
Spain	Tanzania	Venezuela	Mauritania
Sweden	Tunisia	Bangladesh	Mauritius
Switzerland	Zambia	Hong Kong	Mozambique
Turkey	Zimbabwe	India	Niger
U. K.	Costa Rica	Israel	Rwanda
Canada	Dominican Rep.	Jordan	Somalia
U. S.	El Salvador	Korea	Togo
Australia	Guatemala	Malaysia	Uganda
New Zealand	Haiti	Burma	Zaire
	Honduras	Pakistan	Nepal
	Jamaica	Philippines	Papua New Guinea

REFERENCES

1. Balestra, P. and M. Nerlove (1966), "Pooling Cross-Section and Time-Series Data in the Estimation of a Dynamic Economic Model: The Demand for Natural Gas", *Econometrica*, 34, 585-612.
2. Barnard, G. A., G. M. Jenkins and C. B. Winsten (1962), "Likelihood Inference and Time Series", (with discussion), *Journal of the Royal Statistical Society*, Series A, 125, 321-375.
3. Bernard, A. B. and S. N. Durlauf (1996), "Interpreting Tests of the Convergence Hypothesis", *Journal of Econometrics*, 71, 161-173.
4. Bernard, A. B. and S. N. Durlauf (1995), "Convergence in International Output", *Journal of Applied Econometrics*, 10, 97-108.
5. Barro, R. J. (1991), "Economic growth in a Cross-Section of Countries", *Quarterly Journal of Economics*, 106, 407-443.
6. Barro, R. J. and Jong-Wha Lee (1993), "International Comparisons of Educational Attainment", NBER Working Paper No. 4349.
7. Barro, R. J. and X. Sala-I-Martin (1995), *Economic Growth*, New York: McGraw-Hill.
8. Baumol, W. (1986), "Productivity Growth, Convergence, and Welfare: What the Long-Run Data Show", *American Economic Review*, 76, 1072-1085.
9. Binder, M. and M. H. Pesaran (1996), "Stochastic Growth", Working Paper No. 19-18, Department of Economics, University of Maryland.
10. Birnbaum, A. (1962), "On the Foundations of Statistical Inference", (with discussion) *Journal of the American Statistical Association*, 57, 269-306.
11. Breusch, T. S. (1987), "Maximum Likelihood Estimation of Random Effects Models", *Journal of Econometrics*, 36, 383-389.
12. Diebold, F. X. and M. Nerlove (1990), "Unit Roots in Economic Time Series: A Selective Survey", in T.B. Fomby and G.F. Rhodes, eds., *Advances in Econometrics*, Vol. 8: *Co-Integration, Spurious Regressions, and Unit Roots*, Greenwich, CT: JAI Press, 3-69.
13. Greene, W. (1993), *Econometric Analysis*, Second Edition. New York: Macmillan Publishing.
14. Islam, N. (1995), "Growth Empirics: A Panel Data Approach", *Quarterly Journal of Economics*, 110, 1127-1170.
15. Judge, G., R. C. Hill, W. Griffiths, H. Lütkepohl and T-C. Lee (1988), *Introduction to the Theory and Practice of Econometrics*, Second Edition, New York: John Wiley & Sons.
16. Kiviet, Jan F. (1995), "On the Bias, Inconsistency and Efficiency of Various Estimators in Dynamic Panel Models", *Journal of Econometrics*, 68, 53-78.
17. Lee, K., M. H. Pesaran, and R. Smith (1996), "Growth and Convergence: A Multi-country Empirical Analysis of the Solow Growth Model", unpublished.
18. Mankiw, N. G., D. Romer and D. N. Weil (1992), "A Contribution to the Empirics of Economic Growth", *Quarterly Journal of Economics*, 108, 407-437.
19. Mátyás, L. and P. Sevestre (1996), *The Econometrics of Panel Data: Handbook of Theory and Applications*, 2nd. ed., Boston: Kluwer Academic Publishers.
20. Maddala, G. S. (1971), "The Use of Variance Components Models in Pooling Cross-

Section and Time Series Data", *Econometrica* , 39, 341-358.

21. Michelacci, C., and P. Zaffaroni, (1997), "Beta Convergence", unpublished working paper, EM/97/332, Suntory Center, London School of Economics and Political Science.
22. Mundlak, Y. (1978), "On the Pooling of Cross-Section and Time-Series Data", *Econometrica*, 46, 69-86.
23. Nerlove, M. (1971), "Further Evidence on the Estimation of Dynamic Economic Relations from a Time Series of Cross-Sections", *Econometrica*, 39, 359-382.
24. Nerlove, M. (1994), "Reflections on Agricultural Development Population Growth and the Environment." Presented at the Third Conference on Development Economics, Asian Development Bank, Manila, November 23-25. Published in M. G. Quibria and J. M. Dowling, *Current Issues in Economic Development*, New York: Oxford University Press, 1996, 299-347.
25. Nerlove, M. (1997), "Likelihood Inference for Dynamic Panel Models", Presented at the Seventh Conference on Panel Data Econometrics, 19 - 20 June 1997, Paris. *Annales d'Économie et de Statistique de l'INSEE*, (forthcoming, 1999).
26. Nerlove, M. (1998), "Properties of Alternative Estimators of Dynamic Panel Models: An Empirical Analysis of Cross-Country Data for the Study of Economic Growth". Forthcoming in *Analysis of Panels and Limited Dependent Variable Models*, C. Hsiao, K. Lahiri, L-F. Lee and M. H. Pesaran, eds., Cambridge: Cambridge University Press, 1999.
27. Nerlove, M., and P. Balestra (1996), "Formulation and Estimation of Econometric Models for Panel Data", in L. Mátyás and P. Sevestre, op.cit., 3-22.
28. Nerlove, M., and L. K. Raut (1997), "Growth Models with Endogenous Population: A General Framework", in *The Handbook of Family and Population Economics*, ed. by M. R. Rosenzweig and O. Stark, New York: Elsevier Scientific Publishers, 1117-1175.
29. Nickell, S. (1981), "Biases in Dynamic Models with Fixed Effects", *Econometrica*, 49, 1417-1426.
30. Quah, D., 1996, "Empirics for Economic Growth and Convergence", *European Economic Review*, 40, 1353 - 1375.
31. Sevestre, P. and A. Trognon (1983) "Propriétés de grands échantillons d'une classe d'estimateurs des modèles autorégressifs à erreurs composées", *Annales de l'INSEE*, 50, 25-49.
32. Sevestre, P. and A. Trognon (1996), "Linear Dynamic Models", in Mátyás and Sevestre, op. cit., 120-144.
33. Solow, R.M. (1956), "A Contribution to the Theory of Economic Growth", *Quarterly Journal of Economics*, 70, 65-94.
34. Swan, T.W. (1956), "Economic Growth and Capital Accumulation", *Economic Record*, 32, 324-361.
35. Trognon, A. (1978), "Miscellaneous Asymptotic Properties of Ordinary Least Squares and Maximum Likelihood Methods in Dynamic Error Components Models", *Annales de l'INSEE*, 30-31, 631-657.

Panel Data Econometrics: Future Directions
J. Krishnakumar and E. Ronchetti (Editors)

CHAPTER 2

DO PANEL DATA RESCUE THE PURCHASING POWER PARITY (PPP) THEORY ?

G.S. MADDALA, Shaowen WU and Peter C. LIU

Abstract

The unit root tests and cointegration tests applied to individual currencies, broadly speak ing, reject the PPP. This result has been beamed on the low power of unit root tests. Since the appearance of the paper by Levin and Lin (1992) on panel data unit root tests , which argued that panel data unit root tests have higher power than single equation unit root tests, there have been several papers using the Levin-Lin tests to show that PPP holds.

Also Frenkel and Rose (1997) assembled panel data on exchange rates for over 120 countries and estimated dynamic panel data models to show that PPP deviations eroded faster than thought earlier.

This paper provides a detailed critique of the Levin-Lin tests and suggests a better alternative and extends this to panel cointegration tests. The paper also provides a critique of the estimation methods used by Frenkel and Rose. Some deficiencies and gaps on their panel data are corrected and it is shown how their results are very sensitive to the countries used.

The paper summarizes the picture one gets on the validity of PPP based on panel data analysis.

1. INTRODUCTION

A large number of papers have been written on testing the PPP theory. The validity of the theory has been often tested by testing for a unit root in the real exchange rate. It is well known that when the rate of convergence for a stationary series is very slow, long time series are needed to reject the hypothesis that the series follows a random walk. The problem with long time series on exchange rates is that they cover periods when the nominal exchange rate regime shifted from floating to fixed and back again. The panel approach allows a different way of increasing the power of unit root tests using post Bretton Woods data by pooling across different real exchange rates. The literature on using panel data to test the PPP is huge. This can be classified into the following categories:

(i) panel data unit root tests (discussed in Sec. 2)

(ii) panel data cointegration tests (discussed in Sec. 3)

(iii) estimation of cross-country regression based on panel data (discussed in Sec.4). We shall review the literature that falls into these categories, note the deficiencies in the existing work and present some new results.

2. PANEL DATA UNIT ROOT TESTS

In modern time series literature, there are two approaches to test the PPP hypothesis empirically. One is the unit root approach and the other one is the cointegration method. The unit root approach tests the null hypothesis of a unit root in the real exchange rates. If the null cannot be rejected the real exchange is stationary and reverts to its mean in the long-run, thus supporting PPP. With the cointegration approach, one investigates whether there exists a cointegrating relationship between the nominal exchange rates and the relative price indices. If a cointegrating relationship is detected, then PPP is believed to hold. Note the above two methods test relative PPP instead of absolute PPP. In addition to cointegrating relationship between the nominal exchange rates and the price ratio, a cointegrating vector of one will support absolute PPP.

Among the empirical work of testing long-run PPP using unit root tests, only occasional rejections of unit root hypothesis have been reported. This can be attributed to the low power problem of various unit root tests in small samples as argued by many researchers, given the fact that we only have less than 25 years of data for the current float. To solve this problem, it has been argued that adding cross sections by using panel data approach is a good alternative.

The first stage of testing long-run PPP utilizing multiple currencies is featured by the practice of extending the univariate unit root test of the Augmented Dickey and Fuller (ADF) test to panel data models.

Following the convention in the literature, let q be the natural logarithm of real exchange rate, s be the natural log of the nominal exchange rate in local currency units per foreign currency unit, and p and p^* be natural log of the domestic and foreign (the US) price level respectively. Then the real exchange rate is constructed by :

$$q = s + p^* - p$$

Abuaf and Jorion (1990) consider the following model:

$$q_{i,t} = k_0 + k_1 q_{i,t-1} + u_{i,t}$$

where i denotes country and t denotes time period. The null hypothesis under test is $H_0 : k_0 = 0, k_1 = 1$. They estimate the system jointly using GLS and simulate the critical value of the Dickey and Fuller (1979) test with their sample size. Applying the test to both annual data span 1900-1972 and the monthly data covering the period of 1973-1987, they reject the null of a unit root decisively for the long period but only reject the null marginally over the flexible exchange rate period. However, the serial correlation in the disturbances has not been taken into consideration. The estimation method they follow is a pooling one.

Jorion and Sweeney (1996) update the sample and improve the method in Abuaf and Jorion (1990) by including a heterogeneous time trend. Using the empirical distribution obtained via Monte Carlo simulation, they find clear evidence against unit root null for G-10 countries under the current float.

To settle the long time debate of which price index should be used to construct the real exchange rate, Wei and Parsley (1995) study the validity of PPP using a panel of 12 tradable sectors in OECD countries. They apply a traditional unit root test and strongly reject the unit root null thus supporting the long-run PPP.

As mentioned previously, the above studies reviewed use a pooling method to estimate a multi-currency system. The autoregressive parameters are restricted to be the same.

The appearance of panel data unit root tests , such as Quah (1994) and Levin and Lin (1992, 1993) has stimulated more and more researchers to re-investigate the validity of long-run PPP using panel data approach. The Levin and Lin (LL hereafter) test considers a fixed effects model. The procedure of the LL test can be briefly summarized as follows. Consider a model with country specific effects, (LL consider models of no constant and of no time trends as well)

$$\triangle y_{it} = \alpha_i y_{i,t-1} + \delta_i + e_{it}$$

First subtract cross-section average from the data and then apply the Augmented Dickey-Fuller (ADF) test to each individual series. The ADF regression

$$\triangle y_{it} = \alpha_i y_{i,t-1} + \sum_{j=1}^{p_i} \theta_{ij} \triangle y_{i,t-j} + \delta_i + \varepsilon_{it} \tag{1}$$

is equivalent to performing two auxiliary regressions of $\triangle y_{it}$ and $y_{i,t-1}$ on the remaining part of the equation (1). Let the residuals from these two auxiliary regressions be $\hat{e}_{it}$ and $\hat{V}_{i,t-1}$ respectively. Since there is heteroskedasticity in ε_{it}, they suggest a method to normalize $\hat{e}_{it}$ and $\hat{V}_{i,t-1}$ to control it. Call the normalized residuals $\tilde{e}_{it}$ and $\tilde{V}_{i,t-1}$. Now pooling the disturbances for all the cross-sections and time periods, they run the following regression :

$$\tilde{e}_{it} = \alpha \tilde{V}_{i,t-1} + \varepsilon_{it}$$

They then show that the t_α statistic has a standard normal distribution.

MacDonald (1996) applies the Levin and Lin test to the OECD countries and finds strong evidence in favor of PPP. He examines both the level and trend stationary models and assumes independent model innovations throughout his study, which leaves room for improvement. Nevertheless, it is one of the earliest papers exploring the possibility of using panel unit root tests in the literature of PPP, and it deserves credit.

Another application of the LL test can be found in Frankel and Rose (1996). They consider a fixed effects model allowing for both country specific effects and time specific effects. Using data for 150 countries covering 1948-1992, they reject the null of a unit root. However, their real exchange rate data cover both the fixed and floating exchange rate regimes, thus they do not show direct evidence on long-run PPP under the current float.

Oh (1996) applies the LL test to G-6 and OECD countries using data from Penn World Tables. He rejects the unit root null for most of his samples. A demonstration of the power gain by using panel data test is also provided in his paper. (However, as argued later, the direct power comparison is not relevant.)

The above mentioned papers apply the LL test directly, without paying much attention to the structure of the model innovations. Wu (1996) accounts for serial correlation in the disturbance terms. He considers the following panel model:

$$q_{i,t} = \delta_0 + \delta_1 t + \mu_i + nu_t + \rho q_{i,t-1} + \varepsilon_{i,t}$$

After removing the common intercept term, time trend, and the individual and time specific effects from the data, he uses the following panel regression:

$$\Delta\tilde{q}_{i,t} = b\tilde{q}_{i,t-1} + \sum \phi_j \Delta\tilde{q}_{i,t-j} + \tilde{\varepsilon}_{i,t}$$

The lagged difference terms are added to take care of the serial correlation in the disturbance terms. Wu calculated the empirical distribution of the LL test via Monte Carlo simulation to accommodate his sample size. His results show that the null of a unit root can be rejected strongly.

Papell (1997) investigates the problem of serial correlation in the disturbances more carefully. He considers the following model :

$$q_{j,t} = \alpha_j + \rho_j q_{j,t-1} + \sum_{i=1}^{k} \gamma_{j,i} \Delta q_{j,t-i} + \varepsilon_{j,t} \qquad j = 1, \ldots, N \tag{2}$$

He finds that the LL test suffers from size distortion without being able to adequately correct for serial correlation. Using Monte Carlo simulation, he shows that the finite sample critical values are greater than those in Levin and Lin (1992). For quarterly data, the critical values are 11% higher (on average) than those reported by Levin and Lin and for monthly data, they are 3% higher. Using the finite sample critical values he computed, Papell applies the LL test to six samples: the full sample of OECD countries, the sample of European countries, the sample of EC, EMS, G-6, and G-10 countries. He rejects the unit root null at 5% for some of his samples but not all of them. He also pointed out that accounting for serial correlation is important because if the critical values in Levin and Lin were used, it would lead to inappropriate rejections.

So far, the work searching for evidence of long-run PPP using the LL test in the literature has not paid much attention to the existence of cross-sectional correlation in the disturbances. Recently, O'Connell (1998) addresses this problem. By assuming an equi-correlation covariance matrix, he shows that there are dramatic size distortions for the Levin-Lin test in the presence of contemporaneous correlation. In fact, he shows that the size distortion could be as large as 50% when the nominal size is 5% and hence he argues that the earlier findings supporting PPP using panel data may have been spurious. To correct for the problem he estimates the model by GLS and proposes a bootstrap method to control for contemporaneous correlation. His results show that there is no evidence of long-run PPP for all his samples, including the sample of the world as a whole and the subsamples of Europe, Asia, South America and Africa.

However, a common problem with the application of the LL test comes from its restrictive alternative hypothesis. In equation (2), the LL test tests

$$\begin{aligned} & H_0 && : \rho_j = 1, j = 1, \ldots, N \\ Vs. \ & H_1 && : \rho_j = \rho < 1, j = 1, \ldots, N \end{aligned}$$

As pointed out in Maddala and Wu (1998), this alternative hypothesis is implausible in applied work, because it means that under PPP each real exchange rate reverts to its respective mean over time at the same rate. For this reason, Im, Pesaran and Shin (1996) and Maddala and Wu (1998) propose two new tests with a more realistic alternative hypothesis. While we denote the Im, Pesaran and Shin test as the IPS test, Maddala and Wu call their test the Fisher test because they adopted the idea of the test from R. A. Fisher (1932). For the Im, Pesaran and Shin (IPS) and Fisher tests, the alternative hypothesis under study is $H_1 : \rho_j < 1, j = 1, \ldots, N$, which allows different convergence rates toward PPP across countries. Both IPS and Fisher show that their tests have higher power than the LL test via Monte Carlo simulation. Maddala and Wu further show the superiority of the Fisher test to the others in the presence of cross-sectional correlation.

Let t_{ρ_j} be the ADF t-statistic for the j-th currency. The IPS test statistic is defined as $\overline{z} = \frac{\bar{t}-E(\bar{t})}{\sqrt{\text{Var}(\bar{t})}}$, where $\bar{t} = \frac{1}{N}\sum_{j=1}^{n} t_{\rho_j}$, with mean $E(\bar{t})$ and variance Var $(\bar{t})$. It follows the standard normal distribution asymptotically. The Fisher test statistic λ is defined as $\lambda = -2\sum_{j=1}^{N} \log P_j$, where P_j is the p-value ADF test for the j-th country. It has a χ^2 distribution with $2N$ degrees of freedom. Note that the IPS test pools individual test statistics across countries, whereas the Fisher test pools the p-values of each individual test across countries. Both the IPS and Fisher tests are based on individual ADF regressions. Since an appropriate ADF regression will correct for serial correlation in the data, these tests take care of serial correlation automatically.

Despite the popularity of the use of the LL test in testing PPP, there are a few papers applying the IPS and Fisher tests in this literature. One application of the IPS test is by Coakley and Fuertes (1997). They also consider the panel data regression model as in (2) and apply the IPS t-bar and LR-bar tests based on the mean of univariate unit root statistics. To implement the t-bar and LR-bar tests, two adjustment terms (mean and variance of the univariate unit root statistics) are needed and they are adopted from the table tabulated by IPS. The disturbance terms are assumed to be white noise.

Recently, Wu and Wu (1998) have conducted a complete study of testing PPP using both the IPS and Fisher tests. Considering the same model as in (2), they study the similar samples as in Papell (1997). They find that both tests reject the null of a unit root strongly for all samples. Their results are stronger than that of Papell and they suggest that the use of more powerful tests may explain the differences. They further investigate the role of cross-sectional correlation in testing PPP. They first estimate the magnitude of cross-sectional correlation using a SUR technique and show that the correlation is significantly different from zero. Then a non-parametric bootstrap procedure is proposed to correct the cross-sectional correlation. After computing the critical values of the two tests, they conduct the finite sample IPS and Fisher tests on the real exchange rates. Unlike in O'Connell (1998), they still find strong evidence of long-run PPP and hence they conclude that O'Connell's result may be incorrect due to the restrictive estimation and test procedure based on the equi-correlation assumption he used. In addition, they study the size distortions of the conventional IPS and Fisher tests by computing the empirical sizes from the bootstrapped empirical distribution. Comparing the two tests with each other, they find that the IPS test suffers from larger size distortions than the Fisher test. This has also been the finding of Maddala and Wu (1998). The test results of Wu and Wu are summarized in Table 1.

It is well documented in the literature that PPP works better among European countries than between the US and these countries. Jorion and Sweeney (1996) and Papell (1997) report more evidence in favor of long-run PPP when German mark, instead of the US dollar, is used as the base currency. Wu and Wu also apply the IPS and Fisher tests to the German Mark based real exchange rates. They find that the null of a unit root is rejected more strongly for the German mark based real exchange rates. One explanation provided by them is that when the German mark is used as the base currency, the cross-sectional correlation is smaller than that of US dollar based real exchange rates. The smaller cross-sectional correlation reduces the size distortions of the German mark based real exchange rates and hence yields a better test result. The test results using German mark as the base currency are listed in Table 2.

As a summary, applying various panel data unit root tests to multiple currencies to search for evidence of long-run PPP has witnessed more rejections of the unit root null than non-rejections. However, one should be careful in interpreting the results of panel data unit root tests . The panel data unit root tests give a summary picture of whether there exists unit roots for all the cross sections in the panel. A rejection of the unit root hypothesis does not automatically mean that all the real exchange rate series are stationary. To draw that conclusion, one needs to perform a univariate unit root test for each individual series. To gain higher power of the unit root tests, one should refer to efficient unit root tests such as in Elliott *et al.* (1996).

Table 1

Bootstrap Results on P-Values and Empirical Size of IPS and Fisher Tests (US dollar as the numeraire and CPI as price index)

Sample	Quarterly				Monthly			
	IPS		Fisher		IPS		Fisher	
	P-value	Size	P-value	Size	P-value	Size	P-value	Size
All 20	0.029	0.270	0.054	0.203				
All 17					0.118	0.281	0.167	0.209
EC	0.069	0.253	0.095	0.180	0.145	0.231	0.184	0.169
EMS	0.114	0.228	0.131	0.161	0.138	0.203	0.157	0.150
Group 6	0.052	0.119	0.091	0.111	0.183	0.115	0.287	0.099
Group 10	0.040	0.207	0.058	0.162	0.118	0.213	0.178	0.162

Notes:

1. The IPS test statistic $\overline{z}$ is calculated as $\overline{z} = \frac{\overline{t}-E(\overline{t})}{\sqrt{\mathrm{Var}(\overline{t})}}$, where $\overline{t} = \frac{1}{N}\sum_{j=1}^{N} t_{\rho j}$, with mean $E(\overline{t})$ and variance $\mathrm{Var}(\overline{t})$ as its variance and $t_{\rho j}$ is the ADF t-statistic for the j-th currency. The Fisher test statistic λ is defined as $\lambda = -2\sum_{j=1}^{N} \log P_j$, where P_j is the p-value of the ADF test for j-th country.
2. Empirical size is reported for nominal size of 5%.
3. P-values are constructed based on the bootstrapped distributions.

The efficient unit root tests suggested in Elliott *et al.* (which we shall refer as the ERS test) have been used in Cheung and Lai (1993) and Liu (1997). Liu applies them and compares the results with those from the ADF tests for 136 countries in the panel used by Frankel and Rose (1996), both without trend and including trend. He finds the unit root null rejected by the ERS test but not the ADF test in the no trend case for 24 countries (including UK, Belgium, France, Luxembourg, Canada, Finland, Australia, Argentina, Brazil, Hong Kong, Thailand and a few African countries). In the case of 7 countries, both tests rejected the unit root null (these include Bolivia, Paraguay, Korea, Singapore and 3 African countries). In the case where trend was included, both tests rejected the unit root null in 13 cases and ERS test rejected the unit root null but not the ADF test in 10 cases (these include France, Canada, Spain, Argentina, Korea, Singapore and 4 smaller countries). In summary, one finds more support for PPP from individual country regressions also, if one uses more efficient unit root tests than the commonly used ADF test.

Another study worth mentioning is that of Seda *et al.* (1998) who test the PPP using the wholesale price index (WPI) instead of the CPI for 39 countries and find weaker support for PPP.

Table 2
Bootstrap Results on P-Values and Empirical Size of IPS and Fisher Tests (German mark as the numeraire and CPI as price index)

Sample	Quarterly				Monthly			
	IPS		Fisher		IPS		Fisher	
	P-value	Size	P-value	Size	P-value	Size	P-value	Size
All 20	0.002	0.133	0.006	0.114				
All 17					0.016	0.074	0.055	0.074
EC	0.007	0.092	0.017	0.080	0.104	0.062	0.195	0.063
EMS	0.075	0.066	0.141	0.067	0.029	0.088	0.072	0.077
Group 6	0.051	0.093	0.090	0.083	0.007	0.076	0.021	0.074
Group 10	0.012	0.083	0.033	0.082	0.002	0.097	0.012	0.090

Notes: Same as Table 1.

Most of the studies on testing PPP, use unit root tests based on the unit root null (ADF tests etc.). Culver and Papell (1997) test PPP using stationarity as null (KPSS test). It is not true that these tests are more powerful than tests using unit root as null. One can never compare the two tests because the null and alternatives are reversed. They have been suggested for "confirmatory analysis" but confirmation is less frequent than usually assumed and is very often spurious. See Section 4.6 on "confirmatory analysis" in Maddala and Kim (1998). See also section 4.5 on the different tests using stationarity as null. Also, the KPSS test using stationarity as null has the same low power problems as the ADF test (in rejecting the respective nulls).

There have been attempts to extend the KPSS test using stationarity as null to panel data unit root tests . See Hadri (1998). However, all such extensions are unnecessary. The Fisher test suggested by Maddala and Wu (1998) can be used for all the tests, the efficient unit root tests, the tests using stationarity as null and so on, without any new theory for every test.

Coming to the problem of power comparisons, invalid power comparisons are also widely prevalent in the discussion of panel data unit root tests . It is very often argued that tests for unit roots in individual time series have low power and panel data unit root tests increase power. This is sheer nonsense. Consider the unit root test for a single time series : $H_0 : \rho_1 = 1$ *vs.* $H_1 : \rho_1 <$ in

$$y_{it} = \rho_1 y_{1,t-1} + e_{1t}$$

The panel data unit root test tests the hypothesis

$$\begin{array}{rll} & H_0 & : \ \rho_1 = \rho_2 = \ldots = \rho_N = \rho = 1 \\ vs. & H_1 & : \ \rho_1 = \rho_2 = \ldots = \rho_N = \rho < 1 \end{array}$$

in the regression $y_{it} = \rho_i y_{i,t-1} + e_{it}, i = 1, 2, \ldots, N$.

The two hypotheses are different. How can you compare their powers? Suppose I am interested in whether PPP holds for Canada *vs.* the U.S. The ADF test fails to reject the unit root null in the real exchange rate, thus rejecting the PPP. Of what use is it to me if I am told that if I throw in 100 more countries from Angola to Zimbabwe, I won't reject PPP? What is of relevance to me is this particular exchange rate. If the ADF test has low power, then we should try more powerful tests. In this case the ERS test rejects the unit root null in the real exchange rates. Thus, panel data tests are the wrong answer to the low power problem of some commonly used unit root tests.

3. PANEL DATA COINTEGRATION TESTS

Following the definitions in Section 2, a cointegration test can be applied to detect the long-run relationship between the nominal exchange and the price ratio

$$s_t = \alpha + \beta \triangle p_t + e_t \quad .$$

where $\triangle p_t = p_t - p_t^*$. Since it is well documented in the literature that the nominal exchange rates and the price indices are nonstationary, the above equation could be either a spurious regression or a cointegration regression, depending on whether s_t is cointegrated with $\triangle p_t$. Using a residual based test, if e_t is stationary, s_t is said to be cointegrated with $\triangle p_t$. This indicates that there are long run relationships between the nominal exchange rates and the price ratios. Since β is not restricted to be one any more in the weak version of long run PPP, a rejection of the null of no cointegration can be viewed as direct evidence in favor of the weak long run PPP hypothesis.

A spate of papers has appeared in the literature applying various univariate cointegration tests to testing long-run PPP. Similar to the situation of applying unit root tests, the results of cointegration tests with respect to the current float are barely in favor of PPP. Researchers start to turn to the panel data approach to seek for a solution. Kao (1996) proposes a residual-based panel data cointegration test for a fixed effects model. Pedroni (1995) considers a heterogeneous panel data model instead

$$y_{it} = \alpha_i + \delta_i t + \gamma_t + x_{it}\beta_i + e_{it}$$

Under the null of no cointegration, the residual e_{it} will be nonstationary. He proposes a set of test statistics that follow normal distributions asymptotically. Based on a similar model, Wu (1998) proposes two panel data cointegration tests. Following the spirit of the IPS and Fisher tests, she extents the two tests to residual based cointegration tests. The tests can be summarized as follows. First apply a univariate cointegration test to each cross section unit. Then the group mean test combines the individual t-statistic and the Fisher test combines the p-values of individual tests. She investigates the size and power performances of the two tests when various univariate residual based cointegration tests are used in the individual series. She finds that the tests based on Engle and Granger's (1987) ADF test yields the best size and power.

Unlike the growing interest in testing PPP using panel data unit root approaches, applying panel cointegration tests to this problem is still in its infancy. Pedroni (1997) and Wu (1998) are the only efforts so far trying to explore this possibility. Testing PPP using panel cointegration tests considers the following model :

$$s_{i,t} = \alpha_i + \beta_i \triangle p_{i,t} + e_{i,t} \qquad i = 1, \ldots, N$$

Pedroni applies the tests he proposed and he reports more favorable evidence for PPP. Among all the test statistics he used, he could reject the null of no PPP at the 10% level for more than half of the cases.

Wu applies the group mean and Fisher tests to the same samples as in Wu and Wu (1998). She finds strong rejection of the null of no cointegration in most samples using both tests. She also explores the differences in test results by choosing different numeraire. When German mark is chosen as the base currency, the rejection of the null is stronger in European countries than the cases when US dollar is the base currency. Her results can be found in Tables 3 and 4.

Again as argued in Section 2, a rejection of the hypothesis of no cointegration in the panel does not necessarily imply PPP holds for all the series. However, one can claim there is evidence of PPP when the null is rejected because the rejection of the composite null implies there must exist a cointegrating relationship for at least one series. Nevertheless, to claim that PPP holds for a particular currency, one has to resort to univariate cointegartion tests.

Table 3

Panel Data Cointegration Tests for PPP: US as the Base Country

Countries	Quarterly				Monthly			
	Group Mean		Fisher		Group Mean		Fisher	
	$\overline{z}$	p-value	λ	p-value	$\overline{z}$	p-value	λ	p-value
All 20	-3.06	0.001	62.3	0.013				
All 17					-2.16	0.016	44.5	0.107
EC	-1.88	0.030	30.9	0.098	-1.272	0.102	23.3	0.276
EMS	-1.29	0.099	16.7	0.270	-0.967	0.167	12.8	0.386
Group 6	-2.056	0.020	21.7	0.041	-1.78	0.038	19.1	0.086
Group 10	-2.28	0.011	32.4	0.040	-2.038	0.021	29.2	0.084

Note: The IPS test statistic $\overline{z}$ is calculated as $\overline{z} = \frac{\overline{t}-E(\overline{t})}{\sqrt{\mathrm{Var}(\overline{t})}}$, where $\overline{t} = \frac{1}{N}\sum_{j=1}^{N} t_{\rho j}$, with mean $E(\overline{t})$ and variance $\mathrm{Var}(\overline{t})$ as its variance and $t_{\rho j}$ is the t-statistic of univariate cointegration test for the j-th currency. The Fisher test statistic λ is defined as $\lambda = -2\sum_{j=1}^{N} \log P_j$, where P_j is the p-value of univariate cointegration test for j-th country.

Table 4

Panel Cointegration Tests for PPP: Germany as the Base Country

Countries	Quarterly				Monthly			
	Group Mean		Fisher		Group Mean		Fisher	
	$\overline{z}$	p-value	λ	p-value	$\overline{z}$	p-value	λ	p-value
All 20	-2.93	0.002	62.9	0.012				
All 17				-2.44	0.007	53.8	0.017	
EC	-2.18	0.015	32.4	0.039	-2.28	0.011	30.0	0.037
EMS	-1.157	0.124	15.5	0.216	-1.44	0.077	14.5	0.150
Group 6	-0.752	0.226	12.4	0.411	-0.369	0.356	11.0	0.528
Group 10	-1.337	0.091	25.2	0.194	-1.529	0.063	27.3	0.127

Note: the same as in Table 3.

4. PANEL DATA REGRESSION

It is obvious that PPP does not hold exactly and thus the unit root tests and cointegration tests are not very informative on whether PPP holds or not. What is of relevance is how long it takes for PPP deviations to erode. This question can be answered by estimating dynamic equations of the behavior of exchange rates. With panel data one can estimate dynamic equations using panel data but as we shall note presently not all problems with such estimation have been noted in the literature.

Panel data regression have been used by Frankel and Rose (1996) and Lothian (1997) but the study by Frankel and Rose (to be referred to as F-R) is the most influential and often quoted one and hence we shall concentrate on that study. F-R assemble data on 150 countries over a period of 45 years. They estimate the following panel regression model:

$$\Delta q_{it} = \alpha + \gamma q_{i,t-1} + \sum_i \delta_i D_i + \sum_t \phi_t D_t + \varepsilon_{it}$$

where q_{it} is the real exchange rate for country i at time t, and D_i and D_t are country specific and year dummies respectively. ε_{it} is IID $(0, \sigma^2)$ error term. F-R estimated this panel regression with no dummies, country dummies only, time dummies only and both country and time dummies. Their major conclusion is that the analysis provides strong support in favor of PPP and that this support is "masked" in time series data, but can be only found in cross-section data. In particular they argue that PPP deviations are eroded at the rate of approximately 15% annually, i.e. their half-life is around four years, which is consistent with long-horizon time series data.

The results of F-R, often cited as providing strong support for PPP, are flawed in several respects. It is true that long time series data are plagued by the problem of instability over time because of switches between fixed and flexible exchange rate regimes. But cross-section data have the problem of cross-sectional heterogeneity, Liu and Maddala (1996) document this instability in the results obtained by F-R. The results change substantially depending on which countries are deleted from the sample and what country groups are considered.

First of all, Liu and Maddala (1996) deleted countries that have no observations on some variables or have only a couple of observations over the entire period. This leads to 24 countries from the whole sample. On the other hand, they extend the series for some countries using the updated information from the IFS tapes. These included Argentina, Brazil, Cameroon, China, El Salvador, Lebanon, Nicaragua, Peru and Poland. Overall the number of countries they used is 136 compared with 150 in F-R. However, they have more observations (4341) compared with (4109) in F-R.

When they estimated the panel data equation used by F-R, Liu and Maddala found no evidence in favor of PPP unless both country specific and time specific dummies are included. They also found that PPP deviations are eroded more like 12.5% rather than 15% per year giving a half life of 5 years rather than 4. A summary of their results is presented in Table 5.

Table 5

Panel Regression Estimates Using All 136 Countries

$$\Delta a_{it} = \alpha + \gamma q_{i,t-1} + \sum_i \delta_i D_i + \sum_t \phi_t D_t + \varepsilon_{it}$$

	$\hat{\gamma}$	SE
No fixed effects	-.0027	.0026
Country effects only	-.0686	.0221
Year effects only	-.0026	.0026
Both country and year effects	-.1252	.0392

Of greater interest are the results presented in Table 6 using different groups of countries. Since the support for PPP is stronger from the regressions with both country dummies and time dummies, we shall discuss these. The stronger support for PPP comes from the African countries. On the other hand the support for PPP is very weak for the Asian countries (even though there are 22 countries in that panel). As for G-6, there is again no support for PPP. The estimate of γ, with both country and year specific dummies, is -0.0353. The coefficient is almost unchanged when Italy is included in the G-6 (-0.0369). On the other hand, if Greece is included instead of Italy, the estimate of γ rises to -0.1223. This illustrates the argument by Liu and Maddala (1996) that support for PPP depends on countries chosen. Some more interesting questions to ask and investigate are: why is there greater support for PPP when some country is included but not the others? And why is there greater support for PPP in some groups (e.g. African countries) than in some other groups (e.g. the Asian countries)? These differences are some of the interesting results emanating from panel data analysis.

Table 6

Results on Panel Regressions Using Subsets of Countries
(Using both country and time dummies) N = number of observations

	$\hat{\gamma}$	SE	N
Industrial	-0.1192	0.0492	22
Western Hemisphere	-0.1321	0.0462	34
Middle East	-0.0439	0.0441	10
Asian	0.0001	0.0241	22
African	-0.1778	0.0569	42
Eastern Europe	-0.1141	0.0560	6
G-6	-0.0353	0.0239	6
G-6 + Italy	-0.0369	0.0233	7
G-6 + Greece	-0.1223	0.0747	7

Results from Cross-sectional Regressions and Time-series Regressions

F-R state that they also investigated cross-sectional regressions for each year and time-series regressions for each country and that these confirm their conclusion. In their paper, they provide only the histograms of the estimates. Liu and Maddala (1996) present more detailed results of these estimates. Looking at the cross-sectional regressions, they find that except in one single case (1977) in the 42 years considered, the coefficient γ is not significantly less than zero. In the other cases where the t-ratio is greater than 2, the coefficients are positive and not negative (in the year of 1957, 1960, 1969, 1970, 1984, and 1991). Thus, there is no support for PPP in the cross-sectional regressions.

Turning next to the country regressions, the estimates exhibit a wide range with the strongest support for PPP coming from several African countries, Australia and New Zealand, and two Asian countries Thailand and Korea. There are also countries like Egypt and Lebanon and some islands like Antigua, Grenada, St. Vincent, St. Kitts and Nevis and so on. So it is not true that support for the PPP theory cannot be found in post WWII time-series data. In spite of all their limitations, the time series regression give more information than the cross-sectional regressions. Thus, it is not true, as concluded by F-R, that strong support for PPP can be "masked in time series data but are relatively easy to find in cross-section data".

Problems with Fixed Effects Models

One major problem with the fixed effects (or random effects) models is that they are based on the implicit assumption of homogeneity of the slope coefficients across cross-sectional units and over time. The results presented in Liu and Maddala (1996) show substantial cross-country heterogeneity. This means that introducing just country specific dummies is not enough. The fixed effects model is not a valid one with which to make inferences. The nature of the biases, however, can be determined only by making some assumptions about the coefficients. If the true model is a random coefficient model, then Sevestre and Trognon (1996) show that the true autoregressive coefficient is bounded by the coefficient from the pooled estimator and the fixed effects estimator. Thus, for instance, in Table 5, the true value γ lies in between -0.0027 and -0.1252 and so the rate at which PPP deviations are eroded lies between 0% and 12.5% per year.

In a series of papers, Nerlove (1997, 1998 a, b) investigated the nature of the biases in the estimates of the coefficient γ of the lagged dependent variable, arising from the estimation of fixed effects models from panel data. One important problem that he mentions is the bias arising from the use of the conditional likelihood function (conditional on $q_{i,t-1}$) rather than the unconditional likelihood function (taking into account the distribution of $q_{i,0}$). Such biases were noted in a Monte Carlo study by Maddala in the early 1970's. Nerlove shows how the use of the unconditional likelihood function demonstrates the fragility of inferences about convergence in Barro type growth regressions. The convergence noted in these studies is an artifact. Wu and Yin (1998) similarly demonstrate using the panel data on exchange rates that the evidence in favor of PPP in the fixed effects models is an artifact. They find that the estimates of γ from the unconditional likelihood function are all very close to zero. The unconditional MLE showed that PPP deviations erode much slower than what F-R found. The point estimator of γ is -0.01 and they can barely find evidence of mean reversion. They investigated

(i) whole panel, whole time period (1948-92)

(ii) whole panel, post Bretton Woods period (1973-1992)

(iii) OECD countries, whole time period (1948-1992)

(iv) OECD countries, post Bretton Woods period (1973-1992)

The fixed effects model estimates (from the conditional MLE) showed very strong support for PPP in case (ii) and (iv) with estimates of γ around -0.37 and -0.18 respectively, but the unconditional MLE gave estimates of γ around -0.01 in all the four cases, thus indicating that the support for PPP coming from the fixed effects models is a statistical artifact.

5. CONCLUSION

The summary picture we get from all this voluminous work is that panel data *do not* rescue the PPP theory. At first glance the panel data unit root tests and panel data regressions seem to support the PPP theory. But when allowance is made for the deficiencies in the panel data tests and panel estimation methods, the support turns out to be much weaker.

Mark and Sul (1998) investigate the problem of long run predictability of nominal exchange rates from long-horizon regressions using panel data on seventeen countries. They find that the predictions using monetary fundamentals are better than those from a random walk model, but the predictions using PPP are worse than those from a random walk model. Thus, PPP is of no use in forecasting nominal exchange rates.

REFERENCES

1. Abuaf, N. and P. Jorion (1990), "Purchasing Power Parity in the Long Run", *Journal of Finance*, 45, 157-174.
2. Cheung, Y. and K. Lai (1993), "LR PPP During the Recent Float", *Journal of International Economics*, 34, 181-192.
3. Chin, M.D. and L. Johnston (1996), "Real Exchange Rate Levels, Productivity and Demand Shocks, Evidence From a Panel of 14 Countries", Working Paper# 5709, NBER.
4. Coakley, J. and A.M. Fuertes (1997), "New Panel Unit Root Tests of PPP", *Economics Letters*, 57, 17-22.
5. Culver, S.E. and D.H. Papell (1997), "Long Run Purchasing Power Parity With Short-Run Data: Evidence With a Null-Hypothesis of Stationarity", Manuscript, University of Houston.
6. Dickey, D. A. and W. A. Fuller (1979), "Distribution of the Estimators for Autoregressive Time Series with a Unit Root", *Journal of American Statistical Association*, 74, 427-431.
7. Elliott, G., T.J. Rothernberg and J. Stock (1996), "Efficient Tests for An Autoregressive Unit Root", *Econometrica*, 65, 813-834.
8. Engel, C., M.K. Hendrickson and J.H. Rogers (1997), "Intra-National, Intra- Continental and Intra-Planetary PPP", Working Paper, University of Washington.
9. Engel, C. (1996), "Long-Run PPP May Not Hold After All", Working Paper# 5646, NBER.
10. Fisher, R. A. (1932), *Statistical Methods for Research Workers*, Oliver and Boyd, Edinburgh 4th Ed.
11. Frankel, J.A. and A.K. Rose (1996), "A Panel Project on Purchasing Power Parity: Mean Reversion Within and Between Countries", *Journal of International Economics*, 40, 209-224.
12. Hadri, K. (1998), "Testing for Stationarity in Heterogeneous Panel Data", Discussion paper, University of Exeter.
13. Im, K. S., M. H. Pesaran and Y. Shin (1996), "Testing for Unit Roots in Heterogeneous Panels", Discussion Paper, University of Cambridge.
14. Jorion, P. and R. Sweeney (1996), "Mean Reversion in Real Exchange Rates: Evidence and Implications for Forecasting", *Journal of International Money and Finance*, 15, 535-550.
15. Levin, A. and C. F. Lin (1992), "Unit Root Test in Panel Data: Asymptotic and Finite Sample Properties", University of California at San Diego, Discussion paper# 92-93.
16. Levin, A. and C. F. Lin (1993), "Unit Root Test in Panel Data: New Results", University of California at San Diego, Discussion paper# 93-56.
17. Liu, P.C. (1997), "Is the Debate on Purchasing Power Parity Over?", Working Paper, University of Miami.
18. Liu, P.C. and G.S. Maddala (1996), "Do Panel Data Cross-Country Regressions Rescue Purchasing Power Parity Theory?", Manuscript, University of Miami.
19. Lothian, J.R. (1997), "Multi-Country Evidence on the Behavior of Purchasing Power

Parity Under the Current Float", *Journal of International Money and Finance*, 16, 19-35.

20. Maddala, G. S. (1975), "Some Problems Arising in Pooling Cross-Section and Time Series Data", unpublished paper, reprinted as Chapter 3 in *Econometric Methods and Applications*, Volume 1, Edward Elgar Publishing Co., 1994, 223-245.
21. Maddala, G. S. and I. M. Kim (1998), *Unit Roots, Cointegration and Structural Change*, Cambridge University Press.
22. Maddala, G. S. and S. Wu (1998), "A Comparative Study of Unit Root Tests with Panel Data and a New Simple Test", *Oxford Bulletin of Economics and Statistics*, (forthcoming).
23. Mark, N. and D. Sul (1998), "Nominal Exchange Rates and Monetary Fundamentals: Evidence from a Seventeen Country Panel", Manuscript, Dept. of Economics, Ohio State University, Paper presented at the Midwest Econometrics Meetings, Bloomington, Indiana, October 1998.
24. McDonald, R. (1996), "Panel Unit Root Tests and Real Exchange Rates", *Economics Letters*, 50, 7-11.
25. McDonald, R. (1993), "Long-Run Purchasing Power Parity: Is it for Real ?", *Review of Economics and Statistics*, 75, 690-695.
26. Nerlove, M. (1997), "Likelihood Inference for Dynamic Panel Models", *Annales d'Économie et de Statistique de l'INSEE*, (forthcoming, 1999).
27. Nerlove, M. (1998a), "Growth Rate Convergence, Fact or Artifact", (An Essay on the Use and Misuse of Panel Data Econometrics), Havlicek Lecture, Ohio State University, April 16, 1998.
28. Nerlove, M. (1998b), "Properties of Alternative Estimators of Dynamic Panel Models", in C. Hsiao, L. F. Lee, K. Lahiri and H. Pesaran (eds), *Panel Data and Limited Dependent Variables, Essays in Honor of G. S. Maddala*, Cambridge University Press, Cambridge.
29. O'Connell, P. (1998), "The Overvaluation of Purchasing Power Parity", *Journal of International Economics*, 44, 1-19.
30. Oh, K. Y. (1996), "Purchasing Power Parity and the Unit Root Tests Using Panel Data", *Journal of International Money and Finance*, 15, 405-418.
31. Papell, D. H. (1997), "Searching For Stationarity: Purchasing Power Parity Under the Current Float", *Journal of International Economics*, 43 (3-4), 313-32.
32. Papell, D.H. and H. Theodoridis (1998a), "Increasing Evidence of Purchasing Power Parity Over the Current Float", *Journal of International Money and Finance*, 17, 41-50.
33. Papell, D.H. and H. Theodoridis (1998b), "The Choice of Numeraire Currency in Panel Tests of Purchasing Power Parity", Working Paper, University of Houston.
34. Seda, R., J. Devereux and P.C. Liu (1998), "Reconsidering Purchasing Power Parity", Manuscript, University of Miami.
35. Sevestre, P. and A. Trognon (1996), "Linear Dynamic Models" in L. Mátyás and P. Sevestre (eds.), *The Econometrics of Panel Data*, Second Ed., Kluwer, Boston, 120-144.
36. Taylor, M.P. and L. Sarno (1997), "The Behaviour of Real Exchange Rates During the Post-Bretton Woods Period", Working Paper, Oxford University.

37. Wei, S. J. and D. Parsley (1995), "Purchasing Power Disparity During the Floating Rate Period: Exchange Rate Volatility, Trade Barriers and Other Culprits", National Bureau of Economic Research Working Paper: 5032, February 1995.
38. Wu, S. (1998), "Nonstationary Panel Data Analysis", Thesis, the Ohio State University.
39. Wu, S. and J. Wu (1998), "Purchasing Power Parity Under the Current Float: New Evidence From Panel Data Unit Root Tests", Working Paper, Ohio State University.
40. Wu, S. and Y. Yin (1998), "An Unconditional ML Estimation of Panel Data Regressions on Exchange Rates", Manuscript, Dept. of Economics, SUNY at Buffalo.
41. Wu, Y. (1996), "Are Exchange Rates Non-Stationary? Evidence From a Panel-Data Test", *Journal of Money, Credit and Banking*, 28, 54-63.

Panel Data Econometrics: Future Directions
J. Krishnakumar and E. Ronchetti (Editors)

CHAPTER 3

NEGLECTED HETEROGENEITY AND DYNAMICS IN CROSS-COUNTRY SAVINGS REGRESSIONS

Nadeem U. HAQUE, M. Hashem PESARAN and Sunil SHARMA

Abstract

This paper examines the extent to which conclusions of cross-country studies of private savings are robust to allowing for the possible heterogeneity of savings behaviour across countries and to the inclusion of dynamics. It provides a review of the econometric implications of neglected slope heterogeneity and dynamics for the fixed effects estimators routinely used in such studies, and illustrates the nature and extent of the biases involved by a re-examination of time series data from 21 OECD countries previously analysed in the literature. The paper shows that neglecting heterogeneity and dynamics in cross-country savings regressions can lead to misleading inferences about the key determinants of savings behavior. If differences across countries are ignored, one can overestimate the influence of certain factors on the private savings rates and at the same time obtain highly significant, but spurious, nonlinear effects for some of the potential determinants. The results indicate that among the many variables considered in the literature only the fiscal variables – the general government surplus as a proportion of GDP and the ratio of government consumption to GDP– seem to be the key determinants of private savings rates in the industrial countries in the post-World War II period.

1. INTRODUCTION

There are many important empirical issues that the aggregate private savings behavior literature attempts to address. The first is the still unresolved question of whether higher private savings precede increases in growth in the gross domestic product (GDP) or whether higher GDP growth is triggered by other factors and higher private savings are merely a result of higher income levels as well as GDP growth rates. Evidence provided by Carroll and Weil (1994) suggests that growth Granger causes savings and not *vice versa.* But given the difficulties surrounding the interpretation of Granger causality tests, this evidence still accommodates the possibility that while the initial impetus to growth should be sought in other factors, the process of (rapid) development may involve a virtuous circle whereby higher growth leads to higher domestic savings which in turn through raising domestic capital formation leads to even higher growth rates.

The second key question is whether private savings are affected by fiscal policy variables, in particular the public sector fiscal balances and the aggregate level and composition of government expenditures. Recent research seems to suggest that aggregate private savings do offset movements in public savings, although strict Ricardian equivalence does not hold. The focus of the current research has been on identifying the magnitude of this offset and evaluating the channels through which such behavior manifests itself at the microeconomic level. In this context, openness of economies and access to international markets have also been examined to understand how access to foreign savings may influence aggregate private savings.

The third set of issues is related to analyzing the effect of demographic changes and the role played by the provision of social insurance. In particular, interest has focussed on how changes in the dependency ratio are likely to affect private savings and whether such behavior is modified by the presence and design of pension systems and social security.

Other possible determinants of the savings behavior have also been considered; such as the rate of inflation and its variability, changes in the terms of trade, borrowing constraints, the depth of the financial system, and macroeconomic and political stability. Whether such factors have short-term effects or whether the influences are longer lasting has generally not been addressed in the literature. In part this is due to a lack of a theoretical framework for analyzing such factors and in part because good empirical proxies for variables such as financial depth and political and economic stability are not available.

Most recent studies have used multi-country panel data to examine the various issues raised in the literature about aggregate private savings behavior. An early cross-country study of household savings in developing countries was provided by Schmidt-Hebbel, Webb and Corsetti (1992). Other prominent examples are Carroll and Weil (1994) mentioned above and recent studies by Attanasio, Picci and Scorcu (1998), Ogaki, Ostry and Reinhart (1995), Edwards (1996), Masson, Bayoumi and Samiei (1995), Dayal-Gulati and Thimann (1997), and Callen and Thimann (1997). Carroll and Weil (1994) base their analysis on data from 64 countries (OECD and developing) over the period 1958-87. They report fixed-effects regressions of growth on the savings rates and *vice versa* using non-overlapping 5-year averages. Attanasio, Picci and Scorcu (1998) also focus on the growth-investment-saving inter-linkages and estimate country-specific savings/growth rates regressions for a panel of 123 industrial and developing countries over the period 1961-94. Ogaki, Ostry and Reinhart (1995) on the other hand provide an empirical examination of the interest-elasticity of savings in 13 low-income and middle-income countries over 1968-92. Dayal-Gulati and Thimann (1997) consider saving rates across 5 Asian and 9 Latin American countries over the period 1975-95, and report separate static fixed-effects regressions (estimated by least squares and instrumental variables techniques) for the Asian group and Latin American group of countries. Their results show considerable heterogeneity in the parameter estimates across the two country groupings. Callen and Thimann (1997) consider the household saving behaviour across 21 OECD countries over 1975-95, and report static fixed-effects regressions. They do not allow for the possibility of slope heterogeneity in their analysis, but attempt to take account of error variance heterogeneity and a limited degree of dynamics in some of their specifications.

The studies by Edwards (1996) and Masson, Bayoumi and Samiei (1995, 1998) consider a wider class of variables in their analysis of saving behavior. Edwards (1996) uses a 36 country data set (of which eleven are industrialized countries) over the period 1970-92, while Masson, Bayoumi and Samiei (hereafter MBS) examine the determinants of the private savings rate using time series observations on 21 OECD countries over 1971-93, and 40 developing countries over 1982-93. Both of these papers build on the extensive theoretical and empirical literature that exists on savings and consumption behaviour. The study by MBS focuses on six possible determinants of private savings: fiscal variables (general government budget surplus), demographics (the dependency ratio measured as the ratio of the population that is under 20 and 65 and over to that aged between 20-64 years), GDP growth and level of GDP per capita relative to U.S. GDP, the interest rate, the inflation rate and changes in the terms of trade. It reports separate static panel regressions for their sample of industrial and developing countries. Based on the panel regressions and a number of associated cross-section regressions, MBS then conclude that general government surplus, the dependency ratio, GDP growth, and the relative per capita GDP have significant effects on the private savings rate, although with differing degrees of precision. The evidence on the effects of the interest rate and the level of inflation on the savings rate is much weaker and depends on the sample of countries under consideration.

The modelling strategy in these and other cross-country studies of savings rates has generally relied on pooled OLS or static fixed-effects regressions. Little attempt has been made to introduce dynamics, differentiate short-run and long-run parameters or examine the extent to which the diversity in institutional structures across countries can be taken into account while assessing the behavior of aggregate private savings.[1] Clearly, saving and wealth accumulation is a dynamic process and static specifications are unlikely to capture essential features of such processes. Also, cross-country parameter homogeneity restrictions are, at best, likely to hold for long-run parameters with the short-run responses differing across countries. Moreover, while economic theory provides some guidance on long-run parameters it is typically silent on short-run dynamics and the exact nature of the adjustment processes. And most importantly, unless the heterogeneity across countries in short-run responses is taken into account (and allowed for to the extent permitted by the data), the estimation of parameters of interest can be contaminated, vitiating the conclusions drawn about the importance of various factors in determining aggregate private savings.

[1] The studies by Carroll and Weil (1994) and Attanasio, Picci and Scorcu (1998) do allow for dynamics but focus on growth-saving linkages and do not consider the effect of other possible variables such as the dependency ratio, fiscal policy variables, inflation and other variables considered in the studies by Edwards (1996) and Masson, Bayoumi and Samiei (1995, 1998).

The papers mentioned above clearly address an important issue of special concern to policy makers and academics alike. They attempt to isolate the key determinants of the saving rates across a large number of industrialized and developing countries. However, the econometric implementation generally relies on fixed-effects estimation of static panel data models; this raises the question of robustness of their results to the neglected dynamics and the possible heterogeneity across countries of short-run and long-run effects of the various likely determinants of the private savings rate. In this paper we examine the robustness of the conclusions to these two sources of misspecification using the MBS data.

Initially, we consider the consequences of allowing for slope heterogeneity, but continue to use the static specification of the savings rate equations used in the literature.[2] We examine the importance of slope heterogeneity using two different methods: (i) We explicitly model the cross-sectional variations of the slope coefficients in terms of country-specific wealth-GDP ratios and income per capita and estimate augmented fixed-effects regressions. We show that once slope heterogeneity is taken into account the quadratic relationship between private savings and income found in MBS (1998) is no longer statistically significant. The theoretical reasons behind this result are discussed in some detail, with the relevant derivations relegated to an appendix. (ii) Our second approach to the slope heterogeneity problem follows Pesaran and Smith (1995) and compares the average estimates of the slope coefficients from individual country regressions (referred to as the "mean group estimates") to those obtained using the fixed-effects procedure. We also consider different groupings of the coefficient estimates according to whether they are positive or negative and whether they are statistically significant, thus providing a simple and effective way of reporting the extent of the heterogeneity that seems to exist in the underlying parameters.

We then allow for dynamics in individual savings rate equations, and consider two types of estimators: the mean group estimator of the long-run coefficients, and a new pooled estimator that allows for short-run heterogeneity whilst restricting the long-run coefficients to be the same across groups (see Pesaran, Shin and Smith, 1999). As shown in Pesaran and Smith (1995) and Pesaran, Smith and Im (1996), in the presence of dynamics and slope heterogeneity the use of standard panel techniques, such as the fixed-effects estimator or the Anderson-Hsiao estimator, leads to inconsistent estimates and potentially misleading inferences even for large N and T panels. In contrast, the mean group and the pooled estimators of the long-run coefficients (the latter under the assumed homogeneity of the long-run parameters) are consistent when both N (the number of countries) and T (the number of time periods) are reasonably large. Our results show that only the effects of the ratio of general government budget surplus to GDP, and the ratio of general government current expenditure to GDP are reasonably robust to the presence of slope heterogeneity and yield plausible estimates for the off-setting effects of government budget surpluses and government consumption expenditures on private savings across the OECD countries.

The plan of the paper is as follows: Section 2 sets up the econometric framework used in

[2]However, even the "static" models implicitly involve some dynamics through the wealth variable included in many specifications.

cross-country savings studies and reviews the theoretical literature on slope heterogeneity both in static and dynamic panel data models. Section 3 provides a detailed empirical examination of the private savings equation analyzed by MBS (1995, 1998). Section 4 presents a summary of the main results, discusses their economic interpretation and their relevance for policy.

2. CROSS-COUNTRY SAVINGS REGRESSIONS: NEGLECTED HETEROGENEITY

Almost all cross-country studies of savings behavior in the literature make use of linear reduced form models where the savings rate (private or national) is explained in terms of a number of factors such as GDP growth, the real interest rate, inflation, wealth effects, fiscal indicators and demographic variables. In its most general form such a country-specific savings equation can be written as:

$$\lambda_i(L)s_{it} = \mu_i + \sum_{j=1}^{k} \beta_{ij}(L)x_{ijt} + \varepsilon_{it}, \tag{1}$$
$$= \mu_i + \boldsymbol{\beta}_i'(L)\mathbf{x}_{it} + \varepsilon_{it}$$

where s_{it} is the savings rate of country $i = 1, 2, ..., N$ during period $t = 1, 2, ..., T$, $\mathbf{x}_{it} = (x_{i1t}, x_{i2t}, ..., x_{ikt})'$ is a $k \times 1$ vector of factors deemed to be important in the determination of the savings rate in country i. The parameters μ_i represent the fixed-effects, and $\lambda_i(L)$ and $\boldsymbol{\beta}_i(L)$ are the distributed lag functions of orders p and q_i defined by

$$\lambda_i(L) = 1 - \lambda_{i1}L - \lambda_{i2}L^2 - ... - \lambda_{ip}L^p, \tag{2}$$

$$\boldsymbol{\beta}_i(L) = \boldsymbol{\beta}_{i0} + \boldsymbol{\beta}_{i1}L + ... + \boldsymbol{\beta}_{iq_i}L^{q_i}, \tag{3}$$

where $\boldsymbol{\beta}_{is} = (\beta_{i1s}, \beta_{i2s}, ..., \beta_{iks})'$. Finally, ε_{it}, the disturbance term for country i, is intended to capture the effect of a multitude of (remaining) unobserved effects on the saving rate. These disturbances are assumed to be distributed independently (both over time and across countries) with a zero mean and a constant variance, σ_i^2. They are also usually assumed to be distributed independently of the regressors, $\mathbf{x}_{it}$.

For each country (1) represents an autoregressive distributed lag model of order $(p, q_1, q_2, ..., q_k)$, or simply $ARDL(p, q_1, q_2, ..., q_k)$. All the cross-country studies of savings rates are special cases of this $ARDL$ model. Edwards (1996) distinguishes between private and public savings, and applies a static version of (1) to a panel of 36 countries. For the private savings rate he uses pooled OLS which assumes that all the coefficients (slopes as well as the intercepts) are homogenous across countries. For the public savings rate equation he allows for heterogenous intercepts but continues to assume slope homogeneity. In one set of regressions Edwards includes Latin American dummy variables for each regressor in the panel; thus allowing for a limited degree of parameter heterogeneity. Such dummy variable regressions still impose error variance homogeneity across all the countries in the sample as well as parameter homogeneity within the two country groupings. MBS (1995, 1998) also use a homogenous static version of (1) in their analysis of private saving rates.

They consider two separate country groups, one consisting of 21 OECD economies and the other 40 developing economies. The latter is then grouped into high, middle and low income countries. Therefore, they allow for the parameters to differ between the country groupings, but not across the countries within a given group. For each country group they only allow for fixed-effects and assume that all the slope coefficients and error variances are the same across countries. MBS (1998) also experiment with a limited dynamic specification where (implicitly) a common factor restriction is imposed on the distributed lag functions $\lambda_i(L)$ and $\boldsymbol{\beta}_i(L)$. In particular they impose (without testing) the restrictions:

$$\lambda_i(L) = 1 - \lambda L, \text{ and } \quad \beta_{ij}(L) = \beta_{j0}(1 - \lambda L), \tag{4}$$

for all i and j.

In an attempt to address the possible simultaneity problem, many of these cross-country regression studies also provide instrumental variable (IV) estimates using lagged values of the regressors as instruments. Such a procedure is valid in the case of static models. But in the case of the saving process where the dynamics of adjustments can play an important role the application of the IV procedure is problematic as any lagged value that is used as an instrument could itself potentially be an important factor in explaining the short-run dynamics of the saving process. This difficulty with the IV technique is related to the problem of identification and of restrictions in macroeconometric specifications, a problem that was considered in Sims (1980).[3]

The extent to which the results based on cross-country savings regressions are robust to neglected slope heterogeneity depends on (i) whether there are any systematic relationships between the slope coefficients and the regressors, (ii) the importance of the dynamics in the saving process, and (iii) the degree of slope heterogeneity itself. The overall outcome can only be judged in an empirical context by comparing the fixed-effects estimators reported in the literature with those estimators that allow for slope heterogeneity and dynamics. But before proceeding with the empirical analysis it is instructive to examine, at a theoretical level, the consequences of neglected slope heterogeneity on the fixed-effects estimators in the context of simple models.

2.1. Neglected heterogeneity in static models

Consider the following static fixed-effects panel data model:

$$y_{it} = \mu_i + \boldsymbol{\beta}'\mathbf{x}_{it} + u_{it}, \tag{5}$$

where $\boldsymbol{\beta}$ is the vector of unknown slope coefficients assumed to be the same across all the countries in the panel, and u_{it} are unobserved random shocks assumed to be distributed independently (both over time and across countries) and identically with a zero mean and a constant variance, σ^2. It is also usually assumed that the errors, u_{it}, and the regressors, $\mathbf{x}_{it}$, are independently distributed. The only source of heterogeneity allowed for in this framework are the fixed-effects, μ_i.

[3]Edwards (1996) and MBS (1995), for example, estimate their panel data model by instrumental variable (IV) techniques, using lagged values of the regressors as instruments.

The slope and error variance homogeneity assumption that underlie the fixed-effects formulation may be a reasonable first-order approximation for analysis of household or firm behaviour in a given locality or region, but it is less likely to hold across countries that are at different stages of their economic development with different institutions, customs or social norms. This is particularly true of the short-run effects since institutional constraints are likely to be more binding in the short-run and hence can cause the private savings rate across countries to respond differently to its various determinants such as output growth, the real interest rate, inflation, and fiscal deficits.

The consequences of neglecting slope heterogeneity can be quite serious, particularly when the slopes vary systematically across countries. To see this consider the following simple static panel data model with cross-sectionally varying slopes and intercepts:

$$y_{it} = \mu_i + \beta_i x_{it} + u_{it}. \tag{6}$$

For ease of exposition we confine our attention to a model with a single time-varying regressor and continue to maintain the error variance homogeneity assumption. The coefficients, β_i, are allowed to vary freely across countries but are otherwise assumed to be fixed (over time). It proves useful to decompose β_i into a common component, β, and a remainder, η_i, that varies across countries:

$$\beta_i = \beta + \eta_i. \tag{7}$$

The nature of the slope heterogeneity can now be characterized in terms of the properties of η_i. In the panel literature, following the work of Swamy (1970), it is often assumed that η_i are identically independently distributed (i.i.d.) as well as distributed independently of x_{it} and u_{it} for all i and t, with a zero mean and a constant variance, σ^2_η. This specification is known as the random coefficients model (RCM) discussed extensively by Hsiao (1986, Ch. 6). The RCM only allows for a minimal degree of slope heterogeneity. For example, it rules out systematic relationships between β_i and the sample means or variances of the x_{it} process. To cover such possibilities we shall also consider the case where the β_i's are treated as fixed; in exactly the same way that the intercepts, μ_i, are treated in the fixed-effects model, (5).

Consider an investigator that ignores the heterogeneity of the slope coefficients in (6) and instead estimates the following augmented homogenous slope model:

$$y_{it} = \alpha_i + \delta_x x_{it} + \delta_z z_{it} + v_{it}, \tag{8}$$

where z_{it} is an additional regressor spuriously thought to be important by the investigator. For expositional simplicity we assume that for each i, $\mathbf{w}_{it} = (x_{it}, z_{it})'$ is covariance stationary with the variance-covariance matrix

$$\Omega_i = \begin{pmatrix} \omega_{ixx} & \omega_{ixz} \\ \omega_{izx} & \omega_{izz} \end{pmatrix}. \tag{9}$$

It is now easily established that the fixed-effects (FE) estimator of the slope coefficient, $\boldsymbol{\delta} = (\delta_x, \delta_z)'$, is generally inconsistent. The inconsistency of the FE estimator in this set-up is derived in the appendix. Denoting the FE estimator of $\boldsymbol{\delta}$ by $\hat{\boldsymbol{\delta}}_{FE}$, we have

$$\operatorname*{plim}_{N,T\to\infty} (\hat{\delta}_{x,FE} - \beta) = \frac{E(\omega_{izz})Cov(\omega_{ixx}, \beta_i - \beta) - E(\omega_{ixz})Cov(\omega_{ixz}, \beta_i - \beta)}{E(\omega_{ixx})E(\omega_{izz}) - (E(\omega_{ixz}))^2}, \tag{10}$$

$$\underset{N,T\to\infty}{\text{plim}}\ (\hat{\delta}_{z,FE}) = \frac{E(\omega_{ixx})Cov(\omega_{ixz},\beta_i-\beta) - E(\omega_{ixz})Cov(\omega_{ixx},\beta_i-\beta)}{E(\omega_{ixx})E(\omega_{izz}) - (E(\omega_{ixz}))^2}, \tag{11}$$

where[4]

$$Cov(\omega_{ixx},\beta_i-\beta) = \lim_{N\to\infty}\left(\frac{1}{N}\sum_{i=1}^{N}\omega_{ixx}(\beta_i-\beta)\right),$$

$$Cov(\omega_{ixz},\beta_i-\beta) = \lim_{N\to\infty}\left(\frac{1}{N}\sum_{i=1}^{N}\omega_{ixz}(\beta_i-\beta)\right),$$

$$E(\omega_{ixx}) = \lim_{N\to\infty}\left(\frac{1}{N}\sum_{i=1}^{N}\omega_{ixx}\right),\quad E(\omega_{izz}) = \lim_{N\to\infty}\left(\frac{1}{N}\sum_{i=1}^{N}\omega_{izz}\right),$$

$$E(\omega_{ixz}) = \lim_{N\to\infty}\left(\frac{1}{N}\sum_{i=1}^{N}\omega_{ixz}\right).$$

The above results have a number of interesting implications:

1. The fixed-effects estimator of δ_z is robust to slope heterogeneity if the incorrectly included regressors, z_{it}, are on average orthogonal to x_{it}, namely when $E(\omega_{ixz}) = 0$. However, in the presence of slope heterogeneity the fixed-effects estimator of δ_x continues to be inconsistent even if z_{it} and x_{it} are on average orthogonal. The direction of the asymptotic bias of $\hat{\delta}_{x,FE}$ depends on the sign of $Cov(\omega_{ixx},\beta_i-\beta)$. The bias of $\hat{\delta}_{x,FE}$ is positive when $Cov(\omega_{ixx},\beta_i-\beta) > 0$ and *vice versa*.[5]

2. The fixed-effects estimators, $\hat{\boldsymbol{\delta}}_{x,FE}$ and $\hat{\delta}_{z,FE}$, are both consistent if

$$Cov(\omega_{ixz},\beta_i-\beta) = Cov(\omega_{ixx},\beta_i-\beta) = 0. \tag{12}$$

   Clearly, these conditions are met under slope homogeneity. In the present application where the regressors are assumed to be strictly exogenous, the fixed-effects estimators converge to their true values under the RCM where the slope coefficients and the regressors are assumed to be independently distributed.[6] Notice, however, that since the β_i's are assumed to be fixed over time, then any systematic dependence of η_i on $\mathbf{w}_{it}$ over time is already ruled out under model (6). The random coefficients assumption imposes further restrictions on the joint distribution of η_i and the cross-sectional distribution of $\mathbf{w}_{it}$. This result provides a straightforward extension of the misspecification results already familiar from the regression analysis of single series (i.e. when $N = 1$), and which forms the basis of the "general-to-specific" methodology advocated by David Hendry.[7]

---

[4]In the case where the slopes are randomly distributed across i, the limits in the definitions of $Cov(\omega_{ixx},\beta_i-\beta)$ and $Cov(\omega_{ixz},\beta_i-\beta)$ need to be replaced by probability limits.

[5]Notice that $E(\omega_{ixx})E(\omega_{izz}) - (E(\omega_{ixz}))^2 > 0$, unless of course x_{it} and z_{it} are perfectly collinear for all i, which we rule out. See Assumption A.3.

[6]See, for example, Swamy (1970) and Hsiao (1986, Ch. 6).

[7]See, for example, Hendry (1993, Ch's. 6 and 19), and Gilbert (1986).

3. In general, where $E(\omega_{ixz}) \neq 0$ and $Cov(\omega_{ixz}, \beta_i - \beta) \neq 0$ and/or $Cov(\omega_{ixx}, \beta_i - \beta) \neq 0$, the fixed-effects estimators, $\hat{\delta}_{x,FE}$ and $\hat{\delta}_{z,FE}$, are both inconsistent. Therefore, if the slope coefficients are fixed but vary systematically across the groups, the application of the general-to-specific methodology to standard panel data models can lead to misleading results (spurious inference). An important example is provided by the case when attempts are made to check for the presence of nonlinearities by testing the significance of quadratic terms in static panel data models using fixed-effects estimators. In the context of our simple specification this would involve setting $z_{it} = x_{it}^2$, and a test of the significance of z_{it} in (8) will yield sensible results only if the conditions defined by (12) are met. In general, it is possible to falsely reject the linearity hypothesis when there are systematic relations between the slope coefficients and the cross-sectional distribution of the regressors. Therefore, results from nonlinearity tests in panel data models should be interpreted with care. The linearity hypothesis may be rejected not because of the existence of a genuine nonlinear relationship between y_{it} and x_{it}, but due to slope heterogeneity. Finally, it is worth noting that since the β_i's are fixed for each i, the nonlinear specification

$$y_{it} = \alpha_i + \delta_x x_{it} + \delta_z x_{it}^2 + v_{it}, \tag{13}$$

cannot be reconciled with (12), unless it is assumed that β_i varies proportionately with x_{it}. Clearly, it is possible to allow the slopes, β_i, to vary systematically with some aspect of the cross-sectional distribution of x_{it} without requiring β_i to be proportional to x_{it}, and hence time-varying. For example, it could be that

$$\beta_i = \gamma_0 + \gamma_1 \bar{x}_i, \tag{14}$$

where $\bar{x}_i = T^{-1} \sum_{t=1}^{T} x_{it}$. This specification retains the linearity of (12) for each i, but can still yield a statistically significant effect for x_{it}^2 in (13) if slope heterogeneity is ignored and fixed-effects estimates of (13) are used in inference. This feature of fixed-effects regressions under heterogeneous slopes is illustrated in Figure 1. The figure shows scatter points and associated regression lines for three countries with slopes that differ systematically with $\bar{x}_i$. It is clear that the pooled regression based on the scatter points from all the three countries will exhibit strong nonlinearities, although the country-specific regressions are linear. For an empirical illustration of this see section 3.1 below.

2.2. Neglected heterogeneity in dynamic models

The neglect of slope heterogeneity is yet more serious in dynamic panel data models. As shown in Pesaran and Smith (1995), it generates a correlation between the regressors and the error term as well as serial correlation in the disturbances, and hence introduces a bias in the fixed-effects estimator, even for sufficiently large T and N. Also, unlike the static case, the inconsistency of the fixed-effects estimators does not disappear even if we assume that the slope coefficients are distributed independently of the exogenous regressors and

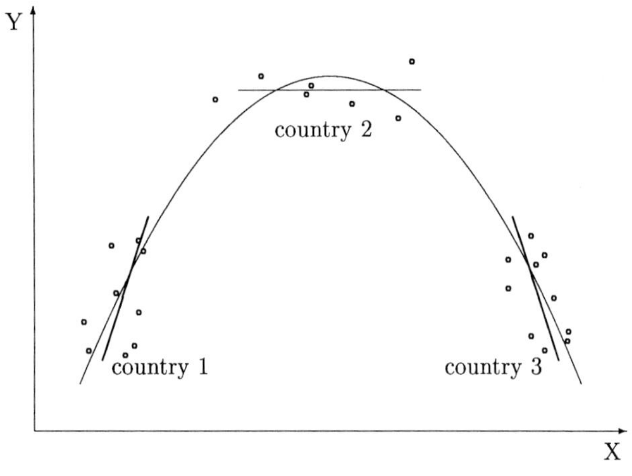

Figure 1. Fixed-Effects Regression under Heterogeneous Slopes

the disturbances. To get some idea of the size and the direction of the asymptotic bias of the fixed-effects estimators, suppose that the y_{it}'s are generated according to the following simple dynamic version of (6):

$$y_{it} = \mu_i + \lambda_i y_{i,t-1} + \beta_i x_{it} + u_{it}, \quad u_{it} \sim iid\ (0, \sigma_i^2), \quad i = 1, 2, ..., N;\ t = 1, 2, ..., T. \qquad (15)$$

To simplify the exposition in what follows we assume that $\lambda_i = \lambda$, and focus on the fixed-effects estimators of λ and β (denoted by $\hat{\lambda}_{FE}$ and $\hat{\beta}_{FE}$) in

$$y_{it} = \mu_i + \lambda y_{i,t-1} + \beta x_{it} + v_{it}, \qquad (16)$$

where

$$v_{it} = \eta_i x_{it} + u_{it}. \qquad (17)$$

We also assume that the η_i's are distributed independently of x_{it} and u_{it} for all i and t, and that they have a zero mean and a constant variance, σ_η^2. It is now easily seen that the fixed-effects estimator of λ and β in (16) will be inconsistent even if both T and N are allowed to increase without bounds. The inconsistency of the fixed-effects estimators is due to the non-zero correlation between v_{it} and $y_{i,t-1}$, and the fact that v_{it}'s are serially correlated, unless x_{it} is serially uncorrelated. Assuming the dynamic processes (16) are stable (namely, $|\lambda| < 1$), and have been in operation for a sufficiently long time we can obtain

$$Cov(v_{it}, y_{i,t-1}) = E([(v_{it} - \bar{v}_i)(y_{i,t-1} - \bar{y}_{i,-1})] = \sigma_\eta^2 \sum_{j=0}^{\infty} \lambda^j \gamma_x(j+1),$$

where $\bar{v}_i = T^{-1}\sum_{t=1}^{T} v_{it}$, $\bar{y}_{i,-1} = T^{-1}\sum_{t=1}^{T} y_{i,t-1}$, and $\gamma_x(j)$ is the $j-th$ order autocovariance function of the x_{it} process. In this simple example $Cov(v_{it}, y_{i,t-1}) = 0$ only if

x_{it} is a serially uncorrelated process, which is very unlikely in the case of most economic time series.[8] The asymptotic bias of the fixed-effects estimators of λ and β are derived in Pesaran and Smith (1995). In the case where x_{it} follows a first-order autoregressive process

$$x_{it} = \kappa_i (1-\rho) + \rho x_{i,t-1} + \xi_{it}, \qquad \xi_{it} \sim iid\ (0, \tau_i^2),$$

they show that

$$\underset{N,T\to\infty}{\text{plim}}\ \hat{\lambda}_{FE} = \lambda + \frac{\rho\,(1-\lambda\rho)\,(1-\lambda^2)\sigma_\eta^2}{\Psi},$$

and

$$\underset{N,T\to\infty}{\text{plim}}\ \hat{\beta}_{FE} = \beta - \frac{\beta\,\rho^2\,(1-\lambda^2)\sigma_\eta^2}{\Psi},$$

where $\hat{\lambda}_{FE}$ and $\hat{\beta}_{FE}$ denote the fixed-effects estimators of λ and β in (16) and[9]

$$\Psi = (\sigma^2/\tau^2)\,(1-\rho^2)\,(1-\lambda\rho)^2 + (1-\lambda^2\rho^2)\,\sigma_\eta^2 + (1-\rho^2)\,\beta^2 > 0.$$

The size of the asymptotic bias depends on β, λ, ρ, σ_η^2, and the means of σ_i^2 and τ_i^2, denoted by σ^2 and τ^2. It is easy to check that $\hat{\beta}_{FE}$ always underestimates β, whereas $\hat{\lambda}_{FE}$ over- or underestimates λ depending on whether ρ is positive or negative, respectively.

Pesaran and Smith also show that in the general case where both λ_i and β_i are allowed to vary across i, it is not possible to obtain consistent estimates of $\lambda = E(\lambda_i)$ and $\beta = E(\beta_i)$ by the application of the traditional instrumental variables or the Generalized Method of Moments (GMM) estimators proposed, for example, by Anderson and Hsiao (1981, 1982), Arellano (1989), Arellano and Bover (1995), Keane and Runkle (1992) and Ahn and Schmidt (1995), to a first-differenced form of (16). Instead, they propose the mean group (MG) estimator, obtained by estimating the coefficients of each cross-sectional unit separately by the ordinary least squares (OLS) and then by taking an arithmetic average of them. The MG estimators of λ and β (which we denote by $\hat{\lambda}_{MG}$ and $\hat{\beta}_{MG}$) are given by

$$\hat{\lambda}_{MG} = \frac{1}{N}\sum_{i=1}^{N} \hat{\lambda}_i, \quad \hat{\beta}_{MG} = \frac{1}{N}\sum_{i=1}^{N} \hat{\beta}_i, \tag{18}$$

where $\hat{\lambda}_i$ and $\hat{\beta}_i$ are the OLS estimates from individual group (country) regressions. The variance-covariance matrix of the MG estimators can then be consistently estimated by

$$\widehat{Cov}(\hat{\boldsymbol{\delta}}_{MG}) = \frac{\sum_{i=1}^{N}(\hat{\boldsymbol{\delta}}_i - \hat{\boldsymbol{\delta}}_{MG})(\hat{\boldsymbol{\delta}}_i - \hat{\boldsymbol{\delta}}_{MG})'}{N(N-1)},$$

[8]In the more general case where the coefficients of the lagged dependent variables, λ_i, also vary across groups $Cov(v_{it}, y_{i,t-1}) \neq 0$ even if the regressors, x_{it}, are serially uncorrelated. For further details see Pesaran and Smith (1995).

[9]The expression for Ψ given here corrects a typo in equation (2.9) of Pesaran and Smith (1995), where $(1-\rho^2)\,\beta^2$ in that equation was incorrectly entered as $(1-\rho^2)\,\beta$.

where $\hat{\boldsymbol{\delta}}_{MG} = (\hat{\lambda}_{MG}, \hat{\beta}_{MG})'$.[10] MG estimation is possible when both T and N are sufficiently large, and is applicable irrespective of whether the slope coefficients are random (in Swamy's sense) or fixed in the sense that the diversity in the slope coefficients across countries cannot be captured by means of a finite parameter probability distribution.[11] When the slopes differ randomly across countries the Swamy estimator (also known as the "empirical Bayes" estimator) computed as weighted averages of $\hat{\lambda}_i$ and $\hat{\beta}_i$, or the Bayes estimator proposed by Hsiao, Pesaran and Tahmiscioglu (1999) can be used. It is shown that all the three estimators; namely the mean group, the Swamy and the Bayes estimators are asymptotically equivalent and have a standard asymptotic normal distribution for large N and large T so long as $\sqrt{N}/T \to 0$, as both N and $T \to \infty$.

Although the MG and the Bayes estimators provide an asymptotically valid distribution theory for making inferences about the average of the slope coefficients, nevertheless they do not take account of the fact that certain parameters may be the same across groups. The traditional pooled estimators, such as the fixed- and random-effects estimators, stand at the other extreme and (with the possible exception of intercepts) assume that the coefficients and error variances are the same across the groups. An intermediate estimator which allows the intercepts, short-run coefficients and error variances to differ across groups, but imposes the equality of one or more of the long-run coefficients across the groups has been recently proposed by Pesaran, Shin and Smith (1999). This estimator is called the Pooled Mean Group (PMG) estimator because it involves both pooling and averaging. Such an intermediate estimation technique is particularly relevant to the cross-country analysis of consumption functions where it is reasonable to assume that aggregate consumption responds very similarly across countries to aggregate disposable income in the long-run, although due to historical and institutional reasons it may not be plausible to assume that aggregate consumption in all countries will adjust similarly and with the same speed to short term changes in income.

3. EMPIRICAL EVIDENCE

In this section we examine the empirical evidence on the determinants of cross country private savings rates using the data from MBS (1995, 1998). We have chosen to focus on this particular study because of the relatively comprehensive list of variables that it considers, and also because it arrives at a number of policy conclusions whose robustness to neglected slope heterogeneity and dynamics are worth checking. As noted earlier, MBS divide their sample into an industrial country group and a developing country group. They present estimates obtained for all the 61 countries taken together as well as those from separate analyses of the two country groups. Homogeneity of the slope coefficients across the two country groupings is strongly rejected possibly also due to important differences between the two groups in terms of data definitions and data reliability. The data for the two groups also cover different time periods. Available time series for the developing

[10]For further details see, for example, Im, Pesaran and Smith (1996).

[11]In situations where N is small and T is large, the Seemingly Unrelated Regression Estimation (SURE) procedure due to Zellner (1962) can be used. In the cross-country savings literature N is often quite large which precludes the use of the SURE procedure. For example, the full data set used by MBS (1995) covers 61 countries.

countries are substantially shorter than for the industrial countries. Since our primary purpose here is to illustrate the importance of dynamics and slope heterogeneity in cross-country analysis of savings behaviour we confine our analysis to the industrial countries where conceivably slope heterogeneity could be less of an issue. For the industrial countries MBS run fixed-effects regressions of

$PSAV$: the private savings rate, defined as the ratio of aggregate private savings to GDP,

on

SUR : the ratio of general government budget surplus to GDP,

$GCUR$: the ratio of the general government current expenditure to GDP,

GI : the ratio of the general government investment to GDP,

GR : GDP growth rate,

$RINT$: real interest rate,

INF : inflation rate,

$PCTT$: percentage change in terms of trade,

$YRUS$: per capita GDP relative to the U.S.,

DEP : dependency ratio, defined as the ratio of those under 20 and 65 and over to those aged 20-64,

W : ratio of private wealth (measured as the cumulative sum of past nominal private savings) to GDP.

The fixed-effects estimates including all the 10 regressors are reported in the first column of table 2 in MBS (1995). This table also reports least squares and IV estimates for a restricted version of their general model where the regressors GR and W are dropped from the model and the coefficients of $GCUR$ and GI are imposed to be the same. In a more recent version of their paper, MBS (1998) report estimates for a slightly more general regression model that also includes the square of the relative income variable (see table 3 in MBS, 1998). They argue that the effect of the income variable on the savings rate is likely to be nonlinear; being positive at low levels of income and then becoming negative at higher income levels. Presumably, similar arguments can also be made with respect to some of the other variables, notably the wealth variable; but such possibilities are not pursued by MBS. Fixed-effects estimates corrected for residual serial correlation, using Cochrane-Orcutt type procedures, are also reported "in order to avoid biasing estimates of standard errors", in the belief that the regression model being estimated is static and does not contain lagged dependent variables. However, their specification implicitly *does* contain lagged dependent variables through the wealth variable. Hence, evidence of significant residual serial correlation can be a problem, and as we suggest below, a likely symptom of dynamic misspecification and neglected slope heterogeneity.[12]

[12]In general, the Cochrane-Orcutt type corrections do not adequately deal with dynamic mis-specification. See Hendry (1993, Ch. 7), and the discussion in Section 2 on testing for common factor restrictions.

3.1. Slope heterogeneity in "static" cross-country savings regressions

For convenience we begin our investigation by reproducing the MBS's (1998) fixed-effects regression for the industrial countries in table 1. We refer to this specification as model M_0. The estimates under "model M_0" in table 1 are identical to those reported in column 1 of table 3 in MBS (1998). Apart from the coefficient of the GDP growth rate (GR), all the estimated coefficients are statistically (some very highly) significant, and in particular suggest a strong quadratic relationship between saving and per capita income. However, as pointed out earlier, the validity of these estimates and the inferences based on them critically depend on the extent to which slope coefficients differ across countries, and in the case of static models whether these differences are systematic. Whether on balance it is reasonable to ignore slope heterogeneity clearly depends on the particular application under consideration, and it is therefore important that the robustness of the fixed-effects estimates to slope heterogeneity is checked, as far as possible, on a case-by-case basis.

As it was shown in section 2.1, one important implication of neglected slope heterogeneity is the possibility of obtaining spurious nonlinear effects. We explored this possibility by adding quadratic terms in W, INF, $PCTT$, and DEP to the regressors already included in model M_0. While there may be some *a priori* argument for a nonlinear wealth effect in the savings equation, the rationale for nonlinear effects in the case of the other three variables seems less clear. Nevertheless, as can be seen from the estimates reported under "model M_1" in table 1, all these quadratic terms are statistically highly significant. The quadratic relationships between the private savings rate and the variables W, $PCTT$, and DEP are in fact much stronger than the quadratic relationship between savings and per capita income that MBS focus on. The $\bar{R}^2$ of the augmented model, 0.801, is also appreciably larger than that obtained for model M_0, 0.766. A similar conclusion is reached using other model selection criteria such as the Akaike Information Criterion (AIC) and the Schwarz Bayesian Criterion (SBC) also reported in table 1.

As an alternative to the quadratic specifications used in model M_1, we investigated the possibility that the slope coefficients in each country are *fixed over time*, but are allowed to vary across countries linearly with the sample means of their wealth to GDP ratio or their income per capita. More specifically, denote the vector of slope coefficients for country i by $\boldsymbol{\beta}_i$, and define

$$\overline{W}_i = T^{-1}\sum_{t=1}^{T} W_{it}, \text{ and } \overline{YRUS}_i = T^{-1}\sum_{t=1}^{T} YRUS_{it}.$$

Then, slope heterogeneity in the present application could be modelled by:

$$\boldsymbol{\beta}_i = \boldsymbol{\beta}_0 + \boldsymbol{\beta}_{01}\overline{W}_i + \boldsymbol{\beta}_{02}\overline{YRUS}_i. \tag{19}$$

Substituting the above expression for $\boldsymbol{\beta}_i$ in (5) we have[13]

$$y_{it} = \mu_i + \boldsymbol{\beta}_0'\mathbf{x}_{it} + \boldsymbol{\beta}_{01}'(\mathbf{x}_{it}\overline{W}_i) + \boldsymbol{\beta}_{02}'(\mathbf{x}_{it}\overline{YRUS}_i) + u_{it}, \tag{20}$$

[13]It is also reasonable to expect that in addition to the systematic effects characterized through the dependence of $\boldsymbol{\beta}_i$ on $\overline{W}_i$ and $\overline{YRUS}_i$, the slope coefficients also differ randomly across i. Such a formulation, however, moves us towards the mean group or weighted mean group estimation procedures discussed in Section 2.2, which we shall consider later in this section.

Table 1

Fixed-Effects Estimates of "Static" Private Saving Equations
(21 OECD Countries, 1971-1993)

	Model M_0		Model M_1	
Regressors	Linear Terms	Quadratic Terms	Linear Terms	Quadratic Terms
SUR	-0.574	-	-0.581	-
	(-9.39)		(-10.30)	
GCUR	-0.467	-	-0.521	-
	(-11.30)		(-13.39)	
GI	-0.603	-	-0.701	-
	(-5.71)		(-6.92)	
GR	-0.060	-	-0.065	-
	(-1.14)		(-1.33)	
RINT	0.212	-	0.281	-
	(4.40)		(5.90)	
W	0.023	-	0.175	-0.00025
	(5.11)		(8.38)	(-7.69)
INF	0.180	-	-0.041	0.011
	(4.63)		(-0.53)	(3.29)
PCTT	0.047	-	0.063	-0.0013
	(3.07)		(4.11)	(-2.81)
YRUS	0.586	-0.0048	0.286	-0.0026
	(3.41)	(-3.90)	(1.70)	(-2.15)
DEP	-0.118	-	-1.201	0.0073
	(-4.12)		(-5.25)	(4.85)
$\overline{R}^2$	0.766		0.801	
$\widehat{\sigma}$	2.325		2.145	
LL	-1076.4		-1035.3	
AIC	-1108.4		-1071.3	
SBC	-1165.3		-1146.5	

The dependent variable (PSAV) is the ratio of private savings to GDP. Model M_0 is the specification estimated by Masson *et al.* (1998)– see column 1 of Table 3 in that paper. The figures in brackets are t-ratios. $\overline{R}^2$ is the adjusted multiple correlation coefficient, $\widehat{\sigma}$ is the standard error of the regression; LL is the maximized value of the log-likelihood function; AIC is the Akaike information criterion, and SBC is the Schwarz Bayesian criterion.

where $y_{it} = PSAV_{it}$,

$$\mathbf{x}_{it} = (SUR_{it}, GCUR_{it}, GI_{it}, GR_{it}, RINT_{it}, W_{it}, INF_{it}, PCTT_{it}, YRUS_{it}, DEP_{it})'.$$

Initially, the elements of $(\boldsymbol{\beta}_0, \boldsymbol{\beta}_{01}, \boldsymbol{\beta}_{02})$ were estimated without any constraints and it was found that in the case of almost all the regressors $\overline{W}_i$ was by far a better proxy than $\overline{YRUS}_i$ for capturing slope heterogeneity in this application. The exception was the coefficient of the real interest variable, $RINT$. The unrestricted estimates of $\boldsymbol{\beta}_0$, $\boldsymbol{\beta}_{01}$,and $\boldsymbol{\beta}_{02}$, together with their t-ratios are given in table 2. Apart from the coefficient of the SUR variable, all the other coefficients show systematic variation across countries. The coefficient of the SUR variable seems to be least affected by slope heterogeneity, and the hypothesis of slope homogeneity cannot be rejected in the case of this variable. However, none of the other estimates are directly comparable to the fixed-effects estimates given in table 1. In particular, the coefficients of output growth variables (GR_{it} and $GR_{it} * \overline{W}_i$) are both statistically significant, while this was not so in the case of the fixed-effects estimates in table 1. Care must also be exercised when interpreting these estimates. For example, the results suggest that the effect of real output growth on the savings rate is likely to be higher in a country with a high wealth-GDP ratio. Similarly, inflation effects on the savings rate are estimated to be higher in countries with higher wealth to GDP ratios. However, these results do not predict, for instance, that an individual country's savings rate will necessarily rise with output growth. Table 3 gives the country-specific estimates together with their cross-sectional averages. Except for the coefficient of the SUR variable all the other estimates show considerable variation across countries. The coefficient of the output growth rate, for example, ranges from -0.211 (for Greece) to 0.172 (for Portugal). The effect of inflation on savings varies across countries even more widely; ranging from -0.142 to 0.374. The same also applies to the relative income variable, $YRUS$. Only the coefficients of the government expenditure variables, $GCUR$ and GI , do not change sign and remain negative across all the 21 countries.

The country-specific estimates in table 3 are obtained on the assumption that the slope coefficients across countries are *exact* linear functions of $\overline{W}_i$ and/or $\overline{YRUS}_i$. The underlying fixed-effects regression in table 2 also assumes that the error variances, $Var(u_{it}) = \sigma_i^2$, are the same across countries. Clearly, these are rather restrictive assumptions, and the consequences of incorrectly imposing them on the parameters of interest need to be examined. Under the alternative assumption of unrestricted slope and error variance heterogeneity country-specific estimates can be obtained from individual country regressions. Mean group (MG) estimates computed as simple averages of country-specific estimates from country specific regressions can then be used to make inferences about $E(\boldsymbol{\beta}_i) = \boldsymbol{\beta}$ along the lines reviewed in section 2.2.

We first estimated the basic MBS specification containing the relative income variable ($YRUS$) and its square ($YRUS^2$) for 20 out of the 21 OECD economies in the panel. We had to exclude the U.S. equation from this analysis since its parameters are not identified.[14] The quadratic terms $YRUS_{it}^2$ were statistically significant only in the case of four countries: Austria, Belgium, Ireland, and Norway. In view of this and bearing in

[14]Notice that $YRUS_{it}$ is defined as the ratio of country i's GDP per capita to that of the U.S., and

Table 2

Fixed-Effects Estimates of Private Savings Equations
with Cross-Sectionally Varying Slopes (Model M_2)
(21 OECD Countries, 1971-1993)

Regressors (x_{it})	β_0	β_{01}	β_{02}
SUR	-0.625	-	-
	(-12.10)		
GCUR	-1.146	0.0022	-
	(-6.91)	(4.26)	
GI	-1.891	0.0039	-
	(-2.44)	(1.60)	
GR	-0.744	0.0023	-
	(-2.69)	(2.71)	
RINT	0.417	-	-0.0052
	(4.36)		(-3.53)
W	0.119	-0.00033	-
	(5.28)	(-4.70)	
INF	-0.860	0.0031	-
	(-5.29)	(6.29)	
PCTT	-0.214	0.00083	-
	(-1.88)	(2.30)	
YRUS	1.435	-0.0046	-
	(6.31)	(-6.72)	
DEP	0.502	-0.0021	-
	(2.54)	(-3.39)	
$\overline{R}^2$	0.838		
$\widehat{\sigma}$	1.934		
LL	-982.9		
AIC	-1022.9		
SBC	-1106.5		

See the notes to table 1. The model estimated is $PSAV_{it} = \mu_i + \beta_0' \mathbf{x}_{it} + \beta_{01}'(\mathbf{x}_{it}\overline{W}_i) + \beta_{02}'(\mathbf{x}_{it}\overline{YRUS}_i) + u_{it}$, where $\overline{W}_i$ and $\overline{YRUS}_i$ are the country-specific means of wealth-GDP ratio and the relative income per capita variable

mind that the statistical significance of the nonlinear effects in fixed-effects regressions could be spurious, possibly reflecting systematic slope heterogeneity, we decided to confine our analysis to linear individual country regressions. The results are summarized in table 4. The estimated slope coefficients differ considerably across countries, both in terms of

hence it is indistinguishable from an intercept in the U.S. saving equation. A more appropriate measure would be to measure income per capita relative to the industrial countries average and thus avoid the identification problem in the case of the U.S. saving equation.

Table 3

Country-Specific Estimates Based on Model M_2

Country	$\overline{Y}_{i0}$	$\overline{W}_i$	SUR	GCUR	GI	GR	RINT	W	INF	YRUS	DEP	PCTT
Greece	34.60	232.0	-0.625	-0.6360	-0.9880	-0.2110	0.2370	0.0426	-0.1420	0.3690	0.0155	-0.0217
Canada	82.50	239.0	-0.625	-0.6210	-0.9600	-0.1950	-0.0120	0.0402	-0.1200	0.3370	0.0007	-0.0159
USA	100.00	280.0	-0.625	-0.5300	-0.7990	-0.1000	-0.1030	0.0266	0.0079	0.1470	-0.0859	0.0184
Finland	66.10	283.0	-0.625	-0.5230	-0.7860	-0.0923	0.0734	0.0255	0.0184	0.1320	-0.0931	0.0212
Spain	50.70	286.0	-0.625	-0.5170	-0.7760	-0.0865	0.1540	0.0247	0.0262	0.1200	-0.0983	0.0233
Norway	69.00	290.0	-0.625	-0.5090	-0.7620	-0.0780	0.0583	0.0234	0.0377	0.1030	-0.1060	0.0264
Denmark	74.80	290.0	-0.625	-0.5080	-0.7600	-0.0773	0.0282	0.0233	0.0386	0.1020	-0.1070	0.0266
Sweden	76.80	290.0	-0.625	-0.5080	-0.7600	-0.0772	0.0177	0.0233	0.0387	0.1010	-0.1070	0.0266
Australia	72.40	297.0	-0.625	-0.4930	-0.7330	-0.0608	0.0407	0.0210	0.0608	0.0687	-0.1220	0.0325
Germany	64.10	299.0	-0.625	-0.4870	-0.7230	-0.0553	0.0836	0.0202	0.0683	0.0575	-0.1270	0.0345
France	77.80	306.0	-0.625	-0.4720	-0.6960	-0.0395	0.0126	0.0179	0.0895	0.0261	-0.1410	0.0402
Netherlands	72.60	314.0	-0.625	-0.4560	-0.6670	-0.0224	0.0395	0.0155	0.1130	-0.0081	-0.1570	0.0464
Austria	72.20	322.0	-0.625	-0.4380	-0.6360	-0.0041	0.0418	0.0128	0.1370	-0.0449	-0.1740	0.0530
Japan	69.90	326.0	-0.625	-0.4290	-0.6200	0.0057	0.0537	0.0114	0.1500	-0.0644	-0.1820	0.0565
New Zealand	67.10	339.0	-0.625	-0.4010	-0.5710	0.0346	0.0682	0.0073	0.1890	-0.1220	-0.2090	0.0670
UK	68.80	357.0	-0.625	-0.3610	-0.5000	0.0765	0.0590	0.0013	0.2460	-0.2060	-0.2470	0.0821
Belgium	71.80	364.0	-0.625	-0.3450	-0.4710	0.0934	0.0435	-0.0011	0.2690	-0.2400	-0.2630	0.0882
Ireland	42.50	373.0	-0.625	-0.3260	-0.4380	0.1130	0.1960	-0.0040	0.2950	-0.2790	-0.2810	0.0953
Italy	69.00	373.0	-0.625	-0.3260	-0.4370	0.1130	0.0580	-0.0040	0.2960	-0.2800	-0.2810	0.0954
Switzerland	97.90	391.0	-0.625	-0.2860	-0.3670	0.1550	-0.0920	-0.0100	0.3520	-0.3630	-0.3190	0.1100
Portugal	35.20	398.0	-0.625	-0.2700	-0.3380	0.1720	0.2340	-0.0124	0.3740	-0.3960	-0.3340	0.1160
Average	68.37	316.62	-0.625	-0.4496	-0.6566	-0.016	0.0615	0.0145	0.1212	-0.0210	-0.1628	0.0487
Standard error	16.71	46.12	0.00	0.1012	0.1799	0.1061	0.0869	0.0152	0.1430	0.2121	0.0969	0.0382

The country-specific estimates are computed as $\beta_i = \hat{\beta}_0 + \hat{\beta}'_{01}\overline{W}_i + \hat{\beta}'_{02}\overline{YRUS}_i$, using the estimates in Table 2.

Table 4
Country-Specific Estimates of "Static" Private Saving Equations (20 OECD countries, 1972-1993)

Country	SUR	GCUR	GI	GR	RINT	W	INF	PCTT	YRUS	DEP
Australia	**-0.81**	-0.18	**-1.00**	0.08	**0.18**	**0.06**	**0.27**	0.04	**0.42**	**0.46**
	(0.18)	(0.27	(0.41)	(0.08)	(0.08)	(0.02)	(0.09)	(0.03)	(0.17)	(0.22)
Austria	-0.48	-0.42	0.35	0.06	0.24	0.04	0.09	0.11	-0.10	-0.03
	(0.56)	(0.40)	(0.84)	(0.32)	(0.32)	(0.05)	(0.54)	(0.16)	(0.24)	(0.21)
Belgium	**-0.68**	**-0.53**	-2.47	0.09	-0.04	-0.02	-0.10	-0.00	**0.17**	-0.22
	(0.23)	(0.15)	(1.51)	(0.11)	(0.14)	(0.03)	(0.13)	(0.02)	(0.09)	(0.35)
Canada	**-1.31**	**-0.56**	1.01	**0.24**	0.10	-0.03	**0.29**	**0.17**	0.07	-0.17
	(0.10)	(0.14)	(1.03)	(0.09)	(0.08)	(0.04)	(0.09)	(0.05)	(0.12)	(0.12)
Denmark	**-1.08**	**-0.64**	0.36	0.03	-0.20	-0.01	0.10	0.02	0.14	**-1.17**
	(0.15)	(0.22)	(0.80)	(0.25)	(0.20)	(0.03)	(0.29)	(0.05)	(0.24)	(0.36)
Finland	**-0.70**	-0.35	0.87	0.14	**0.40**	0.03	**0.52**	0.01	0.02	-0.39
	(0.16)	(0.21)	(1.59)	(0.20)	(0.18)	(0.03)	(0.22)	(0.02)	(0.19)	(0.52)
France	**-1.45**	-0.78	-3.13	0.10	-0.16	-0.04	-0.22	-0.06	0.12	-0.16
	(0.51)	(0.52)	(2.00)	(0.23)	(0.18)	(0.10)	(0.24)	(0.05)	(0.12)	(0.43)
Germany	**-0.80**	**-0.54**	-0.18	0.19	-0.06	0.00	0.02	-0.01	-0.10	**-0.28**
	(0.35)	(0.28)	(0.71)	(0.18)	(0.17)	(0.03)	(0.25)	(0.05)	(0.20)	(0.11)
Greece	-0.69	-0.29	-1.13	0.15	**1.23**	**0.10**	1.05	-0.49	-0.87	1.52
	(0.45)	(0.71)	(1.65)	(0.34)	(0.58)	(0.05)	(0.63)	(0.27)	(1.29)	(1.24)
Ireland	-0.48	**-0.50**	1.33	-0.08	**-0.71**	**-0.13**	**-0.88**	**0.32**	**0.79**	**1.14**
	(0.29)	(0.14)	(1.18)	(0.14)	(0.28)	(0.06)	(0.22)	(0.11)	(0.24)	(0.35)
Italy	**-0.46**	0.05	-0.16	0.13	0.12	-0.00	0.09	-0.00	-0.12	0.32
	(0.18)	(0.21)	(0.48)	(0.15)	(0.11)	(0.03)	(0.13)	(0.04)	(0.15)	(0.19)
Japan	**-0.58**	**-0.79**	**-0.98**	-0.14	-0.05	0.04	0.01	**0.04**	-0.06	0.22
	(0.21)	(0.31)	(0.50)	(0.12)	(0.16)	(0.03)	(0.09)	(0.01)	(0.08)	(0.32)
Netherlands	**-0.75**	-0.43	-1.50	-0.05	0.09	**0.12**	-0.37	0.06	0.30	0.22
	(0.33)	(0.33)	(2.64)	(0.20)	(0.28)	(0.05)	(0.27)	(0.15)	(0.26)	(0.39)
New Zealand	0.02	-0.54	-1.22	-0.12	-0.07	0.02	-0.20	0.07	-0.46	0.24
	(0.29)	(0.45)	(0.78)	(0.22)	(0.20)	(0.03)	(0.19)	(0.07)	(0.33)	(0.18)
Norway	-0.22	0.13	-0.15	-0.06	0.02	-0.07	-0.04	**0.23**	0.12	-0.16
	(0.51)	(0.66)	(0.61)	(0.46)	(0.51)	(0.05)	(0.60)	(0.07)	(0.31)	(0.64)
Portugal	**-1.00**	-0.57	2.91	**0.60**	**0.47**	-0.07	**0.64**	0.21	-0.72	0.16
	(0.20)	(0.32)	(1.64)	(0.24)	(0.20)	(0.05)	(0.19)	(0.13)	(0.37)	(0.41)
Spain	-0.18	-0.06	1.36	-0.01	0.07	-0.09	0.11	0.18	-0.78	-0.28
	(0.55)	(0.59)	(1.58)	(0.31)	(0.38)	(0.05)	(0.42)	(0.12)	(0.32)	(0.57)
Sweden	**-0.84**	**-0.96**	-2.54	-0.53	0.24	0.05	-0.02	0.09	0.00	0.22
	(0.11)	(0.20)	(1.49)	(0.30)	(0.23)	(0.05)	(0.23)	(0.10)	(0.22)	(0.81)
Switzerland	-0.22	-0.09	0.36	**-0.26**	0.02	0.06	**0.21**	-0.04	-0.06	**-0.39**
	(0.50)	(0.16)	(0.76)	(0.13)	(0.14)	(0.03)	(0.11)	(0.05)	(0.12)	(0.09)
UK	**-0.72**	0.03	**-0.79**	**0.37**	**0.18**	-0.04	0.21	0.01	-0.25	**0.34**
	(0.12)	(0.10)	(0.34)	(0.09)	(0.08)	(0.03)	(0.08)	(0.04)	(0.15)	(0.15)
Average	**-0.671**	**-0.401**	-0.335	0.046	0.104	0.001	0.089	0.048	-0.069	0.080
Std error	(.083)	(.067)	(.332)	(.052)	(.081)	(.014)	(.088)	(.036)	(.090)	(.127)

Dependent variable is the private saving rate, PSAV. The regressors are defined at the start of Section 3. The specification of the saving function used in MBS (1995,1998) is not identified for the U.S. Figures in brackets are the standard errors. Statistically significant coefficients are shown in bold.

Table 4 (Continued)

Summary and Diagnostic Statistics

	$\widehat{\sigma}$	$\chi^2_{SC}(1)$	$\chi^2_{FF}(1)$	$\chi^2_N(2)$	$\chi^2_{HE}(1)$	$\overline{R}^2$	LL
Australia	0.573	0.83	0.29	0.70	1.24	0.90	-11.36
Austria	1.210	0.05	2.69	1.56	0.10	0.28	-27.78
Belgium	0.693	18.10	2.84	1.03	0.81	0.69	-15.51
Canada	0.518	0.01	1.27	0.18	0.22	0.76	-9.10
Denmark	1.197	1.63	0.20	1.56	2.32	0.49	-27.55
Finland	1.079	8.32	2.44	1.78	0.38	0.70	-25.27
France	0.689	1.78	12.51	1.80	1.13	0.54	-15.40
Germany	0.817	10.02	0.00	0.76	0.48	0.16	-19.15
Greece	2.439	6.25	0.09	1.05	0.32	0.53	-43.21
Ireland	1.469	3.04	0.59	1.49	0.01	0.77	-32.06
Italy	0.606	2.80	5.09	0.74	2.76	0.72	-12.57
Japan	0.399	0.39	1.59	4.97	0.12	0.77	-3.37
Netherlands	1.052	3.40	1.57	0.20	2.02	0.52	-24.70
New Zealand	1.743	12.38	8.26	0.68	10.45	0.70	-35.82
Norway	1.622	8.47	2.18	0.81	0.53	0.39	-34.23
Portugal	2.042	0.00	1.67	0.80	0.69	0.86	-39.30
Spain	1.319	8.68	5.47	1.20	0.40	0.58	-29.68
Sweden	1.194	6.97	0.76	0.15	1.67	0.68	-27.49
Switzerland	0.535	3.13	3.40	0.70	7.79	0.44	-9.83
UK	0.541	1.63	2.20	1.38	0.50	0.81	-10.07

$\widehat{\sigma}$ is the standard error of the country specific regressions, $\chi^2_{SC}(1)$, $\chi^2_{FF}(1)$, $\chi^2_N(2)$ and $\chi^2_{HE}(1)$ are Chi-squared statistics for tests of residual serial correlation, functional form mis-specification, non-normal errors and heteroskedasticity. The figures in brackets are their degrees of freedom. $\overline{R}^2$ is the adjusted multiple correlation coefficient, and LL is the maximized log-likelihood value of the country-specific regressions.

their magnitude and their statistical significance. Some of the coefficients are statistically significant only in the case of 3 or 4 countries and in general are very poorly estimated.[15] This is true of the coefficients of GI, GR, W, $PCTT$ and $YRUS$. Also the sign of these estimated coefficients vary quite widely across countries. The coefficients of $RINT$ and INF are better estimated, but still differ significantly both in magnitude and in sign across the countries. Only the estimated coefficients of the SUR and $GCUR$ variables are estimated precisely and tend to be similar across countries. The coefficient of SUR is estimated to be negative in 19 out of the 20 countries. The positive estimate (obtained for New Zealand) is very small and not statistically significant. Thirteen of these estimated coefficients are negative and statistically significant. Similarly, 17 out of 20 coefficients estimated for the $GCUR$ variable have a negative sign. None of the three positive coefficients estimated for $GCUR$ are statistically significant, and 7 of the 17 negative coefficients are statistically significant.

[15] In Table 4 the statistically significant estimates (at the 95 per cent level) are shown in bold.

The mean group estimates based on the individual country regressions in table 4 support these general conclusions. Only the MGE of the *SUR* and the *GCUR* variables are statistically significant (see the last two rows of table 4). At -0.671, the MGE of the *SUR* variable is only marginally higher than the corresponding fixed-effects estimate in table 2 that allows for some slope heterogeneity. The MGE of the *GCUR* variable (-0.401) is also similar to the average estimate (-0.450) reported in table 3, computed using the fixed-effects, varying-slope regression of table 2. These results are quite encouraging; but before reaching a conclusion we also need to consider the possible effects of mis-specified dynamics on the estimates.

3.2. Slope heterogeneity in dynamic cross-country savings regressions

The fixed-effects "static" private savings regressions reported in tables 1 and 2 are subject to a substantial degree of residual serial correlation, and as pointed out earlier can lead to inconsistent estimates even under slope homogeneity since the wealth variable, W, is in fact constructed from accumulation of past savings. Presence of residual serial correlation could be due to a host of factors: omitted variables, neglected slope heterogeneity in the case of serially correlated regressors, and of course neglected dynamics. From the diagnostic statistics provided in the second part of table 4 it is clear that even when the slope coefficients are allowed to be estimated freely across countries the residual serial correlation still continues to be a problem, at least in the case of some, if not all the countries.[16] The diagnostic statistics computed for the individual country regressions show statistically significant evidence of residual serial correlation in the case of 8 of the 20 countries: Belgium, Finland, Germany, Greece, New Zealand, Norway, Spain and Sweden.[17] The usual time series technique for dealing with dynamic misspecification is to estimate error correction models based on autoregressive distributed lag (ARDL) models of the type discussed in section 2. ARDL models have the advantage that they are robust to integration and cointegration properties of the regressors, and for sufficiently high lag orders could be immune to the endogeneity problem, at least as far as the long-run properties of the model are concerned.[18] In the present application observations for each individual country are available for too short a period to estimate even a first-order ARDL model including all the 10 regressors for each country separately.[19] Pooling in the form of fixed-effects estimation can compensate for lack of time series observations but as we have shown this can have its own set of problems.

To check the robustness of the "static" fixed-effects estimates presented in table 2 to

[16]The diagnostic statistics are computed using the Lagrange multiplier procedure described, for example, in Pesaran and Pesaran (1997, Section 18.5.2), and are valid irrespective of whether the regressions contain lagged dependent variables, implicitly or explicitly.

[17]Under slope homogeneity restrictions, residual serial correlation is a problem for *all* the countries in the panel.

[18]For a detailed discussion see Pesaran and Shin (1999).

[19]A first-order ARDL model in the private savings rate for each country that contains *all* 10 regressors would involve estimating 22 unknown parameters with only 22 time series observations available per country!

dynamic misspecification we estimated the following first-order dynamic panel data model:

$$y_{it} = \mu_i + \lambda y_{i,t-1} + \boldsymbol{\beta}_0' \mathbf{x}_{it} + \boldsymbol{\beta}_{01}'(\mathbf{x}_{it}\overline{W}_i) + \boldsymbol{\beta}_1' \mathbf{x}_{i,t-1} + u_{it}. \tag{21}$$

The country-specific long-run coefficients are given by

$$\theta_i = (\boldsymbol{\beta}_0 + \boldsymbol{\beta}_1 + \boldsymbol{\beta}_{01}\overline{W}_i)/(1-\lambda). \tag{22}$$

We also considered the inclusion of the weighted lagged variables $\overline{W}_i \mathbf{x}_{i,t-1}$ and $\overline{W}_i y_{i,t-1}$ to the model but did not find them to be statistically significant. The fixed-effects estimates computed using all the 21 countries over the period 1972-1993 are given in table 5.[20] Clearly, there are significant dynamics, particularly in the relationship between changes in the government surplus and expenditure variables (SUR, $GCUR$, and GI) and the private savings rate. There is also important evidence of cross-sectional variations in the coefficients of the wealth, income and demographic variables (W, $YRUS$ and DEP). However, unlike the static estimates in table 2, the coefficients of GDP growth and the real interest rate are no longer statistically significant. Overall, this equation presents a substantial improvement over the static fixed-effects estimates. In fact the estimated standard error of this dynamic regression is 62 percent lower than the standard error of the fixed-effects estimates favoured by MBS (1998), and reproduced in the first column of table 1.

Using the formula (22) the following estimates of the long-run coefficients were obtained:

SUR	-0.432	W	0.224	$-0.00057\ \overline{W}_i$
	(-3.11)		(4.58)	(-3.77)
$GCUR$	-0.398	INF	0.248	
	(-4.65)		(3.10)	
GI	-0.202	$PCTT$	0.136	
	(-0.91)		(4.11)	
GR	-0.004	$YRUS$	1.384	$-0.0047\ \overline{W}_i$
	(-0.03)		(2.58)	(-2.92)
$RINT$	0.154	DEP	0.708	$-0.0027\ \overline{W}_i$
	(1.64)		(2.19)	(-2.64)

According to these estimates the long-run coefficients of the SUR and $GCUR$ variables are still statistically significant, although the coefficient of the SUR variable is now estimated to be much lower than the estimate based on the static regressions. The long-run

[20]For relatively simple dynamic models where T (= 22) is reasonably large and of the same order of magnitude as N (= 21), the application of the IV type estimators to a first differenced version of (21) does not seem necessary, and can lead to considerable loss of efficiency. The estimation of fixed-effects dynamic panel data models when the time dimension is short, say in the range of 3-10, and the cross-sectional dimension is relatively large, say 50 or more, is discussed in Anderson and Hsiao (1981,1982), Arellano and Bond (1991), and more recently in Hsiao, Pesaran, and Tahmiscioglu (1998).

Table 5

Fixed-Effects Estimates of Dynamic Private Savings Equations
with Cross-Sectionally Varying Slopes
(21 OECD Countries, 1972-1993)

Regressors	Coefficients	Regressors	Coefficients
$PSAV_{-1}$	0.670	W	0.074
	(20.80)		(4.41)
SUR	-0.771	$W \times \overline{W}_i$	-0.00019
	(-16.28)		(-3.62)
SUR_{-1}	0.628	INF	0.082
	(11.54)		(3.11)
GCUR	-0.544	PCTT	0.045
	(7.78)		(4.54)
$GCUR_{-1}$	0.412	YRUS	0.456
	(6.16)		(2.49)
GI	-0.666	$YRUS \times \overline{W}_i$	-0.00157
	(-5.54)		(-2.81)
GI_{-1}	0.600	DEP	0.233
	(4.80)		(2.12)
GR	-0.0014	$DEP \times \overline{W}_i$	-0.00089
	(-0.03)		(-2.52)
RINT	0.051		
	(1.60)		
$\overline{R}^2$	0.908		
$\widehat{\sigma}$	1.451		
LL	-807.61		
AIC	-845.61		
SBC	924.18		

See equation (21) in the text. The figures in brackets are t-ratios. For definitions of the variables see the notes to Tables 1 and 2.

coefficients of the GI, GR and $RINT$ variables are no longer statistically significant. It appears that in contrast to government consumption expenditures, the effect of changes in government investment expenditures on private savings is temporary and tends to be zero in the long-run. The inflation and the terms of trade variables (INF and $PCTT$) have the expected signs and are also statistically significant. The long-run coefficients of the remaining variables vary with country-specific average wealth-GDP ratio and when averaged across countries yield the values of 0.043 [0.026], -0.118 [0.219] and -0.148 [0.125] for W, $YRUS$, and DEP variables respectively. The cross-sectional standard errors of these estimates are given in square brackets. The average estimate of the coefficient of the relative income variable has the wrong sign, but it is not statistically significant. The average estimates of the other two coefficients have the expected signs, but are not statistically significant either. It is clear that the effects of many of the regressors considered in the MBS study are not robust to dynamic misspecifications.

But before reaching a final conclusion we also need to examine the consequences of *jointly* allowing for unrestricted short-run slope heterogeneity and dynamics.[21] To this end we estimated individual country regressions containing first-order lagged values of the savings rates, $PSAV_{i,t-1}$. The MG estimates of the long-run coefficients based on these dynamic individual country regressions are given in table 6.[22] For ease of comparison we have also included MGE based on a static version of these regressions, as well as the corresponding fixed-effects estimates. Unlike the fixed-effects estimates the consequences of allowing for dynamics on the MG estimates are rather limited. Once again only the coefficients of the SUR and the $GCUR$ variables are statistically significant; although the dynamic MG estimates suggest the coefficient of the $PCTT$ variable also to be marginally significant.

Finally, in the last column of table 6 we give the pooled mean group estimates of the long-run coefficients recently proposed by Pesaran, Shin and Smith (1999), where the short-run dynamics are allowed to differ freely across countries but equality restrictions are imposed on one or more of the long-run coefficients. The rationale being that due to differences in factors such as adjustment costs or the institutional set-up across countries slope homogeneity is more likely to be valid in the long-run. The pooled mean group estimates (PMGE) in table 6 impose the slope homogeneity restrictions only on the long-run coefficients of the SUR variable. We did try similar restrictions on the other long-run coefficients, but they were rejected using a Hausman-type test that compares the MG and the PMG estimates.[23] Only the homogeneity restrictions on the long-run coefficients of the SUR variable could not be rejected. As expected, the PMGE are generally more precisely estimated and confirm that amongst the various determinants of private savings considered by MBS only the effects of the SUR and the $GCUR$ variables seem to be reasonably robust to the presence of slope heterogeneity and yield plausible estimates for the off-setting effects of government budget surpluses and government consumption expenditures on private savings across OECD countries.

4. CONCLUDING REMARKS

Given the paucity of long time series on individual countries, examination of many macroeconomic hypotheses in the literature relies on cross-country panel data. Much of this literature is based on simple fixed-effects estimators and does not adequately address the possibility that there may be considerable heterogeneity in short-run and long-run parameters across countries. This paper has shown that neglecting heterogeneity and dynamics in cross-country savings regressions can lead to misleading inferences about the key determinants of savings behavior. If differences across countries are ignored, one can

[21] The estimates in Table 5 only allow for a limited degree of slope heterogeneity.

[22] Individual country regressions that underlie the estimation of the MGE are available from the authors on request.

[23] For details of the Hausman test applied to MG and PMG estimates see Pesaran, Shin and Smith (1999).

Table 6

Private Saving Equations: Fixed-Effects, Mean Group and Pooled MG Estimates (20 OECD countries, 1972-1993)

	FE Estimates		Mean Group Estimates		Pooled MGE
Regressors	Static	Dynamic	Static	Dynamic	Dynamic
SUR	-0.518	-0.968	-0.671	-0.911	-0.870
	(-8.50)	(-7.76)	(-8.07)	(-5.48)	(-19.81)
GCUR	-0.461	-0.665	-0.401	-0.394	-0.474
	(-10.76)	(-8.17)	(-5.95)	(-4.38)	(-6.88)
GI	-0.555	-0.789	-0.335	-0.109	-0.401
	(-5.28)	(-4.14)	(-1.01)	(-0.22)	(-1.14)
GR	-0.059	0.091	0.046	0.057	0.029
	(-1.09)	(-0.93)	(0.88)	(0.92)	(0.48)
RINT	0.205	0.127	0.104	0.183	0.139
	(4.11)	(1.41)	(1.28)	(1.61)	(1.66)
W	0.020	0.028	0.001	0.002	-0.004
	(4.51)	(3.49)	(0.061)	(0.115)	(-0.21)
INF	0.161	0.069	0.089	0.137	0.103
	(3.91)	(0.93)	(1.02)	(1.18)	(1.11)
PCTT	0.044	0.094	0.048	0.103	0.077
	(2.83)	(3.31)	(1.34)	(2.21)	(2.37)
YP	-0.087	-0.076	-0.069	-0.056	-0.031
	(-2.54)	(-1.23)	(-0.77)	(-0.60)	(-0.35)
DEP	-0.161	-0.241	0.080	0.058	0.050
	(-5.13)	(-4.22)	(0.63)	(0.45)	(0.39)

The dependent variable is $PSAV_{it}$. The estimates refer to the long-run coefficients. Dynamic fixed effects (FE) estimates are based on a first-order autoregressive panel data model containing the lagged dependent variables, $PSAV_{i,t-1}$. The dynamic Mean Group (MG) estimates are based on country-specific regressions also containing, $PSAV_{i,t-1}$. The Pooled MG estimates impose the restrictions that the long-run coefficients of the SUR variable is the same across countries, but are otherwise comparable to the dynamic MG estimates. Due to the presence of YRUS variable in the model, country-specific parameters for the U.S. are not identified, and the U.S. is dropped from the panel. See the notes to Table 1 for the definition of the variables.

overestimate the influence of certain factors on the private savings rates and at the same time obtain highly significant, but spurious, nonlinear effects for some of the potential determinants.

Our results indicate that fiscal variables – the general government surplus as a proportion of GDP and the ratio of government consumption to GDP– are the key determinants of private savings rates in the industrial countries in the post World War II period. Keeping government consumption constant, the estimated parameters imply that the Ricardian offset in private savings of a decrease in the government surplus is quite large (about 0.9 in table 6). The estimated parameters also imply that changes in government consumption have a different impact on the private savings rate than changes in government investment. In fact, once slope heterogeneity is adequately taken into account the impact of government investment expenditures on private saving is not statistically significant. The results in the paper also provide some support for the Harberger-Laursen-Metzler effect with improving terms of trade having a small positive effect on the private savings rate. For the OECD economies over the period under consideration, we do not find any evidence that the rate of output growth, the inflation rate, the real interest rate, the ratio of wealth to GDP, or the dependency ratio have had a statistically significant (long-term) effect on the private savings rate.

Appendix

Suppose the dependent variables y_{it}, $i = 1, 2, ..., N$, are generated according to the following simple, static panel data model:

$$y_{it} = \mu_i + \beta_i x_{it} + u_{it}, \; i = 1, 2, ..., N; \; t = 1, 2, ..., T. \tag{23}$$

The intercepts, μ_i, as well as the slopes, β_i, are allowed to vary across groups. Intercepts will be treated as fixed-effects. For the slopes we use the random-coefficients model

$$\beta_i = \beta + \eta_i, \; i = 1, 2, ..., N, \tag{24}$$

but allow for the possibility of systematic dependence between η_i and the regressors x_{it} and z_{it}. In this appendix we derive the inconsistency of the fixed-effects estimators of the slope coefficients δ_x and δ_z in the more general panel data model

$$y_{it} = \alpha_i + \delta_x x_{it} + \delta_z z_{it} + v_{it} = \alpha_i + \boldsymbol{\delta}' \mathbf{w}_{it} + v_{it}, \; i = 1, 2, ..., N; \; t = 1, 2, ..., T, \tag{25}$$

when in fact the y_{it}'s are generated according to (23). To simplify the derivations we make the following assumptions:

Assumption A.1: u_{it} is serially uncorrelated and distributed independently of u_{jt} for all $i \neq j$.

Assumption A.2: $\mathbf{w}_{it} = (x_{it}, z_{it})'$ is distributed independently of $u_{it'}$, for all i, t and t'.[24]

Assumption A.3: $\mathbf{w}_{it}$ follows a covariance stationary process with the variance-covariance matrix, $\boldsymbol{\Omega}_i$, defined by (9), such that

$$E(\boldsymbol{\Omega}_i) = \lim_{N \to \infty} \left(\frac{1}{N} \sum_{i=1}^{N} \boldsymbol{\Omega}_i \right), \tag{26}$$

is a positive definite matrix.

Assumption A.4: For each t, $\mathbf{w}_{it}$ is distributed independently across i.

Although, not all the above assumptions are necessary when both N and T are sufficiently large. For example, assumption A.4 is not needed when T is sufficiently large.

[24]These assumptions require $\mathbf{w}_{it}$ to be strictly exogenous, and therefore rule out the case where the model contains lagged dependent variables. The problem of inconsistency of fixed- or random-effects estimators of dynamic panel data models under slope heterogeneity is addressed in Pesaran and Smith (1995).

Assumption A.3 can be relaxed when T is small. It is also worth noting that assumption A.3 does not require the correlation matrix of the regressors for all i to be non-singular, only that the "pooled" covariance matrix, $E(\mathbf{\Omega}_i)$, defined by (26), should be non-singular.

In matrix notations (23) and (25) can be written as:

$$\mathbf{y}_i = \mu_i \boldsymbol{\iota} + \beta_i \mathbf{x}_i + \mathbf{u}_i, \tag{27}$$

and

$$\mathbf{y}_i = \alpha_i \boldsymbol{\iota} + \mathbf{w}_i \boldsymbol{\delta} + \mathbf{v}_i, \tag{28}$$

respectively, where

$$\mathbf{y}_i = (y_{i1}, y_{i2}, ..., y_{iT})', \boldsymbol{\iota} = (1, 1, ..., 1)', \mathbf{x}_i = (x_{i1}, x_{i2}, ..., x_{iT})',$$

$$\mathbf{u}_i = (u_{i1}, u_{i2}, ..., u_{iT})', \boldsymbol{\delta} = (\delta_x, \delta_z)',$$

and

$$\mathbf{w}_i = \begin{bmatrix} x_{i1} & z_{i1} \\ x_{i2} & z_{i2} \\ \vdots & \vdots \\ x_{iT} & z_{iT} \end{bmatrix}, \quad \mathbf{v}_i = \begin{bmatrix} v_{i1} \\ v_{i2} \\ \vdots \\ v_{iT} \end{bmatrix}.$$

The fixed-effects estimators of the slope coefficients in (28) can be written as:

$$\hat{\boldsymbol{\delta}}_{FE} = \begin{pmatrix} \hat{\boldsymbol{\delta}}_{x,FE} \\ \hat{\boldsymbol{\delta}}_{z,FE} \end{pmatrix} = \left(\sum_{i=1}^{N} \mathbf{w}_i' \mathbf{H} \mathbf{W}_i \right)^{-1} \left(\sum_{i=1}^{N} \mathbf{w}_i' \mathbf{H} \mathbf{y}_i \right), \tag{29}$$

where $\mathbf{H} = \mathbf{I}_T - \boldsymbol{\iota}(\boldsymbol{\iota}'\boldsymbol{\iota})^{-1}\boldsymbol{\iota}'$.[25] Under (27) we have

$$\hat{\boldsymbol{\delta}}_{FE} = \left(\frac{1}{NT} \sum_{i=1}^{N} \mathbf{w}_i' \mathbf{H} \mathbf{W}_i \right)^{-1} \left\{ \frac{1}{NT} \sum_{i=1}^{N} (\mathbf{w}_i' \mathbf{H} \mathbf{x}_i) \beta_i + \frac{1}{NT} \sum_{i=1}^{N} \mathbf{w}_i' \mathbf{H} \mathbf{u}_i \right\}. \tag{30}$$

It is now easily seen that under assumptions A.1-A.4 and for N and/or T sufficiently large

$$\frac{1}{NT} \sum_{i=1}^{N} \mathbf{w}_i' \mathbf{H} \mathbf{u}_i \xrightarrow{p} 0, \tag{31}$$

where $\xrightarrow{p}$ denotes convergence in probability. Therefore

$$\text{plim}(\hat{\boldsymbol{\delta}}_{FE}) = \left\{ \text{plim} \left(\sum_{i=1}^{N} \frac{\mathbf{w}_i' \mathbf{H} \mathbf{W}_i}{NT} \right) \right\}^{-1} \text{plim} \left(\sum_{i=1}^{N} \left(\frac{\mathbf{w}_i' \mathbf{H} \mathbf{x}_i}{NT} \right) \beta_i \right). \tag{32}$$

[25]The fixed effects estimator in (29) assumes a balanced panel. But the results readily extend to unbalanced panels

In the case where the slopes are homogenous, namely $\beta_i = \beta$, we have

$$\text{plim}(\hat{\boldsymbol{\delta}}_{FE}) = \begin{pmatrix} \beta \\ 0 \end{pmatrix}. \tag{33}$$

Consider now the case where the slopes are heterogenous. Using (24) in (32), it is easily seen that the consistency result in (33) will follow if and only if

$$\sum_{i=1}^{N} \left(\frac{\mathbf{w}_i'\mathbf{H}\mathbf{x}_i}{NT} \right) \eta_i = \begin{pmatrix} \frac{1}{NT}\sum_{i=1}^{N} \mathbf{x}_i'\mathbf{H}\mathbf{x}_i\eta_i \\ \frac{1}{NT}\sum_{i=1}^{N} \mathbf{z}_i'\mathbf{H}\mathbf{x}_i\eta_i \end{pmatrix} \xrightarrow{p} 0. \tag{34}$$

This condition holds under the random coefficient specification where it is assumed that η_i's are distributed independently of $\mathbf{w}_{it}$ for all i and t. (See also Swamy (1970)). Under assumption A.3 and as $T \to \infty$ we have

$$\frac{1}{NT}\sum_{i=1}^{N} \mathbf{x}_i'\mathbf{H}\mathbf{x}_i\eta_i - \frac{1}{N}\sum_{i=1}^{N} \omega_{ixx}\eta_i \xrightarrow{p} 0,$$

and

$$\frac{1}{NT}\sum_{i=1}^{N} \mathbf{z}_i'\mathbf{H}\mathbf{x}_i\eta_i - \frac{1}{N}\sum_{i=1}^{N} \omega_{izx}\eta_i \xrightarrow{p} 0.$$

Therefore, for the fixed-effects estimators, (29), to be consistent we must have

$$\frac{1}{N}\sum_{i=1}^{N} \omega_{ixx}\eta_i \xrightarrow{p} 0, \quad \text{and} \quad \frac{1}{N}\sum_{i=1}^{N} \omega_{izx}\eta_i \xrightarrow{p} 0, \tag{35}$$

as $N \to \infty$. Namely, any systematic dependence between β_i and the second order moments of the steady state distribution of the regressors $\mathbf{w}_{it}$ must also be ruled out. When the conditions in (35) are not satisfied the inconsistencies of the fixed-effects estimators (for T and N sufficiently large) are given by[26]

$$\text{plim}(\hat{\boldsymbol{\delta}}_{x,FE} - \beta) = \frac{Cov(\omega_{ixx}, \eta_i)E(\omega_{izz}) - E(\omega_{ixz})Cov(\omega_{ixz}, \eta_i)}{E(\omega_{ixx})E(\omega_{izz}) - (E(\omega_{ixz}))^2} \tag{36}$$

$$\text{plim}(\hat{\boldsymbol{\delta}}_{z,FE}) = \frac{Cov(\omega_{ixz}, \eta_i)E(\omega_{ixx}) - E(\omega_{ixz})Cov(\omega_{ixx}, \eta_i)}{E(\omega_{ixx})E(\omega_{izz}) - (E(\omega_{ixz}))^2} \tag{37}$$

where

$$Cov(\omega_{ixx}, \eta_i) = \underset{N\to\infty}{\text{plim}} \left(\frac{1}{N}\sum_{i=1}^{N} \omega_{ixx}\eta_i \right), \quad Cov(\omega_{ixz}, \eta_i) = \underset{N\to\infty}{\text{plim}} \left(\frac{1}{N}\sum_{i=1}^{N} \omega_{ixz}\eta_i \right),$$

$$E(\omega_{ixx}) = \lim_{N\to\infty} \left(\frac{1}{N}\sum_{i=1}^{N} \omega_{ixx} \right), E(\omega_{izz}) = \lim_{N\to\infty} \left(\frac{1}{N}\sum_{i=1}^{N} \omega_{izz} \right), \tag{38}$$

$$E(\omega_{ixz}) = \lim_{N\to\infty} \left(\frac{1}{N}\sum_{i=1}^{N} \omega_{ixz} \right).$$

[26]Notice that under slope heterogeneity the fixed effects estimators are inconsistent when N is finite and only $T \to \infty$.

REFERENCES

1. Anderson, T.W. and C. Hsiao (1981), "Estimation of Dynamic Models with Error Components", *Journal of the American Statistical Association*, 76, 598-606.
2. Anderson, T.W. and C. Hsiao (1982), "Formulation and Estimation of Dynamic Models Using Panel Data", *Journal of Econometrics*, 18, 47-82.
3. Arellano, M. and S. Bond (1991), "Some Tests of Specification for Panel Data: Monte Carlo Evidence and an Application to Employment Equations", *Review of Economic Studies*, 58, 277-297.
4. Attanasio, O.P., L. Picci and A. Scorcu (1998), "Saving, Growth and Investment: A Macroeconomic Analysis Using a Panel of Countries", Unpublished Manuscript, University College London and University of Bologna.
5. Callen, T. and C. Thimann (1997), "Empirical Determinants of Household Saving: Evidence from OECD Countries", *IMF Working Paper*, WP/97/181, (Washington: International Monetary Fund).
6. Carroll, C.D. and D.N. Weil (1994), "Saving and Growth: A Reinterpretation", *Carnegie-Rochester Conference Series on Public Policy*, 40, 133-192.
7. Dayal-Gulati, A. and C. Thimann (1997), "Saving in South East Asia and Latin America Compared: Searching for Policy Lessons", *IMF Working Paper*, WP/97/110, (Washington: International Monetary Fund).
8. Edwards, S. (1996), "Why Are Latin America's Savings Rates so Low? An International Comparative Analysis", *Journal of Development Economics*, 51, 5-44.
9. Gilbert, C.L. (1986), "Professor Hendry's Econometric Methodology", *Oxford Bulletin of Economics and Statistics*, 48, 283-307.
10. Hendry, D.F. (1993), *Econometrics: Alchemy or Science?*, Blackwell, Oxford.
11. Hsiao, C. (1986), *Analysis of Panel Data*, Cambridge University Press, Cambridge.
12. Hsiao, C., M.H. Pesaran and A.K. Tahmiscioglu (1998), "Maximum Likelihood Estimation of Fixed-Effects Dynamic Panel Data Models Covering Short Time Periods", Unpublished Manuscript, University of Southern California and Cambridge University. Available via the Internet: `http://www.econ.cam.ac.uk/faculty/pesaran/`.
13. Hsiao, C., M.H. Pesaran and A.K. Tahmiscioglu (1999), "Bayes Estimation of Short-Run Coefficients in Dynamic Panel Data Models", in C. Hsiao, K. Lahiri, L.-F. Lee and M.H. Pesaran (eds.), *Analysis of Panels and Limited Dependent Variables: A Volume in Honour of G. S. Maddala*, Cambridge University Press, Cambridge.
14. Keane, M.P. and D.E. Runkle (1992), "On the Estimation of Panel Data Models with Serial Correlation when Instruments are not Strictly Exogenous", *Journal of Business and Economic Statistics*, 10, 1-29.
15. Masson, P.R., T. Bayoumi and H. Samiei (1995), "International Evidence on the Determinants of Private Saving", *IMF Working Paper*, WP/95/51, (Washington: International Monetary Fund).
16. Masson, P.R., T. Bayoumi and H. Samiei (1998), "International Evidence on the Determinants of Private Saving", *World Bank Economic Review*, 12, 483-502.
17. Ogaki, M., J. Ostry and C. Reinhart (1996), "Saving Behavior in Low- and Middle-Income Developing Countries", *IMF Staff Papers*, 43, 38-97.
18. Pesaran, M.H. and B. Pesaran (1997), "Working with Microfit 4.0: Interactive Econo-

metric Analysis", Oxford University Press, Oxford.

19. Pesaran, M.H. and R. Smith (1995), "Estimating Long-Run Relationships from Dynamic Heterogeneous Panels", *Journal of Econometrics*, 68, 79-113.
20. Pesaran, M.H. and Y. Shin (1999), "An Autoregressive Distributed Lag Modelling Approach to Cointegration Analysis", in S. Strom, A. Holly, and P. Diamond (eds.), *Econometrics and Economic Theory in the 20th Century: The Ragnar Frisch Centennial Symposium*, Cambridge University Press, Cambridge.
21. Pesaran, M.H., Yongcheol Shin and R. Smith (1999), "Pooled Mean Group Estimation of Dynamic Heterogeneous Panels", *Journal of the American Statistical Association*, 94, 621-634.
22. Pesaran, M.H., R. Smith and K.-S. Im (1996), "Dynamic Linear Models for Heterogeneous Panels", in L. Mátyás and P. Sevestre (eds.), *The Econometrics of Panel Data*, Kluwer.
23. Schmidt-Hebbel, K., S.B. Webb and G. Corsetti (1992), "Household Saving in Developing Countries: First Cross-Country Evidence", *World Bank Economic Review*, 6, 529-547.
24. Sims, C.A. (1980), "Macroeconomics and Reality", *Econometrica*, 48, 1-48.
25. Swamy, P.A.V.B. (1970), "Efficient Inference in a Random Coefficient Regression Model", *Econometrica*, 38, 311-323.
26. Zellner, A. (1962), "An Efficient Method of Estimating Seemingly Unrelated Regressions and Tests of Aggregation Bias", *Journal of the American Statistical Association*, 57, 348-368.

PART I

(contd.)

B. Social Economics

Panel Data Econometrics: Future Directions
J. Krishnakumar and E. Ronchetti (Editors)

CHAPTER 4

PANEL DATA ESTIMATION OF THE INTERGENERATIONAL CORRELATION OF INCOMES*

Ramses ABUL NAGA and Jaya KRISHNAKUMAR

Abstract

We consider the problem of estimating the intergenerational correlation of incomes in the context of a panel data framework with measurement errors. We present single equation estimation methods as well as system methods under various assumptions regarding the serial correlation of the error term and taking into account possible correlations among children of the same family. Application to a sample of US parents and children leads to estimates of the order of 0.42 to 0.60 for the coefficient of income transmission.

1. INTRODUCTION

Ever since President Johnson's declaration of the "War on Poverty" in the United States in the year 1964, economists have increasingly turned their attention and effort to understanding the mechanisms of income transmission. There are several important equity issues underlying the general question of the intensity of intergenerational inheritance of income status.

Equity concerns can be formulated along several lines. One question that often arises concerns the extent to which children raised in poor families are themselves likely to end up in the lower end of the distribution of income during their adult lives (Atkinson *et al.* (1983), ch.1). The continuity problem in low incomes is often also formulated by contrasting the likelihoods that children raised in different social environments face, of

*We would like to thank Pietro Balestra, Christian Schluter and Dirk Van de gaer for their careful reading and valuable comments on an earlier version of the paper. Suggestions from the participants of the Economics Seminar at the University of St.Gallen are also acknowledged.

ending up in poverty. Economists and social scientists also seek to assess the separate contributions of environment-related factors and genetically transmitted traits in the overall transmission of income status (the famous 'nature versus nurture' debate).

In immigration countries such as the United States, another question arises about the rate at which newcomers to the host country are likely to be assimilated in terms of economic and educational attainment (Stokey (1996)). To answer such questions, one needs to make progress both at the theory level, i.e. in the formulation of models of income transmission and the dynamics of wealth distribution (e.g. Galor and Zeira (1993)), as well as in the direction of the empirical analysis of longitudinal income data.

The estimation of the intergenerational correlation of incomes is a particularly complex task, since the variables of interests, namely the permanent incomes of parents and children, are typically unobservable quantities. Instead, the researcher usually possesses a short time-series (in the order of 3 or 4 observations) on some indicator of economic attainment such as hourly earnings, or a family income measure. The resulting measurement error problem has been shown by previous researchers in the area to render the OLS estimator biased towards zero (see e.g. Bowles (1972), Atkinson *et al.* (1983), Behrman and Taubman (1990)).

Of the various approaches proposed in order to deal with this measurement error problem, two methods have received considerable attention. These include (i) averaging the income of parents (i.e. the error-ridden explanatory variable) over the several years of available data in order to reduce the ratio of transitory to total income variance, and (ii) the use of out of equation instruments (typically the father's education) for the income pertaining to the parents' generation (cf. for instance Solon (1992)).

The purpose of the present study is to estimate the intergenerational correlation of incomes within a panel data framework. It is rather surprising that no explicit treatment of this problem has been considered in the panel data perspective[1], since most recent studies (at least the US ones) have been based on samples extracted from longitudinal earnings surveys[2].

There are indeed several good reasons for considering this estimation problem within a panel data framework. Firstly, as shown by Griliches and Hausman (1986), Hsiao and Taylor (1991) and others, a wide range of errors in variables models may be identified without having to appeal to out of equation instruments. Secondly, by controlling for unobserved population heterogeneity, panel data estimators will usually have more explanatory power than their cross-section counterparts. Finally, because we have repeated measurements on the incomes of parents and children, we are able to estimate our various models under alternative scenarios regarding the serial correlation in the transitory components of income and test these scenarios. This latter point extends beyond efficiency considerations, since the choice of instruments itself is dictated by the assumptions regarding the serial correlation in errors of measurements.

[1]Though some insights into this problem are provided in Zimmerman (1992).
[2]See for instance Behrman and Taubman (1990), Altonji and Dunn (1991), Solon (1992), Zimmerman (1992) and Björklund and Jantti (1997)

Our study provides a discussion of two further issues: the pooling of instrumental variable regressions from the various cross-sections into a system (of equations) estimator, and the consequences of allowing for multiple children from the same parent family (entailing cross-sectional correlations across observations) for efficient estimation. When applied to a US sample of parents and children, the various models and estimators considered here provide estimates in the range of 0.42 to 0.60 for the coefficient of income transmission.

The structure of the paper is the following: section 2 discusses the data, section 3 deals with inference issues, section 4 contains the empirical applications, and section 5 concludes with a summary and directions for further research.

2. DATA

The empirical applications contained in this study draw evidence from the panel study of income dynamics (PSID). The PSID is a US longitudinal survey of 5000 families which has been running annually since 1968. A detailed description of the history of the panel, and its main features, can be found in Hill (1993). Our sample was extracted from the merged family-individual tape of wave XXI (1968-1988) of the PSID. A summary of the characteristics of our sample can be found in Abul Naga (1998). Here we discuss three sampling aspects of our data which entail direct consequences for the estimation strategies to be pursued in section 3 below. These are (i) the extent to which our data meet the standard definition of a panel, (ii) the problem of measuring long-run economic status, or permanent income, and (iii) the presence of multiple children from the same parent family. We take up each of these points in turn.

We have a sample of 1426 parent-child pairs. Incomes of parents and children are observed respectively over the five year intervals 1967-71 and 1983-87. On the one hand data on dependent and explanatory variables are not contemporaneously observed, a feature which is not typical of the standard framework adopted in panel data analysis (for instance Hsiao (1986), Chap.3). On the other hand, the income data have a natural time ordering, which is essential for modelling and testing for serial correlation in the disturbances, and also for selecting valid instruments for explanatory variables (see below). As will become apparent in the next section, the estimators we adopt do not require incomes of parents and children to be contemporaneously observed. The estimators will be shown to have obvious panel data interpretations, but more generally, they may also be considered within the framework of multiple (simultaneous) equations systems.

Our main income concept is the total annual family income normalized by the family's needs, and deflated to 1967 dollars (the first year of the panel). The needs standard is the official Orshansky scale which is used in the US in order to quantify the extent of poverty. The price deflator used is the consumer price index. Such income measures may be treated as proxies for a household's long-run economic status, or following Griliches (1986), as random draws from a variable with a population mean equal to the household's permanent income. Thus, in section 3, we propose several instrumental variables procedures in order to deal with the measurement error problem inherent in our data.

Table 1
Summary Statistics

year	Parents		Children	
	mean	coef. variation	mean	coef. variation
1	1.73	0.80	2.86	0.70
2	1.88	0.85	3.00	0.71
3	2.00	0.84	3.05	0.76
4	2.15	0.83	3.15	0.77
5	2.31	0.83	3.25	0.83

1. The resource concept is the family income normalized by the Orshansky needs standard.
2. The first observation year (t=1) pertains to 1967 for parents, and to 1983 for children.

As the income concept we have chosen to use is based on the total family income, we did not find it necessary to restrict our sample to father and son pairs. Thus, for a daughter from an initial sample family, the income of her household is matched to that of the parents whether or not she happens to be the main income earner. We have also allowed for multiple children from the same parent family. We note that because of unobserved family background components, observations on siblings are expected to be correlated. Under such circumstances, efficient estimation will require the adoption of generalized least squares methods, which are also discussed in some length in the following section.

Table 1 provides some summary statistics for the incomes of parents and children. Parents appear to be on the whole poorer than the US population in the late 1960s. This may be explained by noting that approximately a half of the parents originate from the SEO file (a sample of families whose incomes fell short of twice their needs) of the PSID. Bicketti *et al.* (1988) have found that disadvantaged groups were more likely to exit the panel and that on the whole, the PSID has evolved towards a sample of middle class families. This finding may help in accounting for the seemingly lower level of income dispersion experienced by the sample of children, as well as the growth in their average income.

3. THE MODEL AND THE ESTIMATION METHODS

We are interested in estimating a relationship of the form

$$\eta_{c,i} = \beta\eta_{p,i} + \alpha_i \tag{1}$$

where $\eta_{c,i}$ represents the logarithm of the permanent income of the child, $\eta_{p,i}$ the logarithm of the permanent income of the parents and α_i a random disturbance term specific to the individual. If correct measurements of both the variables are available, then a consistent estimation of β would be given by OLS. However the variables in question are not directly observable and the only information one generally has are the actual incomes of the parent and the child at different points in time. Obviously these snapshots do contain a component equal to the permanent income but also include other transitory components. Hence these observations can be thought of as measurements of the permanent income subject to error. Denoting the observed incomes as y_{it} and x_{it}, we can write:

$$y_{it} = \eta_{c,i} + u_{it} \tag{2}$$

$$x_{it} = \eta_{p,i} + v_{it} \tag{3}$$

where u_{it} and v_{it} are uncorrelated random error terms with zero means. Thus the relationship between the observables is

$$y_{it} = \beta x_{it} + \alpha_i + (u_{it} - \beta v_{it}) \tag{4}$$

or

$$y_{it} = \beta x_{it} + \alpha_i + \varepsilon_{it} \tag{5}$$

with

$$\varepsilon_{it} = u_{it} - \beta v_{it} \tag{6}$$

and

$$E(x_{it}\alpha_i) = E(\eta_{c,i}u_{it}) = E(\eta_{p,i}v_{it}) = E(u_{it}v_{it}) = 0 \tag{7}$$

Let us note that if only the dependent variable is measured with error ($\eta_{c,i}$ in our case), OLS would still consistently estimate β, whereas if the *explanatory* variable has a measurement error then OLS produces inconsistent estimates (cf. Greene (1993) e.g.). Though a remedy to this problem is given by the instrumental variable (IV) technique, in the case of pure cross section data, one needs to resort to extraneous instruments and this may pose a real practical difficulty. However there is an easier way out in the case of panel data and Griliches and Hausman (1986) were amongst the first ones to point out that the model can be identified without the use of external information. See also Hsiao and Taylor (1991), Wansbeek and Koning (1991), Biorn (1998) in this regard. Indeed, the observations on the explanatory variable relating to different time periods provide appropriate instruments for the current period, the gap to be chosen depending on the nature of serial correlation assumed for the errors.

In general, two approaches have been proposed in the literature for panel data models with measurement errors. Either the equation can be first differenced (to eliminate the specific effect α_i) and the instruments used in levels, or the equation is kept in levels and the instruments differenced (see Biorn (1998)).

For our model, special care needs to be taken while choosing the instruments as the true unobserved variable is time invariant and hence any differencing operation over time will leave us with only the difference of the corresponding v_{it}'s and any "instrument" correlated with this difference will necessarily be correlated with the same difference appearing in the error term. For instance, upon first differencing we get

$$y_{it} - y_{i,t-1} = \beta(x_{it} - x_{i,t-1}) + \varepsilon_{it} - \varepsilon_{i,t-1} \tag{8}$$

But from (3) we have

$$x_{it} - x_{i,t-1} = v_{it} - v_{i,t-1} \tag{9}$$

which also appears in $\varepsilon_{it} - \varepsilon_{i,t-1}$. Thus any variable correlated with $(x_{it} - x_{i,t-1})$ (condition to be satisfied by a valid instrument) will always be correlated with $(\varepsilon_{it} - \varepsilon_{i,t-1})$.

The above argument thus excludes the possibility of differencing in our case and we will therefore only consider estimating the equation in levels. For the same reasons, differencing of instruments is also inappropriate.

The set of valid instruments varies according to the type of serial correlation assumed for ε_{it}. Let us distinguish two cases, both assuming stationarity: (i) iid errors and (ii) MA(1) errors. More general MA processes will also be considered in the application section. The case of AR(1) errors offers no immediate solution and hence will not be pursued here.

Case 1: iid ε_{it}'s

Assumption A1:

$$\varepsilon_{it} \sim iid(0, \sigma_\varepsilon^2); \quad \alpha_i \sim iid(0, \sigma_\alpha^2); \quad E(\alpha_j \varepsilon_{it}) = 0 \quad \forall i, j, t$$

In terms of the individual components the assumptions would be

$$E(u_{it}u_{js}) = \delta_{ij}\delta_{st}\sigma_u^2 \quad \forall i, j, s, t; \quad E(v_{it}v_{js}) = \delta_{ij}\delta_{st}\sigma_v^2 \quad \forall i, j, s, t$$

$$E(\alpha_j u_{it}) = 0 \quad \forall i, j, t; \quad E(\alpha_j v_{it}) = 0 \quad \forall i, j, t$$

where δ_{ij} is the Kronecker delta. However it should be noted that only the overall variance $\sigma_\varepsilon^2 = \sigma_u^2 + \beta^2\sigma_v^2$ can be identified.

In this case, for any period t, all the observations at least one period apart are valid instruments. Let y_t, x_t, α and ε_t denote $(N \times 1)$ vectors obtained by piling all the individuals for period t, and define $r_t = \alpha + \varepsilon_t$. So for the period 1 equation written as

$$y_1 = x_1\beta + \alpha + \varepsilon_1 \equiv x_1\beta + r_1 \tag{10}$$

$z_1 = [x_2 \quad x_3 \quad \ldots \quad x_T]$ is a valid instrument matrix, assuming that we have observations for T time periods. Furthermore,

$$V(r_1) = V(\alpha) + V(\varepsilon_1) = \sigma_\alpha^2 I_N + \sigma_\varepsilon^2 I_N \equiv \sigma_r^2 I_N$$

Given this, two methods are possible: applying the IV technique equation by equation or combining all periods into a system and then applying IV with the whole set of instruments for all the periods together. Letting z_t denote the instrument set for the t-th period equation, the first method leads to

$$\hat{\beta}_{(t)} = [x_t' z_t (z_t' z_t)^{-1} z_t' x_t]^{-1} x_t' z_t (z_t' z_t)^{-1} z_t' y_t \tag{11}$$

as $V(r_t) = \sigma_r^2 I_N$.

The system estimator will be obtained as follows combining all t's:

$$y_1 = x_1\beta + \alpha + \varepsilon_1$$

$$\vdots$$

$$y_T = x_T\beta + \alpha + \varepsilon_T$$

or using appropriate notations

$$y = X\beta + (\iota_T \otimes I_N)\alpha + \varepsilon \equiv X\beta + r \tag{12}$$

where ι_T is a vector of ones, and y, X and r are $(NT \times 1)$ vectors. The resulting system variance covariance matrix is given by

$$V(r) \equiv \Sigma = \sigma_\alpha^2(\iota_T \iota_T' \otimes I_N) + \sigma_\varepsilon^2 I_{NT}$$

Writing the whole set of instruments as

$$Z = \begin{pmatrix} z_1 & 0 & 0 \\ 0 & z_2 & 0 \\ . & . & . \\ 0 & 0 & z_T \end{pmatrix} \tag{13}$$

we will have

$$\hat{\beta}_{(gls)} = [X'Z(Z'\Sigma Z)^{-1}Z'X]^{-1}X'Z(Z'\Sigma Z)^{-1}Z'y \tag{14}$$

This estimator can be shown to be a weighted average of the "individual" $\hat{\beta}_{(t)}$'s obtained by (11) for each period, with the weights being inversely proportional to the corresponding variance matrix. Needless to say that the same estimator can be derived using a Generalised Method of Moments (GMM) approach (cf. Greene (1993) e.g.) based on the orthogonality conditions between the instruments and the combined error term[3]. Note that we could also write a system OLS estimator as follows:

$$\hat{\beta}_{(ols)} = [X'Z(Z'Z)^{-1}Z'X]^{-1}X'Z(Z'Z)^{-1}Z'y \tag{15}$$

So far we have assumed independence across different individuals in the sample. However our sample of parents and children contains siblings and it will be more realistic to assume that the individual effects of children of the same parents are correlated. This would imply non zero correlation between the specific effects α_i and α_j if i and j belong to the same family. Let us take this into account by means of a variable d_{ij} such that

$$d_{ij} = \begin{cases} 1 & \text{if } i,j \text{ are siblings} \\ 0 & \text{if not} \end{cases} \tag{16}$$

Let us further assume that

$$E(\alpha_i \alpha_j) = d_{ij} c_\alpha$$

This modifies our variance matrix of α as follows:

$$V(\alpha) = \begin{pmatrix} \sigma_\alpha^2 & d_{12}c_\alpha & \dots & d_{1N}c_\alpha \\ d_{21}c_\alpha & \sigma_\alpha^2 & \dots & d_{2N}c_\alpha \\ \cdot & \cdot & \cdot & \cdot \\ \cdot & \cdot & \cdot & \cdot \\ \cdot & \cdot & \cdot & \cdot \\ d_{N1}c_\alpha & \dots & \dots & \sigma_\alpha^2 \end{pmatrix} \equiv \Sigma_\alpha \tag{17}$$

Then

$$V(r_t) = \Sigma_\alpha + \sigma_\varepsilon^2 I_N \equiv \Sigma_0^* \tag{18}$$

and

$$V(r) \equiv \Sigma^* = (\iota_T \iota_T' \otimes \Sigma_\alpha) + \sigma_\varepsilon^2 I_{NT} = \begin{pmatrix} \Sigma_0^* & \Sigma_\alpha & \dots & \Sigma_\alpha \\ \cdot & \cdot & \cdot & \cdot \\ \cdot & \cdot & \cdot & \cdot \\ \cdot & \cdot & \cdot & \cdot \\ \Sigma_\alpha & \Sigma_\alpha & \dots & \Sigma_0^* \end{pmatrix} \tag{19}$$

Thus the single equation estimator of β accounting for correlations across siblings would be given by

$$\hat{\beta}^*_{(t)} = [x_t'z_t(z_t'\Sigma_0^* z_t)^{-1}z_t'x_t]^{-1}x_t'z_t(z_t'\Sigma_0^* z_t)^{-1}z_t'y_t \tag{20}$$

[3]An alternative estimator is the so-called Generalised Instrumental Variables Estimator (GIVE) which is obtained by using the instrument matrix $\Sigma^{-1}Z$ and then applying GLS on the model transformed by the instrument matrix. The relative efficiency of this estimator with respect to the one given in (14) cannot be established in general. We have not considered the GIVE in our empirical analysis due to the computational complications involved in its implementation.

and the system estimator by

$$\hat{\beta}^*_{(gls)} = [X'Z(Z'\Sigma^*Z)^{-1}Z'X]^{-1}X'Z(Z'\Sigma^*Z)^{-1}Z'y \tag{21}$$

Now let us proceed to the MA(1) case.

Case 2: MA(1) errors

Assumption A2: $\varepsilon_{it} = w_{it} + \theta_\varepsilon w_{i,t-1}$

with $w_{it} \sim$ iid $(0, \sigma_w^2)$ and θ_ε an unknown parameter. Here the underlying assumptions on the components are (with similar notations as for the components of ε_{it}):

$$u_{it} = \rho_{it} + \theta_u \rho_{i,t-1} \tag{22}$$

$$v_{it} = \lambda_{it} + \theta_v \lambda_{i,t-1} \tag{23}$$

but once again only the parameters describing the overall error term ε_{it} can be identified. Let us denote

$$\gamma_1 \equiv E(\varepsilon_{it}\varepsilon_{i,t+1}) \qquad \forall t$$

and we know for an MA(1) process

$$E(\varepsilon_{it}\varepsilon_{is}) = 0 \quad \text{for} \quad |s-t| \geq 2$$

The instrument set has to be modified according to the new assumptions as observations one period apart are no longer valid instruments. They have to be at least two periods away. Thus we would have (taking T=5 as is the case in our study):

$$\begin{aligned}
\tilde{z}_1 &= [x_3 \quad x_4 \quad x_5] \\
\tilde{z}_2 &= [x_4 \quad x_5] \\
\tilde{z}_3 &= [x_1 \quad x_5] \\
\tilde{z}_4 &= [x_1 \quad x_2] \\
\tilde{z}_5 &= [x_1 \quad x_2 \quad x_3]
\end{aligned}$$

Having made these changes and assuming for the moment that there are no siblings, the expression of the single equation estimator $\tilde{\beta}_{(t)}$ remains the same (equation(11)) where the new instrument $\tilde{z}_t$ is to be used instead of z_t. In the system estimation procedure, the variance of the vector r changes as we now have non zero correlation between r_t and r_{t-1} or r_{t+1}. Again assuming no siblings, we have

$$E(r_t r_t') = \sigma_\alpha^2 I_N + \sigma_\varepsilon^2 I_N \equiv \Sigma_0 \tag{24}$$

$$E(r_t r'_{t+1}) = \sigma^2_\alpha I_N + \gamma_1 I_N \equiv \Sigma_1 \tag{25}$$

and

$$E(r_t r'_s) = \sigma^2_\alpha I_N \equiv \Sigma_2 \quad \text{for} \quad |s-t| \geq 2 \tag{26}$$

Thus

$$E(rr') = \begin{pmatrix} \Sigma_0 & \Sigma_1 & \Sigma_2 & \dots & \Sigma_2 \\ \Sigma_1 & \Sigma_0 & \Sigma_1 & \dots & \Sigma_2 \\ \cdot & \cdot & \cdot & \cdot & \cdot \\ \cdot & \cdot & \cdot & \cdot & \cdot \\ \cdot & \cdot & \cdot & \cdot & \cdot \\ \Sigma_2 & \Sigma_2 & \dots & \Sigma_1 & \Sigma_0 \end{pmatrix} \equiv \tilde{\Sigma} \tag{27}$$

and the modified system estimator would be written as

$$\tilde{\beta}_{gls} = [X'\tilde{Z}(\tilde{Z}'\tilde{\Sigma}\tilde{Z})^{-1}\tilde{Z}'X]^{-1}X'\tilde{Z}(\tilde{Z}'\tilde{\Sigma}\tilde{Z})^{-1}\tilde{Z}'y \tag{28}$$

where $\tilde{Z}$ now contains the new set of instruments.

Let us now introduce correlations among siblings. We get

$$E(r_t r'_t) = \Sigma_\alpha + \sigma^2_\varepsilon I_N \equiv \Sigma^*_0 \tag{29}$$
$$E(r_t r'_{t+1}) = \Sigma_\alpha + \gamma_1 I_N \equiv \Sigma^*_1 \tag{30}$$
$$E(r_t r'_{t+2}) = \Sigma_\alpha \equiv \Sigma^*_2 \tag{31}$$

Thus

$$E(rr') = \begin{pmatrix} \Sigma^*_0 & \Sigma^*_1 & \Sigma^*_2 & \dots & \Sigma^*_2 \\ \Sigma^*_1 & \Sigma^*_0 & \Sigma^*_1 & \dots & \Sigma^*_2 \\ \cdot & \cdot & \cdot & \cdot & \cdot \\ \cdot & \cdot & \cdot & \cdot & \cdot \\ \cdot & \cdot & \cdot & \cdot & \cdot \\ \Sigma^*_2 & \Sigma^*_2 & \dots & \Sigma^*_1 & \Sigma^*_0 \end{pmatrix} \equiv \tilde{\Sigma}^* \tag{32}$$

Now, the single equation and system estimators taking account of such correlations are given respectively by

$$\tilde{\beta}^*_{(t)} = [x'_t\tilde{z}_t(\tilde{z}'_t\Sigma^*_0\tilde{z}_t)^{-1}\tilde{z}'_t x_t]^{-1}x'_t\tilde{z}_t(\tilde{z}'_t\Sigma^*_0\tilde{z}_t)^{-1}\tilde{z}'_t y_t \tag{33}$$

and

$$\tilde{\beta}^*_{(gls)} = [X'\tilde{Z}(\tilde{Z}'\tilde{\Sigma}^*\tilde{Z})^{-1}\tilde{Z}'X]^{-1}X'\tilde{Z}(\tilde{Z}'\tilde{\Sigma}^*\tilde{Z})^{-1}\tilde{Z}'y \tag{34}$$

Variance - covariance estimators

In order to implement all the above methods in practice, we need prior estimates of the various variance-covariance parameters appearing in the different blocks of $V(r)$. We give below the various sample moments that consistently estimate the relevant parameters.

As

$$r_{it} - r_{i.} = \varepsilon_{it} - \varepsilon_{i.} \tag{35}$$

and

$$V(\varepsilon_{it} - \varepsilon_{i.}) = \frac{(T-1)}{T}\sigma_\varepsilon^2 \tag{36}$$

where a dot in the place of a subscript indicates the average taken over it, σ_ε^2 can be estimated by

$$\hat{\sigma}_\varepsilon^2 = \frac{1}{N(T-1)}\sum_i \sum_t (\hat{r}_{it} - \hat{r}_{i.})^2 \tag{37}$$

where $\hat{r}_{it} = y_{it} - x_{it}\hat{\beta}$ and $\hat{\beta}$ can be either the corresponding estimator for that time period (given by equation (11)) or a first stage system OLS estimator (given by (15)).
Using

$$V(r_{i.}) = V(\alpha_i) + V(\varepsilon_{i.}) = \sigma_\alpha^2 + \sigma_\varepsilon^2/T \tag{38}$$

we can estimate σ_α^2 as follows:

$$\hat{\sigma}_\alpha^2 = \frac{1}{N}\sum_i \hat{r}_{i.}^2 - \frac{1}{T}\hat{\sigma}_\varepsilon^2 \tag{39}$$

Finally, an estimator of c_α is given by

$$\hat{c}_\alpha = \frac{1}{N_J}\sum_{i,j \in J}(\hat{r}_{i.} - \tilde{r}_{..})(\hat{r}_{j.} - \tilde{r}_{..}) \tag{40}$$

where J is the group of individuals who are siblings, N_J is the number of persons in J and $\tilde{r}_{..}$ is the mean over this group.

In the MA(1) case, we need γ_1 in addition to the above. Knowing

$$Cov(r_{it}, r_{i,t+1}) = \sigma_\alpha^2 + \gamma_1$$

and

$$Cov(r_{it} - r_{i.}, r_{i,t+1} - r_{i.}) = \frac{(T-1)}{T}\gamma_1$$

we can obtain

$$\hat{\gamma}_1 = \frac{T}{(T-1)}\frac{1}{(NT)}\sum_i\sum_t(\hat{r}_{it} - \hat{r}_{i.})(\hat{r}_{i,t+1} - \hat{r}_{i.})$$
$$= \frac{1}{(T-1)}\frac{1}{N}\sum_i\sum_t(\hat{r}_{it} - \hat{r}_{i.})(\hat{r}_{i,t+1} - \hat{r}_{i.})$$

The above procedures (single equation and system) can be generalised to MA(2), MA(3),... errors in an exactly analogous way from iid to MA(1) without much difficulty. In fact these possibilities will also be explored empirically.

Specification tests

Before finishing with the methodology, let us look at the different specification tests that can be carried out in this context. The first type of tests that one can think of are those that concern the nature of serial correlation assumed for the errors r_t. For instance, in order to test the assumption of serial independence, denoted as MA(0), against the alternative MA(1), a Hausman test statistic can be constructed based on the difference between $\hat{\beta}$ and $\tilde{\beta}$ denoting the estimator under the null (time independence) as $\hat{\beta}$ and the one under the alternative (MA(1)) as $\tilde{\beta}$. Under the null, both are consistent with $\hat{\beta}$ being more efficient and under the alternative only $\tilde{\beta}$ is consistent. Let us consider the single equation case say for $t = 1$. The instrument will be $z_1 = [x_2 \quad x_3 \quad x_4 \quad x_5]$ under H_0 and $\tilde{z}_1 = [x_3 \quad x_4 \quad x_5]$ under H_a. The two estimators of β are given by:

$$\hat{\beta} = [x_1'z_1(z_1'\hat{\Sigma}_0^*z_1)^{-1}z_1'x_1]^{-1}x_1'z_1(z_1'\hat{\Sigma}_0^*z_1)^{-1}z_1'y_1 \tag{41}$$

and

$$\tilde{\beta} = [x_1'\tilde{z}_1(\tilde{z}_1'\hat{\Sigma}_0^*\tilde{z}_1)^{-1}\tilde{z}_1'x_1]^{-1}x_1'\tilde{z}_1(\tilde{z}_1'\hat{\Sigma}_0^*\tilde{z}_1)^{-1}\tilde{z}_1'y_1 \tag{42}$$

where $\hat{\Sigma}_0^*$ is the estimator of the variance of r_1 under MA(1). It is easily shown that

$$V(\hat{\beta}) = [x_1'z_1(z_1'\hat{\Sigma}_0^*z_1)^{-1}z_1'x_1]^{-1} \tag{43}$$
$$V(\tilde{\beta}) = [x_1'\tilde{z}_1(\tilde{z}_1'\hat{\Sigma}_0^*\tilde{z}_1)^{-1}\tilde{z}_1'x_1]^{-1} \tag{44}$$

with

$$V(\hat{\beta}) < V(\tilde{\beta})$$

and

$$Cov(\hat{\beta}, \tilde{\beta}) = V(\hat{\beta}) \tag{45}$$

Hence

$$V(\tilde{\beta} - \hat{\beta}) = V(\tilde{\beta}) - V(\hat{\beta}) \tag{46}$$

The test statistic is therefore

$$(\tilde{\beta} - \hat{\beta})'[V(\tilde{\beta}) - V(\hat{\beta})]^{-1}(\tilde{\beta} - \hat{\beta}) \sim \chi_1^2$$

with large values rejecting independence.

Similarly, MA(1) can be tested against MA(2) by constructing the test statistic based on the difference between the two corresponding estimators. In this case, the instrument sets for the first period equation are $z_1 = [x_3 \quad x_4 \quad x_5]$ under H_0 and $\tilde{z}_1 = [x_4 \quad x_5]$ under H_a. Other tests such as MA(2) against MA(3) or MA(1) against MA(3), MA(0) against MA(2) or MA(0) against MA(3) can all be devised similarly.

The same results hold for the system estimators too, the basic difference being the dimension of the variables involved. Let us illustrate the case iid against MA(1).

We have the system (see (12))

$$y = X\beta + r \tag{47}$$

and

$$Z = \begin{pmatrix} z_1 & 0 & 0 \\ 0 & z_2 & 0 \\ \cdot & \cdot & \cdot \\ 0 & 0 & z_T \end{pmatrix} \tag{48}$$

for the null and

$$\tilde{Z} = \begin{pmatrix} \tilde{z}_1 & 0 & 0 \\ 0 & \tilde{z}_2 & 0 \\ \cdot & \cdot & \cdot \\ 0 & 0 & \tilde{z}_T \end{pmatrix} \tag{49}$$

for the alternative. The expressions of the estimators will be

$$\hat{\beta} = [X'Z(Z'\Sigma^* Z)^{-1}Z'X]^{-1}X'Z(Z'\Sigma^* Z)^{-1}Z'y \tag{50}$$

and

$$\tilde{\beta} = [X'\tilde{Z}(\tilde{Z}'\Sigma^* \tilde{Z})^{-1}\tilde{Z}'X]^{-1}X'\tilde{Z}(\tilde{Z}'\Sigma^* \tilde{Z})^{-1}\tilde{Z}'y \tag{51}$$

Finally the test statistic will be given by

$$(\tilde{\beta} - \hat{\beta})'[V(\tilde{\beta}) - V(\hat{\beta})]^{-1}(\tilde{\beta} - \hat{\beta}) \sim \chi_K^2$$

Another important category of tests is the so-called overidentification tests of Sargan (1976). These tests use covariances between IV residuals and a set of instruments that need not have been used in the estimation to detect any model misspecification regarding the validity of the instruments. Under the null of no misspecification, the covariance between the residuals and the instrument set in question would be close to zero. More explicitly, let us say we have a model written as

$$y = X\beta + \varepsilon \tag{52}$$

and estimated by IV using W as instruments. Now suppose we have another potential instrument set $\tilde{W}$ of order m ($\tilde{W}$ may or may not overlap with W). Then the test statistic using the covariance matrix $\hat{\Delta}$ of $\hat{\varepsilon}'\tilde{W}$ is given by (see Godfrey (1988))

$$\hat{\varepsilon}'\tilde{W}\hat{\Delta}^{-1}\tilde{W}\hat{\varepsilon} \sim \chi^2_m$$

Now if $\tilde{W}$ is a subset of W (Pagan-Hall (1983) suggestion) then the above test is equivalent to testing $\delta = 0$ in the augmented regression

$$y = X\beta + \tilde{W}\delta + \varepsilon \tag{53}$$

as the above test statistic can be shown to be the same as that of Gallant and Jorgenson (1979) for testing $\delta = 0$ in the above model. The latter is based on the difference between the optimisation criterion in the unrestricted model (53) and the restricted model (with $\delta = 0$). It is given by

$$\tilde{S} - \hat{S} \sim \chi^2_m$$

where

$$\tilde{S} = \tilde{\varepsilon}'W(W\hat{\Sigma}W)^{-1}W'\tilde{\varepsilon}, \quad \tilde{\varepsilon} = y - X\tilde{\beta} - \tilde{W}\tilde{\delta}$$

$$\hat{S} = \hat{\varepsilon}'W(W\hat{\Sigma}W)^{-1}W'\hat{\varepsilon}, \quad \hat{\varepsilon} = y - X\hat{\beta}$$

and both models are estimated using W as instruments and $\hat{\Sigma}$ calculated using $\tilde{\varepsilon}$.

Coming to our model say for the single equation $t = 1$, in the iid case, one can test the validity of $\tilde{W} = [x_2]$ as instruments by estimating the augmented model

$$y_1 = x_1\beta + x_2\delta + r_1 \tag{54}$$

and testing $\delta = 0$. If the test is rejected then x_2 is not a valid instrument and only $[x_3 \quad x_4 \quad x_5]$ should be used as the instrument matrix. This can be repeated for $\tilde{W} = [x_2 \quad x_3]$ or $\tilde{W} = [x_2 \quad x_3 \quad x_4]$. In the MA(1) case, $W = [x_3 \quad x_4 \quad x_5]$ and $\tilde{W}$ can be either $[x_3]$ or $[x_3 \quad x_4]$.

Once again the procedure is easily extended for testing other MA structures and to the case of system estimators.

Let us now go on to look at the empirical results on the various estimators and tests discussed above.

4. RESULTS

This empirical section is divided into three parts. Firstly we examine single equation estimation of the income transmission equation. Then, we consider a system analysis where all the equations are pooled to arrive at a unique estimator. Finally, in the third sub-section we carry out specification tests on the system estimates in an effort to reconcile the various findings and to arrive at general conclusions pertaining to the serial correlation in the error term, and hence the appropriate choice of instruments.

All the regressions results reported below include as explanatory variables a measurement on the parent family's annual income, age controls (age and 'age-squared' of the parent and child family heads) together with a constant. All estimations take account of correlations across siblings, and where appropriate, are robust to serial correlation up to three lags (or leads).

4.1. Single equation results

For the single equation analysis, we can report estimates for up to 5 years (year one pertains to observations on the child's 1983 income and her/his parents' 1967 income, while year 5 pertains to the child's 1987 income and the parents' 1971 resources). Single equation analysis is very popular in the empirical literature on intergenerational mobility (see for instance Tables 2 and 3 of Solon (1992) and Table 2 of Björklund and Jantti (1997)). We note that potentially we could estimate a total of 25 equations, not just 5. This is so, because, in practice, nothing precludes us from using each of x_1 to x_5 to explain y_1 (i.e. five separate regressions), and to use the same variables to explain y_2 etc. Our choice here to regress y_t on x_t is purely expositional, and has been motivated by our interest in formulating our estimation problem in the context of the panel data framework. Below we report results for the first and last year of the panel only, since these will suffice to motivate the need for proceeding in the direction of system level estimation.

In Table 2 we report results for period one of the panel. When x_5, parental income in 1971, is used to instrument x_1, (the corresponding 1967 variable) the coefficient of income inheritance β is estimated as 0.55. As a benchmark, the OLS estimate for this parameter is 0.485 with a standard error of 0.0245. As this latter estimate however is downwardly biased (and its standard error is incorrect), it is expected that IV estimates of β would be higher; this is indeed the case for all the figures reported in Table 2.

All four estimates of Table 2 are within the narrow bracket of 0.53 to 0.55 (less than one standard error from one another). With a sample size of 1426 observations, adding extra instruments can generally be recommended on efficiency grounds, since the resulting finite sample bias (which increases with the number of instruments included in the regression) is small. The results of Table 2 confirm this pattern: standard errors fall from 0.035 to 0.031 as the set of instruments is expanded from x_5 to include x_5 to x_2. Finally, the Sargan tests (last column of the table) do not reject any of the specifications at the 5% level when x_4 to x_2 are included in the set of instruments.

While the findings of Table 2 provide no indication of serial correlation in the disturbances, the story changes somewhat when we turn to period 5 results, reported in Table 3.

Table 2
IV Results for Period One of the Panel

$\hat{\beta}$	instr. set x_5	x_4	x_3	x_2	Sargan test
0.550 (0.035)	×				-
0.544 (0.033)	×	×			0.511
0.539 (0.032)	×	×	×		0.525
0.532 (0.031)	×	×	×	×	1.680

1. The dependent variable is y_1 (the child's 1983 income). The set of explanatory variables contains x_1 (the parents' 1967 income) together with age controls for the parent and child family heads.
2. The single equation estimator of β is as defined in equation (20). A × mark indicates that the corresponding variable is used as an instrument. The set of instruments (x_2 to x_5) contains leads on the parent family's income from 1968 to 1971.
3. Standard errors appear inside parentheses.

The estimates of Table 3 use lags of family income as instruments, while those of Table 2 used leads of parental income. Note first that the estimates of β in Table 3 are generally larger (ranging between 0.55 and 0.60) than those of Table 2, though these differences are not statistically significant. On the basis of the Sargan tests statistics we may also conclude that the findings reject the validity of a one period lagged income as an instrument at the 5% (also at the 1%) significance level. Conditional upon x_1 (income lagged four periods) being a valid instrument, x_2, and $[x_2, x_3]$ are not rejected as over-identifying instruments, while the inclusion of x_4, leads to a rejection of the orthogonality conditions. Thus, period 5 results suggest an MA(1) specification for the regression error term, while those of period 1 give no indication of any potential serial correlation in the disturbances. It is for this reason that we will also subject our system-level estimators to various specification tests, given that the set of instruments may be called to doubt in the light of our findings.

We close this sub-section by reporting some related findings in the literature. Using education of the household head as an instrument, Solon (1992) estimates β at 0.56 using a sub-sample of the PSID. Abul Naga (1998) estimates this same parameter at 0.63 (also using education as an instrumental variable for a sub-sample of the PSID). Some UK results provided by Dearden *et al.* (1997) estimate β to be in the order of 0.55 to 0.6 when education is used to instrument parental income. They also report an interesting finding that the incomes of daughters tend to be more correlated with their parents' economic outcomes than in the case of sons.

Table 3
IV Results for Period Five of the Panel

$\hat{\beta}$	instr. set x_5	x_4	x_3	x_2	Sargan test
0.599 (0.034)	×				-
0.577 (0.033)	×	×			1.796
0.564 (0.032)	×	×	×		2.166
0.545 (0.031)	×	×	×	×	14.040*

1. The dependent variable is y_5 (the child's 1987 income). The set of explanatory variables contains x_5 (the parents' 1971 income) together with age controls.
2. A * mark indicates that the Sargan test of over-identifying restrictions is rejected at the 5% level.

4.2. System estimation

Moving from the single equation framework to the system estimator is analogous to the transition from two-stage to three stage least squares methods in the general simultaneous equations framework. This allows for potential efficiency gains provided the specifications considered are validated using appropriate diagnostics tests.

In comparison to the single equation results of Tables 2 and 3, we may note that the system GLS estimate is substantially smaller under the MA(0) assumption - no serial correlation in the errors - (a value of 0.42) but that this estimate increases to 0.52 with a standard error of 0.027 under the MA(3) specification. The system GLS estimator appears to be somewhat more sensitive to the time-series structure of the error term than the system OLS estimator, though with the OLS estimator we also find that the estimate of β increases as we move from the MA(0) specification to the MA(3) model, with values ranging from 0.50 to 0.57.

As discussed in Section 3, the existence of serial correlation in the residuals reduces the set of potential instruments for parental income. Thus, while under the MA(0) and MA(1) assumptions all equations can be used to arrive at an estimate of β, this is no longer the case under the MA(2) and MA(3) specifications. Under the MA(2) specification, x_3 cannot be instrumented using lags and leads of x (when the panel spans a period of 5 years). Likewise, under the MA(3) structure, x_2, x_3 and x_4 will not possess within-equation instruments. Accordingly, for the MA(2) specification the period 3 equation has been deleted from the system estimator. Likewise, the MA(3) model only pools period one and period 5 data to estimate β. The resulting pattern for the standard errors of the system estimator is to take on increasing values as we move from the MA(0) to the MA(3) models (for both OLS and GLS).

Table 4
System Estimators

Model	System-OLS	System-GLS
MA(0)	0.498 (0.026)	0.417 (0.022)
MA(1)	0.520 (0.027)	0.475 (0.024)
MA(2)	0.538 (0.027)	0.489 (0.025)
MA(3)	0.565 (0.030)	0.522 (0.027)

1. MA(0) denotes a model with serially uncorrelated residuals, while MA(q) denotes a model with a moving average disturbance term of order q.
2. The system-OLS and system-GLS estimators are as defined in equations (14) and (21) or (34) respectively.

Finally, note that the variance of the individual effect accounts for approximately 70% of the total variance in the error term: σ_α^2 is estimated at 0.354, while σ_ε^2 is estimated at 0.166 (results not shown in the table). Viewed under this perspective, it is clear that panel data models will provide a better fit for microdata with a substantial component of unobserved heterogeneity than pure cross-section regressions.

4.3. Hausman specification tests

Our final task in this empirical section of the paper consists in testing various scenarios regarding the time-series structure of the disturbances of the system estimator. Such tests are required in order to provide a sound basis for discriminating among the various estimates of β in Table 4, with values ranging from 0.42 to 0.57.

Our benchmark assumption is that of an MA(3) process: the resulting system estimator will be consistent (but inefficient) under the MA(2), MA(1), or MA(0) specifications, while, the other way around, the MA(q) estimator is inconsistent under the MA(r) scenario, for $r > q$.

Specification tests are carried out using both the system-OLS and system-GLS estimators, as, in practice, a sub-optimal weighting scheme for the GLS estimator need not result is efficiency gains over OLS (Szroeter (1994)). Comparing our test statistics to a χ^2 variable with 6 degrees of freedom, our results (Table 5) can be summarized as follows: the MA(1) and MA(0) specifications are rejected at the 1% level against the null hypothesis of an MA(3) process using both the system OLS and GLS estimators. The MA(2) hypothesis (first line of Table 5) is not rejected using the system OLS estimator, though it is rejected at the 5% level (but not at 1%) using GLS. In this sense, the MA(1) and MA(0) assumptions appear to be inadequate, while, provided the MA(3) hypothesis is a valid one, the MA(2) model appears to be more plausible.

Table 5
Hausman Specification Tests

Specification	System-OLS	System-GLS
MA(2) *vs.* MA(3)	11.525	16.539*
MA(1) *vs.* MA(3)	16.942**	19.897**
MA(0) *vs.* MA(3)	25.232**	52.449**
MA(1) *vs.* MA(2)	8.649	7.199
MA(0) *vs.* MA(2)	18.661**	46.828**
MA(0) *vs.* MA(1)	0.0127	49.246**

A * (**) indicates that the null hypothesis is rejected at a 5% (1%) probability of type-I error.

The last three lines of Table 5 provide further results when the null specification is modified. A test of the MA(1) specification against the MA(2) model does not lead to a rejection (using both estimators) while the MA(0) assumption is rejected against MA(2) at the 1% level. Finally, the GLS estimator rejects the assumption of no serial correlation in the error term, against the MA(1) model, while OLS fails to reject the MA(0) model against MA(1). The overall pattern, then, is that both estimators reject the MA(q-2) model against MA(q), while system-OLS never rejects the MA(q-1) scenario against MA(q). Adopting a more global perspective, the system-GLS estimator is perhaps to be recommended over system-OLS on such grounds.

5. CONCLUSIONS

In this study, we have carried out the estimation of the intergenerational correlation of permanent incomes within the framework of a panel data model with measurement errors. This has enabled us to implement new estimators as well as specification tests, as the problem has not been explicitly considered from this perspective so far.

The availability of time-series on a cross-section of families has allowed us to exploit within-sample information to deal with the errors in variables problem as well as to develop system estimators for the parameters of interest. The panel data context has also been useful in testing various scenarios regarding the time-series structure of the error term and its implications for the choice of instruments. Our estimators have also taken into account possible correlations among children belonging to the same family.

For the various methods used in this study, we have estimated the coefficient of income inheritance to be in the range of 0.42 to 0.60. Single equation estimates vary between 0.53 and 0.60. Results vary depending on the choice of instruments for a given time period, but also from one period to another. System estimates were found to be between 0.42 and 0.57, with the system OLS yielding higher values than the GLS counterpart. On the basis of our specification tests we find that MA(0) (no serial correlation) is definitely rejected compared to MA(3), MA(2) and MA(1) (at least in the system-GLS case). Turning to MA(1), it is rejected compared to MA(3) but not compared to MA(2). Finally MA(2) is accepted against MA(3). Given that MA(3) is the least restricted model that our data permit and hence using this as a reference for comparing the other scenarios, we can say that there is some supporting evidence for an MA(2) structure of the errors.

These results are taken to imply a substantial amount of income continuity from one generation to the next. A slope value in the order of 0.5 to 0.55, while indicative of a process of regression towards the mean, is nonetheless far remote from an idealized equal opportunities situation.

In general, panel data models allow the researcher to relax the independence assumption between the specific effect and the explanatory variable. However, this was not possible in our study because the variable of interest subject to errors (namely permanent income of the parent family) is time-invariant. Furthermore, we have not considered other dynamic structures for the error term such as AR or ARMA processes, which could provide a useful direction for further work.

REFERENCES

1. Abul Naga, R. (1998), " Estimating the Intergenerational Correlation of Incomes: an Errors in Variables Framework", Discussion paper No.9812, DEEP, University of Lausanne.
2. Altonji, J. and T. Dunn (1991), "Relationships Among the Family Incomes and Labor Market Outcomes of Relatives", *Research in Labor Economics*, 12, 269-310.
3. Atkinson, A., A. Maynard and C. Trinder (1983), *Parents and Children: Incomes in Two Generations*, London, Heinemann.
4. Behrman, J. and P. Taubman (1990), "The Intergenerational Correlation between Children's Adult Earnings and their Parents Income: Results from the Michigan Panel of Income Dynamics", *Review of Income and Wealth*, 36, 115-127.
5. Bicketti, S., W. Gould, L. Lillard and F. Welch (1988), "The Panel Study of Income Dynamics after Fourteen Years: an Evaluation", *Journal of Labor Economics*, 6, 472-92.
6. Biorn, E. (1998), "Panel Data with Measurement Errors: Instrumental Variables and GMM Procedures Combining Levels and Differences", Invited Paper at the Eighth International Conference on Panel Data, Goteberg.
7. Bjorklund, A. and M. Jantti (1997), "Intergenerational Income Mobility in Sweden Compared to the United States", *American Economic Review*, 87, 1009-1018.
8. Bowles, S. (1972), "Schooling and Inequality from Generation to Generation", *Journal of Political Economy*, 80, S219-S251.
9. Dearden, L., S. Machin and H. Reed (1997), "Intergenerational Mobility in Britain", *Economic Journal*, 107, 47-66.

10. Gallant, A. and D. Jorgenson, (1979), " Statistical Inference for a System of Simultaneous, Non-linear, Implicit Equations in the Context of Instrumental Variable Estimation", *Journal of Econometrics*, 11, 275-302.
11. Galor, O. and J. Zeira (1993), " Income Distribution and Macroeconomics", *Review of Economic Studies*, 60, 35-52.
12. Godfrey, L. (1988), *Misspecification Tests in Econometrics*, Cambridge, Cambridge University Press.
13. Greene, W.H. (1993), *Econometric Analysis*, Second Edition, Macmillan Publishing Company, New York.
14. Griliches, Z. (1986), "Economic Data Issues" in Z. Griliches and M. Intriligator (eds): *Handbook of Econometrics*, Vol. 3, North Holland, Amsterdam.
15. Griliches, Z. and J. Hausman (1986), "Errors in Variables in Panel Data", *Journal of Econometrics*, 31, 93-118.
16. Hill, M. (1993), *The Panel Study of Income Studies: a User's Guide*, New York, Sage Publications.
17. Hsiao, C. (1986), *Analysis of Panel Data*, Cambridge University Press, Cambridge.
18. Hsiao, C. and G. Taylor (1991), "Some Remarks on Measurement Error and the Identification of Panel Data Models", *Statistica Neerlandica*, 45, 187-194.
19. Pagan, A. and A. Hall (1983), "Diagnostic Tests as Residual Analysis", *Econometric Reviews*, 2, 159-218.
20. Sargan, D. (1976), "Testing for Misspecification after Estimating using Instrumental Variables", mimeo, London School of Economics.
21. Solon, G. (1992), "Intergenerational Income Mobility in the United States", *American Economic Review*, 82, 393-408.
22. Stokey, N. (1996), "Shirtsleeves to Shirtsleeves: The Economics of Social Mobility", reprinted in D. Jacobs, E. Kalai and M. Kamian (eds) (1998): *Frontiers of Research in Economic Theory: Nancy L. Schwartz Memorial Lectures 1983-1997*, Cambridge University Press, Cambridge .
23. Szroeter, J. (1994), "Exact Finite-Sample Relative Efficiency of Suboptimally Weighted Least Squares Estimators in Models with Ordered Heteroscedasticity", *Journal of Econometrics*, 64, 29-43.
24. Wansbeek, T. and R. Koning (1991), "Measurement Error and Panel Data", *Statistica Neerlandica*, 45, 85-92.
25. Zimmerman, D. (1992), "Regression Toward Mediocrity in Economic Status", *American Economic Review*, 82, 409-429.

Panel Data Econometrics: Future Directions
J. Krishnakumar and E. Ronchetti (Editors)

CHAPTER 5

LIFE EXPECTANCY AND RELATED INDICATORS AS MEASURES OF DEVELOPMENT: The Case of Switzerland

Gabrielle ANTILLE and Jacques SILBER

1. INTRODUCTION

Finding an adequate measure of development allowing comparisons over time and across countries is not an easy task. Many proposals have been made during the past fifty years and although the G.D.P. per capita (or some related measure derived from national accounts) remains probably the most popular measure, it is not without problems. Summers and Heston (1991) have provided what is probably the best data base for international comparisons but it is limited to the period 1950–1988.

For those who wish to go back in time, the use of national accounts to make international comparisons is an extremely difficult task. One may then prefer to rely on other indicators, among which the life expectancy remains an attractive choice. It has in particular the advantage of measuring results rather than inputs. It is however not very sensitive to the distribution of the benefits of development in the population. This is why Silber (1983) had suggested the use of an indicator derived from the life expectancy, which he called E.L.L., the "Equivalent Length of Life", a measure which also takes into account the dispersion of the durations of life.

The purpose of this paper is to use the life expectancy, as well as the indicator E.L.L., to make comparisons over time and across countries. More precisely Swiss data for the period 1930–1990 will be analyzed and the performance of Switzerland will be compared with that of seven other European countries in 1970 and in 1990.

The paper is organized as follows. The following section describes the advantages and shortcomings of using life expectancy as an indicator of development. Section 3 then shows how uncertainty theory may be applied to the comparison of life tables while Section 4 explains how the measure E.L.L. is computed. Section 5 gives the definition of a more sophisticated version of the indicator E.L.L. while Section 6 shows how to apply the tools previously presented to the analysis of gender differentials in mortality. Section 7 looks at the evolution of mortality in Switzerland between 1930 and 1990 and derives implications concerning the pace of development in this country during this period. Using a similar approach Section 8 compares the levels of development in Switzerland and seven other European countries in 1970 and 1990. The paper ends with some concluding remarks.

2. LIFE EXPECTANCY AS AN INDICATOR OF DEVELOPMENT

Numerous indicators of development have been proposed during the past 50 years. Though per capita income or GDP remains the most popular measure, several attempts have been made to devise a better measure. These efforts have taken mainly two directions.

On one hand, there has been a search for a measure which would not only look at the efficiency of providing goods and services or at the "standard of living" (what GDP or income per capita do) but also reflect various aspects of the quality of life. Nordhaus and Tobin (1972) and Usher (1973), for example, suggested the inclusion of leisure in the measure of welfare. Others tried to take into account the negative impact of the level of pollution. There were many attempts to devise composite development indices which would weight, in one way or another, several more basic indicators. This was the approach taken by the U.N.R.I.S.D when it proposed its "Development Index" (see Drewnowski and Scott, 1966 or McGranahan *et al.*, 1972) or by Morris and Liser (1977) and the Overseas Development Council when they launched the idea of a "Physical Quality of Life" Index (P.Q.L.I.), a measure combining infant mortality, life expectancy at age one and the degree of literacy. This idea was extended by Ram (1982) when he suggested using Principal Component Analysis to derive the exact weights of the three components previously mentioned. Hirschberg *et al.*, (1991) used clustering analysis to derive measures of the quality of life which would take into account much more than three elements, but the Human Development Index (see Paul, 1996) which is computed each year and has become quite popular, represents a return to the idea of devising a measure derived from a small number of basic indicators of the quality of life.

A second type of criticism was used against per capita GDP or income, one which argued that pure growth was not the only aim of development and that such a goal could be in conflict with the search for a more fair distribution of incomes. Sen (1976) had already stressed that one cannot say what total national income is until one knows its distribution, and suggested (see Sen, 1974) an index of welfare combining per capita income and the inequality of incomes. Chenery *et al.*, (1974) adjusted the growth rates of developing countries for changes in their income distribution, but such weighting procedures have been subject to serious criticism (see, Beckerman, 1978).

Given the problems raised by these various attempts of devising a composite index of development, one may wonder whether Hicks and Streeten (1979) were not right when they presented arguments in favor of the use of a single measure. They favored life expectancy rather than per capita income:

"Therefore, it could be argued that some measure of health, such as life expectancy at birth, would be a good single measure of basic needs. In a sense, life expectancy is a kind of weighted 'composite' of progress in meeting physiological basic needs. It has the advantage of capturing the impact on individuals, not only of non-market factors but also of income net of taxes, transfer payments and social services, without raising all the difficulties of income per head measures, such as the appropriate unit (individual, household or family), the appropriate magnitude (capital, consumption, income), the appropriate set of prices (market prices, international prices), what to value as final goods and what as costs, etc... For these purposes it might be regarded as superior not only to a composite index of social indicators but also to GNP and to indices of income distribution[1]".

More recently Sen (1998) suggested also to use mortality as an indicator of economic success and failure. More precisely he argued that "mortality information has intrinsic importance (since a longer life is valued in itself), enabling significance (since being alive is a necessary condition for our capabilities) and associative relevance (since many other valuable achievements relate – negatively – to mortality rates[2])".

The next section will recommend the use of a development indicator that is derived from mortality data, more precisely from life tables. However rather than choosing life expectancy, we suggest to adopt an approach originally suggested by Atkinson (1970) and Kolm (1966, 1976) in the context of income inequality analysis. The general idea is to take into account the effect of uncertainty on the utility which individuals may derive from the duration of their lives.

3. UNCERTAINTY AND THE ORDINAL COMPARISON OF LIFE TABLES

The comparison of the level of mortality in two countries is generally based on the use of one indicator, life expectancy at birth. Some studies have attempted to build indices based on two measures of mortality, such as the infant mortality rate and life expectancy at age one (e.g., the Physical Quality of Life Index, put forth originally by Morris and Liser, 1977, or the Human Development Index published annually in the Human Development Report).

But a correct comparison of mortality in two countries should be based on the whole mortality schedule (i.e., the whole life table). The same kind of issue is evidently faced in finance where it is well known that decision making cannot be based only on the comparison of expected returns. This is why use is often made of what is called mean-variance analysis (see Markowitz, 1959), but although the latter has the advantage of not requiring a detailed knowledge of the whole distribution, it cannot always be applied (see Levy and Sarnat, 1972). To solve this problem, specialists of finance have devised a more

[1]Dreze and Sen (1995) also argue that GDP and growth must only be viewed as means to achieving greater capabilities (see, Sen, 1985, for more details on the concept of "capabilities").

[2]In a recent study on famines and economics Ravallion (1997) attempted to analyze survival prospects in developing countries and suggested that "the ability to avoid starvation depends in part on current consumptions, but also on the health-relevant aspects of the individual's environment, and various idiosyncratic attributes of the individual which may depend on past health and consumptions".

general criterion called "Stochastic Dominance" (see Hadar and Russel, 1969; Hanoch and Levy, 1969, Rotschild and Stiglitz, 1970 and 1971). This approach has been also applied to the comparison of life tables (see Paroush and Silber, 1980) and the main steps of such an analysis will now be summarized.

Let l_i and l_j be the survivorship curves in countries i and j. The "First Order Stochastic Dominance" criterion then states that the mortality schedule of country i will be preferred to that of country j if the curve l_i lies above the curve l_j for at least one age group, and does not lie below for any of the other age groups.

An alternative way of defining "First Order Stochastic Dominance" is to use the schedule $d(x)$ defining the number of individuals, dying at age x. If $s(x)$ denotes the number of survivors at age x, it is clear that $s(x+1) - s(x) = d(x)$. By constructing the cumulative function, $D(y) = \sum_{x \leq y} d(x)$, we can evidently state, calling D_i and D_j the schedules $D(y)$ in countries i and j, that if D_i lies below D_j for at least one age group and does not lie above for any of the other age groups, the "First Order Stochastic Dominance" criterion implies that mortality in country i is to be "preferred" to that in country j.

When the survivorship curves l_i and l_j (or the cumulative curves D_i and D_j) intersect, it is not possible to apply this criterion. Use is then made of the "Second Order Stochastic Dominance" principle. Calling F(y) the cumulative function $F(y) = \sum_{x \leq y} D(x)$, we will then state that according to the "Second Order Stochastic Dominance" principle, mortality in country i will be preferred to that in country j, if F_i and F_j (the schedules $F(x)$ in countries i and j) are such that F_i is below F_j for at least one age group, and does not lie above for any other age group. It should be emphasized that whereas "First Order Stochastic Dominance" implies neutrality towards risk, "Second Order Stochastic Dominance" assumes risk aversion in the sense that the utility of an individual which depends on the duration of his life, is a concave function (in other words the marginal utility of duration of life is positive, but decreasing). This second criterion is therefore stronger than the first, but it is more powerful since it may be also applied to the case where two survivorship curves l_i and l_j intersect, provided they do not intersect more than once.

These concepts of Stochastic Dominance have also implications concerning the use of cardinal measures summarizing the mortality schedule in two countries. Yitzhaki (1982) and Shalit and Yitzhaki (1984) have derived two interesting propositions which, though originally applied to portfolio analysis, are also useful in the analysis of mortality schedules (see Silber, 1988).

Let e_i and e_j be respectively the life expectancy at birth in country i and j and Δ_i and Δ_j, the mean differences[3] derived from the distributions d_i and d_j of the ages at death in

[3]Let a_i be the average age at death in group i, d_i the number of individuals dying at the average age at death a_i and n the number of groups distinguished. If $l_0 = \sum_{h=1}^{n} d_h$ is the so-called radix of the life table, the mean difference of the distribution of ages at death in a given population will then be defined (see, Kendall and Stuart, 1969) as

$$D = \sum_{h=1}^{n} \sum_{k=1}^{n} d_k \, d_h |a_h - a_k| / (l_0)^2$$

countries i and j, implied by the survivorship curves l_i and l_j.

The first proposition then states that $e_i \geq e_j$ and $e_i - (1/2)\triangle_i \geq e_j - (1/2)\triangle_j$ are necessary conditions for the distribution l_i to dominate the distribution l_j, according to both "First and Second Order Stochastic Dominance".

The second proposition states that if $e_i = e_j$ and if the survivorship curves l_i and l_j do not intersect more than once, the inequality $e_i - (1/2)\triangle_i \geq ej - (1/2)\triangle_j$ is a sufficient condition for l_i to dominate l_j according to stochastic dominance rules. In other words, it might often be possible to base the comparison of mortality in two countries on the use of only two summary measures, the life expectancy at birth e_0 and Gini's mean difference $\triangle$. The next section will show that by combining these two indicators e_0 and $\triangle$, it is possible to devise a new measure of economic development.

4. FROM THE CONCEPT OF LIFE EXPECTANCY TO THAT OF "EQUIVALENT LENGTH OF LIFE" (E.L.L)

In his widely cited paper on the analysis of income inequality, Atkinson (1970) defined what he called the "equally distributed equivalent level of income", which is the income which, if equally distributed among all individuals, would give society the same level of welfare as the one enjoyed presently with an unequal distribution. This idea has been applied by Silber (1983) to the case where social welfare is a function, not of the incomes of the individuals, but of the duration of their life.

Let a_i be the duration of life of individual i and let $W(a_1, \ldots, a_n) = W_0$ be the actual level of social welfare of society where n is the number of individuals. If everybody had the same duration of life a_E, society would enjoy this same level of social welfare W_0 only if $W(a_E, \ldots, a_E) = W_0$. Silber (1983) has called "Equivalent Length of Life" (E.L.L.), this duration of life which if equally enjoyed by all the individuals would give society the same level of social welfare W_0 as that presently enjoyed when durations of life are unequal. The value of a_E depends hence both on the distribution $(a_1, \ldots, a_n)$ of the durations of life (that is on the life table) and on the social welfare function W, which is chosen. Silber (1983) suggested the use of either the social welfare function proposed by Atkinson[4] (1970) or of that devised by Kolm[5] (1976). In another paper Silber (1988) used the social welfare function corresponding to the Gini Index and it can be shown (see, Donaldson and Weymark, 1980) that in such a case the "Equivalent Length of Life" a_E may be expressed as

$$a_E = e_0 - (1/2)\triangle \qquad (1)$$

[4]Using the notations of footnote 3 and adopting the social welfare function suggested by Atkinson, it can be shown (see, Silber, 1983) that if e_0 is the life expectancy at birth, the inequality I_A of the durations of life may be expressed as $I_A = 1 - (a_{ATK}/e_0)$ where $a_{ATK} = [(1/l_0)\sum_{i=1}^{n} d_i(a_i)^{1-\varepsilon}]^{1/(1-\varepsilon)}$. ε is a parameter measuring the "relative aversion to inequality" while I_{ATK} is known as Atkinson's index (see, Silber, 1983, for more details).

[5]Using again the notations of footnote 3 and adopting this time the social welfare function suggested by Kolm, it can be shown (see, Silber, 1983) that in such a case the inequality of the duration of life may be expressed as $I_{KOLM} = a_{KOLM} - e_0$ where $a_{KOLM} = (-1/\theta)ln[(1/l_0)\sum_{i=1}^{n} d_i e^{-\theta a_i}]$. θ is a parameter measuring the "absolute aversion to inequality" while I_{KOLM} is what is known as Kolm's inequality index (see, Silber, 1983, for more details).

where $\triangle$ is the mean difference of the duration of life (see footnote 4).

Since the Gini Index G of the Inequality of the durations of life may be expressed as

$$G = \frac{1}{2}\frac{\triangle}{e_0} \tag{2}$$

the life expectancy at birth e_0 and the equivalent length of life a_E are related (see, Silber, 1988) by the relation

$$a_E = e_0(1 - G) \tag{3}$$

The equivalent length of life a_E may therefore be considered as a better measure of the structure of mortality than the life expectancy at birth e_0 since it takes the inequality of the durations of life into account[6]. Therefore, if e_0 (see Hicks and Streeten, 1979) may be considered as a good indicator of economic development, the equivalent length of life should be considered as an even better indicator (see Silber, 1983).

The next section will show that it is possible to further improve the definition of a development indicator, by taking into account the asymmetry of the distribution of the durations of life.

5. THE "EQUIVALENT LENGTH OF LIFE" AND THE ASYMMETRY OF THE DISTRIBUTION OF AGES AT DEATH

In a study analyzing some of the properties of the Gini Index, Berrebi and Silber (1987) have suggested the use of a new index to measure the skewness or asymmetry of a distribution. This index A is defined as

$$A = \frac{1}{2}\frac{\triangle_R - \triangle_L}{\triangle} \tag{4}$$

where $\triangle_R$ and $\triangle_L$ are respectively the mean differences of the ages at death of those who live more or less than the median age of death, $\triangle$ being as before the mean difference of the whole distribution. Berrebi and Silber (1987) proved that $-1 \leq A \leq +1$ and that it had properties similar to those of Pearson's measure of skewness. Silber (1988) then proposed to extend the concept of "Equivalent Length of Life" by defining a summary measure of the life table which would take into account the dispersion as well as the asymmetry of ages at death. Since in uncertainty theory, other things constant, an increase of the degree of asymmetry to the right of a distribution, should have a positive effect on utility, Silber (1988) defined this "Extended Equivalent Length of Life" [7] as

$$a_A = e_0 - \frac{1}{2}\triangle(1 - A) \tag{5}$$

It may be observed that when the distribution is symmetric, $A = 0$ and $a_A = a_E$. When $A > 0$, $a_A > a_E$; in particular when $A = 1$, $a_A = e_0$. Similarly, when $A < 0$, $a_A < a_E$

[6] Note that e_0 and a_E will coincide either when the inequality of the durations of life is nil (everybody lives the same number of years) or when a linear utility function is adopted.

[7] We have not attempted to derive the social welfare function underlying the concept of "Extended Equivalent Length of Life" given in expression (5).

and when A reaches its lowest value -1, $a_A = e_0 - \triangle$. Over time there have been drastic changes in the asymmetry of the distribution of ages at death (an increase in the degree of skewness to the left) but Silber (1988), in a study of mortality in Italy between 1881 and 1970, showed that despite this negative effect, the increase in the life expectancy at birth and the decrease in the mean difference of ages at death $\triangle$ were so important, that the "Extended Equivalent Length of Life" a_A increased very significantly over time.

Whereas the study of mortality has hitherto been limited to the analysis of a given life table (e.g., comparing the summary measures derived from the life tables of males and females, as was done by Silber (1988) from Italy), it is also possible to combine the life tables corresponding to various subgroups (e.g., regions or genders) and decompose the overall mortality into mortality between and within the subgroups, as will be explained in the following section.

6. GENDER DIFFERENTIALS AND THE DECOMPOSITION OF OVERALL MORTALITY

Following earlier works, such as those of Bhattacharya and Mahalanobis (1967), Rao (1969), Pyatt (1976), Fei, Ranis and Kuo (1979), Silber (1989) has shown that the Gini Index G of overall inequality could be decomposed into the sum of a "between groups component" G_B, a "within groups component" G_W and an interaction term G_o, which somehow measures the degree of overlapping of the distributions corresponding to the various population subgroups. In his analysis, Silber (1989) derived a definition of the Gini Index based on the use of a mathematical operator which he called the G-matrix. The latter is a square matrix whose typical element g_{ij} is equal to zero if $i = j$, to -1 if $j > i$ and to $+1$ if $j < i$. When applied to life tables, such an approach defines the overall inequality G (Gini Index) of ages at death as

$$G = e' G_M s \tag{6}$$

where e is the one by k row vector of the proportions $(d_i / \sum_{i=1}^{k} d_i)$ of individuals dying at age i, k being the number of age groups, while s is a $k \times 1$ column vector of the shares $(a_i d_i / \sum_{i=1}^{k} a_i d_i)$ of the various age groups in the overall number of years lived by the population analyzed[8]. Note that G_M is a k by k G-matrix and that both e' and s are ranked by decreasing values of the ages at death a_i.

If we apply such an analysis to the study of gender differentials in mortality, it can be shown (see Silber, 1989) that the between genders inequality before death (inequality G_B of the ages at death) may be expressed as

$$G_B = \frac{1}{2} \frac{e_M - e_F}{e_M + e_F} \tag{7}$$

where e_M and e_F are respectively equal to the male and female life expectancies.

In the definition given in (7), it was assumed that the "sizes of the male and female populations" are equal, which is generally true since life tables are constructed by starting

[8]The product $a_i d_i$ is also called the persons-years T_i.

with a given number of births, the so-called radix of the life table (usually 10'000 or 100'000, depending on the degree of precision desired).

Silber (1989) has also proven that the within-genders Gini index of the inequality of the ages at death (G_W) could be written as

$$G_W = (1/2) \sum_{h=1}^{2} b_h G_h \tag{8}$$

where (1/2) is, as just indicated, the weight of gender h in the total population, b_h its weight in the total number of person-years, while G_h is the Gini Index of the Inequality of the ages at death among persons of gender h.

The overall Gini Index is then defined as

$$G = G_B + G_W + G_o \tag{9}$$

where G_o measures the overlapping of the two distributions (males and females) of ages at death. Silber (1989) showed how to compute G_o while more details on this concept of overlapping are given in Deutsch and Silber (1996) and Deutsch and Silber (1999).

In the following sections an analysis of the evolution over time (1930-1990) of mortality in Switzerland and in particular of the changes in the Equivalent Lengths of Life a_E and a_A will be presented. We will also compare the changes which occurred during the more recent period (1970-1990) in Switzerland and seven other European countries (Austria, Belgium, Denmark, Finland, France, Sweden and the United Kingdom).

7. THE EQUIVALENT LENGTHS OF LIFE AS INDICATORS OF THE DEVELOPMENT OF SWITZERLAND DURING THE PAST SIXTY YEARS

An ordinal approach to the study of the evaluation of mortality in Switzerland, based on the concepts summarized in Section 2, is presented in Table 1. A sign + in a given case comparing years t and t' indicates that mortality was lower in year t' (on the basis of the criterion of First Order Stochastic Dominance). It appears that male as well as female mortality decreased over time. The data indicate clearly that for both genders the distribution of ages at death in year t was "better" than that in year $t-1$, this being true for all t, except in three cases. First when comparing the mortality schedules (male and female) of 1960 and 1970, we observed that they intersected and this was also the case when we tried to apply the rules of Second Order Stochastic Dominance. Second no clear conclusion could be drawn when comparing the male mortality schedules for the years 1986 and 1990 on the basis of First Stochastic Dominance Rules. When Second Order Stochastic Dominance were applied, we could however conclude that in 1990 male mortality was lower than 1986.

Table 2 indicates that there was for both genders an increase over time in life expectancy as well as in the Equivalent Length of Life, whether the latter takes only the dispersion of ages at death into account (E.L.L.) or also the asymmetry of the distribution (E.L.L.').

Table 1

First Order Stochastic Dominance and Mortality Comparisons
(Switzerland, 1930-1990)

I - Male Mortality

Year \ Year'	1941	1951	1960	1970	1975	1980	1986	1990
1930	+	+	+	+	+	+	+	+
1941		+	+	+	+	+	+	+
1951			+	+	+	+	+	+
1960				?	+	+	+	+
1970					+	+	+	+
1975						+	+	+
1980							+	+
1986								?

II - Female Mortality

Year \ Year'	1941	1951	1960	1970	1975	1980	1986	1990
1930	+	+	+	+	+	+	+	+
1941		+	+	+	+	+	+	+
1951			+	+	+	+	+	+
1960				?	+	+	+	+
1970					+	+	+	+
1975						+	+	+
1980							+	+
1986								+

Table 2

Life Expectancy at Birth and Equivalent Lengths of Life
(Switzerland, 1930-1990)

Year	Men			Women		
		Equivalent Lengths of Life			Equivalent Lengths of Life	
	Life Expectancy e_0	E.L.L.	E.L.L.'	Life Expectancy e_0	E.L.L.	E.L.L.'
1930	59.10	46.17	41.93	63.32	51.04	46.41
1941	62.75	50.94	46.74	66.89	55.86	51.48
1951	66.39	56.16	52.53	70.82	61.69	58.21
1960	68.73	59.33	56.14	73.94	65.99	62.99
1970	69.33	59.66	56.21	75.47	67.49	63.98
1975	70.98	61.86	58.66	77.26	69.90	66.44
1980	71.87	63.08	60.01	78.14	71.12	67.68
1986	73.41	65.09	62.17	79.45	72.95	69.43
1990	73.88	65.83	63.05	79.96	73.83	70.56

Table 3
Annual Growth Rates (in %) of Life Expectancy and Equivalent Lengths of Life in Switzerland, (1930-1990)

Period	Life Expectancy e_0		Equivalent Lengths of Life			
			E.L.L.		E.L.L.'	
	Men	Women	Men	Women	Men	Women
1930-41	0.546	0.500	0.897	0.824	0.992	0.947
1941-51	0.565	0.573	0.980	0.998	1.175	1.233
1951-60	0.386	0.480	0.612	0.751	0.741	0.881
1960-70	0.090	0.205	0.055	0.225	0.012	0.156
1970-75	0.466	0.470	0.727	0.704	0.857	0.757
1975-80	0.250	0.227	0.391	0.347	0.456	0.371
1980-86	0.354	0.277	0.524	0.424	0.591	0.426
1986-90	0.160	0.160	0.283	0.300	0.352	0.404

Table 3 gives the annual growth rates, for both genders, of the life expectancy and Equivalent Lengths of Life. It appears that for all indicators the growth rates were higher between 1930 and 1960 than afterwards, the growth rates being exceptionally low during the period 1960-1970[9]. As a whole, the growth was highest for the indicator E.L.L.' and lowest for the life expectancy. During the period 1970-1990, there was an overall, though not uniform, decrease in growth rates and here again for each subperiod growth rates were highest for E.L.L.' and lowest for life expectancy at birth. As a whole the picture concerning these growth rates is quite similar for both genders.

Table 4 gives detailed information on the components of inequality before death, the overall inequality being decomposed, as indicated earlier, into between (G_{BET}) and within (G_{WITH}) genders inequality, with a residual term (G_{OVER}) measuring the degree of overlap between the distribution of ages at death of both genders. The data indicate that overall inequality (G_{TOT}) as well as within genders inequality (G_{WITH}) decreased over time. A decrease in inequality is also observed for each gender separately (G_{MEN} and G_{WOMEN}), though for males there was a temporary increase between 1960 and 1970[10]. The degree of overlap between the distribution of ages at death of both genders also decreased over time and this change took place in parallel with an *increase* in the between genders inequality (G_{BET}) of ages at death. Table 4 gives also the value of an absolute measure of dispersion, the mean difference, for both genders. Here again, for both genders, there is a clear decrease over time in this mean difference ($MDIF_{MEN}$ and $MDIF_{WOMEN}$). Finally, Table 4 gives the value of the asymmetry index that was defined in Section 5 and it appears that in the 1970's and 1980's there was a higher degree of skewness to the left than in the 1930's or 1940's, although there seems to have been a slight decrease in this asymmetry between 1986 and 1990. Such an increase over time in the degree of asymmetry to the left is to be expected, as more and more people tend to live longer, so that the dispersion of ages at death among those who have a high duration

[9]This increase may be due to the fact that different data sources were used in 1960 and 1970.
[10]Here again this may be a consequence of the use of different data sources.

of life is much smaller than that of those who die at a younger age (for more details, see again the definition of the asymmetry index A in Section 5).

Table 4

Inequality Before Death in Switzerland (1930 - 1990)

Year	Total G_{TOT}	Between Genders G_{BET}	Within Genders G_{WITH}	Overlap G_{OVER}	Within Male Population G_{MEN}	Within Female Population G_{WOMEN}
1930	0.207	0.017	0.103	0.087	0.219	0.194
1941	0.177	0.016	0.088	0.073	0.188	0.165
1951	0.142	0.016	0.071	0.056	0.154	0.129
1960	0.123	0.018	0.061	0.044	0.137	0.108
1970	0.125	0.021	0.061	0.043	0.140	0.106
1975	0.114	0.021	0.056	0.037	0.128	0.095
1980	0.109	0.021	0.053	0.035	0.122	0.090
1986	0.100	0.020	0.048	0.032	0.133	0.082
1990	0.095	0.020	0.046	0.030	0.109	0.077

Year	Mean Difference Among Men $MDIF_{MEN}$	Mean Difference Among Women $MDIF_{WOMEN}$	Assymetry Index A for Men	Assymetry Index A for Women
1930	25.86	24.56	-0.328	-0.377
1941	23.62	26.06	-0.355	-0.397
1951	20.46	18.26	-0.354	-0.381
1960	18.80	15.90	-0.340	-0.378
1970	19.39	15.96	-0.356	-0.440
1975	18.24	14.72	-0.351	-0.470
1980	17.58	14.04	-0.349	-0.489
1986	16.64	13.02	-0.351	-0.540
1990	16.10	12.27	-0.346	-0.531

Instead of looking at the changes over time in the value of various indicators of development in Switzerland, it is also possible to compare the situation of Switzerland during the period 1970–1990 with that of seven other European countries. Such an approach will be taken in the following section.

8. COMPARING THE LEVELS OF DEVELOPMENT IN SWITZERLAND AND SEVEN OTHER EUROPEAN COUNTRIES IN 1970 AND 1990

In this section we compare for the years 1970 and 1990 the life tables of Switzerland with those of Austria, Belgium, Denmark, Finland, France, Sweden and the United Kingdom, for these two years. These are the only Western European Countries for which a comparison could be made. Table 5 gives the results obtained when the comparison of the mortality schedules is based on First and Second Order Stochastic Dominance Rules.

$A + (-)$ sign in a given case indicates that in the country that is compared with Switzerland mortality is higher (lower). As a whole very few clear-cut conclusions may be drawn. One may only say that on the basis of First Order Stochastic Dominance Rules, male mortality in 1970 was higher in Denmark and lower in Sweden than in Switzerland whereas female mortality in 1970 was lower in Sweden than in Switzerland. When Second Order Stochastic Dominance Rules are applied, two additional countries have a lower female mortality than Switzerland: Denmark and France.

Table 5
Comparing the Mortality Schedules in Switzerland and Seven Other European Countries in 1970 and 1990

Other Countries	1970				1990			
	Male Mortality		Female Mortality		Male Mortality		Female Mortality	
	FOSD	SOSD	FOSD	SOSD	FOSD	SOSD	FOSD	SOSD
Austria	?	?	?	?	?	+	?	?
Belgium	?	?	?	?	?	?	?	?
Denmark	+	+	?	-	?	?	?	?
Finland	?	?	?	?	?	?	?	?
France	?	?	?	-	+	+	?	?
Sweden	-	-	-	-	?	-	?	?
UK	?	?	?	?	?	?	?	+

A look at the 1990 data indicates that the relative situation of Switzerland improved since Swedish mortality in 1990 was lower than that of Switzerland only when Second Order Stochastic Dominance Rules are applied and this being true only for males. On the other hand male mortality in Switzerland was lower than in France according to F.O.S.D. Rules; male mortality was also lower in Switzerland than in Austria according to S.O.S.D. Rules. Finally female mortality in Switzerland was lower than that of the United Kingdom according to S.O.S.D.

Rather than looking at the whole mortality schedules, one may also compare summary measures. Tables 6 and 8 indicate that in 1970 the ranking of Switzerland was quite low, whatever indicator one looks at, this being true for males and females. For male mortality Switzerland had the third rank for life expectancy, the fourth rank for the Equivalent Length of Life E.L.L. and the fifth rank for E.L.L.' The ranking was quite similar for females.

In 1990 however for both genders and all indicators Switzerland had either the first or second rank. One may also note that in 20 years, life expectancy at birth in Switzerland increased by 4.5 years (for men and women). For the Equivalent Length of Life the increase was even higher (5.5 to 6 years for E.L.L. and almost 7 years for E.L.L.'), for both genders. Table 9 confirms this improvement. It gives the annual growth rates of the three indicators and it turns out that for life expectancy at birth the growth rate was around 0.3% for both genders. For the Equivalent Length of Life it was between 0.45% and 0.5% for E.L.L. and 0.49% and 0.58% for E.L.L.'.

Table 6

Life Expectancy at Birth and Equivalent Lengths of Life in 8 European Countries around 1970 and 1990

Year	Country	Men			Women		
		e_0	E.L.L.	E.L.L.'	e_0	E.L.L.	E.L.L.'
1970	Austria	66.50	56.86	53.76	73.31	65.05	61.93
1970	Belgium	67.77	58.56	55.81	73.95	65.92	62.92
1970	Denmark	70.73	61.98	59.33	75.54	67.90	64.97
1970	Finland	66.13	57.03	54.69	74.29	66.91	64.42
1970	France	68.53	59.26	56.53	75.66	67.88	64.67
1970	Sweden	72.08	63.71	61.01	76.77	69.68	66.83
1970	Switzerland	69.35	59.66	56.21	75.47	67.49	63.98
1970	UK	68.65	59.99	57.59	74.65	66.73	63.78
1991	Austria	72.40	64.02	61.34	78.63	72.18	69.30
1989	Belgium	72.34	64.39	62.03	78.51	71.92	68.94
1990	Denmark	72.04	63.95	61.65	77.15	70.01	67.14
1990	Finland	70.87	62.46	60.15	78.40	71.97	69.26
1990	France	72.54	63.87	61.01	79.96	73.74	70.31
1991	Sweden	74.76	67.33	64.94	79.68	73.56	70.54
1990	Switzerland	73.88	65.83	63.05	79.96	73.83	70.57
1989	UK	72.58	64.90	62.77	77.60	70.80	68.10

This important improvement in the relative ranking of Switzerland shows up also in Tables 7 and 8, when looking at the various components of Inequality before death. Concerning overall inequality (G_{TOT}) and within genders inequality (G_{WITH}), the relative position of Switzerland clearly improved between 1970 and 1990, this being also true for the Gini Index of ages at death for men (G_{MEN}) and women (G_{WOMEN}) as well as for the absolute measures of dispersion ($MDIF_{MEN}$) and $MDIF_{WOMEN}$). On the other hand, one may note that the position of Switzerland concerning inequality between the genders (G_{BET}) deteriorated over time as in 1970, among the seven countries, it had the third smallest inequality level, while in 1990 it had only the fifth rank.

9. CONCLUDING REMARKS

Using life expectancy and a mesure related to the latter called E.L.L., the "Equivalent Length of Life", as measures of development, this paper has shown how important the decrease in mortality has been in Switzerland during the period 1930- 1990. This progress concerns both genders, the growth rates in life expectancy and in the Equivalent Length of Life being generally higher for women than for men. It also appears that a greater improvement is observed on the basis of the measure E.L.L. than on that of life expectancy, a result which indicates that there was a decrease in the dispersion of the durations of life at the same time as there was an increase in the mean duration. As a whole growth was stronger during the period 1930- 1960 than during the following thirty years.

Table 7

Inequality Before Death in Eight European Countries around 1970 and 1990

Year	Country	G_{TOT}	G_{BET}	G_{WITH}	G_{OVER}	G_{MEN}	G_{WOMEN}	$MDIF_{MEN}$	$MDIF_{WOMEN}$	Asymmetry Index A Men	Asymmetry Index A Women
1970	Austria	0.131	0.024	0.064	0.043	0.145	0.113	19.28	16.52	-0.322	-0.377
1970	Belgium	0.125	0.022	0.061	0.042	0.136	0.109	18.42	16.06	-0.298	-0.373
1970	Denmark	0.114	0.016	0.056	0.041	0.124	0.101	17.50	15.28	-0.303	-0.383
1970	Finland	0.123	0.029	0.059	0.035	0.138	0.099	18.20	14.76	-0.257	-0.338
1970	France	0.122	0.025	0.059	0.038	0.135	0.103	18.54	15.56	-0.294	-0.412
1970	Sweden	0.106	0.016	0.052	0.038	0.116	0.092	16.74	14.18	-0.323	-0.401
1970	Switzerland	0.125	0.021	0.061	0.043	0.140	0.106	19.38	15.96	-0.356	-0.440
1970	UK	0.119	0.021	0.058	0.040	0.126	0.106	17.32	15.84	-0.278	-0.369
1991	Austria	0.101	0.021	0.049	0.032	0.116	0.082	16.76	12.90	-0.320	-0.445
1989	Belgium	0.100	0.020	0.048	0.031	0.110	0.084	15.90	13.18	-0.297	-0.453
1990	Denmark	0.104	0.017	0.051	0.036	0.112	0.092	16.18	14.28	-0.283	-0.403
1990	Finland	0.104	0.025	0.050	0.029	0.119	0.082	16.82	12.86	-0.274	-0.422
1990	France	0.102	0.024	0.049	0.029	0.120	0.078	17.34	12.44	-0.330	-0.551
1991	Sweden	0.090	0.016	0.044	0.030	0.099	0.077	14.86	12.24	-0.323	-0.492
1990	Switzerland	0.095	0.020	0.046	0.030	0.109	0.077	16.10	12.26	-0.346	-0.531
1989	UK	0.099	0.017	0.048	0.034	0.106	0.088	15.36	13.60	-0.277	-0.397

Table 8

Comparing the Ranking of Eight European Countries for Various Indicators around 1970 and 1990

Country	Life Expectancy[1]				E.L.L.				E.L.L.'			
	Men		Women		Men		Women		Men		Women	
	1970	1990	1970	1990	1970	1990	1970	1990	1970	1990	1970	1990
Austria	7	5	8	4	8	5	8	4	8	6	8	4
Belgium	6	6	7	5	6	4	7	6	6	4	7	6
Denmark	2	7	3	8	2	6	2	8	2	5	2	8
Finland	8	8	6	6	7	8	5	5	7	8	4	5
France	5	4	2	1	5	7	3	2	4	7	3	3
Sweden	1	1	1	3	1	1	1	3	1	1	1	2
Switzerland	3	2	4	1	4	2	4	1	5	2	5	1
UK	4	3	5	7	3	3	6	7	3	3	6	7

Country	G_{TOT}		G_{BET}		G_{WITH}		G_{MEN}		G_{WOMEN}		$MDIF_M$		$MDIF_W$	
	1970	1990	1970	1990	1970	1990	1970	1990	1970	1990	1970	1990	1970	1990
Austria	8	5	6	6	8	5	8	6	8	4	7	6	8	5
Belgium	6	4	5	4	6	3	5	4	7	6	5	3	7	6
Denmark	2	7	1	2	2	8	2	5	3	8	3	5	3	8
Finland	5	7	8	8	4	7	6	7	2	5	4	7	2	4
France	4	6	7	7	5	6	4	8	4	3	6	8	4	3
Sweden	1	1	2	1	1	1	1	1	1	1	1	1	1	1
Switzerland	7	2	3	5	7	2	7	3	5	1	8	4	6	2
UK	3	3	3	3	3	4	3	2	6	7	2	2	5	7

[1] The ranking of the Life Expectancy and of the Equivalent Length of Life (E.L.L. and E.L.L.') is by decreasing order, that of the other indicators by increasing order.

Table 9
Annual Growth Rates (in %) of Life Expectancy and Equivalent Lengths of Life in Eight European Countries during the Period 1970 - 1990

Period	Country	Life Expectancy at birth e_0		Equivalent Lengths of Life E.L.L.		Equivalent Lengths of Life E.L.L.'	
		Men	Women	Men	Women	Men	Women
1970-91	Austria	0.406	0.334	0.566	0.496	0.630	0.537
1970-89	Belgium	0.344	0.315	0.501	0.460	0.558	0.482
1970-90	Denmark	0.092	0.106	0.157	0.153	0.192	0.164
1970-90	Finland	0.347	0.270	0.456	0.365	0.477	0.363
1970-90	France	0.285	0.277	0.375	0.415	0.382	0.419
1970-91	Sweden	0.183	0.186	0.277	0.271	0.313	0.271
1970-90	Switzerland	0.317	0.289	0.493	0.450	0.576	0.491
1970-89	UK	0.293	0.204	0.415	0.312	0.454	0.346

This study has also shown that, as a whole, during the period 1970- 1990, progress in Switzerland was greater than in the other seven European countries for which data were available. This is particularly true for the overall inequality of the durations of life and for the gender-specific inequality before death. The data indicate however that for the between genders inequality in the duration of life, improvement in Switzerland was weaker than in several other countries.

REFERENCES

1. Atkinson, A. B. (1970), "On the Measurement of Inequality", *Journal of Economic Theory*, 2, 46-68.
2. Beckerman, W. (1978), *Measures of Leisure, Equality and Welfare*, Paris, O.E.C.D.
3. Berrebi, Z. M. and J. Silber (1987), "Dispersion, Asymmetry and the Gini Index of Inequality", *International Economic Review*, 28, 331-338.
4. Bhattacharya, N. and B. Mahalanobis (1967), "Regional Disparities in Consumption in India", *Journal of the American Statistical Association*, 62:
5. Chenery, H., M Ahluwalia, C. L. E. Bell, J. H. Duloy and J. Jolly (1974), *Redistribution with Growth*, London.
6. Deutsch, J. and J. Silber (1996), "The Overlapping of Distributions: Alternative Measures and their Application to the Analysis of Consumption Patterns", in Chakravarty, Condoo and Mukherjee, editors, *Econometrics; Theory and Practice, Essays in Honor of Professor N. Bhattacharya*, New Delhi, Allied Publishers.
7. Deutsch, J. and J. Silber (1999), "The Decomposition of Inequality by Population Subgroups and the Analysis of Interdistributional Inequality", in J. Silber, *Handbook on Income Inequality Measurement*, Boston, Kluwer Academic Publishers.
8. Donaldson, D. and J. Weymark (1980), "A Single Parameter Generalization of the Gini Indices of Inequality", *Journal of Economic Theory*, 22, 67-87.

9. Drewnowsky, J. and W. Scott (1966), "The Level of Living Index", United Nations Research Institute for Social Development, report No. 4, Geneva.
10. Dreze, J. and A. K. Sen (1995), *India: Economic Development and Social Opportunity*, Delhi, Oxford University Press.
11. Fei, J. C. H., G. Ranis and S. W. Y. Kuo (1979), *Growth with Equity: the Taiwan Case*, Oxford University Press, New York.
12. Hadar, J. and W. R. Russel (1969), "Rules for Ordering Uncertain Prospects", *American Economic Review*, 59, 25-34.
13. Hanoch, G. and H. Levy (1969), "The Efficiency Analysis of Choices Involving Risks", *Review of Economic Studies*, 36, 335-346.
14. Hicks, N. and P. Streeten (1979), "Indicators of Development, The Search for a Basic Needs Yardstick", *World Development*, 7: 567-580.
15. Hirschberg, J. G. ,E. Maasoumi and D. J. Slottje (1991), "Cluster Analysis for Measuring Welfare and Quality of Life Across Countries", *Journal of Econometrics*, 50, 131-150.
16. Kendall, M. G. and A. Stuart (1969), *The Advanced Theory of Statistics*, London, Charles Griffin and Company Ltd.
17. Kolm, S. C. (1976), "Unequal Equalities: I and II", *Journal of Economic Theory*, 22:416-442 and 23, 72-111.
18. Levy, H. and M. Sarnat (1972), *Investment and Portfolio Analysis*, New Yok, Wiley.
19. Markowitz, H. M. (1959), *Portfolio Selection*, A Cowles Foundation Monograph, New Haven, Yale University Press.
20. McGranahan, D. V. , C. Richard-Proust, N. V. Sovani and M. Subramanian (1972), *Contents and Measurement of Socio-Economic Development*, New York, Praeger.
21. Morris, M. D. and F. B. Liser (1977), "The P.Q.L.I.: Measuring Progress in Meeting Human Needs", Communiqué on Development Issues, No. 32, Overseas Development Council.
22. Nordhaus, W. and J. Tobin (1972), "Is Growth Obsolete", in *Economic Growth*, New York: National Bureau of Economic Research, Columbia University Press.
23. Paroush, J. and J. Silber (1980), "The Stochastic Dominance Criteria, Mortality Risk and Investment in Education: A Cross-Country Comparison", *Research in Finance*, 2, 111-120.
24. Paul, S. (1996), "A Modified Human Development Index and International Comparison", *Applied Economics Letters*, 3, 677-682.
25. Pyatt, G. (1976), "On the Interpretation and Disaggregation of Gini Coefficients", *Economic Journal*, 86, 243-255.
26. Ram, R. (1982), "Composite Indices of Physical Quality of Life, Basic Needs Fulfilment and Income: A 'Principal Component' Representation", *Journal of Development Economics*, 11, 227- 247.
27. Rao, C. R. (1969), "Two Decompositions of the Concentration Ratio", *Journal of the Royal Statistical Society*, Series A, 132:
28. Ravallion, M. (1997), "Famines and Economics", *Journal of Economic Literature*, XXXV, 1205-1242.
29. Rotschild, M. and J. Stiglitz. (1970 and 1971). "Increasing Risk: I, A Definition and II, Its Economic Consequences", *Journal of Economic Theory*, II, 225-243, and III,

66-84.
30. Sen, A. K. (1974), "Informational Bases of Alternative Welfare Approaches", *Journal of Public Economics*, 3, 387-403.
31. Sen, A. K. (1976), "Real National Income", *Review of Economic Studies*, 43, 19-39.
32. Sen, A.K. (1985), *Commodities and Capabilities.* Professor Dr. P. Hennipman Lectures in Economics, Theory, Institutions, Policy. Amsterdam, North Holland.
33. Sen, A.K. (1998), "Mortality as an Indicator of Economic Success and Failure", *Economic Journal*, 108, 1-25.
34. Shalit, H. and S. Yitzhaki (1984), "Mean-Gini, Portfolio Theory and the Pricing of Risky Assets", *Journal of Finance*, 39, 1449- 1468.
35. Silber, J. (1983), "E. L. L. (The Equivalent Length of Life) or Another Attempt of Measuring Development", *World Development*, 11, 21-29.
36. Silber, J. (1988), "On Inequality before Death and Life Tables Summary Measures", *Genus*, 44, 25-39.
37. Silber, J. (1989), "Factor Components, Population Subgroups and the Computation of the Gini Index of Inequality", *Review of Economics and Statistics*, 71, 107-115.
38. Summers, R. and A. Heston (1991), "The Penn World Table (Mark 5), An Expanded Set of International Comparisons, 1950-1988", *Quarterly Journal of Economics*, 106, 327-268.
39. Usher, D. (1973), "An Imputation to the Measure of Economic Growth for Changes in Life Expectancy", in M. Moss, editor, *The Measure of Economic and Social Performance*, New York, National Bureau of Economic Research.
40. Yitzhaki, S. (1982), "Stochastic Dominance, Mean-Variance and Gini's Mean Difference", *American Economic Review*, 72, 178-185.

PART I

(contd.)

C. Finance

Panel Data Econometrics: Future Directions
J. Krishnakumar and E. Ronchetti (Editors)

CHAPTER 6

NONLINEAR PANEL DATA MODELS WITH DYNAMIC HETEROGENEITY

Christian GOURIEROUX and Joanna JASIAK

Abstract

We introduce nonlinear panel data models for the management and control of individual risks. Our approach extends the traditional methods by allowing for nonlinearities in input variables and unobserved individual heterogeneity with possible temporal dependence. This permits us to develop nonlinear models of individual risks in the presence of moral hazard and adverse selection. In practice, these phenomena are confronted by banks and insurance companies in their basic activities of fund supply and loss coverage. Although moral hazard and adverse selection are not perfectly controllable, their effects can be alleviated by adjustments to the pure premiums and an updating scheme based on the approximated risk.

1. INTRODUCTION

An important area of application of nonlinear panel models involves the assessment of individual risks[1]. Recently, a growing concern of financial institutions is the increasing liability and falling insurance efficiency attributable in part to moral hazard and adverse selection[2]. These phenomena are difficult to control and impede appropriate risk evaluation. As they arise because of insufficiency of information available to financial institutions, a straightforward remedy consists in acquiring more knowledge about borrowers or policyholders. The strategy of banks and insurance companies is focused on learning from past experiences. Indeed, various financial and insurance products have been developed which maintain the customers wealth but allow the companies to accumulate data on the history of borrowers or policyholders. Revolving credit, where the borrower is offered a

[1]See selected applications in Mátyás, Sevestre (1996).
[2]See, Geneva Papers on Risk and Insurance, No.77, October 1995, or Loubergé (1998).

permanent varying debt, is an example of such product, since it eliminates the cost of multiple individual decisions on borrowing and new agreements on repayment. Similarly, motor vehicle insurers reward low risk customers by updating their policy premiums and granting them bonuses. These examples show that banks and insurers seek to create an environment favoring long term commitments of individuals.

It is commonly assumed that the distribution of individual risks depends on three types of factors:

i) Observed exogenous characteristics of the individual or of the contract selected by that person reveal her/his risk category.

The standard practice of credit institutions or insurance companies consists in using these characteristics to define a priori classes of homogenous risks. Within these classes any residual effect of the exogenous variables can be neglected.

ii) Updated approximations of unobserved individual factors are necessary to alleviate the asymmetry of information in favour of the individual.

This unobserved component is more accurately approximated when the observed risk history increases. The updating of this approximation underlies the current bonus-malus scheme introduced, for instance, in car insurance.

iii) Individual effort to prevent losses is unobserved and features temporal dependence.

The individual may adjust his/her effort for loss prevention according to his/her experience with past claims, the price of the contract and awareness of future consequences of an incident. The effort variable determines the moral hazard and is modeled as a dynamic unobserved factor.

The total amount of claims, confronted by companies in a fixed period of time, is an outcome of several variables of different types. The dichotomous qualitative variables indicate the occurrence of claims, the discrete variables measure the number of claims, and finally the quantitative variables with a point mass at zero, capture the total cost of claims. Due to this variety of components, *nonlinear models* are necessary to represent the magnitude of covered losses incurred in a given period.

In this paper we introduce nonlinear panel models with dynamic heterogeneity for individual risk analysis. Our approach allows for unobserved individual factors and permits us to evaluate the comparative effects of adverse selection and moral hazard. We emphasize the consequences of model specification for insurance pricing in terms of pure premiums, the premium updating and the Value at Risk.

The paper is organized as follows. In section 2, we present the linear credibility theory introduced into the actuarial literature by Bailey (1945), (1950), Buhlmann (1967), (1979), and Buhlmann and Straub (1970). We give the explicit form of the associated linear panel model and discuss its limitations affecting both the premium updating scheme and the description of individual structural behavior [see, Balestra, Nerlove (1996), Balestra (1996)].

Significant improvements are obtained by extending the model and introducing dynamic heterogeneity. In particular, we illustrate the advantage of including an unobserved, autoregressive factor of order one. In section 3, we propose nonlinear panel models with dynamic heterogeneity. In this approach, the unobserved heterogeneity is not uniquely defined. We use the example of car insurance, where the risk is measured by a bivariate endogenous variable consisting of the number of claims and their total cost to explain how the initial heterogeneity factors can be transformed into gaussian heterogeneity factors.

This paper presents an analysis performed within a class of homogenous risks, eliminating the presence of explanatory variables. The partition of risks into homogenous classes is out of the scope of this paper. We refer interested readers to Gourieroux (1998a).

2. LINEAR CREDIBILITY THEORY

We consider a set of individuals $i = 1, \ldots, n$. For each period $t = 1, \ldots, T$, the risk associated with individual i is measured by a unidimensional quantitative variable $Y_{i,t}$. In applications to loan and insurance management, the individuals i are assumed to belong to the same homogenous class of risk. This implies in particular that their contracts are of the same type, start at approximately the same date, and the individuals are of the same age when the contract becomes effective. The variable t is the index measuring the time since the beginning of the contract and $Y_{i,t}$ denotes the total cost of the claims for period t. The linear credibility theory assumes implicitly that these variables admit continuous distributions on the real line (in some cases an even stronger assumption of gaussian distributions is imposed). This assumption is quite unrealistic considering the nature of dependent variables in the credit and insurance analysis. It is introduced in the next subsection for simplicity of exposition, and is later relaxed in the context of complex nonlinear panel models.

2.1. The basic model

In general, the basic model is presented in the literature in a semi-parametric framework [see, Buhlmann (1967), (1969), Buhlmann, Straub (1970)]. Nevertheless, its implementation requires the full specification of the distribution, especially when the Value at Risk needs to be determined. A possible choice is the gaussian distribution, which underlies the model discussed below. The model is a simple linear panel model with individual heterogeneity and without explanatory variables. The endogenous variables are such that:

$$Y_{i,t} = m + u_i + v_{i,t}, \quad i = 1, \ldots, n, \ t = 1, \ldots, T, \tag{1}$$

where:

i. the two error terms u_i, $i = 1, \ldots, n$, $v_{i,t}$, $i = 1, \ldots, n$, $t = 1, \ldots, T$ are independent;

ii. the term u_i representing heterogeneity is gaussian, has zero mean and a fixed variance η^2;

iii. the error terms $v_{i,t}$ are gaussian with zero mean, and a fixed variance σ^2.

The main objective of risk analysis is prediction of future risks. It becomes feasible whenever the risks are observed over some period of time, say from time 0 until time T, and no attrition is involved. More precisely, for a given horizon h we evaluate the expected total cost $E_T(Y_{i,T+h})$, also called the pure premium, along with the variability of this cost $V_T(Y_{i,T+h})$, and the corresponding quantiles, called the Values at Risk and defined by: $P_T[Y_{i,T+h} > VaR(T,h,\alpha)] = \alpha$. The indexed variables E_T, V_T, P_T indicate that computations are performed conditional on the information available at time T.

Under the basic specification the conditional distribution of $(Y_{i,T+h})$ given $I_T = [Y_{i,t},\ i = 1,\dots,n,\ t = 1,\dots,T]$ is gaussian. Its mean is:

$$\begin{aligned} E[Y_{i,T+h}|\, I_T] &= E[Y_{i,T+h}|\, Y_{i,1},\dots,Y_{i,T}] \\ &= m + E[u_i|\, Y_{i,1},\dots,Y_{i,T}] \\ &= m + E[u_i|\, \overline{Y}_{i,T}] \end{aligned} \tag{2}$$

$$\text{(where:} \quad \overline{Y}_{i,T} = \frac{1}{T}\sum_{t=1}^{T} Y_{i,t})$$

$$\begin{aligned} &= m + \frac{Cov(u_i, \overline{Y}_{i,T})}{V(\overline{Y}_{i,T})}(\overline{Y}_{i,T} - m) \\ &= m + \frac{\eta^2}{\eta^2 + \sigma^2/T}(\overline{Y}_{i,T} - m). \end{aligned} \tag{3}$$

The conditional variance is given by:

$$V[Y_{i,T+h}|\, I_T] = \frac{\sigma^2/T}{\eta^2 + \sigma^2/T}. \tag{4}$$

The equation (2) defines the pure premium formula, i.e. the basic concept of the credibility theory. The pure premium is a weighted average of the expected cost m for the specific class of risks and the individual empirical average cost $\overline{Y}_{i,T}$:

$$\pi_{i,T}(h) = E(Y_{i,T+h}|\, I_T) = \frac{\eta^2}{\eta^2 + \sigma^2/T}\overline{Y}_{i,T} + \frac{\sigma^2/T}{\eta^2 + \sigma^2/T}m. \tag{5}$$

During the coverage period, data are collected while the observed history is increasing. Simultaneously, the pure premium is being modified:

$$\begin{aligned} \pi_{i,T+1}(h-1) - \pi_{i,T}(h) &= E(Y_{i,T+h}|\, I_{T+1}) - E(Y_{i,T+h}|\, I_T) \\ &= \left[\frac{\eta^2}{\eta^2 + \sigma^2/(T+1)} - \frac{\eta^2}{\eta^2 + \sigma^2/T}\right][\overline{Y}_{i,T} - m] \\ &\quad + \frac{\eta^2}{\eta^2 + \sigma^2/(T+1)}[\overline{Y}_{i,T+1} - \overline{Y}_{i,T}]. \end{aligned} \tag{6}$$

The modification is determined by two terms. The first one is related to the adjustment of weights assigned to the amount of experience. It indicates that a long contract history is more reliable than a short one. The second component results from the updating of individual average costs.

Recall that this section is based on a restrictive model, which assumes that the individual heterogeneity u_i is independent of the time t. This implies several drawbacks:

i. From a structural point of view the basic model cannot account for an individual effort, which is endogenously modified in time. In particular the additional risk due to the moral hazard is neglected and its price is set equal to zero arbitrarily.

ii. The informational advantage of the individual vanishes when a long history is observed. Indeed, when T tends to infinity, we get $\lim_{T\to\infty} \overline{Y}_{i,T} - m = u_i$, and the unobserved heterogeneity becomes known.

iii. Moreover, when T is large, the pure premium becomes $\pi_{i,T}(h) \approx \overline{Y}_{i,T}$. If the price of the contract is based on this pure premium, each individual will asymptotically finance his/her own losses and not those of other insured persons. Asymptotically the insurer creates a balance between the claims and payments of a given individual over various periods, instead of a balance between claims and payments of different individuals in a fixed period. In some sense, the task of insurance company becomes management of spendings and savings of individuals. The insurer is not capable to spread the risk between individuals.

iv. Finally the basic model implies that the conditional distribution of future risks does not depend on the horizon h.

2.2. Dynamic individual heterogeneity

An immediate extension of the basic model is obtained by introducing a time varying effort variable $u_{i,t}$. To illustrate this technique we represent the dynamics of the effort variable as an autoregressive process of order one. The rationale behind this approach is to incorporate in the model consistent adjustments to individual behavior in order to prevent incidents. The model becomes:

$$Y_{i,t} = m + u_{i,t} + v_{i,t}, \quad i = 1, \ldots, n, \ t = 1, \ldots, T, \ldots, \tag{7}$$

where:

i. $u_{i,t} = \phi u_{i,t-1} + \eta\sqrt{1-\phi^2}\epsilon_{i,t}$, $i = 1, \ldots, n$, $t = 1, \ldots, T$ with $|\phi| < 1$;

ii. the two error terms $\epsilon_{i,t}$ and $v_{i,t}$, $i = 1, \ldots, n$, $t = 1, \ldots, T$ are independent as are the initial values of the individual heterogeneity $u_{i,0}$, $i = 1, \ldots, n$;

iii. the error terms $\epsilon_{i,t}$, $i = 1, \ldots, n$, $t = 1, \ldots, T, \ldots$ are gaussian with zero mean and unit variance;

iv. the error terms $v_{i,t}$, $i = 1, \ldots, n$, $t = 1, \ldots, T, \ldots$ are gaussian with zero mean and variance σ^2;

v. the initial heterogeneity factors $u_{i,0},\ i = 1,\dots,n$ are gaussian with zero mean and variance η^2.

The specification given above differs from the standard panel model with individual effects and autocorrelated errors which is usually written as :

$$Y_{i,t} = m + u_i + v_{i,t},$$

where $v_{i,t}$ is autoregressive of order one. It seems important for the purpose of interpretation to impose temporal dependence of the u term while keeping the intrinsic error term $v_{i,t}$ unchanged. Indeed, even if the effort component and the intrinsic component cannot be identified in the linear framework, they are easily distinguished in the nonlinear framework considered in section 3. Moreover we introduce in the model (7) a specific parametrization of the autoregressive process, which ensures that the marginal distribution of $u_{i,t}$ is gaussian, with zero mean and variance η^2. In particular, the marginal distribution does not depend on the autoregressive coefficient ϕ. In the limiting case $\phi = 1$, the process $u_{i,t}$ is time independent: $u_{i,t} = u_{i,0},\ t = 1,\dots,T$, and stationary. The unit root case corresponds to the basic model of subsection 2.1. The parameter ϕ can be viewed as a coefficient of effort updating by the individual: the lower ϕ, the stronger is the individual effort adjustment.

The serial correlation of effort variables results in significant modifications of prediction formulas. Let us consider the pure premium prediction at horizon h. We get:

$$\begin{aligned} E_T(Y_{i,T+h}) &= m + E_T(u_{i,T+h}) \\ &= m + \phi^h E_T[u_{i,T}] \\ &= m + \phi^h Cov[u_{i,T}, (Y_{i,T},\dots,Y_{i,1})'] \left[V \begin{pmatrix} Y_{i,T} \\ \vdots \\ Y_{i,1} \end{pmatrix} \right]^{-1} \begin{bmatrix} Y_{i,T} - m \\ \vdots \\ Y_{i,1} - m \end{bmatrix}. \end{aligned}$$

Let us denote by $J(\phi)$ the $T \times T$ matrix defined by:

$$J(\phi) = \begin{bmatrix} 1 & \phi & \dots & \phi^{T-1} \\ \phi & \ddots & \ddots & \vdots \\ \vdots & \ddots & \ddots & \phi \\ \phi^{T-1} & \dots & \phi & 1 \end{bmatrix},$$

we get:

$$\pi_i(T,h) = m + \phi^h \eta^2 [1, \phi, \dots, \phi^{T-1}][\sigma^2 Id + \eta^2 J(\phi)]^{-1} \begin{bmatrix} Y_{i,T} - m \\ \vdots \\ Y_{i,1} - m \end{bmatrix}.$$

We note that the pure premium in general depends on the prediction horizon. For a long horizon $[h \to \infty]$ and a regression coefficient $|\phi| < 1$, the pure premium coincides with the population parameter m and the individual contract history provides no useful information. The informational advantage of the insured person depends on the prediction horizon.

When the individual effort $u_{i,T+1}$ is unknown, then even for a short prediction horizon ($h = 1$) and a long contract history ($T \to \infty$) the pure premium $\pi_i(T, 1)$ would not be equivalent to $m + u_{i,T+1}$. For instance, when $\phi = 0$, $u_{i,t}$ and $v_{i,t}$ cannot be distinguished by the econometrician and the observations are not informative to predict $Y_{i,T+1}$. Therefore the informational advantage of the individual also depends on his/her effort modification.

In a neighbourhood of fixed effort, i.e. for ϕ close to 1, we can derive the first order expansion of the pure premium [see Appendix].

3. NONLINEAR PANEL MODEL WITH HETEROGENEITY

We consider now the extension of linear credibility theory to a nonlinear framework. In the first subsection we describe the case of independent heterogeneity, illustrated by the Poisson-Gamma model with heterogeneity, used in the insurance industry. In the second subsection, we allow for temporal dependence of the heterogeneity components.

3.1. Static individual heterogeneity

As in the previous section, the risk variables are denoted by $Y_{i,t}$, whereas the individual heterogeneity is denoted by u_i. These variables may be multidimensional. The model is defined under the following set of assumptions:

i. The risk variables are independent conditional on the individual heterogeneity components u_i, $i = 1, \ldots, n$.

ii. The conditional distribution of $Y_{i,t}$ given u_i, $i = 1, \ldots, n$ depends on the conditioning variables through u_i only. Its p.d.f. belongs to a given parametric class of distributions: $f(y | u_i; \theta)$ (say), where θ is a p-dimensional parameter.

iii. The heterogeneity components u_i, $i = 1, \ldots, n$ are independent, identically distributed.

iv. The distribution of u_i is gaussian with zero mean and an identity variance covariance matrix.

Under assumptions i., ii., iii., the heterogeneity components are not uniquely defined. One can easily see that assumption iv. is also satisfied by an appropriately chosen transform of the initial heterogeneity component. Let us assume that the distribution of u_i belongs to a parametric family with the continuous p.d.f. $g(u; \alpha)$, (say). It is always possible to transform u_i into a standard gaussian variable: $u_i = G(u_i^*; \alpha)$, (say) where $u_i^* \sim N(0, Id)$ and G is a one to one function. Therefore assumption (iv) is satisfied for u_i^* as new heterogeneity component.

Under assumptions i.-iv. the sequences of risk measures corresponding to two different individuals are independent, and identically distributed. The p.d.f. of $Y_{i,1}, \dots, Y_{i,T}$ is given by:

$$l(y_{i,1}, \dots, y_{i,T}; \theta) = \int \dots \int \prod_{t=1}^{T} f(y_{i,t} | u; \theta) \psi(u) du, \tag{8}$$

where ψ denotes the p.d.f. of the (multivariate) standard gaussian distribution. The determination of the p.d.f. l may require integration by Monte Carlo methods, except for some specific models, like for example, the Poisson-Gamma model [3].

Example 3.1 : The Poisson-Gamma model with static heterogeneity.

In car insurance the risk at period t can be measured by a bidimensional variable, whose first component $Z_{i,t}$ is the number of claims and second component $X_{i,t}$ is the total cost of the claims. A common assumption is a Poisson distribution of Z [see, Hausman, Hall, Griliches (1984), Gourieroux, Monfort, Trognon (1984), Dionne, Vanasse (1989), Lemaire (1995)], and a Gamma-type distribution of X [Gourieroux (1998a)], and usually a heterogeneity factor is introduced for each component of the risk. The distribution of the heterogeneity is usually selected from the conjugate families of Poisson and Gamma distributions. We denote by $u^*_{1,i}, u^*_{2,i}$ the initial heterogeneity components and by $u_{1,i}, u_{2,i}$ their gaussian transforms. The distributional assumptions of the complete model are given below:

i. The risk variables $(Z_{i,t}, X_{i,t})$, i, t varying, are independent conditional on the heterogeneity components $u^*_{1,i}, u^*_{2,i}$, i varying.

ii. The heterogeneity components $u^*_{1,i}, u^*_{2,i}$, i varying are independent.

iii. The conditional distribution of the count variable $Z_{i,t}$ given the heterogeneity components is the Poisson distribution $\mathcal{P}[u^*_{1,i}\theta_1]$.

iv. The conditional distribution of the cost variable $X_{i,t}$ given $Z_{i,t}$ and the heterogeneity component is the Gamma distribution $\gamma[\theta_3 Z_{i,t},\ \theta_2 u^*_{2,i}]$.

v. The marginal distributions of the heterogeneity components are:

$$u^*_{1,i} \sim \gamma[\theta_4, \theta_4],$$
$$u^*_{2,i} \sim \gamma[\theta_5, \theta_5].$$

Let us denote by $H(.; \theta)$ the quantile function of the $\gamma(\theta, \theta)$ distribution. Their gaussian transformed heterogeneity components are:

$$u_{1,i} = \Psi^{-1}[H(u^*_{1,i};\ \theta_4)],$$
$$u_{2,i} = \Psi^{-1}[H(u^*_{2,i};\ \theta_5)], \tag{9}$$

[3]The case of qualitative data has been discussed, for instance, by Albert, Chib (1993).

where Ψ is the c.d.f. of the standard normal distribution. Under these specific distributional assumptions we obtain explicit formulas of the conditional distribution of future risks $Y_{i,T+h} = (Z_{i,T+h}, X_{i,T+h})'$ given the contract history $Y_{i,t}, t = 1, \ldots, T$. In particular the pure premium is independent of the horizon h and is given by: [Gourieroux (1998b)]

$$\begin{aligned}\pi_{i,T}(h) &= E[X_{i,T+h} | Z_{i,t}, X_{i,t}, \, i = 1, \ldots, n, \, t = 1, \ldots, T] \\ &= \frac{\theta_3\theta_1}{\theta_2} \frac{\overline{Z}_{i,T} + \theta_4/T}{\theta_1 + \theta_4/T} \frac{\theta_2\overline{X}_{i,T} + \theta_5/T}{\theta_3\overline{Z}_{i,T} + (\theta_5 - 1)/T}.\end{aligned} \tag{10}$$

Like in the static linear credibility theory, for a long history ($T \to \infty$) the pure premium no longer depends on the population parameters θ, but instead on the individual historical summary variables $\overline{Z}_{i,T}, \overline{X}_{i,T}$ only.

3.2. Dynamic individual heterogeneity

The nonlinear panel model with static heterogeneity is extended by allowing the individual components to be time dependent. To obtain a tractable model with simple interpretation, we consider a gaussian autoregressive heterogeneity of order one. The set of assumptions becomes:

i. The risk variables are independent conditional on the individual heterogeneity components $u_{i,t}$, i, t varying.

ii. The conditional distribution of $Y_{i,t}$ given the heterogeneity components depends on the conditioning variables through $u_{i,t}$ only, and belongs to a given parametric class of distributions: $F(y | u_{i,t}; \theta)$, (say).

iii. The individual processes of heterogeneity $(u_{i,t}, \; t \geq 0)$, i varying, are independent, identically distributed.

iv. They satisfy a gaussian autoregressive model:

$$u_{i,t} = \Phi u_{i,t-1} + (Id - \Phi\Phi')^{\frac{1}{2}} \epsilon_{i,t}, \quad t \geq 1,$$

where $u_{i,0}, \epsilon_{i,t}, t \geq 1$ are independent, gaussian variables $N(0, Id)$.

4. STATISTICAL INFERENCE

Let us assume that the available information consists of observations $Y_{i,t}$, $t = 1, \ldots, n$, $t = 1, \ldots, T$. The statistical analysis of a nonlinear panel model with dynamic heterogeneity concerns: i. the estimation of the unknown parameter including the static parameter θ and the dynamic parameter Φ; ii. the approximation of the unobserved heterogeneity variables $u_{i,t}$, $i = 1, \ldots, n$, $t = 1, \ldots, T$, which may provide a criterion for classification of individuals according to the dynamics of their heterogeneity; iii. the prediction of future values of the process $Y_{i,T+h}$ used for the future risk pricing.

These various problems are rather complex due to the unobservability of the u variables. The unobservability implies that the likelihood function, which underlies the maximum likelihood method, and the conditional expectations, which are used for predicting the u [smoothing] and the future Y [filtering], involve multiple integrals. For instance, the likelihood function conditional on the initial values of heterogeneity is:

$$\prod_{i=1}^{n} \int \cdots \int \prod_{t=1}^{T} \left\{ f(y_{i,t} | u_{i,t}; \theta) \frac{\exp -\frac{1}{2}(u_{i,t} - \Phi u_{i,t-1})'(Id - \Phi\Phi')^{-1}(u_{i,t} - \Phi u_{i,t-1})}{(2\pi)^{\frac{p}{2}} det(Id - \Phi\Phi')^{\frac{1}{2}}} du_{i,t} \right\},$$

where p is the dimension of the heterogeneity. It is an integral of dimension pT proportional to the number of dated observations. The complexity of this formula suggests to replace analytical computations by simulation based approaches [Gourieroux, Monfort (1996), Richard (1996)]. Fortunately, the nonlinear factor models are easy to simulate.

Let us denote by $\epsilon_{i,t}^{s}$, $i = 1, \ldots, n$, $t = 1, \ldots, T$ independent drawings from the standard normal distribution. We define recursively simulated heterogeneity values corresponding to the parameter value Φ by : $u_{i,t}^{s}(\Phi) = \Phi u_{i,t-1}^{s}(\Phi) + (Id - \Phi\Phi')^{\frac{1}{2}} \epsilon_{i,t}^{s}$, $i = 1, \ldots, n$, $t = 1, \ldots, T$. The simulated values of the process corresponding to parameter values Φ, θ are found by independent drawings $y_{i,t}^{s}(\Phi, \theta)$ from the distribution $F[\cdot \,|\, u_{i,t}^{s}(\Phi); \theta]$. Note that the length of the simulated path can be equal to the length of the observed path, or even longer.

4.1. Estimation method

Various simulation based methods can be applied to estimate the parameters θ and Φ. We describe below two approaches based on the maximum likelihood function and the bounded memory likelihood function.

i. Simulated maximum likelihood function

The idea is to replace the intractable likelihood function by an approximation obtained from simulations. The estimator is defined by:

$$(\hat{\theta}_{T,n}^{s}, \hat{\Phi}_{T,n}^{s}) = \underset{\theta,\Phi}{Argmax} \sum_{i=1}^{n} \log \left[\frac{1}{S} \sum_{s=1}^{S} \prod_{t=1}^{T} f(y_{i,t} | u_{i,t}^{s}(\Phi), \theta) \right], \tag{11}$$

where the above multidimensional integral is replaced by an empirical average of simulations. The estimator is consistent, when n or T tends to infinity, jointly with the number of replications S [see, Gourieroux, Monfort (1996)].

ii. Bounded memory likelihood method

The simulated maximum likelihood can be quite cumbersome to implement numerically. This is due to the fact that the likelihood function is a nonlinear function of parameters, and that the initial distribution has been replaced by a mixture of conditional distributions. However it is possible to consider a simplified approach based on the marginal likelihood:

$$\prod_{i=1}^{n}\prod_{t=1}^{T} f(y_{i,t};\theta), \tag{12}$$

where $f(y;\theta)$ denotes the marginal distribution of $y_{i,t}$, and on the likelihood with memory limited to lag one: [see, Azzalini (1983)]

$$\prod_{i=1}^{n}\prod_{t=1}^{T} f(y_{i,t}, y_{i,t-1};\theta,\Phi), \tag{13}$$

where $f(y_{i,t}, y_{i,t-1};\theta,\Phi)$ denotes the marginal distribution of $y_{i,t}, y_{i,t-1}$. We propose the following two-step approach:

(a) First step: estimation of θ by a marginal maximum likelihood approach
It is interesting to note that $f(y_{i,t};\theta)$ corresponds to the so-called static model, where $\Phi = 0$. In particular the analytical form of the marginal distribution is often known, like in the example of car insurance. A first step estimator of θ is:

$$\hat{\theta}_{T,n} = \underset{\theta}{Argmax} \sum_{i=1}^{n}\sum_{t=1}^{T} \log f(y_{i,t};\theta). \tag{14}$$

(b) Second step: estimation of Φ by a bounded memory maximum likelihood approach
The joint p.d.f. $f(y_{i,t}, y_{i,t-1};\theta,\Phi)$ is a multidimensional integral, since we have to integrate out the unobservable heterogeneity $u_{i,t}, u_{i,t-1}$. However the dimension of this integral does not depend any longer on the number of observations, and is quite low. In the car insurance example it is equal to two, since obviously two integrations can be performed analytically. The second step estimators of Φ is defined by:

$$\hat{\Phi}_{T,n} = \underset{\Phi}{Argmax} \sum_{i=1}^{n}\sum_{t=1}^{T} \log f(y_{i,t}, y_{i,t-1}, \hat{\theta}_{T,n}, \Phi). \tag{15}$$

The asymptotic properties of these estimators can be found in [Azzalini (1983), Gourieroux, Jasiak (1998a)].

4.2. Prediction of future risks

As shown in the example of car insurance, the premium is obtained from the conditional distribution of $Y_{i,T+1}$ given $\underline{Y_{i,T}}$. Moreover the computations described in subsections 2.2 and 3.1 on credibility theory can be performed separately for each individual, and the predictive distribution can be found after having determined the conditional distribution of future heterogeneity $u_{i,T+1}$ given the individual history $\underline{Y_{i,T}}$.

We explain below how to obtain these distributions by using approximated bayesian updating equations. Since the computations are performed for a fixed individual, we omit the index i.

The bayesian updating equations recursively define the conditional distribution in the following steps:

i. input: the filtering distribution: $l_0(u_t|\underline{y_t})$;

ii. factor predictive distribution: $l_1(u_{t+1}|\underline{y_t}) = \int g(u_{t+1}|u_t)l_0(u_t|\underline{y_t})du_t$, where g denotes the conditional normal p.d.f. of u_{t+1} given u_t;

iii. output: the updated filtering distribution:

$$l_0(u_{t+1}|\underline{y_{t+1}}) = l_1(u_{t+1}|\underline{y_t})f(y_{t+1}|u_t)\left[\int l_1(u_{t+1}|\underline{y_t})f(y_{t+1}|u_{t+1})du_{t+1}\right]^{-1}.$$

We now replace in this recursive scheme all distributions by discrete approximations derived by simulations. The procedure is outlined below:

i. input: an approximated filtering distribution: $\hat{l}_0(u_t|\underline{y_t})$, where $\hat{l}_0$ is the empirical distribution corresponding to some values $u_t^{0,1}, \ldots, u_t^{0,S}$;

ii. approximated factor predictive distribution: $\hat{l}_1(u_{t+1}|\underline{y_t})$.
To each value $u_t^{0,s}$, we associate a value $u_t^{1,s}$ drawn from the distribution $g(.|u_t^{0,s})$. The approximation $\hat{l}_1(.|\underline{y_t})$ is the empirical distribution of $u_{t+1}^{1,1}, \ldots, u_{t+1}^{1,S}$.

iii. output: an approximated updated filtering distribution $\hat{l}_0(u_{t+1}|\underline{y_{t+1}})$.

Since the filtering distribution $l_0(u_{t+1}|\underline{y_{t+1}})$ is approximately proportional to $\hat{l}_1(u_{t+1}|\underline{y_t})$ $f(y_{t+1}|u_t)$ whose analytical form is known, we apply a standard acceptance-rejection method based on the latter function [see, e.g. Richard (1996)].

Let us compute $f_{t+1}^{\max} = \max_{s=1,\ldots,S} f(y_{t+1}|u_{t+1}^{1,s})$. Then, for each s we consider a first draw from $u_{t+1}^{1,1}, \ldots, u_{t+1}^{1,S}$ yielding $u_{1,s}^*$, say. This draw is retained with probability $\frac{f(y_{t+1}|u_{1,s}^*)}{f_{t+1}^{\max}}$, rejected otherwise. If it is rejected, we consider a second draw in $\hat{l}_1$, getting $u_{2,s}^*$, say, and reapply a selection with probability $\frac{f(y_{t+1}|u_{2,s}^*)}{f_{t+1}^{\max}}$, and so on, until we obtain a first accepted value $u_{t+1}^{1,s}$. The approximated distribution $\hat{l}_0(\cdot \mid \underline{y_{t+1}})$ is the empirical distribution of $u_{t+1}^{0,1}, \ldots, u_{t+1}^{0,S}$.

The algorithm can be continued to provide an approximated predictive distribution:

iv. approximated predictive distribution of y_{t+1} : $\hat{l}_1^P(y_{T+1}|\underline{y_T})$.

To each value $u_{T+1}^{1,s}$ corresponds a drawing y_{T+1}^s in the distribution $f(y_{T+1}|u_{T+1}^{1,s})$. The predictive distribution is approximated by the empirical distribution of y_{T+1}^s, $s = 1, \ldots, S$.

4.3. Reconstruction of past heterogeneity

It is also interesting to develop a simulation based approach to determine the conditional distribution of past heterogeneity values $u_1, \ldots, u_T$ given the observations $y_1, \ldots, y_T$. Drawings in the conditional distribution $l(u_1, \ldots, u_T|\underline{y_T})$, say, can be obtained from a Gibbs sampler [see Chib (1996) for applications to panel data models]. This procedure consists of the following steps:

i. We select initial values $u_1^0, \ldots, u_T^0$ for the past heterogeneity.

ii. Let us denote by $u_1^{j-1}, \ldots, u_T^{j-1}$ the values available at the beginning of step j. Then we draw recursively the next values u_t^j, t varying, in the conditional distribution of u_t given $u_1 = u_1^j, \ldots, u_{t-1} = u_{t-1}^j, u_{t+1} = u_{t+1}^{j-1}, \ldots, u_T = u_T^{j-1}, \underline{y_T}$. When j is sufficiently large $u_1^j, \ldots, u_T^j$ is close to a drawing from the conditional distribution $l(u_1, \ldots, u_T|\underline{y_T})$.

The advantage of Gibbs sampling is that only drawings from a conditional distribution of the type $l(u_t|u_1, \ldots, u_{t-1}, u_{t+1}, \ldots, u_T, \underline{y_T})$ have to be performed. Such drawings are easy to perform since the conditional distribution is proportional to:

$$\begin{aligned} l(u_t|u_1, \ldots, u_{t-1}, u_{t+1}, \ldots u_T, \underline{y_T}) &= l(u_t|u_{t-1}, u_{t+1}, y_t) \\ &\propto g(u_t|u_{t-1})g(u_{t+1}|u_t)f(y_t|u_t), \end{aligned}$$

which has a simple analytical form. It allows us to perform drawings using a standard acceptance-rejection method as shown in the previous subsection.

5. IMPULSE RESPONSE FUNCTIONS

5.1. Definition

The impact of heterogeneity on the observed variables can be analyzed through appropriate impulse response functions. Contrary to the suggestion by Gallant, Rossi, Tauchen (1993) to consider only consequences of a shock to y_T, say, on the future values $y_{T+1}, \ldots, y_{T+H}$, it seems more appropriate in our framework to distinguish various basic shocks, which may influence the y variable. They include the components of heterogeneity factors and the residual randomness associated with the conditional distribution $f(y_t|u_t)$, encountered in the static case $\Phi = 0$. We are essentially concerned in this section about the transmission of transitory or permanent shocks to the innovation term of the heterogeneity factor dynamics at the individual level [4].

[4] As before, the individual index is omitted.

In this experiment we fix at a constant level the individual past heterogeneity factors and the observables until date T, or alternatively the most recent realizations $u_T = u_T^0, y_T = y_T^0$, say. The future values of the observable process depend both on the sequence of future heterogeneity shocks $\epsilon_{T+1}, \dots, \epsilon_{T+H}$, and the sequence of conditional shocks $\eta_{T+1}, \dots, \eta_{T+H}$, corresponding to the drawings of y_{T+h} given u_{T+h}. These conditional shocks can be represented by independent variables with identical standard gaussian distributions [5]. The future value y_{T+H} can be written as a deterministic function of these shocks and the initial state values:

$$y_{T+H} = a_H(u_T^0, y_T^0; \epsilon_{T+1}, \eta_{T+1}, \dots, \epsilon_{T+H}, \eta_{T+H}). \tag{16}$$

Let us now assume the occurrence of some deterministic shocks to the innovation term of the heterogeneity process.

If this shock is of magnitude δ and transitory, occurring at date $T+1$, the future values become:

$$y_{T+H}^{tr}(\delta) = a_H(u_T^0, y_T^0; \epsilon_{T+1} + \delta, \eta_{T+1}, \dots, \epsilon_{T+H}, \eta_{T+H}). \tag{17}$$

If this shock is of magnitude δ and permanent, the future values become:

$$y_{T+H}^{p}(\delta) = a_H(u_T^0, y_T^0; \epsilon_{T+1} + \delta, \eta_{T+1}, \epsilon_{T+2} + \delta, \eta_{T+2}, \dots, \epsilon_{T+H} + \delta, \eta_{T+H}). \tag{18}$$

To analyse the effects of shocks we can consider the joint distribution of the benchmark variable y_{t+H} and the perturbed variable $y_{T+H}^{tr}(\delta)$ or $y_{T+H}^{p}(\delta)$ conditional on u_T^0, y_T^0, and study how it varies with the magnitude of shock δ and the horizon H [Gourieroux, Jasiak (1998)].

In practice, these joint distributions are approximated by simulations, i.e. by the empirical distributions of: $(y_{T+H}^s, y_{T+H}^{tr,s}(\delta))$ or $(y_{T+H}^s, y_{T+H}^{p,s}(\delta))$, where the simulated y values are obtained by replacing the terms $\epsilon_{T+1}, \dots, \epsilon_{T+H}$, $\eta_{T+1}, \dots, \eta_{T+H}$ in equations (16), (17), (18) by independent drawings $\epsilon_{T+1}^s, \dots, \epsilon_{T+H}^s$, $\eta_{T+1}^s, \dots, \eta_{T+H}^s$, $s = 1, \dots, S$ in the standard gaussian distribution.

It may also be of interest to describe these distributions and compare some selected moments $E\, b(y_{T+H})$ and $E\, b(y_{T+1}^{tr}(\delta))$, where b is given, or their simulated counterparts [see, e.g. Koop, Pesaran, Potter (1996)].

5.2. Impulse response analysis of the Poisson-Gamma model with dynamic heterogeneity

i) The model

We now consider the impulse response analysis for the Poisson-Gamma model with dynamic heterogeneity. The observable variable is bidimensional with two heterogeneity

[5] This is always possible using the standard inversion technique.

factors. We have: $Y_t = (X_t, Z_t)$, where X_t is the annual cost of accidents and Z_t the annual number of accidents. The conditional distributions are:

$$Z_t | u_t^*, v_t^* \sim \mathcal{P}[u_t^* \theta_1],$$

$$X_t | Z_t, u_t^*, v_t^* \sim \gamma(\theta_3 Z_t,\ \theta_2 v_t^*),$$

$$u_T^* = H^{-1}(\Psi(u_t), \theta_4),$$

$$v_t^* = H^{-1}(\Psi(v_t), \theta_5),$$

$$\begin{pmatrix} u_t \\ v_t \end{pmatrix} = \Phi \begin{pmatrix} u_{t-1} \\ v_{t-1} \end{pmatrix} + (Id - \Phi\Phi')^{1/2} \begin{pmatrix} \epsilon_{1,t} \\ \epsilon_{2,t} \end{pmatrix}.$$

The parameters θ_1 and θ_4 are set at $\theta_1 = 0.2$ and $\theta_4 = 0.1$. This implies that the expected number of accidents is $EZ_t = \theta_1 = 20\%$, while its variance $VZ_t = V(\theta_1 u_t^*) + E(\theta_1 u_t^*) = \theta_1[1 + \frac{\theta_1}{\theta_4}]$ allows for an overdispersion of $\theta_1/\theta_4 = 2$.

The parameters θ_3 and θ_2 are set at $\theta_3 = 100, \theta_2 = 0.1$. In absence of heterogeneity $v_t^* = 1 (\Leftrightarrow \theta_5 = +\infty)$, the expected cost per accident is $\theta_3/\theta_2 = 1000\$$, whereas the corresponding variance is $\theta_3/\theta_2^2 = 10000$. The magnitude of the heterogeneity v_t^* is fixed at the same level as for $u_t^* : \theta_5 = 0.1$.

Finally we introduce the independent dynamics of heterogeneity factors:

$$u_t = 0.8 u_{t-1} + \sqrt{1 - 0.8^2}\epsilon_{1t},$$
$$v_t = 0.5 v_{t-1} + \sqrt{1 - 0.5^2}\epsilon_{2t}.$$

ii) The experiment

The initial values of the heterogeneity factors are fixed at their marginal expected values: $u_T = v_T = 0$. In the next step, we perform the following experiments to examine consequences of:

experiment I:	a transitory shock of $\delta = 1$ on ϵ_{1t}.
experiment II:	a transitory shock of $\delta = -1$ to ϵ_{1t}.
experiment III:	a transitory shock of $\delta = 1$ to ϵ_{2t}.
experiment IV:	a transitory shock of $\delta = -1$ to ϵ_{2t}.
experiment V:	a permanent shock of $\delta = 1$ to ϵ_{1t}.
experiment VI:	a permanent shock of $\delta = 1$ to ϵ_{2t}.

We focus on the prediction of the total cost at horizon H. Figure 5.1 displays scatters representing joint distributions of the cost and perturbed cost for the first experiment at horizons $H = 1, 5, 10$.

FIG 5.1 : Scatterplots of costs and perturbed costs

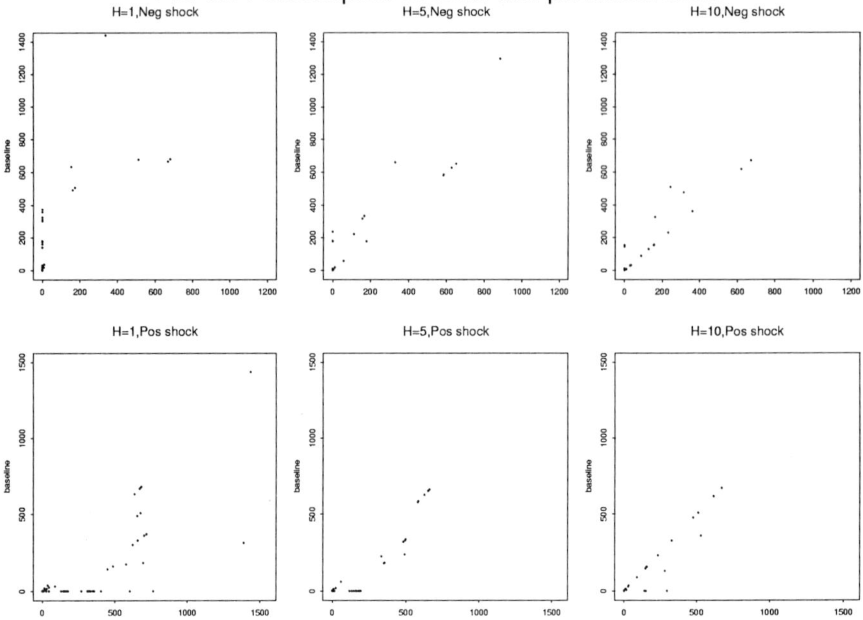

We note that under a negative [resp. positive] shock the observations tend to cluster above [resp. below] the 45 degree line. They approach the 45 degree line when the horizon increases. Since the dynamics is nonlinear, we do not observe symmetric effects of positive and negative shocks of the same magnitude. In particular, responses to positive shocks are more persistent than responses to negative shocks.

In the insurance analysis we are mainly interested in finding the expected total cost and its variance. We provide in Figures 5.2 and 5.2a the expected costs as functions of the horizon for the experiments outlined above, and in Figures 5.3 and 5.3a the associated variances.

In each figure, we plot the baseline corresponding to the absence of shock, and the moments perturbed by negative and positive shocks, respectively. We find that shocks to both heterogeneity factors impact the first and second order moments of the total cost, with effects of shocks hitting the occurrence heterogeneity being stronger. The asymmetric responses to positive and negative shocks are also observed and even more pronounced in the experiment involving the permanent shocks.

FIG 5.2 : Comparison of expected costs
shock to u1

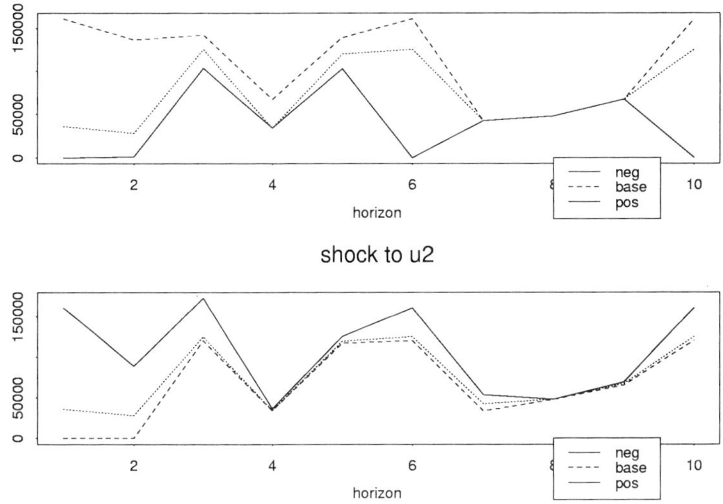

FIG 5.2a : Comparison of expected costs
permanent shock to u1

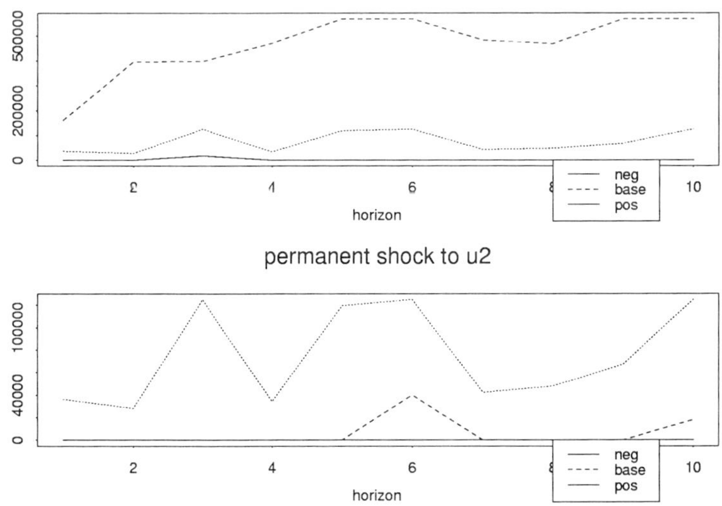

FIG 5.3 : Comparison of st.dev. of costs
shock to u1

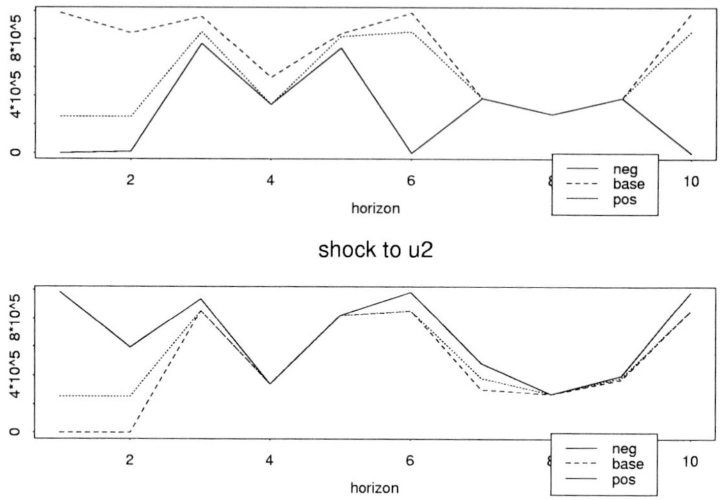

FIG 5.3a : Comparison of std.dev. of costs
permanent shock to u1

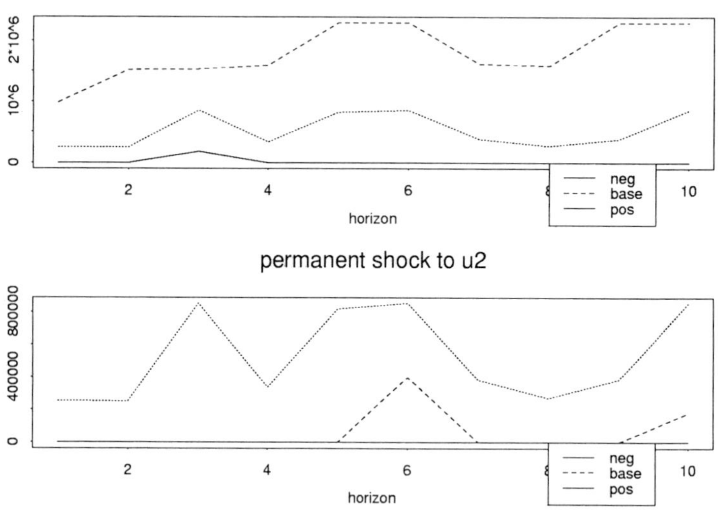

Appendix: Linear credibility theory in a neighbourhood of static individual heterogeneity

We perform the first order expansion of the pure premium given in (2.7), when $\phi \approx 1$. We denote by:

$$J(\phi) = J - (1-\phi)K + o(1-\phi),$$

the first order expansion of the matrix $J(\phi)$. The J matrix is equal to $J = ee'$, where e is the T-dimensional vector with unitary elements. The K matrix is:

$$K = \begin{bmatrix} 0 & 1 & 2 & \dots & T-1 \\ 1 & 0 & \ddots & \ddots & \vdots \\ 2 & \ddots & \ddots & \ddots & \vdots \\ \vdots & \ddots & \ddots & \ddots & 1 \\ T-1 & \dots & \dots & 1 & 0 \end{bmatrix},$$

and its first column will be denoted by k. Then we get:

$$\begin{aligned}
\pi_i(T,h) &= m + [1-h(1-\phi)]\eta^2[e' - (1-\phi)k'] \\
&\qquad [\sigma^2 Id + \eta^2 J - (1-\phi)\eta^2 K]^{-1} \begin{bmatrix} Y_{i,T}-m \\ \vdots \\ Y_{i,1}-m \end{bmatrix} + o(1-\phi) \\
&= m + [1-h(1-\phi)]\eta^2[e' - (1-\phi)k'] \\
&\qquad \{Id - (1-\phi)\eta^2(\sigma^2 Id + \eta^2 J)^{-1}K\}^{-1}[\sigma^2 Id + \eta^2 J]^{-1} \begin{bmatrix} Y_{i,T}-m \\ \vdots \\ Y_{i,1}-m \end{bmatrix} + o(1-\phi) \\
&= m + [1-h(1-\phi)]\eta^2[e' - (1-\phi)k'] \\
&\qquad \{Id + (1-\phi)\eta^2(\sigma^2 Id + \eta^2 J)^{-1}K\}[\sigma^2 Id + \eta^2 J]^{-1} \begin{bmatrix} Y_{i,T}-m \\ \vdots \\ Y_{i,1}-m \end{bmatrix} + o(1-\phi) \\
&= m + \eta^2 c'[\sigma^2 Id + \eta^2 J]^{-1} \begin{bmatrix} Y_{i,T}-m \\ \vdots \\ Y_{i,1}-m \end{bmatrix} - (1-\phi)h\eta^2 e'[\sigma^2 Id + \eta^2 J]^{-1} \begin{bmatrix} Y_{i,T}-m \\ \vdots \\ Y_{i,1}-m \end{bmatrix} \\
&\qquad -(1-\phi)\eta^2 k'[\sigma^2 Id + \eta^2 J]^{-1} \begin{bmatrix} Y_{i,T}-m \\ \vdots \\ Y_{i,1}-m \end{bmatrix} \\
&\qquad +(1-\phi)\eta^4 e'[\sigma^2 Id + \eta^2 J]^{-1} K [\sigma^2 Id + \eta^2 J]^{-1} \begin{bmatrix} Y_{i,T}-m \\ \vdots \\ Y_{i,1}-m \end{bmatrix} + o(1-\phi).
\end{aligned}$$

Moreover we have:

$$[\sigma^2 Id + \eta^2 J]^{-1} = \frac{1}{\sigma^2}[Id - \frac{\eta^2}{\sigma^2 + \eta^2 T} J],$$

$$[\sigma^2 Id + \eta^2 J]^{-1} e = \frac{1}{\sigma^2 + \eta^2 T} e.$$

We deduce that

$$\begin{aligned}
\pi_i(T,h) &= m + \frac{\eta^2}{\sigma^2+\eta^2 T} e' \begin{bmatrix} Y_{i,T}-m \\ \vdots \\ Y_{i,1}-m \end{bmatrix} - (1-\phi)h \frac{\eta^2}{\sigma^2+\eta^2 T} e' \begin{bmatrix} Y_{i,T}-m \\ \vdots \\ Y_{i,1}-m \end{bmatrix} \\
&\quad -(1-\phi)\frac{\eta^2}{\sigma^2} k' \left[Id - \frac{\eta^2}{\sigma^2+\eta^2 T} ee' \right] \begin{bmatrix} Y_{i,T}-m \\ \vdots \\ Y_{i,1}-m \end{bmatrix} \\
&\quad + \frac{(1-\phi)}{\sigma^2} \frac{\eta^4}{\sigma^2+\eta^2 T} e'K \left[Id - \frac{\eta^2}{\sigma^2+\eta^2 T} ee' \right] \begin{bmatrix} Y_{i,T}-m \\ \vdots \\ Y_{i,1}-m \end{bmatrix} + o(1-\phi) \\
&= m + \frac{\eta^2 T}{\sigma^2+\eta^2 T} (\overline{Y}_{i,T}-m) - (1-\phi)h \frac{\eta^2 T}{\sigma^2+\eta^2 T} (\overline{Y}_{i,T}-m) \\
&\quad -(1-\phi)\frac{\eta^2}{\sigma^2} k' \begin{bmatrix} Y_{i,T}-m \\ \vdots \\ Y_{i,1}-m \end{bmatrix} + (1-\phi) \frac{\eta^4 T}{\sigma^2(\sigma^2+\eta^2 T)} \frac{T(T-1)}{2} (\overline{Y}_{i,T}-m) \\
&\quad + \frac{1-\phi}{\sigma^2} \frac{\eta^2}{\sigma^2+\eta^2 T} e'K \begin{bmatrix} Y_{i,T}-m \\ \vdots \\ Y_{i,1}-m \end{bmatrix} \\
&\quad - \frac{(1-\phi)\eta^6 T}{\sigma^2(\sigma^2+\eta^2 T)^2} e'Ke(\overline{Y}_{i,T}-m) + o(1-\phi).
\end{aligned}$$

REFERENCES

1. Albert, J., and S. Chib (1993), "Bayesian Analysis of Binary and Polytochomous Response Data", *Journal of the American Statistical Association*, 88, 669-679.
2. Azzalini, A. (1983), "Maximum Likelihood Estimation of Order m for Stationary Stochastic Processes", *Biometrika*, 70, 381-387.
3. Bailey, A. (1945), "A Generalized Theory of Credibility", *Proc. Cas. Act. Soc.*, 32, 13-20.
4. Bailey, A. (1950), "Credibility Procedures, Laplace's Generalization of Bayes Rule and the Combination of Collateral Knowledge with Observed Data", *Proc. Cas. Act. Soc.*, 37, 7-23.
5. Balestra, P. (1996), "Introduction to Linear Models for Panel Data", in Mátyás, L. and P. Sevestre ed., *The Econometrics of Panel Data*, Kluwer, 23-33.
6. Balestra, P. and M. Nerlove (1966), "Pooling Cross-Section and Time Series Data in the Estimation of a Dynamic Model: The Demand for Natural Gas", *Econometrica*, 34, 585-612.
7. Balestra, P. and M. Nerlove (1996), "Formulation and Estimation of Econometric

Models for Panel Data", in Mátyás, L. and P. Sevestre ed., *The Econometrics of Panel Data*, Kluwer, 3-22.

8. Buhlmann, H. (1967), "Experience Rating and Credibility: I", *ASTIN Bulletin*, 4, 199-207.
9. Buhlmann, H. (1969), "Experience Rating and Credibility: II", *ASTIN Bulletin*, 5, 157-165.
10. Buhlmann, H., and E. Straub (1970), "Glaubwurdigkeit fur Schadensatze", Mitteilungen der Schweizerischen Vereinigung den Versicherungsmathematiken, 111-133.
11. Chib, S. (1996), "Inference in Panel Data Models via Gibbs Sampling", in Mátyás, L. and P. Sevestre ed., *The Econometrics of Panel Data*, Kluwer, 639-650.
12. Dannenburg, D. (1994), "Some Results on the Estimation of the Credibility Factor in the Classical Buhlmann Model", *Insurance: Mathematics and Economics*, 14, 39-50.
13. Dionne, G. and C. Vanasse (1989) , "A Generalization of Actuarial Automobile Insurance Rating Models: The Negative Binomial Distribution with a Regression Component", *Actuarial Bulletin*, 19, 199-212.
14. Gallant, A., P. Rossi and G. Tauchen (1993), "Nonlinear Dynamic Structures", *Econometrica*, 61, 871-908.
15. Goovaerts, M., T. Bauwelinck and C. Stoop (1989), "The Practical Application of Credibility Theory", *Insurance: Mathematics and Economics*, 8, 77-96.
16. Gourieroux, C. (1997), "Econometrics of Insurance", Geneva Papers for Risk and Insurance, (forthcoming).
17. Gourieroux, C. (1998a), *Statistique de l'assurance*, Economica.
18. Gourieroux, C. and J. Jasiak (1998a), "Dynamic Factor Models", CREST, D.P.
19. Gourieroux, C. and J. Jasiak (1998b), "Nonlinear ARMA Models", CREST, D.P.
20. Gourieroux, C. and A. Monfort (1996), *Simulation Based Econometric Methods*, Oxford University Press.
21. Heilmann, W. (1989), "Decision Theoric Foundations of Credibility Theory", *Insurance: Mathematics and Economics*, 8, 77-96.
22. Jewell, W. (1983), "A Survey of Credibility Theory", Operation Research Center, 76.31, University of California, Berkeley.
23. Koop, G., H. Pesaran and S. Potter (1996), "Impulse Response Analysis in Nonlinear Multivariate Models", *Journal of Econometrics*, 74, 119-147.
24. Lemaire, J. (1995), *Bonus-Malus Systems in Automobile Insurance*, Kluwer.
25. Loubergé, H. (1998), "Risk and Insurance Economics 25 Years After", Geneva Papers on Risk and Insurance, 23, 540-567.
26. Mátyás, L. and P. Sevestre (1996), *The Econometrics of Panel Data*, second edition, Kluwer.
27. Richard, J.F. (1996), "Simulation Techniques", in Mátyás, L. and P. Sevestre, ed., *The Econometrics of Panel Data*, 613-638, Kluwer.
28. Sundt, B. (1989), "Bonus Hunger and Credibility Estimators with Geometric Weights", *Insurance: Mathematics and Economics*, 8,119-126.

Panel Data Econometrics: Future Directions
J. Krishnakumar and E. Ronchetti (Editors)

CHAPTER 7

ON THE USEFULNESS OF BANKS PANEL DATA IN THE EMPIRICAL ANALYSIS OF CREDIT MARKETS: A Note

Patrick SEVESTRE

Abstract

Because data about new credit production of banks are lacking, most empirical studies of the credit markets use, instead, those available about their observable credit stock. This substitution has been pointed out to be likely to generate biases (e.g. see Lown and Peristiani (1996)). In this paper, we show that under quite unrestrictive conditions, this substitution does not lead to biased estimates of any log-linear model coefficients, as long as banks panel data are used and fixed effects are included in the estimated equation.

1. INTRODUCTION

The last few years have seen a come-back of the monetary policy efficiency issue. Studies by Berger and Udell (1994), Elyasani, Kopecky and Van Hoose (1995), Kashyap and Stein (1994), Lown and Peristiani (1996), Peek and Rosengren (1995) etc. are examples of the many recent studies devoted to analysing banks loan supply behavior and/or the link between the quantity of loan supplied and non financial firms' investment. One of the common features of these studies is their use of data taken from banks balance sheets.[1] Using individual bank balance sheets presents numerous advantages, among which one can mention the adequation between the (generally micro-) theoretical model and the data used to check its empirical relevance. Moreover, as long as repeated observations over time are available, the possibility to deal with potential unobserved heterogeneity and/or parameter instability is another well-known advantage of this type of data.

[1] An exception is a recent paper by Lown and Peristiani (1996) where data are obtained from a specific survey

However, when studying credit markets, this data source presents a drawback: while the variable appearing in most theoretical models is the *new credit production,* the variable used in the empirical estimation of these models is generally either the *credit stock* or its variation because it is the only available measured variable. Obviously, the latter can hardly be considered as an accurate measure of the former.[2] One can then wonder whether this substitution is neutral with respect to the obtained coefficient estimates. As emphasized by Lown and Peristiani (1996): "Still, a major criticism of the reduced form loan equations that we (and others) have estimated is that the dependent variable - the stock of outstanding loans - does not measure new loans issued." Moreover, this substitution also raises the problem of correcting for inflation since it is clearly invalid to deflate the credit stock by any current price index.[3]

The aim of this note is to clarify the econometric consequences of using the credit stock instead of the new credit production in econometric models, either as the dependent variable or as a regressor. A particular focus is directed to panel data models since it appears that they allow such a substitution to be rather inocuous under quite unrestrictive conditions. The plan of the paper is as follows: in Section 2, we make explicit the link that exists between the new credit production and the stock. In particular, it is clearly shown that this link is much less tight for long term credit than it is for short term ones. Section 3 deals with the problem arising from the substitution of the former by the latter in an econometric model, either as the dependent variable or as a regressor. Conditions under which this substitution is neutral with respect to the estimation of the coefficients are exhibited. Section 4 is devoted to an empirical check. Some conclusions are drawn in Section 5.

2. THE RELATIONSHIP BETWEEN NEW CREDITS AND THE CREDIT STOCK

The amount of credit appearing in banks balance sheets is a measure of all the credits they granted in the past and which remains to be reimbursed. In other words, the *observable* amount of outstanding loans is the sum of all *unobservable* past credit productions minus their already repaid part. Denoting C_{it} the amount of credit stock appearing in bank i's balance sheet at time t and NC_{it} that of new credits provided during the period ending at time t, and ignoring, for the sake of simplicity, the impact of provisions for possible payment default,[4] one can write

$$C_{it} = NC_{it} + \alpha_1 NC_{it-1} + \alpha_2 NC_{it-2} + \alpha_3 NC_{it-3} + \ ... \ + \alpha_p NC_{it-p}$$

where the α_j's $(0 \leq \alpha_j \leq 1)$ form a decreasing sequence accounting for the fact that, due to their repayment, loans granted in the past contribute less and less to the outstanding

[2]See Bernanke and Lown (1991), Lown and Peristiani (1996) and Baumel (1996).

[3]E.g. see Bernanke and Lown (1991). Indeed, one faces here the same problem as the one encountered for deflating the physical capital stock.

[4]Taking these into account can be shown to affect the coefficients α_j $j = 1, ..., p$ in the equation below.

level of loans as time goes by. This equation can be rewritten as

$$C_{it} = NC_{it}\left(1 + \alpha_1\frac{NC_{it-1}}{NC_{it}} + \alpha_2\frac{NC_{it-2}}{NC_{it}} + \alpha_3\frac{NC_{it-3}}{NC_{it}} + \ ... \ + \ \alpha_p\frac{NC_{it-p}}{NC_{it}}\right) \quad .$$

Given that the variable of interest in most economic models is the real value of the new credit production, it is interesting to write this expression as

$$\frac{NC_{it}}{P_t} = \frac{C_{it}}{P_t} \Bigg/ \left(1 + \alpha_1\frac{NC_{it-1}}{NC_{it}} + \alpha_2\frac{NC_{it-2}}{NC_{it}} + \alpha_3\frac{NC_{it-3}}{NC_{it}} + \ ... \ + \ \alpha_p\frac{NC_{it-p}}{NC_{it}}\right)$$

where P_t is a price index. This relationship shows that substituting the total amount of the credit stock for the new credit production will have no undesirable consequence as long as the α coefficients are close to zero; which will be the case for short term credits as their duration is not likely to be longer than the observation periodicity. On the contrary, this substitution can be quite problematic for long term credits, where the credits granted in the past have a strong influence on the current amount of credit outstandings. Moreover, this formula shows that the relationship between new credits and the stock has no reason to be stable over time nor across banks since the ratios NC_{it-j}/NC_{it} depend on the past credit production growth.

One can then wonder about the econometric consequences of substituting credit outstandings taken from balance sheets for new credit production. In this respect, it is worth noticing that the discrepancy between these two quantities can hardly be assimilated to a purely random measurement error. Indeed, it has a non-null expectation which varies across individuals and over time. Moreover, this error is clearly strongly serially correlated over time.[5]

3. ECONOMETRIC CONSEQUENCES OF SUBSTITUTING THE CREDIT STOCK FOR THE NEW CREDIT PRODUCTION

3.1. Credit as the dependent variable

First of all, let us consider the case where the new credit production is the dependent variable in the model, that is, the model under consideration can be written as

$$\frac{NC_{it}}{P_t} = X_{it}\beta + u_{it} \tag{1}$$

where u_{it} is assumed to have all desirable properties.[6]

[5] The extent of the serial correlation makes it difficult to find valid instruments, contrarily to the usual case where past and/or future values of the variable can serve as instruments because of the absence of such a correlation.

[6] Assuming a possible serial correlation or heteroscedasticity of the disturbances does not change the conclusions. The only difference would be that the estimated model would have to be transformed using the $\Omega^{-1/2}$ transformation. Moreover, in the case where some regressors are endogenous, the conclusion still remains valid, given that these variables are correctly instrumented.

Then, obviously, if one estimates the model

$$\frac{C_{it}}{P_t} = X_{it}\gamma + v_{it} \tag{2}$$

instead of model (1), the estimated γ will be a downward biased estimation of β since the expression $\left(1+\alpha_1\frac{NC_{it-1}}{NC_{it}}+\alpha_2\frac{NC_{it-2}}{NC_{it}}+\alpha_3\frac{NC_{it-3}}{NC_{it}}+\ ...\ +\ \alpha_p\frac{NC_{it-p}}{NC_{it}}\right)$ is clearly greater than 1. In fact, the relationship between β and γ just expresses the degree of proportionality that exists between the stock and flow of credit. Unfortunately, it is not necessarily the case that this relationship is stable over time and/or across banks, which makes it difficult to get an unbiased estimate of β whatever data is used, time-series, cross-section or panel. Nevertheless, let us assume that the logarithm of $\left(1+\alpha_1\frac{NC_{it-1}}{NC_{it}}+\alpha_2\frac{NC_{it-2}}{NC_{it}}+\alpha_3\frac{NC_{it-3}}{NC_{it}}+\ ...\ +\ \alpha_p\frac{NC_{it-p}}{NC_{it}}\right)$ can be correctly approximated by the following sum of time and bank effects, i.e.

$$\ln\left(1+\alpha_1\frac{NC_{it-1}}{NC_{it}}+\alpha_2\frac{NC_{it-2}}{NC_{it}}+\alpha_3\frac{NC_{it-3}}{NC_{it}}+\ ...\ +\ \alpha_p\frac{NC_{it-p}}{NC_{it}}\right) \simeq f_i + g_t \quad .$$

This approximation allows to account for the instability of the relationship between the credit stock and the new credit production both over time and across banks. Although one could consider these effects to be random, they are likely to be correlated with some regressors. For example, unobservable differences in the structure of banks credit supply, due to their clientele or their size, may be at the origin of a correlation between banks specific effects and some of the regressors, e.g. the interest rate. This is why we put some emphasis, here, on the fixed effects specification.[7]

Given the previous approximation, model (1) can be rewritten as:

$$\ln\left(\frac{C_{it}}{P_t}\right) = \ln(X_{it}\beta + u_{it}) + f_i + g_t$$

which can be estimated as a non linear model or can be approximated by a log-linear model. Indeed, using the first order Taylor expansion of $\ln(X_{it}\beta + u_{it})$ around $X_{it}\beta$, it is easy to show that the previous model can be approximated by

$$\ln\left(\frac{C_{it}}{P_t}\right) = \ln(X_{it}\beta) + f_i + g_t + v_{it}$$

where $v_{it} = u_{it}/X_{it}\beta$. The linear approximation thus results in heteroscedastic disturbances, which can be easily tackled using feasible-GLS or, if necessary, GMM estimators.

If the model to be estimated is originally in logarithm, the advantage of using banks panel data is even more easily seen. Indeed, in that case, the model to be estimated is defined as

$$\ln\left(\frac{NC_{it}}{P_t}\right) = \ln(X_{it})\beta + u_{it} \tag{3}$$

[7] Anyway, testing the absence of correlation of these effects with the regressors can easily be done in the usual way.

which can be rewritten as

$$\ln\left(\frac{NC_{it}}{P_t}\right) = \ln\left(\frac{C_{it}}{P_t}\right) + \ln\left(1 + \alpha_1\frac{NC_{it-1}}{NC_{it}} + \alpha_2\frac{NC_{it-2}}{NC_{it}} + \alpha_3\frac{NC_{it-3}}{NC_{it}} + \ldots + \alpha_p\frac{NC_{it-p}}{NC_{it}}\right) = \ln(X_{it})\beta + u_{it} \quad .$$

Then, assuming that the second logarithm can be approximated by time and/or bank specific effects, this model can be rewritten as

$$\ln\left(\frac{C_{it}}{P_t}\right) = \ln(X_{it})\beta + f_i + g_t + u_{it} \tag{4}$$

which can be estimated using time and/or bank dummies or rewriting the model in first differences to discard the banks specific effects if one is not directly interested in those coefficients. This is, for example, the approach followed by Berger and Udell (1994) who estimate their model in terms of growth rates (which are not very different from differences in logs). In doing so, they implicitly allow for the existence of individual effects, which make less problematic the substitution of the new credit production by the stock of oustanding loans.

Moreover, it is interesting to note that in this kind of model, it is completely indifferent to deflate or not the stock of credit. Indeed, model (4) can be written as

$$\ln(C_{it}) - \ln(P_t) = \ln(X_{it})\beta + f_i + g_t + u_{it}$$

the estimation of which, given the presence of the time-dummies, can be shown, using the Frisch-Waugh theorem, to be equivalent to that of the model:

$$\ln(C_{it}) = \ln(X_{it})\beta + f_i + h_t + u_{it} \quad .$$

Clearly, using panel data and including time (and banks) dummies in the model allows both to reduce the bias that can be caused by replacing the unobserved new credit production by the observed credit stock and to eliminate the question of correctly deflating this stock. In that case, the difficulty of correctly deflating loans as outlined by Bernanke and Lown (1991) does not exist anymore. A good illustration of this result is provided by Kashyap and Stein (1994) who did not find any significant difference in their estimation of a loan equation using either deflated or nominal values. Indeed, their model contains some macroeconomic variables whose impact on their estimates is probably close to that which would have been obtained with time effects. Moreover, the model is specified in terms of growth rates (which is, again, very similar to a model written in logarithm differences), thus allowing implicitly for individual effects.

As we are now going to see, this set of results extends to the case where loans appear as an explanatory variable instead of being the dependent variable of the model.

3.2. Credit as an explanatory variable

Indeed, consider now that the model to be estimated is

$$y_{it} = \left(\frac{NC_{it}}{P_t}\right)\beta + w_{it} \tag{5}$$

whereas one estimates the model

$$y_{it} = \left(\frac{C_{it}}{P_t}\right)\gamma + w_{it} \quad . \tag{6}$$

Then, again, the estimated coefficient $\hat{\gamma}$ will be biased as long as the $\alpha's$ are not close to zero. But, again in this case, things get better if the model depends on the variables' logarithm, i.e.

$$\ln(y_{it}) = \ln\left(\frac{NC_{it}}{P_t}\right)\beta + u_{it} \quad . \tag{7}$$

Indeed, in that case too, one can rewrite the model as

$$\ln(y_{it}) = \ln\left(\frac{C_{it}}{P_t}\right)\beta + f_i + g_t + u_{it} \quad . \tag{8}$$

Thus, one gets unbiased estimates as long as the approximation of the stock/flow proportionality factor by the sum of time and/or bank specific effects works well. One can find an illustration of this result in Lown and Peristiani (1996). They define the dependent variable of their model as the difference between the bank interest rate at a given point in time and its average over banks, thus allowing implicitly for time effects. Moreover, they include in their model several bank specific variables which probably have on the regression results an effect similar to that which would have been obtained with bank dummies.

It is interesting to note that, in this situation too, the question of deflating or not the loan variable is not important, given that inflation effects are captured by time dummies.[8]

Then, it appears that, if individual banks panel data are available, one can expect the often made substitution of new credit production by the credit stock not to have harmful consequences; the condition being that the proportionality factor linking them can be decomposed into the sum of time and bank specific effects.

If one has doubts about the quality of this approximation, it is possible to consider a further way to deal with the measurement error induced by the substitution. Indeed, one can write

$$\ln\left(1 + \alpha_1\frac{NC_{it-1}}{NC_{it}} + \alpha_2\frac{NC_{it-2}}{NC_{it}} + \alpha_3\frac{NC_{it-3}}{NC_{it}} + \ \dots\ + \alpha_p\frac{NC_{it-p}}{NC_{it}}\right) + \varepsilon_{it} = f_i + g_t \tag{9}$$

[8] In order for these results to remain valid when using time series or cross-section data, it would be necessary for the correcting term to be constant in the time dimension or across banks, respectively.

where ε_{it} is a measurement error. Here, one does not assimilate the total discrepancy between the credit stock and new credits to a random measurement error, but only the difference from its systematic part, approximated by the fixed effects, difference which is more likely to resemble a "basic" measurement error. In the case where the credit production variable is the dependent variable of the model, this has no other consequence than increasing the variance of the model disturbance. When this variable appears in the model as a regressor, one is then faced with an error in variables problem. Indeed, the estimation of model (8) by least squares leads to inconsistent estimates; it is well-known that the absolute value of the bias is an increasing function of the ratio of the measurement error variance to that of the measured variable. In our case, this means that the least squares estimates bias gets stronger as the previous approximation (given by equation (9)) gets worse. Nevertheless, it is still possible to get consistent estimates of the parameters by using an instrumental variables or a GMM estimation technique.[9]

In other words, whatever the quality of the approximation, substituting the credit stock to the new credit production is not an obstacle to obtaining consistent estimates, as long as one takes this substitution into account by adding banks and time dummies to the model and, if necessary, by using an appropriate estimation technique.

However, the question remains to see whether the previous approximation can be considered as acceptable. In order to answer this question, we have used a sample of 15 French large banks for which we have observations of both the credit stock and the new credit production, observations that cover the period 1978-1992 (Baumel (1996)).

4. AN EVALUATION OF THE QUALITY OF THE APPROXIMATION

In this section we want to check whether one can consider the following approximation

$$\ln\left(1+\alpha_1\frac{NC_{it-1}}{NC_{it}}+\alpha_2\frac{NC_{it-2}}{NC_{it}}+\alpha_3\frac{NC_{it-3}}{NC_{it}}+\ \dots\ +\alpha_p\frac{NC_{it-p}}{NC_{it}}\right)\simeq f_i+g_t$$

as acceptable. This amounts to evaluating the quality of the following analysis of variance regression

$$\ln\left(\frac{C_{it}}{NC_{it}}\right)=f_i+g_t+\varepsilon_{it} \quad .$$

As said above, this regression has been run on a panel of 15 large French banks observed quarterly over the period 1978-1992. The table below contains the results of four sets of regressions, corresponding to total loans, as well as short term, medium term and long term ones.

The first interesting result to note is that the ratio of total new loans to total loans assets is quite well explained by the individual and time effects; indeed, 86% of the total variance is explained by these effects. Then, the above claim that replacing the (generally

[9] e.g. past or future values of the credit stock, as well as other balance sheet items are likely to constitute valid instruments. Obviously, the validity of these instruments can be tested for using a Sargan test.

Table 1
Empirical Evaluation of the Approximation.

Dependent variable	R^2	F-value for time effects*	F-value for indiv. effects
Total loans	0.858	4.47	337.98
Short term loans	0.869	2.49	379.74
Medium term loans	0.567	3.57	62.33
Long term loans	0.364	4.45	15.07

* F-statistics are given to provide information about the relative importance of time and banks specific effects. They are not used for explicitly testing their significance.

unobserved) new loans by the (observed) total loan assets in econometric models should not lead to important biases as long as the model includes individual (and time) specific effects appears to be justified.

As could be expected, this approximation works even slightly better for short term loans. This is not really surprising because, for this category of credit, the difference beween new credit and the credit stock is not as strong as it is for longer term credit. Indeed, if all short term loans were one quarter long, we would have an almost exact correspondence between these two measures, at least in a stationary state. Another reason why the previous approximation is almost as good for total loans as it is for short term ones is that short term loans appear to be the most important part of new credits (cf. Baumel (1996)).

The fact that, for medium and long term loans, the previous approximation does not work as well is not really surprising. Then, if one is interested in long term credit, replacing new loans by assets should lead to both the inclusion of bank and time dummies and the use of an instrumental variables or GMM estimation technique. It is worth noticing that we have checked that the sometimes proposed solution consisting in the replacement of these new credits by the first difference in assets does not lead to better results.

5. CONCLUSION

In this paper, we support the use of bank panel data when studying behaviors on the credit markets. Indeed, we show that, using such data, one can replace the unobserved new loans by the observed corresponding stock of outstanding loans without inducing strong biases, as long as bank and time specific effects are included in the model; a solution that cannot be used when working with either time series or cross-section data. The validity of such a substitution, evaluated on a panel of 15 French large banks, observed over the period 1978-1992, and for which we have measures of both the new credit and the corresponding stocks, proves to be quite satisfactory .

Moreover, it is argued that, even when this approximation does not work well, and credit is the dependent variable in the model, least squares estimates are not really affected, at least in terms of consistency; when credit enters the model as a regressor, it is still possible to get consistent estimates of the parameters by using instrumental variables or GMM estimation techniques.

REFERENCES

1. Baumel L. (1996), "Les crédits nouveaux mis en place par les banques AFB de 1978 à 1992. Une évaluation des montants et des durées initiales", *NER N° 40, Banque de France.*
2. Berger A.N. (1995), "The relation between capital and earnings in banking", *Journal of Money, Credit and Banking*, 27, 2, 432-456.
3. Berger A.N. and G.F. Udell (1994), "Did risk-based capital allocate bank credit and cause a "credit crunch" in the United States?", *Journal of Money, Credit and Banking*, 26, 3, 585-628.
4. Bernanke B.S. and C.S. Lown (1991), "The credit crunch", *Brookings Papers on Economic Activity*, 2, 205-247.
5. Elyasani E., K.J. Kopecky et D. Van Hoose (1995), "Costs of adjustment, portfolio separation, and the dynamic behavior of bank loans and deposits", *Journal of Money, Credit and Banking*, 27, 4, 957-974.
6. Kashyap A.K. and J.C. Stein (1994), "The impact of monetary policy on bank balance sheets", NBER Working Paper No. 4821.
7. Lown C. and S. Peristiani (1996), "The behavior of consumer loan rates during the 1990 credit slowdown", *Journal of Banking and Finance*, 20, 1673-1694.
8. Peek J. and E. Rosengren (1995), "The capital crunch: neither a borrower nor a lender be", *Journal of Money, Credit and Banking*, 27, 3, 625-638.

PART I

(contd.)

D. Energy Economics

Panel Data Econometrics: Future Directions
J. Krishnakumar and E. Ronchetti (Editors)

CHAPTER 8

AGGREGATING TIME UNBALANCED PANEL OBSERVATIONS: Methodology and Application to Oil Consumption of Boiler Rooms

Fabrizio CARLEVARO and Jean-Luc BERTHOLET

Abstract

This paper solves the problem of converting a time unbalanced series of panel observations into a corresponding series of time balanced observations according to a calendar periodicity in order to enable their aggregation. To this end, we specify a continuous time regression model, describing the instantaneous rate of change of the observable flow variable and derive a regression model accounting for observations of this variable of any time length. Using this discrete time regression model, we perform the desired allocation through a best linear unbiased predictor. Our approach is applied to estimate an oil consumption statistic for the Canton of Geneva (Switzerland) based on the extrapolation of consumption observations of a stratified random sample of boiler rooms.

1. INTRODUCTION

This paper presents an econometric methodology devised in the course of a mandate commissioned to the Geneva University Center for the Study of Energy Problems (CUEPE) by the Geneva Cantonal Office of Energy (OCEN). The aim of this mandate is to help, on a methodological and technical ground, the Geneva Cantonal Office of Statistics (OCSTAT) in developing and managing a statistic of fuel oil consumption for the Canton of Geneva . At the beginning of the project, CUEPE's contribution had consisted in designing a random panel of boiler rooms allowing to estimate, with a given sampling error, the annual fuel oil consumption of the Geneva population of buildings. More recently, we were asked to implement the methodology to produce official figures of this statistic from the consumption meter readings of the boiler rooms of the panel and the data base recording the boiler room population of the Canton. In this setting we were faced with the problem of converting, according to a calendar periodicity, oil consumption observations recorded on time periods of varying length, in order to allow the computation of the average oil consumption of the panel on a calendar unit time period (month, quarter or year).

This paper focuses on the methodology devised to solve this interpolation problem and discusses the results of its application to the consumption data provided by the boiler room panel during the period 1990-1997. Our presentation is structured as follows. In section 2, we specify a continuous time regression model describing the oil consumption behaviour of a boiler room and derive, from this model, a conventional general linear regression model explaining observable consumptions over time periods of any length. Using this conventional regression model, we formulate, in section 3, the interpolation problem as one of finding the best linear unbiased predictor of an unknown vector of time balanced oil consumptions within the class of linear transformations of the vector of observed time *un*balanced oil consumptions. We suggest an interpretation of this predictor and prove that it intrinsically fulfils three consistency properties. In section 4, we suggest and develop two estimation strategies to render this optimal predictor feasible. Section 5 presents and discusses the results of the application of this methodology in the evaluation of monthly oil consumption figures for the Canton of Geneva based on the panel of observed consumptions. Conclusions summarize our contribution and outline the most promising developments we plan to carry out.

2. THE CAUSAL MODEL

In a residential building, the production of heat essentially satisfies two needs, namely : the heating of residential areas and the preparation of hot water for sanitary installations. The oil consumption for room heating services depends on the area of the heated surface as well as on the gap between indoor and outdoor temperature. Therefore, we can model this first component of oil consumption of a boiler room using the following relation :

$$q_H(t) = \alpha_H(t) S \; H(t) \tag{1}$$

where

$q_H(t)$ denotes the instantaneous rate of oil consumption at (continuous) time t

$\alpha_H(t)$ the instantaneous oil specific consumption of the building for room heating at time t, namely, the instantaneous rate of oil consumption per unit of heated area and per heating-degree

S the fixed area of the heated surface

$H(t)$ the number of heating-degrees to be provided by the heating system at time t, computed according to following formula[1] :

$$H(t) = [\theta_1 - \theta(t)] \ \max \left\{ \frac{\theta_2 - \theta(t)}{|\theta_2 - \theta(t)|}; 0 \right\} \tag{2}$$

where θ_1 is the fixed requested indoor temperature, $\theta_2 < \theta_1$ the outdoor threshold temperature at which the heating system is operated and $\theta(t)$ the outdoor temperature at time t.

Similarly, we model the instantaneous rate of oil consumption for hot water production at time t, $q_W(t)$, as a proportion of the fixed number N of representative hot water consumers in the building. Hence :

$$q_W(t) = \alpha_W(t)N \tag{3}$$

where α_W stands for the instantaneous oil specific consumption of the building for hot water preparation at time t.

Finally, we obtain the instantaneous rate of oil consumption of a boiler room, $q(t)$, by adding up these two components. Taking into account that some buildings are not equipped with a central hot water production system and, therefore, the heat production of their boiler rooms is entirely devoted to the heating of the residential area, this leads to the following combined relation :

$$q(t) = q_H(t) + q_W(t)A \tag{4}$$

where A is a dummy variable taking value 1 for those buildings equipped with a central hot water production installation and value 0 otherwise.

We incorporate random disturbances in this functional relationship by assuming stochastic oil specific consumption, namely :

$$\alpha_H(t) = \alpha_H + \varepsilon_H(t) \quad \text{and} \quad \alpha_W(t) = \alpha_W + \varepsilon_W(t) \tag{5}$$

where α_H, α_W are time invariant coefficients and $\varepsilon_H(t)$, $\varepsilon_W(t)$ two uncorrelated continuous time gaussian white noise disturbances[2], i.e. such that their stochastic integral over a finite time interval[3] $\triangle = [t_0, t_1)$:

$$\varepsilon_H(\triangle) = \int_{t_0}^{t_1} \varepsilon_H(t)dt \quad \text{and} \quad \varepsilon_W(\triangle) = \int_{t_0}^{t_1} \varepsilon_W(t)dt \tag{6}$$

are normally distributed random variables with :

[1] A discussion of this measure of room heating needs used in Switzerland may be found in Spierer (1978) and Carlevaro and Spierer (1986).

[2] For a more rigourous definition see Bergstrom (1984).

[3] For the purpose of our analysis, we consider left-close and right-open time intervals in order to define couples of connected but disjoint time intervals.

- zero expectation :

$$E(\varepsilon_H(\triangle)) = E(\varepsilon_W(\triangle)) = 0 \quad ; \tag{7}$$

- variance proportional to the length $\delta(\triangle) = t_1 - t_0$ of the time interval $\triangle$:

$$E(\varepsilon_H(\triangle)^2) = \sigma_H^2\delta(\triangle) \quad , \quad E(\varepsilon_W(\triangle)^2) = \sigma_W^2\delta(\triangle); \tag{8}$$

- zero serial covariances, for two non overlapping time intervals $\triangle$ and $\triangle^* = [t_0^*, t_1^*)$ $(\triangle \cap \triangle^* = \emptyset)$, and serial covariances proportional to the length $\delta(\triangle \cap \triangle^*)$ of the common time span of two overlapping time intervals[4] $(\triangle \cap \triangle^* = [\max\{t_0, t_0^*\}, \min\{t_1, t_1^*\}) \neq \emptyset)$:

$$\begin{aligned} E(\varepsilon_H(\triangle)\varepsilon_H(\triangle^*)) &= \sigma_H^2\delta(\triangle \cap \triangle^*), \\ E(\varepsilon_W(\triangle)\varepsilon_W(\triangle^*)) &= \sigma_W^2\delta(\triangle \cap \triangle^*); \end{aligned} \tag{9}$$

- zero cross-covariances :

$$E(\varepsilon_H(\triangle)\varepsilon_W(\triangle^*)) = 0 \quad . \tag{10}$$

Inserting equations (1), (3), (5) into relation (4), leads to the continuous time regression model :

$$q(t) = \beta_H H(t) + \beta_W A + \varepsilon(t) \tag{11}$$

with unknown parameters $\beta_H = \alpha_H S$, $\beta_W = \alpha_W N$ and continuous time disturbance :

$$\varepsilon(t) = \varepsilon_H(t)SH(t) + \varepsilon_W(t)NA \quad . \tag{12}$$

By integrating this relationship over a non zero measurable finite time interval $\triangle$, we obtain a regression model explaining the observable oil consumption of a boiler room during this period. This conventional regression model is written as :

$$Q(\triangle) = \beta_H H(\triangle) + \beta_W A\delta(\triangle) + \varepsilon(\triangle), \tag{13}$$

where

$$Q(\triangle) = \int_{t_0}^{t_1} q(t)dt \quad , \quad H(\triangle) = \int_{t_0}^{t_1} H(t)dt \quad , \quad \varepsilon(\triangle) = \int_{t_0}^{t_1} \varepsilon(t)dt \tag{14}$$

stand for the oil consumption of the boiler room, the number of heating-degrees and the stochastic integral of random disturbances during time interval $\triangle$, respectively.

[4] These covariances are also nil if $\triangle \cap \triangle^*$ is a zero measurable non empty interval.

By using the rules of stochastic calculus, one can easily prove, that $\varepsilon(\triangle)$ is a normally distributed random disturbance with zero expectation and second order moments :

$$\begin{aligned} &E(\varepsilon(\triangle)^2) = \sigma^2[H^2(\triangle) + A\delta(\triangle)\lambda^2], \\ &E(\varepsilon(\triangle)\varepsilon(\triangle^*)) = \sigma^2[H^2(\triangle \cap \triangle^*) + A\delta(\triangle \cap \triangle^*)\lambda^2] \end{aligned} \tag{15}$$

where

$$H^2(\triangle) = \int_{t_0}^{t_1} H(t)^2 dt \quad , \quad \sigma^2 = S^2\sigma_H^2 \quad \text{and} \quad \lambda^2 = \frac{N^2\sigma_W^2}{S^2\sigma_H^2} \quad . \tag{16}$$

At this stage, it is worthy to pinpoint that our specification (5) of oil specific consumption quantities $\alpha_H(t)$ and $\alpha_W(t)$, is compatible with the assumption of no randomness of one of these two quantities, namely with the two limit cases where $\varepsilon_H(t) = 0$ or $\varepsilon_W(t) = 0$. Yet, these polar cases have to be handled separately from the general case, because they lead to the disappearance of either σ_H^2 or σ_W^2 present in the definition (16) of the derived parameters σ^2 and λ^2.

As $\sigma_W^2 = 0$ implies $\lambda^2 = 0$, this limit case simply rules out the second term of moments (15). In the other case, where $\sigma_H^2 = 0$, a similar simplification occurs. Indeed, by redefining expressions (15) as :

$$\begin{aligned} &E(\varepsilon(\triangle)^2) = \rho^2 \left[\mu^2 H^2(\triangle) + A\delta(\triangle)\right] \quad , \\ &E\left(\varepsilon(\triangle)\varepsilon(\triangle^*)\right) = \rho^2 \left[\mu^2 H^2(\triangle \cap \triangle^*) + A\delta(\triangle \cap \triangle^*)\right] \end{aligned} \tag{17}$$

where

$$\rho^2 = N^2\sigma_W^2 \quad \text{and} \quad \mu^2 = \frac{S^2\sigma_H^2}{N^2\sigma_W^2} \quad , \tag{18}$$

it is clear that $\sigma_H^2 = 0$, by implying $\mu^2 = 0$, makes the first term of these two moments vanish.

3. OPTIMAL PREDICTION OF TIME BALANCED OIL CONSUMPTIONS

Our goal consists in converting time unbalanced observations of oil consumption of a boiler room, namely a series of quantities $Q_i = Q(\triangle_i), i = 1, \ldots, n$, observed over n connected but disjoint time intervals $\triangle_i = [t_{i-1}, t_i)$, $i = 1, \ldots, n$, into time balanced quantites, i.e. into a series $Q_i^* = Q(\triangle_i^*), i = 1, \ldots, m$, where $\triangle_i^* = [t_{i-1}^*, t_i^*)$ are unit time intervals.[5] As $t_0^* = t_0$ and $t_m^* = t_n$, the first and the last interval of this series may not fulfil this requirement. This arises when the initial or the terminal date of the observation period does not coincide with the beginning or the ending date of the selected time unit period (the month, in our application).

[5]In our application, unit time intervals $\triangle_i^*, i = 1, \ldots, m$, are not all of equal length, as we choose the month as discrete time unit.

According to Goldberger (1962), we formulate this allocation problem as one of finding the minimum variance unbiased predictor for vector y_* of time balanced unknown oil consumptions $Q_i^*, i = 1, \ldots, m$, within the class of linear transformations of vector y of time unbalanced oil consumption observations $Q_i, i = 1, \ldots, n$. To find this best linear unbiased predictor we need to specify the causal model jointly explaining the vector y_* to be predicted with the sample vector y of observations. This combined model is a general linear prediction model which may be written, in a stacked matrix form, as :

$$\begin{bmatrix} y \\ y_* \end{bmatrix} = \begin{bmatrix} X \\ X_* \end{bmatrix} \beta + \begin{bmatrix} \varepsilon \\ \varepsilon_* \end{bmatrix} \tag{19}$$

where

X denotes either the $n \times 2$ matrix $[H_i \ \delta_i]_{i=1,\ldots,n}$, where $H_i = H(\triangle_i)$ and $\delta_i = \delta(\triangle_i), i = 1, \ldots, n$, or the $n \times 1$ vector $[H_i]_{i=1,\ldots,n}$, depending on $A = 1$ (the boiler room produces both room heating and hot water for sanitary purposes) or $A = 0$ (the boiler room produces only room heating);

X_* a matrix similar to X but containing the m known values of the explanatory variables for vector y_*, namely $H_i^* = H(\triangle_i^*)$ and $\delta_i^* = \delta(\triangle_i^*)$, $i = 1, \ldots, m$, if $A = 1$ and only H_i^* if $A = 0$;

ε a $n \times 1$ vector of normal random disturbances with zero expectation and a diagonal variance-covariance matrix :

$$E(\varepsilon\varepsilon') = \sigma^2 \text{Diag}\left(H_1^2 + A\delta_1\lambda^2, \ldots, H_n^2 + A\delta_n\lambda^2\right) = \sigma^2 V(\lambda^2) \tag{20}$$

where $H_i^2 = H^2(\triangle_i)$, $i = 1, \ldots, n$;

ε_* a $m \times 1$ vector of normal random disturbances, similar to ε, having zero expectation, a diagonal variance-covariance matrix :

$$E(\varepsilon_*\varepsilon_*') = \sigma^2 \ \text{Diag}(H_1^{*2} + A\delta_1^*\lambda^2, \ldots, H_m^{*2} + A\delta_m^*\lambda^2) = \sigma^2 V_*(\lambda^2) \tag{21}$$

where $H_i^{*2} = H^2(\triangle_i^*)$ and $\delta_i^* = \delta(\triangle_i^*), i = 1, \ldots m$, and a covariance matrix, with respect to ε :

$$E(\varepsilon\varepsilon_*') = \sigma^2[H_{ij}^2 + A\delta_{ij}\lambda^2]_{i=1,\ldots,n;j=1,\ldots,m} = \sigma^2 W(\lambda^2) \tag{22}$$

where $H_{ij}^2 = H^2(\triangle_i \cap \triangle_j^*)$ and $\delta_{ij} = \delta(\triangle_i \cap \triangle_j^*), i = 1, \ldots, n, j = 1, \ldots, m.$[6]

A well known result of the econometric literature[7] states that, within the framework of this model, the best linear unbiased predictor for y_* takes the following form :

$$\hat{y}_* = X_*\hat{\beta} + B(y - X\hat{\beta}) \tag{23}$$

[6]An alternative parametrisation of matrices $V(\lambda^2), V_*(\lambda^2)$ and $W(\lambda^2)$ may be based on expressions (17) of variances and covariances of random disturbances ε and ε_*.

[7]See i.e. Theil (1971), p.280.

where $\hat{\beta}$ denotes the generalized least squares estimator for β, namely :

$$\hat{\beta} = \left(X'V(\lambda^2)^{-1}X\right)^{-1} X'V(\lambda^2)^{-1}y \tag{24}$$

and B a $m \times n$ matrix defined as :

$$B = W(\lambda^2)'V(\lambda^2)^{-1} = \left[\frac{H_{ij}^2 + A\delta_{ij}\lambda^2}{H_i^2 + A\delta_i\lambda^2}\right]_{j=1,\ldots,m;i=1,\ldots,n} \quad . \tag{25}$$

This allocation formula is the sum of two components which may be easily interpreted. The first component is a **calibration** term, providing a first evaluation $X_*\hat{\beta}$ of time balanced oil consumptions y_* that we are interested in. This first evaluation is based on the deterministic causal explanation present in regression model (13) and it uses the general least squares estimate (24) of unknown parameters β_H and β_W. The second component is an **adjustment** term, that corrects the calibration in order to reset the equality between the total of time unbalanced oil consumption observations and the sum of predicted time balanced oil consumptions, i.e. between :

$$\sum_{i=1}^{n} Q_i = \iota_n' y \quad \text{and} \quad \sum_{i=1}^{m} \hat{Q}_i^* = \iota_m' \hat{y}_* \quad , \tag{26}$$

where ι_n and ι_m stand for vectors of ones of order $n \times 1$ and $m \times 1$, respectively.

This intrinsic adding-up property of $\hat{y}_*$ can be checked by observing that :

$$\iota_m' X_* = \iota_n' X \quad \text{and} \quad \iota_m' B = \iota_n' \tag{27}$$

because

$$\cup_{i=1}^{m} \Delta_i^* = \cup_{i=1}^{m} \Delta_i \Longrightarrow \sum_{i=1}^{m} H_i^* = \sum_{i=1}^{n} H_i \quad , \quad \sum_{i=1}^{m} \delta_i^* = \sum_{i=1}^{n} \delta_i$$

and

$$\sum_{j=1}^{m} H_{ij}^2 = H_i^2 \quad , \quad \sum_{j=1}^{m} \delta_{ij}^2 = \delta_i \Longrightarrow \sum_{j=1}^{m} \frac{H_{ij}^2 + A\delta_{ij}\lambda^2}{H_i^2 + A\delta_i\lambda^2} = 1, \quad i = 1, \ldots, n \quad .$$

Hence :

$$\iota_m' \hat{y}_* = \iota_m' X_* \hat{\beta} + \iota_m' B(y - X\hat{\beta}) = \iota_n' X\hat{\beta} + \iota_n'(y - X\hat{\beta}) = \iota_n' y \quad . \tag{28}$$

The best linear unbiased predictor (23) also enforces two other consistency properties on the predictions $\hat{y}_*$.

- The first one states that the best linear unbiased prediction of Q_j^* is equal to observation Q_l when $\Delta_j^* = \Delta_\ell$. This **invariance** property follows from the fact that :

$$\Delta_j^* = \Delta_\ell \quad \Longrightarrow \quad H_j^* = H_\ell \quad \text{and} \quad \delta_j^* = \delta_\ell \quad ,$$

as well as

$$\Delta_\ell \cap \Delta_j^* = \Delta_\ell \Longrightarrow H_{\ell j}^2 = H_\ell^2 \text{ and } \delta_{\ell j} = \delta_\ell$$

$$\Delta_i \cap \Delta_j^* = \emptyset, i \neq \ell \Longrightarrow H_{ij}^2 = \delta_{ij} = 0, i \neq \ell \quad .$$

Indeed, as a consequence of these particular values of the elements of row j of matrices X_* and B, namely $e_j'X_* = [H_\ell \; \delta_\ell]$ and $e_j'B = e_\ell'$, where e_j and e_ℓ stand for columns j and l of the $m \times m$ identity matrix, we obtain :

$$\hat{Q}_j^* = e_j'\hat{y}_* = [H_\ell \; \delta_\ell] \, \hat{\beta} + e_\ell'(y - X\hat{\beta}) = Q_\ell \quad . \tag{29}$$

- The second consistency property leads to predict a zero time balanced consumption Q_j^*, as it shall be, whenever the boiler room does not provide sanitary hot water ($A = 0$) and the time period Δ_j^* under consideration does not comprise any room heating needs ($H_j^* = 0$). Indeed, in such a peculiar situation, the j-th row of both matrices X_* and B are null and, therefore :

$$\hat{Q}_j^* = e_j'\hat{y}_* = 0\hat{\beta}_H + 0'(y - X\hat{\beta}) = 0 \quad . \tag{30}$$

The main weakness of predictor $\hat{y}_*$ comes from the fact that it cannot avoid negative time balanced oil consumption estimates.

4. FEASIBLE OPTIMAL PREDICTION

In implementing the optimal predictor developed in the previous section, we are faced with the problem of estimating the unknown derived parameter λ^2.

To perform such an estimation, two strategies may be considered :

- the simultaneous estimation of all the model parameters, namely β, σ^2 and λ^2;
- a separate estimation of parameter λ^2 from the other parameters.

The first strategy may be made operational through the application of the maximum likelihood principle. This approach provides a consistent and asymptotically efficient estimator for λ^2 and leads to an estimator for β compatible with that present in the optimal predictor (23), namely the generalized least squares estimator (24).

To compute this estimate we write the likelihood function of the random sample y of observed oil consumptions. It is a vector of normally distributed random variables with mean $E(y) = X\beta$ and variance-covariance matrix $V(y) = \sigma^2 V(\lambda^2)$. Hence, the log-likelihood function is written as :

$$\begin{aligned}\log L(\beta, \sigma^2, \lambda^2) &= -\frac{n}{2}\log(2\pi) - \frac{1}{2}\log \mid \sigma^2 V(\lambda^2) \mid \\ &-\frac{1}{2}(y - X\beta)'[\sigma^2 V(\lambda^2)]^{-1}(y - X\beta) \\ &= -\frac{n}{2}\log(2\pi) - \frac{n}{2}\log\sigma^2 - \frac{1}{2}\sum_{i=1}^{n}\log(H_i^2 + A\delta_i\lambda^2) \\ &-\frac{1}{2\sigma^2}(y - X\beta)'V(\lambda^2)^{-1}(y - X\beta) \quad . \end{aligned} \tag{31}$$

Clearly, conditional on λ^2, the maximum likelihood estimates of β and σ^2 may be written in explicit form as :

$$\hat{\beta}(\lambda^2) = (X'V(\lambda^2)^{-1}X)^{-1}X'V(\lambda^2)^{-1}y \tag{32}$$

and

$$\hat{\sigma}^2(\lambda^2) = \frac{(y - X\hat{\beta}(\lambda^2))'V(\lambda^2)^{-1}(y - X\hat{\beta}(\lambda^2))}{n} \quad . \tag{33}$$

This allows to concentrate the likelihood function with respect to these parameters and, therefore, to simplify the maximization of this function by performing, first, the numerical computation of the maximum likelihood estimate of λ^2, $\hat{\lambda}^2$, through the maximization of the single parameter concentrated likelihood function :

$$\begin{aligned}\log \mathcal{L}^*(\lambda^2) = \log \mathcal{L}(\hat{\beta}(\lambda^2), \hat{\sigma}^2(\lambda^2), \lambda^2) &= -\frac{n}{2}(1 + \log(2\pi)) - \frac{n}{2}\log\hat{\sigma}^2(\lambda^2) \\ &-\frac{1}{2}\sum_{i=1}^{n}\log(H_i^2 + A\delta_i\lambda^2)\end{aligned} \tag{34}$$

and, secondly, once this optimization is performed, by computing

$$\hat{\beta} = \hat{\beta}(\hat{\lambda}^2) \quad \text{and} \quad \hat{\sigma}^2 = \hat{\sigma}^2(\hat{\lambda}^2) \tag{35}$$

using formulas (32) and (33).

The second strategy is a two step procedure based on a preliminary consistent estimate of λ^2. Contrary to the first approach, it does not rely on the normality assumption and, hence, it is more robust with respect to a possible specification error of the likelihood function.

To implement this approach we start from ordinary least squares residuals :

$$e = y - Xb = y - X(X'X)^{-1}X'y = My = M\varepsilon \tag{36}$$

where $b = (X'X)^{-1}X'y$ denotes the ordinary least squares estimate of β and $M = I - X(X'X)^{-1}X'$. The square and cross products of these residuals allow to specify a linear regression model from which we can derive an indirect least squares estimate of λ^2. Indeed :

$$E(ee') = ME(\varepsilon\varepsilon')M = \sigma^2 MV(\lambda^2)M \quad . \tag{37}$$

This expectation matrix may be written in vector form as :

$$\begin{aligned} \text{vec }(E(ee')) &= (M \otimes M) \text{ vec } (\sigma^2 V(\lambda^2)) = (M \otimes M)(\sigma^2 h + \sigma^2\lambda^2 A\delta) \\ &= [(M \otimes M)h \qquad A(M \otimes M)\delta] \begin{bmatrix} \sigma^2 \\ \sigma^2\lambda^2 \end{bmatrix} = Z\gamma \end{aligned} \tag{38}$$

where $h = \text{vec (Diag } (H_1^2, \ldots, H_n^2))$ and $\delta = \text{vec (Diag } (\delta_1, \ldots, \delta_n))$. Hence, we can associate with vec $(ee') = e \otimes e$ the following regression model :

$$e \otimes e = Z\gamma + \eta \tag{39}$$

which is linear with respect to parameters $\gamma' = [\gamma_1 \ \gamma_2]$, where η denotes a vector of zero expectation random disturbances.

As $\lambda^2 = \gamma_2/\gamma_1$, a consistent estimate of λ^2 can be derived from the ordinary least squares estimate of γ, namely :

$$c = \begin{bmatrix} c_1 \\ c_2 \end{bmatrix} = (Z'Z)^{-1}Z'(e \otimes e) \quad , \tag{40}$$

using ratio c_2/c_1.

5. APPLICATION TO THE MEASUREMENT OF BOILER ROOM OIL CONSUMPTION IN THE CANTON OF GENEVA

The demand for statistical information on energy consumption in the Canton of Geneva has developed in the wake of setting a Swiss energy policy, in the aftermath of the seventies oil shocks and the eighties Chernobyl nuclear power plant accident. As a consequence of the federal structure of Switzerland, the implementation of energy policies in the buildings sector is of the competence of cantonal governments. During the eighties, many of them adopted energy laws and created energy delegates or offices in charge of conceiving and implementing such policies. In the Canton of Geneva, this evolution led to the creation of a Cantonal Office of Energy (OCEN) and to the adoption of a cantonal law on energy calling for, in particular, a development of energy statistical information allowing to assess the effectiveness of public energy policy measures.

The statistic of fuel oil consumption is the last born of a series of energy statistics implemented by the Cantonal Office of Statistics (OCSTAT (1998)) on behalf of and in collaboration with OCEN in response to this need[8]. This statistic is intended to complement that of fuel oil sales, set up since 1975, which hardly allows to highlight the short and medium-term evolution of oil consumption, as a consequence of stock variations and unrecorded transcantonal purchases and sales.

The frequently used collective system of distribution (by group of buildings or residential district) of heat produced by oil-fired furnaces at work in a higly urban area as the city of Geneva, does not allow to collect reliable information on final fuel oil consumption at the building level. This information should be grasped directly at the level of boiler room plants, where furnace burners may be equipped by an oil meter, or the agent in charge of monitoring and managing these plants may be asked to record oil tank refillings and measure the stock present in these reservoirs. For this reason, it was decided to measure final fuel oil consumption at the stage of the furnace feeding and hence to survey the population of boiler rooms recorded by the Cantonal Inspection of the Service of Fire (ICSF) of Geneva.

Faced with the exorbitant cost of performing an exhaustive census of this population (about 28'000 boiler rooms in 1994), the initiators of the project decided to opt for a random sampling technique and, therefore, to extrapolate to the entire population the oil consumption of a representative panel of boiler rooms. The design of a random panel allowing to estimate the oil consumption of the Geneva population of boiler rooms, with a given theoretical sampling error was commissioned to the authors of the present paper.

To minimize the panel size, we designed a stratified random sample according to the total nominal power of boilers present in the boiler room, chosen as sampling unit. This stratification variable is recorded for each boiler room by the census of these plants set up by the ICSF. We did not attempt to optimize the stratification with respect to the number and the limits of strata. Instead, we allocated the total sample size among 15 strata according to the Neyman rule[9] leading to the minimization of the variance of the sampling error of extrapolation and, therefore, the minimization of the panel size for a given sampling error. The standard errors of oil consumption within the strata needed to compute such optimal sampling rates were modeled as a logistic function of the nominal power of the strata and estimated using oil consumption data of a non random sample of 71 boiler rooms previously surveyed by the OCEN during the heating season 1979/1980, completed with data provided for the same period by a company in charge of monitoring and managing 238 other boiler rooms.

According to the logic of a stratified random sampling scheme, panel units are chosen within each strata through a simple random sampling, in our case without replacement

[8]We would like to pay hommage to Charles Corajod, who died tragically in 1995, for his perspicacity and tenacity in conceiving and carrying out this project, at first as a civil servant at the OCSTAT, in charge of the energy statistics, and then as administrator at the OCEN. Without his contribution this project would probably have never been realized.

[9]According to this rule, the sample size in a stratum should be proportional to the product of the size of the stratum and the standard deviation of the stratum. See Cochran (1953, chapter 5).

(exhaustive sample). The number of units thus selected in each strata is determined as a proportion of the total sample size using Neyman's sampling rates.

Table 1 presents the stratified sample designed to achieve a 5% sampling error, when estimating annual oil consumption in Geneva. It is worth mentioning that our design includes a complete census of the units pertaining to the last strata of boiler rooms with nominal power exceeding 4000 kW. We also focus our sampling design only on the sub-population of building boiler rooms excluding villas (single family houses). Compared to a simple random sampling scheme of the same precision this stratified sample allows to reduce the panel size from 1592 units to 165.

Table 1 also compares this optimally designed sample to the panel of boiler rooms actually implemented by OCSTAT. The actual panel was set up during year 1989 and reached its full size in 1990. Since then it has significantly decreased in size and modified in structure as a consequence of the desertion of many informants. For this reason, we evaluate the size of the actual panel at a given month according to the collected number of consumption observations covering this month. Annual mean values of the panel presented in Table 1 are averages of these monthly figures.

Finally, we also present in Table 1 the number of boiler rooms per stratum recorded by ICSF in 1987 and 1994 over the canton territory. These strengths are used to extrapolate the oil consumption of the panel to the whole population by multiplying these figures by the corresponding panel average consumption per stratum and by adding up all these estimates of oil consumption per stratum, including the estimate for villas. The design of the stratified panel was based on 1987 population, whereas fuel oil consumption estimates published by OCSTAT are computed according to 1994 figures. The methodology presented in the previous sections were developed to compute average oil consumption per stratum on a monthly base, starting from January 1990. The first oil consumption observations were collected since January 1989, but the number of panel respondents reached a threshold of reliability only at the beginning of 1990. Therefore, for each panel boiler room, oil consumption observations span a period between January 1989 and December 1997.

The number of observations per boiler room vary dramatically due to large differences in the length of the time period covered by each observation. This length ranges between 1 and 30 months for a total of 6197 observations collected for the 382 building's boiler rooms. Fortunately, most of these observations are of a few months, namely : 55,4% up to 3 month, 39% between 3 and 6 month, 4,6% between 6 and 12 month and only 1% more than 1 year. As a consequence of this diversity, it proved impossible to estimate the regression model (13) for each boiler room of the panel, because of an insufficient number of observations for some of them. For those units having less than 3 observations (it was the case for 27 boiler rooms over a total of 382, including villas), we used simple interpolation rules, namely :

Table 1
Population and OCSTAT Panel of Boiler Rooms in the Canton of Geneva

Category of nominal	Population in 1987		Population in 1994		Designed Panel		Mean Panel 1990		Mean Panel 1997	
power (kW)	Size	(%)	Size	(%)	Size	(%)	Size	(%)	Size	(%)
<100	218	3.9	418	8.2	2	1.2	7.8	3.9	2.3	2.0
100-200	1,833	32.5	1,638	32.0	24	14.5	23.0	11.5	13.3	11.8
200-300	1,208	21.4	1,100	21.5	20	12.1	24.8	12.4	17.5	15.5
300-400	644	11.4	508	9.9	14	8.5	16.7	8.3	7.5	6.7
400-500	367	6.5	283	5.5	10	6.1	13.3	6.6	7.6	6.7
500-600	286	5.1	230	4.5	10	6.1	11.6	5.8	4.8	4.3
600-700	177	3.1	151	3.0	7	4.2	10.6	5.3	8.0	7.1
700-800	120	2.1	119	2.3	6	3.6	9.4	4.7	4.6	4.1
800-900	90	1.6	79	1.5	6	3.6	8.5	4.3	7.8	6.9
900-1,000	104	1.8	90	1.8	7	4.2	8.8	4.4	2.9	2.6
1,000-1,500	244	4.3	221	4.3	23	13.9	26.3	13.2	15.0	13.3
1,500-2,000	174	3.1	154	3.0	18	10.9	15.1	7.6	6.0	5.3
2,000-3,000	125	2.2	98	1.9	13	7.9	12.9	6.5	6.4	5.7
3,000-4,000	44	0.8	29	0.6	5	3.0	10.9	5.5	9.1	8.1
Sub-total	**5,634**	**100.0**	**5,118**	**100.0**	**165**	**100.0**	**199.8**	**100.0**	**112.8**	**100.0**
>4,000	41	*0.2*	64	*0.3*	41		**38**	*15.2*	33.1	*21.6*
Villas	11,229	*66.4*	15,024	*74.4*			11.6	*4.6*	7.6	*4.9*
Total	**16,904**		**20,206**				**249.3**		**153.4**	

Proportions in italics are computed with respect to total population or total panel size.

- an allocation where surface heating needs, measured by heating-degrees (the $H(\triangle)$ explanatory variable of model (13)), account for 2/3 of total oil consumption and hot water production for 1/3;

- an allocation proportional to the number of heating-degrees for boiler rooms entirely devoted to space heating, or to the length of the observation period $\triangle$ if the number of heating-degrees for such a period turns out to be zero.

In estimating regression model[10] (13) a distinction should be made between boiler rooms producing hot water (324 in our panel) and those without such a function (31 cases). For the latter, $A = 0$ and therefore parameter λ^2, calling for one of the heavy estimating procedure presented in section 4, is ruled out of the model. One can also easily check that in this particular case the generalized least squares estimator for parameter β_H cannot be negative. Still, the best linear unbiaised predictor (23) for monthly observations of oil consumption can produce negative values. In these uncommon but inconsistent situations, we decided to replace predictor (23) by the second above mentioned simple allocation rule.

When the boiler room provides heat for warming up both residential areas and sanitary water, the econometric estimates of parameters β_H, β_W and λ^2 can show other inconsistencies. Firstly, best linear predictions of monthly oil consumptions may be the consequence of a negative estimate of one of the β coefficients. Once again, when such inconsistent estimates occured (10 times, as a consequence of 3 negative estimates of β_H and 7 estimates of β_W), we decided to apply the first above stated simple interpolation rule.

Secondly, the maximum likelihood estimate of λ^2 can tend to infinity or to zero and the least squares residuals estimate of this parameter may be negative. Clearly, these results are indications of dominance of one of disturbances $\varepsilon_H(t)$ and $\varepsilon_W(t)$ over the other, supporting the assumption $\sigma_H^2 = 0 \Longrightarrow \mu^2 = 0$ ($\varepsilon_W(t)$ dominates $\varepsilon_H(t)$) when λ^2 estimate tends to infinity and the opposite assumption $\sigma_W^2 = 0 \Longrightarrow \lambda^2 = 0$ ($\varepsilon_H(t)$ dominates $\varepsilon_W(t)$) when λ^2 estimate tends to zero or is negative, according to the adopted method of estimation. Using the maximum likelihood method of estimation[11], these limiting cases arose very often, leading to 110 reestimations of model constrained by $\mu^2 = 0$ and 167 reestimations with the restraint $\lambda^2 = 0$ over 355 estimations entailing this parameter.

Still, some of these coherent model estimates generated negative best linear unbiaised monthly oil consumption predictions (206 over 20965). These too were replaced by non negative estimates obtained by allocating observed oil consumptions monthly according to the first simple interpolation rule.

To conclude, we present in Table 2 two estimates of fuel oil consumption statistic for the Canton of Geneva performed according to the methodology described earlier. Monthly estimates for the period 1990-1997, computed according to the number of boiler rooms

---

[10]The number of heating-degrees used to compute the explanatory variables $H(\triangle)$ and $H^2(\triangle)$ are based on a series of daily heating-degrees for the canton of Geneva published by the Swiss meteorological office.
[11]We did not experiment the least squares residuals estimation of λ^2.

Table 2

Quarterly Fuel Oil Consumption Estimates and Sales in the Canton of Geneva (millions of liters)

		Consumption estimate according to boiler room population in :			
Year	Quarter	1987	1994	Discrepancy (%)	Sales
1990	1	149,436	145,984	2.3	138,805
	2	73,211	72,315	1.2	91,071
	3	37,455	37,178	0.7	76,257
	4	133,767	131,938	1.4	120,501
1991	1	161,381	159,157	1.4	142,135
	2	80,773	80,169	0.7	95,718
	3	40,509	40,263	0.6	76,812
	4	149,010	147,947	0.7	130,214
1992	1	168,651	165,422	1.9	162,148
	2	65,880	64,801	1.6	85,990
	3	37,619	37,701	-0.2	80,776
	4	147,567	143,591	2.7	119,242
1993	1	156,982	155,543	0.9	144,820
	2	66,790	67,214	-0.6	78,577
	3	40,355	40,648	-0.7	75,159
	4	144,110	141,003	2.2	134,057
1994	1	133,865	131,109	2.1	128,118
	2	71,058	70,027	1.5	82,153
	3	37,024	37,539	-1.4	62,543
	4	124,403	122,129	1.8	122,670
1995	1	182,982	177,291	3.1	116,637
	2	65,212	66,309	-1.7	83,024
	3	39,666	40,518	-2.1	62,642
	4	120,312	119,351	0.8	118,252
1996	1	164,517	163,829	0.4	137,119
	2	69,355	70,905	-2.2	69,353
	3	45,738	47,846	-4.6	63,916
	4	140,169	138,204	1.4	122,088
1997	1	144,533	143,401	0.8	136,796
	2	67,784	67,121	1.0	82,852
	3	42,681	42,565	0.3	79,883
	4	127,946	127,233	0.6	120,781

in 1987 and 1994, respectively, were aggregated on a quarterly basis in order to compare them with the available figures of the corresponding fuel oil sales statistic. As one can see, little discrepancies appear between estimates based on boiler room population in 1987 and 1994 respectively, even though this population has significantly changed in size and structure during this period (see Table 1)[12]. On the contrary, significant differences are visible if we compare consumption estimates to oil sales, as a consequence of a different seasonal pattern in these two series. Indeed, it is during summer that oil reserves are restored while in winter oil consumption is usually larger than oil sales.

6. CONCLUSIONS

In this paper we solve the problem of converting a time unbalanced series of observations, namely observations of a flow variable for time intervals of varying length, into a corresponding series of observable values, time balanced according to a calendar periodicity. To this end, we specify a continuous time regression model, describing the instantaneous rate of change of the observable flow, that allows to derive a regression model accounting for flow values of any time length. By collecting such stochastic relations written for all the observations at hand as well as for the reallocation of the total of these observations according to a calendar periodicity, we came out with a general linear prediction model allowing to perform the desired allocation through a best linear unbiased predictor entailing additivity of allocated values to the allocation total.

Though general in scope, this methodology is developed and experimented in this paper as an interpolation procedure allowing to aggregate, on a calendar periodicity, the oil consumption of a panel of boiler rooms set up to carry out a statistic of fuel oil consumption for the canton of Geneva based on a sampling technique. In this framework, our approach suggests many useful developments allowing to enlarge the scope of this statistic and to improve its precision. Among the most promising, we shall mention :

- the evaluation of a series of fuel oil consumption reflecting an unchanged annual profile of temperatures for Geneva;
- the splitting up of oil consumption according to the services provided, namely, on one hand, for room heating purposes and, on the other hand, for sanitary hot water production;
- the extension of our continuous time regression model, providing a causal explanation of oil consumption of a single boiler room to multiple boiler rooms by the addition of a cross-section dimension encompassing the individual behaviour of all the boiler rooms of the reference population.

These are the main directions in which we are currently developing this research project.

[12]This measurement error will disappear in the future as a consequence of the computerization of the boiler room population file, allowing to regularly update the sampling frame and therefore to compute each new oil consumption estimate according to the more recent figures of boiler rooms population.

REFERENCES

1. Bergstrom, A.R. (1984), "Continuous Time Stochastic Models and Issues of Aggregation over Time", Chapter 20 in *Handbook of Econometrics, Volume 2*, ed. Zvi Griliches and Michael D. Intriligator, North-Holland, Amsterdam, 1145-1212.
2. Carlevaro, F. and C. Spierer (1986), "Choix d'une mesure de l'intensité de froid pour l'analyse macro-économique de la demande d'énergie : L'évidence empirique", *Revue de l'énergie*, No. 386, 828-833.
3. Cochran W.G. (1953), *Sampling Techniques*, J. Wiley & Sons, New York.
4. OCSTAT (1998), *Statistique de l'énergie à Genève. Une rétrospective commentée (1987-1996)*, Etudes et documents No. 25, Office cantonal de la statistique, Genève.
5. Spierer, C. (1978), "Elaboration d'une variable mesurant l'intensité de froid : Application à la Suisse", *Bulletin ASE/UCS*, 69, 7, 318-320.
6. Theil, H. (1971), *Principles of Econometrics*, Wiley, New York.

PART II

Theoretical Issues

Panel Data Econometrics: Future Directions
J. Krishnakumar and E. Ronchetti (Editors)

CHAPTER 9

TO POOL OR NOT TO POOL PANEL DATA*

Cheng HSIAO and Baohong SUN

Abstract

Issues of pooling panel data are discussed. We argue that the fixed versus random effects specification to capture unobserved heterogeneity across cross-sectional units over time is better treated as an issue of model selection rather than hypothesis testing. A recursive predictive density approach is proposed and Monte Carlo studies are conducted to compare the feasibility of this approach and compare its performance versus BIC and AIC criteria.

1. INTRODUCTION

Panel data, by combining interindividual differences with intra-individual dynamics, offer many advantages over cross-sectional or time series data (e.g. Hsiao (1985, 86, 95)). However, the ability to exploit the information contained in panel data depends critically on the plausibility of poolability. If individual observations are more appropriately viewed as generated from heterogeneous populations, there is no justification to pool the data, hence cannot explore the many advantages associated with the use of panel data.

To pool or not to pool panel data is an issue of whether the ith individual outcome at tth time period, y_{it}, conditional on variables of interest, say $\underset{\sim}{x}$, can be viewed as a random draw from a common population. If it is, the individual and time subscript, it, can be viewed as purely a labelling device and *a priori*, $E(y_{it} \mid \underset{\sim}{x}) = E(y_{js} \mid \underset{\sim}{x})$. (This is what de Finetti (1964) called exchangeability criterion). By pooling the data we can draw more precise inference on the population characteristics (e.g. Hsiao *et al.* (1993)). On the other hand, if conditional on $\underset{\sim}{x}$, individual outcomes are more appropriately viewed as generated from heterogeneous population, then the subscript, it, contains specific information with

*Research support by National Science Foundation is gratefully acknowledged.

regard to which heterogeneous population the particular observation is generated from. In other words, conditional on $\underset{\sim}{x}$, it makes no sense to pool the data. The heterogeneity among cross-sectional units over time is not completely captured by $\underset{\sim}{x}$.

A model is a simplification of reality to capture the essential factors affecting the outcome. Panel data, by nature, focus on individual outcomes. Factors affecting individual outcomes are numerous. It is neither feasible nor desirable to include all the factors affecting the outcome in a model. If it deems appropriate to include $\underset{\sim}{x}$ as the set of important explanatory variables in explaining the outcome of y, then in a linear regression framework we will have

$$y = \underset{\sim}{\beta}'\underset{\sim}{x} + u, \tag{1}$$

with u representing the effects of all excluded variables. The standard assumption is that u possesses the property of random variable and is independent of (or uncorrealted with) $\underset{\sim}{x}$. However, if the heterogeneity among cross-sectional unit over time is not completely captured by $\underset{\sim}{x}$, then the standard assumption about the error of the equation (1) is violated.

Given the framework of (1), there are only two ways to capture the unobserved heterogeneity among cross-sectional units over time. One is to represent the heterogeneity in the error term, the other is to let the coefficients vary across cross-sectional units over time. The former leads to the variable intercept or error components formulation (Balestra and Nerlove (1966), Kuh (1963), Mundlak (1978), Wallace and Hussain (1969)). The latter leads to variable coefficients specification (e.g. Hsiao (1974,75,92), Swamy (1970)).

Within this framework, then the issue of poolability is an issue of random effects versus fixed effects specification. In the situation that unobserved heterogeneity can be treated as random, then (unconditional) pooling is desirable. In the case that unobserved heterogeneity is more appropriately treated as fixed and different among individual observations, then unconditional pooling will yield misleading inferences (e.g. Ashenfelter (1978), Hausman (1978)). However, the fact that unobserved heterogeneity should be treated as fixed does not automatically lead to the rejection of pooling. For instance, in the case of a variable intercept model (e.g. Kuh (1963)) or a mixed fixed and random coefficients model (e.g. Hsiao and Tahmiscioglu (1997)), conditional on the individual effects, we may still draw inference about certain features of the population (e.g. coefficients that are common across individuals, and/or over time). We shall refer to this situation as partial poolability.

In section 2 we will present the issue of poolability in terms of random versus fixed effects specification in a linear regression framework. Section 3 discusses the criteria for selecting fixed versus random effects specification. Section 4 presents Monte Carlo studies to evaluate the usefulness of the various criteria. Conclusions are in section 5.

2. THE MODEL

For ease of exposition, we shall use a linear model to illustrate the issue of poolability. Suppose we have panel observations of $(1 + k_1 + k_2)$ variables $(y_{it}, x'_{it}, z'_{it})$, $i = 1, \ldots, N$, and $t = 1, \ldots, T$, where we wish to explain the variation of y in terms of x and z. If the heterogeneity of y among cross-sectional units over time can be captured by x and z, then we have complete (or unconditional) poolability and the model takes the form

$$y_{it} = \beta' x_{it} + \gamma' z_{it} + v_{it}, \tag{2}$$

where v are uncorrelated with x and z. It should be noted that (2) does not preclude the possibility that the coefficients of x and z vary across individuals and/or over time as long as these variations can be viewed as random outcome from a common probability distribution (or satisfies de Finetti's exchangeability criteria). For instance, we can have a model that takes the form

$$y_{it} = \beta'_{it} x_{it} + \gamma'_{it} z_{it} + u_{it}, \tag{3}$$

where $\beta_{it} = \beta + \eta_{it}$, $\gamma_{it} = \gamma + w_{it}$, $E\eta_{it} = 0$, $Ew_{it} = 0$, Cov $\begin{pmatrix} \eta_{it} \\ w_{it} \end{pmatrix} = \Delta$, Cov $(\eta_{it}, x_{js}) = 0$, Cov $(\eta_{it}, z_{js}) = 0$, Cov $(w_{it}, x_{js}) = 0$, Cov $(w_{it}, z'_{js}) = 0$. (e.g. Swamy (1970), Hsiao (1974, 75)). Substituting $\beta_{it} = \beta + \eta_{it}$, $\gamma_{it} = \gamma + w_{it}$ into (3), we have a common model (2) for all NT observations, with $v_{it} = \eta'_{it} x_{it} + w'_{it} z_{it} + u_{it}$. The best linear unbiased estimator (BLUE) of β and γ is the generalized least squares estimator (GLS). In the extreme case that $\Delta = 0$, $\eta_{it} = 0$ and $w_{it} = 0$, we have a usual linear regression model and the least squares estimator is the BLUE.

If the unobserved heterogeneity cannot be treated as random draws from a common population, then β_{it} and γ_{it} are fixed and different. Model (3) is not estimable because we have more parameters than the degrees of freedom. A structure has to be introduced. Suppose the unobserved heterogeneity varies across individuals but not over time, then we have

$$y_{it} = \beta'_i x_{it} + \gamma'_i z_{it} + u_{it}, \qquad i = 1, \ldots, N, \; t = 1, \ldots, T. \tag{4}$$

In this case, each individual has a different behavior pattern. It makes no sense to pool the data except that one may put the model in the Zellner's (1962) seemingly unrelated regression framework to exploit the common information among individual shocks in each of the N equations to improve the efficiency of the individual parameter estimates. The inference is individual specific. There is no way one can make any general statement about the population.

An intermediate case between complete poolability and non-poolability is the case of conditional pooling, namely, conditional on individual specific effects, one may still draw inference about certain aspects of a population. For instance, we may consider z_{it} to be representing country specific factors. The impact of z_{it} on y_{it} is fixed and different for different countries. Suppose x_{it} represents the price and income variables. Suppose people's response to price and income changes are similar, then the impact of $\underset{\sim}{x}_{it}$ on y_{it} will be randomly distributed with mean $\underset{\sim}{\beta}$ so we can write

$$\underset{\sim}{\beta}_i = \underset{\sim}{\beta} + \underset{\sim}{\eta}_i \tag{5}$$

where $\underset{\sim}{\eta}_i$ is a $k_1 \times 1$ vector of random variables that is distributed independently of $\underset{\sim}{x}_{it}$ and $\underset{\sim}{z}_{it}$ with mean $\underset{\sim}{0}$ and covariance matrix Δ_{11}. In other words, although we cannot make any general statement about the impact of $\underset{\sim}{z}_{it}$ on y_{it}, we are able to infer the impact of $\underset{\sim}{x}$ on y conditional on the effects of $\underset{\sim}{\gamma}_i' \underset{\sim}{z}_{it}$. For instance, the variable intercept model (Mundlak (1972)) or the mixed fixed and random coefficients model (Hsiao *et al.* (1989), Hsiao and Tahmiscioglu (1997)) falls into this category. Substituting (5) into (4), we have

$$y_{it} = \underset{\sim}{\beta}' \underset{\sim}{x}_{it} + \underset{\sim}{\gamma}_i' \underset{\sim}{z}_{it} + v_{it}^*, \tag{6}$$

where $v_{it}^* = \underset{\sim}{\eta}_{it}' \underset{\sim}{x}_{it} + u_{it}$ and the coefficients of $\underset{\sim}{x}$ are the same across individuals.

3. FIXED VERSUS RANDOM EFFECTS SPECIFICIATION

As we have argued, the issue of pooling is tantamount to whether unobserved heterogeneity is better treated as random or fixed. Moreover, the formulation in (5) presupposes that we know which coefficients are more appropriately modeled as random draws from a common population and which coefficients are more appropriately modeled as fixed (and different) constants. In practice, we have very little knowledge about how to dichotomize the explanatory variables into x and z. However, the issue of whether to treat unobserved heterogeneity as fixed or random has paramount importance in panel data modelling (e.g. Ashenfelter (1978), Hausman (1978), Hsiao, Mountain, Tsui and Chan (1989)).

In certain special cases, formal statistical testing procedures have been proposed. For instance, in the case of error-components formulation when β is orthogonal to $\underset{\sim}{z}$, both the LSDV estimator and the generalized least squares (GLS) estimator of $\underset{\sim}{\gamma}$ are consistent with the GLS estimator achieving Cramer-Rao lower bound. When β is not orthogonal to $\underset{\sim}{z}$, the LSDV variable estimator of $\underset{\sim}{\gamma}$ is consistent but the GLS estimator is not. Thus, Hausman (1978) suggests testing fixed versus random effects formulation using the statistic

$$s = \underset{\sim}{\hat{q}}' \widehat{\text{var}}\,(\underset{\sim}{\hat{q}})^{-1} \underset{\sim}{\hat{q}}, \tag{7}$$

where $\underset{\sim}{\hat{q}}$ denotes the difference between the LSDV estimator and the GLS estimator of $\underset{\sim}{\gamma}$, Var $(\underset{\sim}{\hat{q}})$ denotes the difference of the covariance matrix of the LSDV and the GLS estimator. Under the null hypothesis of independence between β and $\underset{\sim}{z}$, (7) is asymptotically chi-square distributed with degrees of freedom equal to that of the rank of $\widehat{\text{Var}}\,(\underset{\sim}{\hat{q}})$. Similarly, Breusch and Pagan (1979) exploit the fact that under a random coefficients formulation, the error terms will have heteroscedastic variances and suggest a Lagrange Multipler test.

However, in a hypothesis testing framework the null is well specified, the alternative is typically composite. All these tests essentially exploit the implication of a random effects formulation in a specific framework. In other words, the tests are indirect in nature. Rejection of the null does not automatically imply the acceptance of a specific alternative.

In fact, it would be more useful to view fixed effects and random effects as *different models*. When we are confronted with different models, the classical sampling theory approach does not appear very satisfactory because the distribution of a test statistic is derived under an assumed true null hypothesis. It would appear more appropriate to view the choice of fixed *vs.* random effects formulations as an issue of model selection.

There are various model selection criteria. For instance, the well known Akaike (1973) and Schwartz (1978) information criteria can be used to select an appropriate formulation. Alternatively, we may follow a Bayesian approach. In the Bayesian approach, prior probabilities are assigned to hypotheses or models that reflect the degree of confidence associated with them and Bayes' theorem is employed to compute and consider a posterior odds ratio. Therefore, for two hypotheses H_0 or H_1 with prior odds π_0 and π_1 the posterior odds ratio is defined as

$$K_{01} = \frac{\text{Prob}\ (H_0 \mid \underset{\sim}{y})}{\text{Prob}\ (H_1 \mid \underset{\sim}{y})} = \frac{\pi_0}{\pi_1} \cdot \frac{f(\underset{\sim}{y} \mid H_0)}{f(\underset{\sim}{y} \mid H_1)}, \tag{8}$$

where $f(\underset{\sim}{y} \mid H_i)$ denotes the conditional probability density for $\underset{\sim}{y}$ given hypothesis H_i,

$$f(\underset{\sim}{y} \mid H_i) = \int f(\underset{\sim}{y} \mid \underset{\sim}{\theta}_i)p(\underset{\sim}{\theta}_i)d\underset{\sim}{\theta}_i. \tag{9}$$

If the probability density function of y, $f(\underset{\sim}{y} \mid \underset{\sim}{\theta}_i)$, is normal and the prior probability of $\underset{\sim}{\theta}_i, p(\underset{\sim}{\theta}_i)$, is either diffuse or normal, $f(\underset{\sim}{y} \mid H_i)$ will be proportional to $f(\underset{\sim}{y} \mid \hat{\underset{\sim}{\theta}}_i)$, where $\hat{\underset{\sim}{\theta}}_i$ is the Bayes estimates of $\underset{\sim}{\theta}_i$. Under the fixed effects formulation, the prior of $\underset{\sim}{\theta}_i$ is diffuse, $\hat{\underset{\sim}{\theta}}_i$ will be equal to their maximum likelihood estimates of $\underset{\sim}{\theta}_i$, and $f(\underset{\sim}{y} \mid \hat{\underset{\sim}{\theta}}_i)$ is the maximum likelihood value of $\underset{\sim}{y}$ given H_i. For the random effects formulation the prior of $\underset{\sim}{\theta}_i$ is informative and $\hat{\underset{\sim}{\theta}}_i$ will not be equal to the maximum likelihood estimate (e.g. Hsiao *et al.* (1993) eq. (3.14)). Since, in general, the specification of the fixed effects model includes more independent parameters and $\hat{\underset{\sim}{\theta}}_i$ is the maximum likelihood estimate of $\underset{\sim}{\theta}_i$, one would expect that $f(\underset{\sim}{y} \mid H_i)$ will be larger for the fixed effects than the random effects specification. Thus, if $\pi_0/\pi_1 = 1$, the posterior odds ratio is more likely to favor the fixed effects formulation. On the other hand, if an informative prior is used, the posterior odds ratio will be heavily dependent on the prior.

An alternative to the use of the posterior odds ratio is to use the predictive density ratio (e.g. Hsiao and Tahmiscioglu (1997), Min and Zellner (1993)). In this framework, we can first divide the time series observations into two periods, 1 to T_1, denoted by $\underset{\sim}{y}^1$ and $T_1 + 1$ to T, denoted by $\underset{\sim}{y}^2$ and use the first T_1 observations to obtain the probability distribution of the parameters associated with H_0 and H_1, say $P(\theta_0 \mid \underset{\sim}{y}^1)$ and $P(\underset{\sim}{\theta}_1 \mid \underset{\sim}{y}^1)$. We then construct the predictive density ratio as

$$\frac{\int f(\underset{\sim}{y}^2 \mid \underset{\sim}{\theta}_0, \underset{\sim}{y}^1)P(\underset{\sim}{\theta}_0 \mid \underset{\sim}{y}^1)d\underset{\sim}{\theta}_0}{\int f(\underset{\sim}{y}^2 \mid \underset{\sim}{\theta}_1, \underset{\sim}{y}^1)P(\underset{\sim}{\theta}_1 \mid \underset{\sim}{y}^1)d\underset{\sim}{\theta}_1}, \tag{10}$$

where $f(y^2 \mid \theta_i, y^1)$ is the conditional density of $\underset{\sim}{y}^2$ given $\underset{\sim}{\theta}_i$ and $\underset{\sim}{y}^1$. The advantage of using (10) is that the impact of prior, $P(\underset{\sim}{\theta}_i)$, on the choice of the model is mitigated by the sample information. It is also consistent with the theme that "a severe test for an economic theory, the only test and the ultimate test is its ability to predict" (Klein (1988, p. 21)) and Zellner's (1988, p. 31) view of the "predictive principle that predictive performance is central in evaluating hypotheses" (also see Friedman (1953) and Geisser (1980)). The disadvantage is that if $\underset{\sim}{y}^2$ only contains a limited number of observations, the choice of the model becomes heavily sample dependent. If the number of observations in $\underset{\sim}{y}^2$ is large, then a lot of sample information is not utilized to estimate unknown parameters. One remedy to this is to modify (10) by recursively updating the estimates when constructing the predictive density ratio:

$$\frac{\int f(y_T \mid \underset{\sim}{\theta}_0, \underset{\sim}{y}^{T-1}) P(\underset{\sim}{\theta}_0 \mid \underset{\sim}{y}^{T-1}) d\underset{\sim}{\theta}_0 \cdot \int f(y_{T-1} \mid \underset{\sim}{\theta}_0, \underset{\sim}{y}^{T-2}) \cdot P(\underset{\sim}{\theta}_0 \mid \underset{\sim}{y}^{T-2}) d\underset{\sim}{\theta}_0}{\int f(y_T \mid \underset{\sim}{\theta}_1, \underset{\sim}{y}^{T-1}) P(\underset{\sim}{\theta}_1 \mid \underset{\sim}{y}^{T-1}) d\underset{\sim}{\theta}_1 \cdot \int f(y_{T-1} \mid \underset{\sim}{\theta}_1, \underset{\sim}{y}^{T-2}) \cdot P(\underset{\sim}{\theta}_1 \mid \underset{\sim}{y}^{T-2}) d\underset{\sim}{\theta}_1}$$

$$\frac{\cdots \int f(y_{T_1+1} \mid \underset{\sim}{\theta}_0, \underset{\sim}{y}^1) P(\underset{\sim}{\theta}_0 \mid \underset{\sim}{y}^1) d\underset{\sim}{\theta}_0}{\cdots \int (y_{T_1+1} \mid \underset{\sim}{\theta}_1, \underset{\sim}{y}^1) P(\underset{\sim}{\theta}_1 \mid \underset{\sim}{y}^1) d\underset{\sim}{\theta}_1}, \tag{11}$$

where $P(\underset{\sim}{\theta} \mid \underset{\sim}{y}^T)$ denotes the posterior distribution of $\underset{\sim}{\theta}$ given observations from 1 to T.

Although (11) may appear quite laborious to compute, given the normality assumption of the likelihood function and the prior of $\underset{\sim}{\theta}$ is either normal or diffuse, the computation is actually quite manageable. As shown in Hsiao and Tahmiscioglu (1997), we can obtain the Bayes updating formulae as follows:

Lemma 1 *Suppose that* $p(\underset{\sim}{\theta} \mid \underset{\sim}{y}^{t-1})$ *is* $N(\hat{\underset{\sim}{\theta}}^{t-1}, D_{t-1})$, *then* $p(\underset{\sim}{\theta} \mid \underset{\sim}{y}^t)$ *is* $N(\hat{\underset{\sim}{\theta}}^t, D_t)$, *where*

$$\hat{\underset{\sim}{\theta}}^t = D_t(W_t'\Omega^{-1}\underset{\sim}{y}_t + D_{t-1}^{-1}\hat{\underset{\sim}{\theta}}^{t-1}), \tag{12}$$

$$D_t = (W_t'\Omega^{-1}W_t + D_{t-1}^{-1})^{-1}, \ \text{for } t = T_1+1, \ldots, T. \tag{13}$$

where $\underset{\sim}{y}_t' = (y_{1t}, \ldots, y_{Nt})$, $\hat{\underset{\sim}{\theta}}^t$ *and* D_t *are the posterior mean and variance of* $\underset{\sim}{\theta}$ *based on the first t observations, and*

$$W_t = \begin{pmatrix} \underset{\sim}{x}_{1t}' & \underset{\sim}{0} & \cdots & & \underset{\sim}{z}_{1t}' & 0 & \cdots & 0 \\ 0 & \underset{\sim}{x}_{2t}' & & & \underset{\sim}{0} & \underset{\sim}{z}_{2t}' & & \\ \vdots & & \ddots & & & & \ddots & \\ 0 & & & \underset{\sim}{x}_{Nt}' & & & & \underset{\sim}{z}_{Nt}' \end{pmatrix}.$$

Lemma 2 *Suppose that* $p(\underset{\sim}{\theta} \mid \underset{\sim}{y}^t)$ *is* $N(\hat{\underset{\sim}{\theta}}^t, D_t)$, *then*

$$\begin{aligned} p(\underset{\sim}{y}_{t+1} \mid \underset{\sim}{y}^t) &= \int f(\underset{\sim}{y}_{t+1} \mid \underset{\sim}{\theta}, \underset{\sim}{y}^t) p(\underset{\sim}{\theta} \mid \underset{\sim}{y}^t) d\underset{\sim}{\theta} \\ &\sim N(W_{t+1}\hat{\underset{\sim}{\theta}}^t, \Omega + W_{t+1}D_tW_{t+1}') \end{aligned} \tag{14}$$

4. A MONTE CARLO STUDY

In this section we provide a Monte Carlo study to evaluate the usefulness of different model selection criteria to distinguish fixed versus random effects formulation.

We first consider the experiments for the random effects model in a univariate regression framework as done in Hsiao and Lightwood (1994). Each experiment consisted of one hundred trials. Each trial consisted of observations on N cross-sectional units over T time periods, with N equal to 50, 75 and 100 and $T = 10$. The panels were generated in the following way. First, one series of a normally distributed explanatory variable x_{it} was generated for the whole panel. Then a series of regression errors were generated with a different variance for each cross-sectional unit. The experiments were designed so only one seed for the random number generator was needed for each experiment and this was changed periodically. The panel generated for each Monte Carlo trial can be summarized as follows.

$$y_{Rit} = x_{it}\beta_{Ri} + u_{it}, \tag{15}$$

where

$$\begin{aligned} x_{it} &\sim \mathrm{N}(0, 2.6), \\ \beta_{Rt} &\sim \mathrm{N}(1, \sigma_R^2), \\ u_{it} &\sim \mathrm{N}(0, \sigma_{ui}^2), \\ \sigma_{ui} &\sim \mathrm{N}(2, .125), \\ i &= 1, \dots, N, \\ t &= 1, \dots, T. \end{aligned} \tag{16}$$

The absolute value of σ_{ui} was used to generate the u_{it}. This was done to avoid the rare but possible occurrence of a negative value for the variance. For the different trials we let σ_R take the following values

$$\sigma_R = .1, .2, .6, .8, 1.5, 2.0,$$

to reflect different dispersions of β_{R_i} or the informativeness of the prior.

Table 1

F-Test for Homogeneity of Slope Coefficients for Random Effects Data: Percentage of Rejections

Standard Deviation of β	0.1	0.2	0.4	0.6	0.8	1.5	2.0
Number of Individuals							
50	.76	1.0	1.0	1.0	1.0	1.0	1.0
75	.80	1.0	1.0	1.0	1.0	1.0	1.0
100	.92	1.0	1.0	1.0	1.0	1.0	1.0

[1] Based on 5% significance level

[2] The trial number is 25

Table 2

Breusch-Pagan Test for Homoskedasticity of Residuals for Random Effects Data: Percentage of Rejections

Standard Deviation of β	0.1	0.2	0.4	0.6	0.8	1.5	2.0
Number of Individuals							
50	.20	.36	.68	.88	.96	1.0	1.0
75	.44	.56	.92	1.0	1.0	1.0	1.0
100	.52	.60	1.0	1.0	1.0	1.0	1.0

The modelling of the fixed effects formulation is a difficult one. Since the implication of fixed effects modelling is most related to the issue of heterogeneous population and correlations between the effects and explanatory variables in this simple simulation we choose two ways to generate the fixed effects data. The first is to generate β_i by modelling the fixed coefficients as a mixture of two normally distributed populations which can be summarized as

$$\begin{aligned}\beta_{Fi} &\sim \mathrm{N}(1,1) \qquad i = 1,\dots,\left[\frac{N}{2}\right],\\ &\sim \mathrm{N}(5,.25) \quad i = \left[\frac{N}{2}\right]+1,\dots,N,\end{aligned} \tag{17}$$

where $[N]$ is the largest integer less than or equal to N. The explanatory variables x_{it} were adjusted to prevent the coefficient of variation for the two groups from taking extreme values, so we have

$$\begin{aligned}x_{it} &\sim (5,2.6), \quad i = 1,\dots,\left[\frac{N}{2}\right],\\ x_{it} &\sim (1,2.6), \quad i = \left[\frac{N}{2}\right]+1,\dots,N.\end{aligned} \tag{18}$$

The second is to generate β_i as correlated with x_i. This is done by modelling

$$\begin{aligned}x_{it} &\sim N(\bar{x}_i,1),\\ b_{F_i} &\sim N(0.5\bar{x}_i,0.16),\end{aligned} \tag{19}$$

and $\bar{x}_i$ is generated by either

$$\bar{x}_i \sim N(3,1), \quad i = 1,\dots,N, \tag{20}$$

or

$$\bar{x}_i \sim N(1,1), \quad \text{for} \quad i = 1,\dots,\left[\frac{N}{2}\right],$$

and

$$\bar{x}_i \sim N(5,1), \quad \text{for} \quad i = \left[\frac{N}{2}\right]+1,\dots,N. \tag{21}$$

The fixed coefficient data were then generated by

$$y_{F_{it}} = x_{it}\beta_{Fi} + u_{it}. \tag{22}$$

As the variance of the regression residuals decreases one would expect the fixed effects estimation to be more accurate and the fixed effects formulation to be favored, the variance of the error terms was also varied to explore the sensitivity of the procedure to this. The distributions for the standard deviations of the error terms are generated from

$$\sigma_{ui} \sim N(\bar{\sigma}_u, .125),$$

with

$$\bar{\sigma}_u = 1, 2, 4.$$

It was found that fifty trials were sufficient to determine the outcome of 100 trials very accurately, therefore fifty trials were used for the fixed effects trials. The results of the fixed effects were spot checked with 100 trials and found to be accurate, with the maximum deviation being one trial out of one hundred. The experiments were conducted for N=10, 25, 50, 75, 100. The small N were included to see how well various procedures perform when there were only a few observations from each group of coefficients.

For the rest of this section the data generated using the fixed coefficients will be called the fixed effects data, and that generated using the random coefficients will be called the random effects data.

Given the generated fixed and random effects data, we first follow the sampling approach by testing the homogeneity of slope coefficients ($\beta_i = \beta_j$) using the statistic

$$\sum_{i=1}^{N} \frac{(\hat{\beta}_i - \hat{\beta}^*)' X_i' X_i (\hat{\beta}_i - \hat{\beta}^*)}{\hat{\sigma}_i^2}, \tag{23}$$

where $\hat{\beta}^* = \left[\sum_{i=1}^{N} \frac{1}{\hat{\sigma}_i^2} X_i' X_i\right]^{-1} \left[\sum_{i=1}^{N} \frac{1}{\hat{\sigma}_i^2} X_i' y_i\right]$ and testing heteroskedasticity of the least squares residuals of the model

$$\frac{1}{\sigma_i}\bar{y}_i = \frac{1}{\sigma_i}\bar{x}_i\beta + \omega_i \quad \text{for} \quad i = 1, \ldots, N, \tag{24}$$

using the modified Breusch-Pagan (1979) statistic, which in this case is equal to the predicted sum of squares of the model (Hsiao (1986))

$$(T\omega_i^2 - 1) = \frac{1}{\sigma_i^2}\bar{x}_i^2\Delta + \epsilon_i, \quad i = 1, \ldots, N, \tag{25}$$

where $\bar{y}_i = \frac{1}{T}\sum_{t=1}^{T} y_{it}$ and $\bar{x}_i = \frac{1}{T}\sum_{t=1}^{T} x_{it}$. Based on 5% significance level and 25 trials for each case, both classical procedures reject homogeneity of slope coefficients and homoskedasticity 100% no matter whether the data are generated from random effects or fixed effects formulations. However, they cannot tell whether the data are indeed generated from the fixed or random effects formulation.

To compute the AIC or SIC, we use the complete time series observations. Unfortunately, because of the computational difficulties, we cannot obtain the MLEs for the random coefficients or mixed random and fixed coefficients models. Since our emphasis is not just on the reliability of a model selection criterion but also on computational tractability, we replace the MLE by the following estimator in evaluating the likelihood value.

Noting that $f(\underset{\sim}{y}_i \mid \bar{\beta}, \Delta, \sigma_i^2) = \int f(\underset{\sim}{y}_i \mid \beta_i, \sigma_i^2) \cdot f(\beta_i \mid \bar{\beta}, \Delta) d\beta_i$, we suggest using the following convergent iterative estimator to evaluate the likelihood value for the derivation of approximate AIC or SIC values:

Step 1: Apply the least squares estimator to each individual's time series data to obtain initial estimator of β_i (and or γ_i).

Step 2: Conditional on β_i (and/or γ_i), compute

$$\Delta = \frac{1}{N} \sum_{i=1}^{N} (\beta_i - \bar{\beta})(\beta_i - \bar{\beta})', \tag{26}$$

and

$$\sigma_i^2 = \frac{1}{T} \sum_{t=1}^{T} (y_{it} - \beta_i x_{it} - \gamma_i z_i)^2. \tag{27}$$

Step 3: Conditional on Δ and σ_i^2, compute the generalized least squares estimator of $\bar{\beta}$ (and/or $\bar{\gamma}$).

$$\begin{pmatrix} \bar{\beta} \\ \bar{\gamma} \end{pmatrix} = \left[\begin{pmatrix} X' \\ Z' \end{pmatrix} (\Omega + X\Delta X')^{-1} (X \quad Z) \right]^{-1} \left[\begin{pmatrix} X' \\ Z' \end{pmatrix} (\Omega + X\Delta X')^{-1} \underset{\sim}{y} \right], \tag{28}$$

where Ω and $X\Delta X'$ are $NT \times NT$ block diagonal matrices with the ith block taking the form $\sigma_i^2 I_T$ and $X_i \Delta X_i'$, respectively, Z is an $NT \times N$ block diagonal matrix with the ith block corresponding to the ith individual's time series observation of z, and y is an $NT \times 1$ vector by stacking each individual time series observations of $\underset{\sim}{y}_i$ one after another.

Step 4: Conditional on $\bar{\beta}, \Delta$ and σ_i^2, compute $\beta = (\beta_i, \ldots, \beta_N)$ by the Bayes estimator

$$\beta = D(X'\Sigma y + (I_N \otimes \Delta^{-1})\bar{\beta}] \tag{29}$$

$$D = [X'\Sigma X + (I_N \otimes \Delta^{-1})]^{-1}, \tag{30}$$

$$\Sigma = \Omega^{-1} - \Omega^{-1} Z (Z'\Omega^{-1} Z)^{-1} Z' \Omega^{-1}. \tag{31}$$

(Of course, in the case of no fixed effects specification, $Z = \underset{\sim}{0}$).

Repeat steps 2-4 until the solution converges. Substitute the convergent $\bar{\beta}, \Delta$, and σ_i^2 into the likelihood function to evaluate the approximate likelihood value.

In the case of using predictive density ratio under the hypothesis that the data are generated from fixed effects, we use the least squares estimator for each individual. Under the hypothesis that the data are generated from the random effects, we use the Bayes estimator developed in Hsiao *et al.* (1992). The fixed and random data series were each estimated using the fixed and random coefficient methods in each trial. The first four observations were used for each group to form $p(\beta_i \mid \underset{\sim}{y}^1)$, and the fifth through the ninth observations were used to update. The fixed coefficient was updated through recursive ordinary least squares. The logarithm of the one step ahead predictive density was calculated for each estimator on both the fixed and random data for observations five through ten. At the tenth observation the predictive density ratio was calculated and a record was kept of the choice of each trial. For ease of computation, the predictive density is evaluated conditional on consistent estimates of Ω and C. The predictive density for the fixed coefficient estimator for each i at each period t is proportional to

$$\left(\frac{1}{\hat{\sigma}_{fit}}\right) \exp\left(-\frac{1}{2}\frac{e_{fit}^2}{\hat{\sigma}_{fit}^2}\right) \tag{32}$$

where

$$\hat{\sigma}_{fit}^2 = \hat{\sigma}_{it}^2\left(1 + x_{it}'(\tilde{X}_{i,t-1}'\tilde{X}_{i,t-1})^{-1}x_{it}\right)$$

and x_{it} is the explanatory variable at t, $\tilde{X}_{i,t-1}'\tilde{X}_{i,t-1}$ is the sum of the cross product of the explanatory variables over the estimation period (i.e. up to $t-1$), $\hat{\sigma}_{it}$ is the standard error of the regression using observations from 1 to t, and e_{fit} is the one step ahead forecast error,

$$e_{fit} = y_{it} - x_{it}\hat{\beta}_{i,t-1}, \tag{33}$$

where $\hat{\beta}_{i,t-1}$ is the estimated coefficient using observations from 1 to $t-1$.

The predictive density for the random coefficient estimator is proportional to

$$\mid \Omega_t + X_t'C_tX_t \mid^{-\frac{1}{2}} \cdot \exp\left\{-\frac{1}{2}(\underset{\sim}{y}_t - X_t\hat{\underset{\sim}{\beta}}_{Rt-1})'(\Omega_t + X_t'C_tX_t)^{-1}(\underset{\sim}{y}_t - X_t\hat{\underset{\sim}{\beta}}_{Rt-1})\right\} \tag{34}$$

where $\underset{\sim}{y}_t = (y_{it}, \ldots, y_{Nt})'$, $\Omega_t = \text{ diag } (\hat{\sigma}_{1t}^2, \ldots, \hat{\sigma}_{Nt}^2)$,

$$X_t = \begin{pmatrix} x_{1t} & & 0 \\ & \ddots & \\ 0 & & x_{Nt} \end{pmatrix},$$

$$\hat{\underset{\sim}{\beta}}_{Rt} = (X_t'\Omega_t^{-1}X_t + C_{t-1}^{-1})^{-1}(X_t'\Omega_t^{-1}\underset{\sim}{y}_t + C_{t-1}^{-1}\hat{\underset{\sim}{\beta}}_{R,t-1}), \tag{35}$$

$$C_t - (X_t'\Omega_t^{-1}X_t + C_{t-1}^{-1})^{-1}, \tag{36}$$

and Ω_t = diag $(\hat{\sigma}_{it}^2)$. The initial C_t is obtained using the formula

$$\left\{X'\hat{\Omega}^{-1}X + \frac{1}{\hat{\Delta}}(I_N - \frac{1}{N}\underset{\sim}{e}_N\underset{\sim}{e}'_N)\right\}^{-1}, \tag{37}$$

with

$$\hat{\Delta} = \frac{1}{N-1}\sum_{i=1}^{N}(\hat{\beta}_{io} - \hat{\bar{\beta}})^2, \tag{38}$$

where $\hat{\underset{\sim}{\beta}}_{i0}$ are the least squares estimates of β_i based on the initially observed y and x and $\hat{\bar{\beta}}$ is the weighted average of $\hat{\beta}_{io}$. The predictive density for the mixed random and fixed effects model is of a similar form to (34) with the proper modification of the presence of fixed effects (e.g. Hsiao *et al.* (1993)).

The results for the random data are shown in Table 3. The entries show the percentage of the 100 trials that the procedures chose the random coefficients correctly. As one might expect, larger N tends to favor more the random effects formulation. For smaller N, the criteria work better for a smaller dispersion in the distribution of the coefficients than when the distribution of the coefficients is dispersed. This is also to be expected. However, the methods work fairly well for N=50 when σ_i is as low as .4. If N is as large as 100, then the random formulation is chosen even for very large variances of the coefficient distribution.

Table 3

RPD, AIC and Schwartz Tests for Random Data:
Percentage Correctly Predicted

Standard Deviation of β		0.1	0.2	0.4	0.6	0.8	1.5	2.0
Number of Individuals								
50	RPD	.95	.91	.77	.50	.31	.17	.14
	AIC	.90	.88	.76	.60	.38	.16	.12
	SIC	.90	.88	.80	.64	.38	.20	.12
75	RPD	.99	.96	.89	.73	.62	.57	.54
	AIC	.90	.88	.85	.70	.52	.44	.41
	SIC	.94	.90	.85	.71	.55	.49	.45
100	RPD	1.0	1.0	1.0	1.0	1.0	1.0	1.0
	AIC	1.0	1.0	1.0	1.0	.96	.94	.93
	SIC	1.0	1.0	1.0	1.0	.99	.95	.95

Tables 4-6 show the results for the fixed data. These tables show that the procedures perform quite well over a wide range of N and $\bar{\sigma}_u$. However, the entries in Tables 4-6 also indicate that the behavior of our procedure is more complex for fixed than for random coefficient data. In general, if the signal-to-noise ratio is high (R^2 above .6) the recursive predictive density ratio approach performs well in distinguishing fixed effects data from random effects data. If the signal-to-noise ratio is low (R^2 below 0.4) and N is large, then the recursive predictive density ratio approach is not able to distinguish fixed effects data from random effects data. The poor performance of recursive predictive density ratio approach to correctly pick up the fixed effects data is probably due to the power of Bayesian shrinkage factor in generating good prediction when the data does not contain much information about the unknown parameters. On the other hand, the approximate AIC and SIC perform very well in this situation, with SIC dominating the other criteria.

Table 4

RPD, AIC and Schwartz Tests for Fixed Data:
Percentage Correctly Predicted

Mean Standard Deviation of the Error Term β		2.0	1.0	0.5
Number of Individuals				
10	RPD	.88	.86	.84
	AIC	.88	.86	.84
	SIC	.88	.88	.80
50	RPD	.98	.94	.94
	AIC	.92	.90	.90
	SIC	.96	.92	.88
75	RPD	1.0	1.0	1.0
	AIC	1.0	.96	.92
	SIC	1.0	1.0	.96
100	RPD	.70	.98	.98
	AIC	.96	.92	.90
	SIC	1.0	1.0	1.0

We also examine the performance of recursive predictive density ratio in distinguishing fixed effects from random effects in a multivariate framework as in (6). For simplicity, we assume that there are two explanatory variables. We have, therefore, four possibilities — both coefficients are random (random-random), both coefficients are fixed (fixed-fixed), the first coefficient is random and the second coefficient is fixed (random-fixed), and the first coefficient is fixed and the second coefficient is random (fixed-random). We generate data for two cases. One is to assume that the data are generated from a random coefficients model with β_{1i} generated from a normal distribution with mean 1 and standard deviation of 0.3 and β_{2i} generated from a normal distribution with mean 2 and standard deviation of 0.3, respectively. The other case is to assume that the data are generated from a mixed random-fixed coefficients model with the random coefficients generated from a normal distribution with mean 1 and standard deviation of 0.3 and the fixed coefficients are

Table 5

RPD, AIC and Schwartz Tests for Fixed Data:
Mean of X-N(3, 1.0)
Percentage Correctly Predicted

Mean of R-square (M.S.D. of Error Term)		2.0 (1.0)	1.0 (2.0)	0.5 (4.0)
Number of Individuals				
50	RPD	.98	1.0	.92
	AIC	.96	1.0	.96
	SIC	.96	.92	.76
75	RPD	1.0	.60	.36
	AIC	1.0	.90	.76
	SIC	1.0	.92	.80
100	RPD	1.0	.12	.04
	AIC	1.0	.92	.80
	SIC	1.0	.96	.84

Table 6

RPD, AIC and Schwartz Tests for Fixed Data:
Mean of X-N(1, 1.0) and Mean of X-N(5, 1.0)
Percentage Correctly Predicted

Mean of R-square (M.S.D. of Error Term)		2.0 (1.0)	1.0 (2.0)	0.5 (4.0)
Number of Individuals				
50	RPD	.98	.92	.84
	AIC	1.0	1.0	.80
	SIC	1.0	.96	.72
75	RPD	1.0	.44	.36
	AIC	1.0	.96	.84
	SIC	1.0	.96	.88
100	RPD	1.0	.36	.28
	AIC	1.0	.96	.88
	SIC	1.0	1.0	1.0

generated from a mixed normal with mean -1 and 2, respectively and standard deviation of 0.3. The two explanatory variables for each individual i are generated by a bivariate normal distribution with standard deviation equal to 1 and correlation coefficient of 0.25. The mean of these two explanatory variables for each cross-sectional unit are generated from two independent normal distributions with mean 3 and standard deviation 1. The error term u_{it} is generated from a normal distribution with mean zero and variance σ_{ui}^2, where σ_{ui} is normally distributed with mean $\bar{\sigma}_u$ and standard deviation 0.125. We let $\bar{\sigma}_u$ be 0.5, 1.0, 2.0. We consider the cases where $N = 25, 35, 50$ and 75, respectively. Again we let $T = 10$.

Tables 7 and 8 present the percentage of choices of 25 trials for random coefficients (RR), fixed coefficients (FF), random-fixed (RF) and fixed-random (FR) coefficients models for data generated from random coefficients and random-fixed coefficients model, respectively. Again, all three criteria appear to do well in distinguishing these cases.

Table 7

RPD, AIC and Schwartz Tests for Random-Random Data:
Mean of β_1 – $N(1, 0.3)$ and Mean of β_2 – $N(2, 0.3)$
Percentage Correctly Predicted

Mean of R-square (M.S.D. of Error Term)		.861 (.5)			.746 (1.0)			.640 (2.0)		
		RPD	AIC	SIC	RPD	AIC	SIC	RPD	AIC	SIC
Number of Individuals										
N=25	RR	.48	.56	.56	.88	.92	.92	.96	1.0	0
	FF	.04	.08	0	0	0	0	0	0	0
	RF	.28	.16	.16	.08	.08	.08	0	0	0
	FR	.20	.20	.28	.04	0	0	.04	0	0
N=35	RR	.60	.60	.60	.88	.92	.96	.92	.96	.96
	FF	.04	.04	.04	0	0	0	0	0	0
	RF	.20	.20	.24	.08	.04	.04	.04	.04	.04
	FR	.16	.16	.12	.04	.04	0	.04	0	0
N=50	RR	.72	.72	.72	.88	.92	.92	.80	.96	1.0
	FF	0	.04	.04	0	0	0	0	0	0
	RF	.12	.12	.12	.08	.08	.08	.12	.04	0
	FR	.16	.12	.12	.04	0	0	.08	0	0
N=75	RR	.76	.76	.88	.64	.92	.96	.72	.96	1.0
	FF	0	.16	.12	0	0	0	0	0	0
	RF	.12	.04	0	.16	.04	.04	.20	0	0
	FR	.12	.04	0	.20	.04	0	.08	.04	0

While simulation results demonstrate the applicability of a recursive predictive density approach as well as our approximation formula for the AIC and SIC, they also provide useful guidance for empirical modelling. We note that other things being held constant, the larger the variance of $\underset{\sim}{\beta}$, the greater the appeal of the fixed effects formulation. On the other hand, the greater the number of cross-sectional units, the more appealing the random effects formulation. Thus, if conventional F or likelihood ratio test rejects the

Table 8

RPD, AIC and Schwartz Tests for Random-Random Data:
Mean of $\beta_1 - N(1, 0.3)$, Mean of $\gamma - N(-1, 0.3)$ and Mean of $\gamma - N(2, 0.3)$
Percentage Correctly Predicted

Mean of R-square (M.S.D. of Error Term)		.861 (1.0)			.746 (1.5)			.640 (2.0)		
		RPD	AIC	SIC	RPD	AIC	SIC	RPD	AIC	SIC
Number of Individuals										
N=25	RR	.16	.16	.16	.24	.12	.12	.24	.12	.12
	FF	.12	.04	0	0	0	0	0	0	0
	RF	.72	.60	.60	.76	.76	.76	.76	.84	.88
	FR	0	.20	.24	0	.12	.12	0	.04	0
N=35	RR	.16	.08	.04	.28	.20	.16	.32	.04	.04
	FF	.04	.04	.04	0	0	0	0	.04	0
	RF	.80	.84	.84	.72	.80	.84	.68	.92	.92
	FR	0	.04	.08	0	0	0	0	0	.04
N=50	RR	.04	0	0	.20	.04	.04	.16	0	0
	FF	.08	.04	.04	0	0	0	0	0	0
	RF	.88	.92	.92	.80	.92	.96	.80	.96	1.0
	FR	0	.04	.04	0	.04	0	.04	.04	0
N=75	RR	0	0	0	.16	.04	0	.04	0	0
	FF	0	0	0	0	0	0	0	0	0
	RF	1.0	1.0	1.0	.80	.96	1.0	.96	1.0	1.0
	FR	0	0	0	.04	0	0	0	0	0

homogeneity hypothesis (namely, $H_0 : \underset{\sim}{\beta}_i = \underset{\sim}{\beta}_j, \ \forall\, i, j$), we could narrow down the possible model choices by assuming those coefficients that are more closely clustered together as random and those coefficients that are more spread out as fixed, then use the recursive predictive density ratio to select the most appropriate representation.

5. CONCLUSION

In this paper we consider the issue of whether to pool the panel data set to draw inference about the population from the perspective of whether conditional on the variables of interest, the outcome variables can be viewed as random draws from a common population. If they are, then we can pool. If they are not, then the panel data should not be pooled to draw inference about the population. Within this framework, the issue of pooling can be viewed as random effects versus fixed effects specification. We also argue that the issue of fixed effects versus random effects specification is more appropriately viewed as an issue of model selection rather than hypothesis testing. We have suggested a recursive predictive density ratio criterion for model selection. Computationally tractable formula for approximating the AIC or SIC criterion for the random or mixed fixed and random coefficients formulation are also suggested. The Monte Carlo results indicate that all three criteria perform fairly well in finite sample in selecting the correct formulation, with the approximate SIC being the more reliable of the three.

REFERENCES

1. Akaike, H. (1973), "Information Theory and an Extension of the Maximum Likelihood Principle", in *Proc. 2nd Int. Symp. Information Theory* ed. by B.N. Petrov and F. Csaki, 267-281, Budapest: Akademiai Kiado.
2. Ashenfelter, O. (1978), "Estimating the Effect of Training Programs on Earnings", *Review of Economics and Statistics*, 60, 47-57.
3. Balestra, P. and M. Nerlove (1966), "Pooling Cross-Section and Time Series Data in the Estimation of a Dynamic Model: The Demand for Natural Gas", *Econometrica*, 34, 585-612.
4. Breusch, T.S. and A.R. Pagan (1979), "A Simple Test for Heteroscedasticity and Random Coefficient Variation", *Econometrica*, 47, 1287-94.
5. de Finetti, B. (1964), "Foresight: Its Logical Laws, Its Subjective Sources", in *Studies in Subjective Probability*, ed. by H.E. Kyburg, Jr. and H.E. Smokler, New York: Wiley, 93-158.
6. Friedman, M. (1953), *Essays in Positive Economics*, Chicago: University of Chicago Press.
7. Garcia-Ferrer, A., R.A. Highfield, F. Plam and A. Zellner (1987), "Macroeconomic Forecasting Using Pooled International Data," *Journal of Business and Economic Statistics*, 5, 53-67.
8. Geisser, S. (1980), "A Predictivistic Primer", in *Bayesian Analysis in Econometrics and Statistics: Essays in Honor of Harold Jeffreys*, Amsterdam: North Holland, 363-382.
9. Hausman, J.A. (1978), "Specification Tests in Econometrics," *Econometrica*, 46, 1251-71.
10. Hsiao, C. (1974), "Statistical Inference for a Model with Both Random Cross-Sectional and Time Effects", *International Economic Review*, 15, 12-30.
11. Hsiao, C. (1985), "Benefits and Limitations of Panel Data", *Econometric Reviews*, 4, 121-174.
12. Hsiao, C. (1986), *Analysis of Panel Data*, Cambridge, Cambridge University Press.
13. Hsiao C. (1990), "A Mixed Fixed and Random Coefficients Framework for Pooling Cross-Section and Time Series Data", paper presented at the Third Conference on Telecommunication Demand Analysis With Dynamic Regulation, Hilton Head, S. Carolina.
14. Hsiao, C. (1992), "Random Coefficients Models", ed. by L. Mátyás and P. Sevestre, Kluwer, 1st edition, 223-241, 2nd ed. (1996), 410-428.
15. Hsiao, C. (1995), "Panel Analysis for Metric Data", *Handbook of Statistical Modelling in the Social and Behavioral Sciences*, ed. by G. Arminger, C.C. Clogg and M.E. Sobel, Plenum, 361-400.
16. Hsiao, C. and J. Lightwood (1994), "Specification Analysis for Panel Data",

Cuaderuos Economicios de ICE (in Spanish), 56, 7-27.

17. Hsiao, C. and D.C. Mountain (1994), "A Framework for Regional Modeling and Impact Analysis — An Analysis of the demand for Electricity by Large Municipalities in Ontario, Canada", *Journal of Regional Science*, 34, 361-385.
18. Hsiao, C. and A.K. Tahmiscioglu (1997), "A Panel Analysis of Liquidity Constraints and Firm Investment", *Journal of the American Statistical Association*, 92, 455-465.
19. Hsiao, C., Appelbe and C.R. Dineen (1993), "A General Framework for Panel Data Models — With an Application to Canadian Customer-Dialed Long Distance Telephone Service", *Journal of Econometrics*, 59, 63-86.
20. Hsiao, C., D.C. Mountain, K.Y. Tsui and M.W. Luke Chan (1989), "Modeling Ontario Regional Electricity System Demand Using a Mixed Fixed and Random coefficients Approach", *Regional Science and Urban Economics*, 19, 567-587.
21. Klein, L.R. (1988), "The Statistical Approach to Economics," *Journal of Econometrics*, 37, 7-26.
22. Kuh, E. (1963), *Capital Stock Growth: A Micro-Econometric Approach*, Amsterdam, North-Holland.
23. Lindley, D.V. and A.F.M. Smith (1972), "Bayes Estimates for the Linear Model", *Journal of the Royal Statistical Society*, B, 34, 1-41.
24. Mundlak, Y. (1978), "On the Pooling of Time Series and Cross Section Data", *Econometrica*, 46, 69-85.
25. Min, C.K. and Z. Zellner (1993), "Bayesian and Non-Bayesian Methods for Combining Models and Forecasts with Applications to Forecasting International Growth Rates", *Journal of Econometrics*, 56, 89-118.
26. Schwarz, G. (1978), "Estimating the Dimension of a Model", *Annals of Statistics*, 6, 461-464.
27. Swamy, P.A.V.B. (1970), "Efficient Inference in a Random Coefficient Regression Model", *Econometrica*, 38, 311-323.
28. Wallace, T.D. and A. Hussain (1969), "The Use of Error Components Models in Combining Cross-Section and Time Series Data", *Econometrica*, 37, 55-72.
29. Zellner, A. (1962), "An Efficient Method of Estimating Seemingly Unrelated Regressions and Tests for Aggregation Bias", *Journal of American Statistical Association*, 57, 348-368.
30. Zellner, A. (1988), "Bayesian Analysis in Econometrics", *Journal of Econometrics*, 37, 27-50.

Panel Data Econometrics: Future Directions
J. Krishnakumar and E. Ronchetti (Editors)

CHAPTER 10

A SCORE TEST FOR INDIVIDUAL HETEROSCEDASTICITY IN A ONE-WAY ERROR COMPONENTS MODEL

Alberto HOLLY and Lucien GARDIOL

Abstract

The purpose of this paper is to derive a Rao's efficient score statistic for testing for heteroscedasticity in an error components model with only individual effects. We assume that the individual effect exists and therefore do not test for it. In addition, we assume that the individual effects, and not the white noise term may be heteroscedastic. Finally, we assume that the error components are normally distributed. We first establish, under a specific set of assumptions, the asymptotic distribution of the Score under contiguous alternatives. We then derive the expression for the Score test statistic for individual heteroscedasticity. Finally, we discuss the asymptotic local power of this Score test statistic.

1. INTRODUCTION

In the analysis of error-components models it is customary to assume that the individual effects are homoscedastic. In some situations, however, it may be appropriate to generalize the error components model context to the heteroscedastic case, as first suggested by Mazodier and Trognon (1978). Misspecification errors in presence of heteroscedasticity can produce misleading results. However, if no heteroscedasticity exists, standard estimation and specification test procedures can be applied straightforwardly. It would therefore simplify the analysis considerably if one were to test for heteroscedasticity before implementing more elaborate inference procedures to deal with the possible heteroscedasticity situation.

For this testing purpose, a natural procedure consists in using Rao's efficient score statistic [Rao (1948)], or its Lagrange Multipier (LM) interpretation provided by Silvey (1959), as its computation is based on the usual error components model in the homoscedastic case. In another setting, Breusch and Pagan (1980) have considered the standard linear regression model with non–spherical disturbances and took the error-components model of Balestra and Nerlove (1966) as an example. They presented an LM test for the null hypothesis that the individual effect is missing. Gourieroux, Holly and Monfort (1982) derived the asymptotic distribution of the LM test of Breusch and Pagan (1980) by taking into account the fact that the parameter defining the null hypothesis is on the boundary of the parameter set. They showed that the standard asymptotic distribution theory does not apply in this case and derived the appropriate nonstandard results.[1]

In a recent paper, Lejeune (1998) developed a pseudo-LM test procedure for jointly testing the null hypothesis of no individual effects and homoscedasticity against the alternative of random individual effects and heteroscedasticity in the white noise error term.[2] The pseudo-LM test derived by Lejeune (1998) is distribution-free in the sense that it does not rely on any distribution assumption such as normality. In this paper we consider a different setting than in Lejeune (1998). Firstly, we assume that the individual effect exists and therefore do not test for it. Secondly, we assume that the individual effects, and not the white noise term may be heteroscedastic. Thirdly, we assume that the error components are normally distributed. In addition, not only the specification considered in this paper differs from that of Lejeune (1998) but also the method of derivation of the main results, which we believe to be useful in other contexts as well.

The paper is organized as follows. The specification of the model as well as some preliminary assumptions are presented in Section 2. The derivation of the asymptotic distribution of the Score under contiguous alternatives is contained in Section 3. The expression of the heteroscedaticity test statistic is derived in Section 4 and its asymptotic local power is discussed in Section 5.

Throughout this paper, we tried to adhere to widely accepted set of notations in the context of Panel Data models. In particular, the unit vector (all elements $= 1$) of size $T \times 1$ is denoted by ι_T and the unit matrix (all elements $= 1$) of size $T \times T$ is denoted by J_T $(= \iota_T \iota_T')$. For a review of the main matrices used in this paper as well as their properties, see Crépon and Mairesse [(1996), Appendix].[3]

The notation $\mathbb{D}$ and $\mathbb{AD}$ are used throughout to mean the distribution and asymptotic distribution, respectively, of a random variable or a random vector. The noncentral chi–square distribution with p degrees of freedom and noncentrality parameter δ^2 is defined as the distribution of the scalar product of a random p–variate normal vector with covariance equal to the identity matrix and mean vector having a norm of δ, and is denoted by $\chi^2_p(\delta^2)$.

[1]See also Baltagi, Chang and Li (1992) for an analysis of the behavior of one–sided LM tests.
[2]We would like to thank B. Lejeune for making his unpublished manuscripts available to us.
[3]Appendix based on an unpublished manuscript by Alain Trognon (1984).

2. SPECIFICATION OF THE MODEL AND PRELIMINARY ASSUMPTIONS

We consider the one-way error components linear regression model

$$y_{nt} = x'_{nt}\beta^0 + u^0_{nt} \qquad n = 1, \ldots, N; \; t = 1, \ldots, T$$

where y_{nt} is the (scalar) observation of the dependent variable, x_{nt} a $K \times 1$ vector of non-stochastic explanatory variables, and u^0_{nt} the unobservable error term which is decomposed as

$$u^0_{nt} = \mu^0_n + v^0_{nt},$$

where μ^0_n is the unobservable random variable of individual effects and v^0_{nt} the usual unobservable error term.

We assume that

Assumption 1 *μ^0_n and v^0_{nt} are independent for all n and t; the v^0_{nt} are independent identically distributed as $\mathcal{N}(0, \sigma^{02}_v)$ and the μ^0_n are independent and distributed as $\mathcal{N}\left(0, \sigma^{02}_\mu h\left(z'_n\theta^0\right)\right)$ where z_n is a $p \times 1$ vector of explanatory variables such that $z'_n\theta^0$ does not contain a constant term; $h : \mathbb{R} \to \mathbb{R}$ is a strictly positive twice differentiable function satisfying $h(0) = 1$, $h^{(s)}(0) \neq 0$ where $h^{(s)}$ denotes the derivative of order s of h for $s = 1, 2$.*

Let

$$\delta^0 = (\beta^{0\prime}, \sigma^{02}_v, \sigma^{02}_\mu)'$$

Assumption 2 *$\delta^0 \in \Delta$ where Δ is a compact subset of $\mathbb{R}^K \times \mathbb{R}_+ \times \mathbb{R}_+$ and $\theta^0 \in \Theta$ where Θ is a compact subset of $\mathbb{R}^p$.*

Assumption 3 *(δ^0, θ^0) is an interior point of $\Delta \times \Theta$.*

It is important to observe that we assume that σ^{02}_μ is *strictly* positive - in other words, that σ^{02}_μ is *not* on the boundary of the parameter set Θ. Therefore, we shall not question the existence of individual effects. Instead, we shall test for heteroscedasticity of the individual effects by testing $H^0 : \theta^0 = 0$ against $H^a : \theta^0 \neq 0$.

The T observations for individual n can be expressed in the following matrix form:

$$y_n = X_n\beta^0 + u^0_n,$$

where y_n is the $T \times 1$ vector of the y_{nt}, X_n is the $T \times K$ matrix whose n-th row is x'_{nt} and u^0_n is the $T \times 1$ vector of the u^0_{nt}.

In this paper we deal with the so-called semi-asymptotic case where T is fixed and N goes to infinity.

Assumption 4 *The empirical distribution of (X_n, z_n), denoted by F_n, converges completely to a nondegenerate distribution function $F(X, z)$. The marginal (limiting) distribution of z will be denoted by F_z.*

More assumptions will be introduced in the following section.

Stacking the individuals one after the other, we have:

$$\begin{pmatrix} y_1 \\ \vdots \\ y_n \\ \vdots \\ y_N \end{pmatrix} = \begin{pmatrix} X_1 \\ \vdots \\ X_n \\ \vdots \\ X_N \end{pmatrix} \beta^0 + \begin{pmatrix} u_1^0 \\ \vdots \\ u_n^0 \\ \vdots \\ u_N^0 \end{pmatrix}$$

or more compactly:

$$y = X\beta^0 + u^0$$

where

$$\mathbb{D}(u) = \mathcal{N}\left(0, \Omega^0\right)$$

and

$$\Omega^0 = \sigma_v^{02} I_{NT} + \sigma_\mu^{02} \mathrm{diag}\left(h\left(z_n'\theta^0\right)\right) \otimes J_T$$

which may be conveniently written as

$$\Omega^0 = \sigma_v^{02} W_n + \mathrm{diag}\left[\sigma_v^{02} + T\sigma_\mu^{02} h\left(z_n'\theta^0\right)\right] \otimes \frac{J_T}{T}$$

where

$$W_n = I_N \otimes \left(I_T - \frac{J_T}{T}\right)$$

3. ASYMPTOTIC DISTRIBUTION OF THE SCORE UNDER CONTIGUOUS ALTERNATIVES

The log-likelihood function is:

$$\mathcal{L} = \text{constant} - \frac{1}{2}\ln\det(\Omega) - \frac{1}{2}u'\Omega^{-1}u$$

where

$$\Omega^{-1} = \frac{1}{\sigma_v^2} W_n + \mathrm{diag}\left(\frac{1}{\sigma_v^2 + T\sigma_\mu^2 h\left(z_n'\theta\right)}\right) \otimes \frac{J_T}{T} \tag{1}$$

Let

$$\gamma = \left(\beta, \sigma_v^2, \sigma_\mu^2, \theta\right)' \tag{2}$$

and consider contiguous alternatives of the form :

$$\gamma_N^a = \gamma^0 + N^{-1/2}\gamma^a \tag{3}$$

where, since we consider contiguous alternatives only for the heteroscedasticity coefficients,

$$\gamma^a = (\ 0,\ \ 0,\ \ 0,\ \ \theta'^a\ )' \tag{4}$$

The purpose of this section is to show that under specific regularity assumptions, $N^{-1/2}\partial\mathcal{L}(\gamma_N^a)/\partial\gamma$ is asymptotically normally distributed. This is the key result for the asymptotic distribution of the heteroscedasticity test to be derived in the following section.

The first differential of $\mathcal{L}$ is:

$$\mathrm{d}\mathcal{L} = -\frac{1}{2}\mathrm{tr}\left(\Omega^{-1}\mathrm{d}\Omega\right) - u'\Omega^{-1}\mathrm{d}u + \frac{1}{2}u'\Omega^{-1}\mathrm{d}\Omega\Omega^{-1}u \tag{5}$$

whcrc

$$\begin{aligned} \mathrm{d}u &= -X\mathrm{d}\beta \\ \mathrm{d}\Omega &= I_{NT}\mathrm{d}\sigma_v^2 + T\left(\mathrm{diag}\left(h\left(z_n'\theta\right)\right)\otimes\frac{J_T}{T}\right)\mathrm{d}\sigma_\mu^2 \\ &\quad + T\sigma_\mu^2\left(\mathrm{diag}\left(h'\left(z_n'\theta\right)z_n'\mathrm{d}\theta\right)\otimes\frac{J_T}{T}\right) \end{aligned}$$

By using the properties of the matrices W_n and J_T, it is not difficult to show that $\mathrm{d}\mathcal{L}$ may be written as

$$\mathrm{d}\mathcal{L} = \frac{\partial\mathcal{L}}{\partial\beta}(\gamma)d\beta + \frac{\partial\mathcal{L}}{\partial\sigma_v^2}(\gamma)d\sigma_v^2 + \frac{\partial\mathcal{L}}{\partial\sigma_\mu^2}(\gamma)d\sigma_\mu^2 + \frac{\partial\mathcal{L}}{\partial\theta}(\gamma)d\theta$$

where

$$\frac{\partial\mathcal{L}}{\partial\beta}(\gamma) = X'\Omega^{-1}u, \tag{6}$$

$$\begin{aligned} \frac{\partial\mathcal{L}}{\partial\sigma_v^2}(\gamma) = \frac{1}{2}\Bigg\{ & -\frac{N(T-1)}{\sigma_v^2} - \sum_{n=1}^{N}\left(\frac{1}{\left[\sigma_v^2 + T\sigma_\mu^2 h\left(z_n'\theta\right)\right]}\right) + \frac{1}{\sigma_v^4}u'W_n u \\ & + u'\left[\mathrm{diag}\left(\frac{1}{\left[\sigma_v^2 + T\sigma_\mu^2 h\left(z_n'\theta\right)\right]^2}\right)\otimes\frac{J_T}{T}\right]u\Bigg\}, \end{aligned} \tag{7}$$

$$\frac{\partial \mathcal{L}}{\partial \sigma_\mu^2}(\gamma) = \frac{T}{2}\left\{ -\sum_{n=1}^{N} \left(\frac{h(z_n'\theta)}{\sigma_v^2 + T\sigma_\mu^2 h(z_n'\theta)} \right) + u' \left[\operatorname{diag}\left(\frac{h(z_n'\theta)}{\left[\sigma_v^2 + T\sigma_\mu^2 h(z_n'\theta)\right]^2} \right) \otimes \frac{J_T}{T} \right] u \right\} \tag{8}$$

$$\frac{\partial \mathcal{L}}{\partial \theta}(\gamma) = \frac{1}{2}\sum_{n=1}^{N} \left\{ \frac{T\sigma_\mu^2 h^{(1)}(z_n'\theta)\, z_n}{\left[\sigma_v^2 + T\sigma_\mu^2 h(z_n'\theta)\right]} + \frac{1}{2}u' \left[\operatorname{diag}\left(\frac{T\sigma_\mu^2 h^{(1)}(z_n'\theta)\, z_n}{\left[\sigma_v^2 + T\sigma_\mu^2 h(z_n'\theta)\right]^2} \right) \otimes \frac{J_T}{T} \right] u \right\} \tag{9}$$

In order to derive the asymptotic distribution of $N^{-1/2}\partial\mathcal{L}(\gamma_N^a)/\partial\gamma$, it is necessary to evaluate the second differential of $\mathcal{L}$.

Using the fact that the second differential of u is equal to zero, the second differential of $\mathcal{L}$ is equal to:

$$\begin{aligned} \mathrm{d}^2\mathcal{L} = {} & \frac{1}{2}\operatorname{tr}\left(\Omega^{-1}\mathrm{d}\Omega\Omega^{-1}\mathrm{d}\Omega\right) - \frac{1}{2}\operatorname{tr}\left(\Omega^{-1}\mathrm{d}^2\Omega\right) \\ & - u'\Omega^{-1}\mathrm{d}\Omega\Omega^{-1}\mathrm{d}\Omega\Omega^{-1}u + \frac{1}{2}u'\Omega^{-1}\mathrm{d}^2\Omega\Omega^{-1}u \\ & + 2u'\Omega^{-1}\mathrm{d}\Omega\Omega^{-1}\mathrm{d}u - \mathrm{d}u'\Omega^{-1}\mathrm{d}u \end{aligned} \tag{10}$$

By taking the expectation of $\mathrm{d}^2\mathcal{L}$, we obtain after obvious simplification, that:

$$\mathbb{E}\left(-\mathrm{d}^2\mathcal{L}\right) = \frac{1}{2}\operatorname{tr}\left(\Omega^{-1}\mathrm{d}\Omega\Omega^{-1}\mathrm{d}\Omega\right) + \mathrm{d}\beta' X'\Omega^{-1}X\mathrm{d}\beta \tag{11}$$

It is not difficult to show that

$$\begin{aligned} \operatorname{tr}\left(\Omega^{-1}\mathrm{d}\Omega\Omega^{-1}\mathrm{d}\Omega\right) = {} & \mathrm{d}\sigma_v^2 \left(\frac{N(T-1)}{\sigma_v^4} + \sum_{n=1}^{N} \frac{1}{\left[\sigma_v^2 + T\sigma_\mu^2 h(z_n'\theta)\right]^2} \right) \mathrm{d}\sigma_v^2 \\ & + \mathrm{d}\sigma_v^2 \left(2T \sum_{n=1}^{N} \frac{h(z_n'\theta)}{\left[\sigma_v^2 + T\sigma_\mu^2 h(z_n'\theta)\right]^2} \right) \mathrm{d}\sigma_\mu^2 \\ & + \mathrm{d}\sigma_v^2 \left(2T\sigma_\mu^2 \sum_{n=1}^{N} \frac{h^{(1)}(z_n'\theta)}{\left[\sigma_v^2 + T\sigma_\mu^2 h(z_n'\theta)\right]^2} z_n' \right) \mathrm{d}\theta \\ & + \mathrm{d}\sigma_\mu^2 \left(T^2 \sum_{n=1}^{N} \frac{\left[h(z_n'\theta)\right]^2}{\left[\sigma_v^2 + T\sigma_\mu^2 h(z_n'\theta)\right]^2} \right) \mathrm{d}\sigma_\mu^2 \end{aligned}$$

$$+ \mathrm{d}\sigma_\mu^2 \left(2T^2\sigma_\mu^2 \sum_{n=1}^{N} \frac{h(z_n'\theta)\, h^{(1)}(z_n'\theta)}{\left[\sigma_v^2 + T\sigma_\mu^2 h(z_n'\theta)\right]^2} z_n' \right) \mathrm{d}\theta$$

$$+ \mathrm{d}\theta' \left(T^2\sigma_\mu^4 \sum_{n=1}^{N} \frac{\left[h^{(1)}(z_n'\theta)\right]^2}{\left[\sigma_v^2 + T\sigma_\mu^2 h(z_n'\theta)\right]^2} z_n z_n' \right) \mathrm{d}\theta$$

We shall first prove the following result:

Lemma 1 *The loglikelihood $\mathcal{L}$ is regular with respect to its first and second derivatives, i.e.*

$$\mathbb{E}\left(-d^2\mathcal{L}\right) = \mathbb{E}\left(d\mathcal{L}\right)^2$$

Proof. [4]
From (5) we have

$$(\mathrm{d}\mathcal{L})^2 = \frac{1}{4}\left[u'\Omega^{-1}\mathrm{d}\Omega\Omega^{-1}u - \mathbb{E}(u'\Omega^{-1}\mathrm{d}\Omega\Omega^{-1}u)\right]^2 + \mathrm{d}u'\Omega^{-1}uu'\Omega^{-1}\mathrm{d}u$$
$$- \left[u'\Omega^{-1}\mathrm{d}\Omega\Omega^{-1}u - \mathbb{E}(u'\Omega^{-1}\mathrm{d}\Omega\Omega^{-1}u)\right] u'\Omega^{-1}\mathrm{d}u$$

The expectation of the third term of the right-hand side is equal to zero. Thus,

$$\begin{aligned}
\mathbb{E}\,(\mathrm{d}\mathcal{L})^2 &= \frac{1}{4}V\,(u'\Omega^{-1}\mathrm{d}\Omega\Omega^{-1}u) + \mathrm{d}u'\Omega^{-1}\mathrm{d}u \\
&= \frac{1}{2}\mathrm{tr}\left(\Omega^{-1}\mathrm{d}\Omega\Omega^{-1}\mathrm{d}\Omega\right) + \mathrm{d}u'\Omega^{-1}\mathrm{d}u \\
&= \mathbb{E}\left(-\mathrm{d}^2\mathcal{L}\right)
\end{aligned}$$

as stated. ■

Let z_j be the j−th component of z, $j = 1, \ldots, p$. We introduce the following additional assumptions.

Assumption 5 $\int |\frac{h^{(1)}(z'\theta)}{h(z'\theta)} z_j| dF_z(z) < \infty$ *for every* $j = 1, \ldots, p$.

Assumption 6 $\int |\frac{h^{(2)}(z'\theta)}{h(z'\theta)} z_j z_k| dF_z(z) < \infty$ *for every* $j, k = 1, \ldots, p$.

Assumption 7 $\int \frac{h^{(1)2}(z'\theta)}{h^2(z'\theta)} |z_j z_k| dF_z(z) < \infty$ *for every* $j, k = 1, \ldots, p$.

Proposition 1 *Let Assumptions 1 through 7 hold. Then*

i. $\mathbb{E}[-(1/N)\partial^2\mathcal{L}(\gamma)/\partial\gamma\partial\gamma']$ *converges uniformly on* Γ *to the asymptotic information matrix* $\mathcal{I}(\gamma)$;

[4]This result holds in a more general situation than the specific one considered in this paper. The proof we provide is simpler than the corresponding proof in Magnus (1978).

ii. $-(1/N)\partial^2\mathcal{L}(\gamma)/\partial\gamma\partial\gamma'$ *converges almost surely and uniformly on* Γ *to* $\mathcal{I}(\gamma)$.

Proof. Let $e^0 = \Omega^{0-1/2}u^0$ and suppose that Assumptions 1 through 7 hold. Then, by inspection, one may easily verify that all the elements of $-(1/N)\partial^2\mathcal{L}(\gamma)/\partial\gamma\partial\gamma'$ which, to save space, are not reproduced here, are of the form $(1/N)\sum_{n=1}^{N} f(X_n, z_n, e_n^0, \gamma)$ where the functions $f(X, z, e^0, \gamma)$ are either uniformly bounded or dominated by a function independent of γ which is integrable with respect to the product measure

$$\nu(A) = \int\int \mathbb{I}_A(X, z, e^0)\mathrm{d}F(X, z)\mathrm{d}\Phi(e^0)$$

where $\Phi(e^0)$ is the $\mathcal{N}(0,1)$ distribution, and $\mathbb{I}_A(X, z, e^0) = 1$ if $(X, z, e^0) \in A$, 0 otherwise.

The assertion of the proposition follows from the version of the Uniform strong law of large numbers proved in Gallant [(1987), Theorem 1, pp. 159–162]. ■

Note that the asymptotic information matrix $\mathcal{I}(\gamma)$ is of the form

$$\mathcal{I}(\gamma) = \begin{pmatrix} \mathcal{I}_{\beta\beta}(\gamma) & 0 & 0 & 0 \\ 0 & \mathcal{I}_{\sigma_v^2\sigma_v^2}(\gamma) & \mathcal{I}_{\sigma_v^2\sigma_\mu^2}(\gamma) & \mathcal{I}_{\sigma_v^2\theta}(\gamma) \\ 0 & \mathcal{I}_{\sigma_\mu^2\sigma_v^2}(\gamma) & \mathcal{I}_{\sigma_\mu^2\sigma_\mu^2}(\gamma) & \mathcal{I}_{\sigma_\mu^2\theta}(\gamma) \\ 0 & \mathcal{I}_{\theta\sigma_v^2}(\gamma) & \mathcal{I}_{\theta\sigma_\mu^2}(\gamma) & \mathcal{I}_{\theta\theta}(\gamma) \end{pmatrix}$$

where, when evaluated at γ^0,

$$\mathcal{I}_{\beta\beta}(\gamma^0) = \lim_{N\to\infty} \frac{1}{N} X'\Omega^{0-1}X,$$

$$\mathcal{I}_{\sigma_v^2\sigma_v^2}(\gamma^0) = \frac{1}{2}\left[\frac{(T-1)}{\sigma_v^{04}} + \frac{1}{\left(\sigma_v^{02} + T\sigma_\mu^{02}\right)^2}\right],$$

$$\mathcal{I}_{\sigma_v^2\sigma_\mu^2}(\gamma^0) = \mathcal{I}_{\sigma_\mu^2\sigma_v^2}(\gamma^0) = \frac{T}{2\left(\sigma_v^{02} + T\sigma_\mu^{02}\right)^2}$$

$$\mathcal{I}_{\sigma_v^2\theta}(\gamma^0) = \mathcal{I}'_{\theta\sigma_v^2}(\gamma^0) = \frac{T\sigma_\mu^{02}h^{(1)}(0)}{2\left(\sigma_v^{02} + T\sigma_\mu^{02}\right)^2} \lim_{N\to\infty} \frac{1}{N}\iota'_N Z$$

$$\mathcal{I}_{\sigma_\mu^2\sigma_\mu^2}(\gamma^0) = \frac{T^2}{2\left(\sigma_v^{02} + T\sigma_\mu^{02}\right)^2}$$

$$\mathcal{I}_{\sigma_\mu^2\theta}(\gamma^0) = \mathcal{I}'_{\theta\sigma_\mu^2}(\gamma^0) = \frac{T^2\sigma_\mu^{02}h^{(1)}(0)}{2\left(\sigma_v^{02} + T\sigma_\mu^{02}\right)^2} \lim_{N\to\infty} \frac{1}{N}\iota'_N Z$$

$$\mathcal{I}_{\theta\theta}(\gamma^0) = \frac{T^2\sigma_\mu^{04}\left[h^{(1)}(0)\right]^2}{2\left(\sigma_v^{02} + T\sigma_\mu^{02}\right)^2} \lim_{N\to\infty} \frac{1}{N} Z'Z$$

Let

$$\underline{Z} = \left(I_N - \frac{J_N}{N} \right) Z \tag{12}$$

be the matrix obtained by centering each column of Z.

We introduce the following additional assumptions:

Assumption 8 $\lim_{N\to\infty} \frac{1}{N} X'\Omega^{0-1}X$ *is nonsingular.*

Assumption 9 $\lim_{N\to\infty} \frac{1}{N}\ \underline{Z}'\underline{Z}$ *is nonsingular.*

Lemma 2 *Under Assumptions 8 and 9,* $\mathcal{I}(\gamma^0)$ *is nonsingular.*

Proof. We may write $\mathcal{I}(\gamma^0)$ as

$$\mathcal{I}(\gamma^0) = \begin{pmatrix} \mathcal{I}_{\delta\delta}(\gamma^0) & \mathcal{I}_{\delta\theta}(\gamma^0) \\ \mathcal{I}_{\theta\delta}(\gamma^0) & \mathcal{I}_{\theta\theta}(\gamma^0) \end{pmatrix}$$

It is easy to verify that if Assumption 8 is satisfied, then $\mathcal{I}_{\delta\delta}(\gamma^0)$ is nonsingular. Therefore, $\mathcal{I}(\gamma^0)$ is nonsingular if and only if $\mathcal{I}_{\delta\delta}(\gamma^0) - \mathcal{I}_{\delta\theta}(\gamma^0)\mathcal{I}_{\theta\theta}(\gamma^0)^{-1}\mathcal{I}_{\theta\delta}(\gamma^0)$ is nonsingular. In turn, this property is implied by Assumption 9. ■

Proposition 2 *Under Assumptions 1 through 9*

$$\mathbb{AD}[N^{-1/2}\partial\mathcal{L}(\gamma_N^a)/\partial\gamma] = \mathcal{N}(0, \mathcal{I}(\gamma^0))$$

Proof. If Assumptions 1 through 9 hold, then one can verify that, without additional assumptions, the Central limit theorem for contiguous alternatives proved in Gallant and Holly (1980) applies. Hence, $N^{-1/2}\partial\mathcal{L}(\gamma_N^a)/\partial\gamma$ converges in distribution to the stated normal distribution. ■

4. THE HETEROSCEDASTICITY SCORE TEST STATISTIC

The necessary first-order conditions system for the maximization of the log-likelihood function subject to the constraint $\theta = 0$ boils down to the familiar estimating equation for the homoscedastic one-way error components model; that is:

$$\widetilde{\beta}^{(c)} = \left(X'\widetilde{\Omega}^{(c)\text{-}1}X\right)^{-1}\left(X'\widetilde{\Omega}^{(c)\text{-}1}y\right)$$

$$\widetilde{\sigma}_v^{2(c)} = \frac{\widetilde{u}^{(c)\prime}W_n\widetilde{u}^{(c)}}{N(T-1)}$$

$$\widetilde{\sigma}_\mu^{2(c)} = \frac{\widetilde{u}^{(c)\prime}\overline{B}_n\widetilde{u}^{(c)}}{N(T-1)} - \frac{\widetilde{u}^{(c)\prime}\widetilde{u}^{(c)}}{NT(T-1)}$$

where

$$\widetilde{u}^{(c)} = y - X\widetilde{\beta}^{(c)}$$
$$\overline{B}_n = I_N \otimes \frac{J_T}{T}$$

It is useful to note that

$$\widetilde{\sigma}_v^{2(c)} + T\widetilde{\sigma}_\mu^{2(c)} = \frac{\widetilde{u}^{(c)\prime}\overline{B}_n\widetilde{u}^{(c)}}{N} \tag{13}$$

Let

$$\widetilde{\gamma}^{(c)} = \left(\widetilde{\beta}^{(c)}, \widetilde{\sigma}_v^{2(c)}, \widetilde{\sigma}_\mu^{2(c)}, 0\right)'$$

All the components of the score vector $\partial\mathcal{L}(\gamma)/\partial\gamma$ evaluated at the constrained estimator $\widetilde{\gamma}^{(c)}$ are equal to zero, except $\partial\mathcal{L}(\widetilde{\gamma}^{(c)})/\partial\theta$ which is equal to:

$$\frac{\partial\mathcal{L}}{\partial\theta}(\widetilde{\gamma}^{(c)}) = \frac{T}{2}\frac{\widetilde{\sigma}_\mu^{2(c)}h^{(1)}(0)}{\left(\widetilde{\sigma}_v^{2(c)} + T\widetilde{\sigma}_\mu^{2(c)}\right)^2} \times \left[\sum_{n=1}^{N}\left(u_n^{(c)\prime}\frac{J_T}{T}u_n^{(c)}\right)z_n - \left(\widetilde{\sigma}_v^{2(c)} + T\widetilde{\sigma}_\mu^{2(c)}\right)\sum_{n=1}^{N} z_n\right] \tag{14}$$

It is convenient to write $\partial\mathcal{L}(\widetilde{\gamma}^{(c)})/\partial\gamma$ more compactly in matrix notation. To this purpose, let $\widetilde{s}^{(c)}$ be the $N \times 1$ vector of the $\widetilde{s}_n^{(c)}$ where $\widetilde{s}_n^{(c)} = \widetilde{u}_n^{(c)\prime}(J_T/T)\widetilde{u}_n^{(c)}$.

Using (13), it is easy to verify that $\widetilde{\sigma}_v^{2(c)} + T\widetilde{\sigma}_\mu^{2(c)}$ is the mean of the $\widetilde{s}_n^{(c)}$. We may thus write,

$$\sum_{n=1}^{N}\left[\widetilde{u}_n^{(c)\prime}\frac{J_T}{T}\widetilde{u}_n^{(c)}\left(z_n - \frac{1}{N}\sum_{n=1}^{N} z_n\right)\right] = \underline{Z}'\widetilde{s}^{(c)}$$

We may thus write $\partial\mathcal{L}(\widetilde{\gamma}^{(c)})/\partial\gamma$ more compactly as:

$$\frac{\partial\mathcal{L}}{\partial\gamma}(\widetilde{\gamma}^{(c)}) = \left(0, 0, 0, \frac{\partial\mathcal{L}}{\partial\theta}(\widetilde{\gamma}^{(c)})\right)' \tag{15}$$

where

$$\frac{\partial\mathcal{L}}{\partial\theta}(\widetilde{\gamma}^{(c)}) = \frac{1}{2}\frac{T\widetilde{\sigma}_\mu^{2(c)}h^{(1)}(0)}{\left(\widetilde{\sigma}_v^{2(c)} + T\widetilde{\sigma}_\mu^{2(c)}\right)^2}\underline{Z}'\widetilde{s}^{(c)} \tag{16}$$

As usual, the information matrix evaluated at γ is defined as

$$\mathcal{I}_N(\gamma) = -\mathbb{E}\left\{\frac{\partial^2\mathcal{L}(\gamma)}{\partial\gamma\partial\gamma'}\right\}$$

We may write $\mathcal{I}_N^{-1}(\gamma)$ as

$$\mathcal{I}_N^{-1}(\gamma) = \begin{pmatrix} \mathcal{I}_N^{\delta\delta}(\gamma) & \mathcal{I}_N^{\delta\theta}(\gamma) \\ \mathcal{I}_N^{\theta\delta}(\gamma) & \mathcal{I}_N^{\theta\theta}(\gamma) \end{pmatrix} \tag{17}$$

By using (12) and (17), we easily verify that

$$\mathcal{I}_N^{\theta\theta}(\widetilde{\gamma}^{(c)}) = \frac{2\left(\widetilde{\sigma}_v^{2(c)} + T\widetilde{\sigma}_\mu^{2(c)}\right)^2}{T^2\widetilde{\sigma}_\mu^{4(c)}\left[h^{(1)}(0)\right]^2}\left(\underline{Z}'\underline{Z}\right)^{-1} \tag{18}$$

We are now in position to derive the expression for the Score test statistic ξ^S given by:

$$\xi^S = \frac{\partial\mathcal{L}}{\partial\gamma}\left(\widetilde{\gamma}^{(c)}\right)'\mathcal{I}_N^{-1}(\widetilde{\gamma}^{(c)})\frac{\partial\mathcal{L}}{\partial\gamma}\left(\widetilde{\gamma}^{(c)}\right) \tag{19}$$

Straightforward computation shows, by using (15), (16) and (18), that

$$\xi^S = \frac{1}{2(\widetilde{\sigma}_v^{2(c)} + T\widetilde{\sigma}_\mu^{2(c)})^2}\widetilde{s}^{(c)\prime}\underline{Z}\left(\underline{Z}'\underline{Z}\right)^{-1}\underline{Z}'\widetilde{s}^{(c)} \tag{20}$$

Alternatively, by using the fact that $\widetilde{\sigma}_v^{2(c)} + T\widetilde{\sigma}_\mu^{2(c)}$ is the mean of the $\widetilde{s}_n^{(c)}$, we may write the expression for the Score test statistic ξ^S as follows,

$$\xi^S = \frac{1}{2}\left(\frac{\widetilde{s}^{(c)}}{\overline{s}} - \iota_N\right)'\underline{Z}\left(\underline{Z}'\underline{Z}\right)^{-1}\underline{Z}'\left(\frac{\widetilde{s}^{(c)}}{\overline{s}} - \iota_N\right) \tag{21}$$

where $\overline{s}$ is the mean of $\widetilde{s}^{(c)}$.

The Score test statistic ξ^S is thus one half of the explained sum of squares of the OLS regression of $\widetilde{s}^{(c)}/\overline{s} - \iota_N$ against $\underline{Z}$ as in Breusch and Pagan (1979)).[5]

5. ASYMPTOTIC LOCAL POWER

Since, according to Proposition 2, $\mathbb{AD}[N^{-1/2}\partial\mathcal{L}(\gamma_N^a)/\partial\gamma] = \mathcal{N}(0, \mathcal{I}(\gamma^0))$, one can show that, under contiguous alternatives, the distribution of the Score test statistic ξ^S converges to the noncentral chi–square distribution with p degrees of freedom and noncentrality parameter $\gamma^{a\prime}A\gamma^a$, that is,

$$\mathbb{AD}\left(\xi^S\right) = \chi_p^2\left(\gamma^{a\prime}A\gamma^a\right)$$

where

$$A = \begin{pmatrix} 0 & 0 & 0 & 0 \\ 0 & 0 & 0 & 0 \\ 0 & 0 & 0 & 0 \\ 0 & 0 & 0 & \mathcal{I}^{\theta\theta}(\gamma^0) \end{pmatrix}$$

For a proof see, for example, Holly (1987).

[5]Notice also the difference and similarity with the particular expression of the Pseudo-LM test in Lejeune (1998) when the normality assumption is assumed to hold.

The asymptotic power of the test is given by the noncentrality parameter $\gamma^{a\prime}A\gamma^{a}$. Its expression is given by:

$$\gamma^{a\prime}A\gamma^{a} = \lim_{N\to\infty} \frac{1}{2}\frac{T^2\sigma_\mu^4\left(h^{(1)}(0)\right)^2}{\left(\sigma_v^2+T\sigma_\mu^2\right)^2}\theta^{a\prime}(\underline{Z}'\underline{Z}/N)\theta^{a}$$

The asymptotic power is influenced by three factors. Firstly, not surprisingly, the power is influenced by θ^a , the test is more powerful to detect alternatives which are away from the null hypothesis. Secondly, although the Score test statistic itself does not depend on $h(0)$ or $h^{(1)}(0)$, the asymptotic power is an increasing function of $\left(h^{(1)}(0)\right)^2$ for any given alternative. Thirdly, the power increases with T, as the multiplicative constant $T\sigma_\mu^2/\left(\sigma_v^2+T\sigma_\mu^2\right)$ converges to 1 when T goes to infinity. This last effect shows that the test is improved when the number of observations for each individual sample increases. One could also note that the local power of the test tends to zero when σ_μ^2 tends to zero and will tend to be small if $T\sigma_\mu^2$ is small compared to σ_v^2. Thus, as one should expect, the test will be powerful in situations where the individual heteroscedasticity is high.

REFERENCES

1. Balestra, P. and M. Nerlove (1966), "Pooling cross-section and time series data in the estimation of a dynamic model", *Econometrica*, 34, 85–612.
2. Baltagi, B. H., Y. J. Chang and Q. Li (1992), "Monte Carlo results on several new and existing tests for the error component model," *Journal of Econometrics*, 54, 95–120.
3. Breusch, T. S. and A. R. Pagan (1979), "A simple test of heteroscedasticity and random coefficient variation", *Econometrica*, 47, 1287– 1294.
4. Breusch, T. S. and A. R. Pagan (1980), "The Lagrange multiplier test and its applications to model specification in econometrics", *Review of Economic Studies*, 47, 239–253.
5. Crépon, B. and J. Mairesse (1996), "The Chamberlain approach", in *The econometrics of panel data. A handbook of the theory with applications*, L. Mátyás and P. Sevestre eds, The Netherlands: Kluwer.
6. Gallant, A. R. (1987), *Nonlinear statistical models*, New York: Wiley.
7. Gallant, A.R., and A. Holly (1980), "Statistical inference in an implicit, nonlinear, simultaneous equation model in the context of maximum likelihood estimation", *Econometrica*, 48, 697–720.
8. Gourieroux, Ch., A. Holly and A. Monfort (1982), "Kuhn-Tucker, Likelihood Ratio and Wald tests for nonlinear models with inequality constraints on the parameters", *Discussion Paper Series* , 770, Harvard University.
9. Holly, A. (1987), "Specification tests: an overview", in *Advances in econometrics – Fifth World Congress*, Volume I, T. F. Bewley ed., New York: Cambridge University Press.
10. Lejeune, B. (1998), "A distribution-free joint test for random individual effects and heteroscedasticity allowing for incomplete panels," *Mimeo*.
11. Magnus, J. R. (1978), "Maximum likelihood estimation of the GLS model with unknown parameters in the disturbance covariance matrix," *Journal of Econometrics*, 7, 281–312. Corrigenda, *Journal of Econometrics*, 10, 261.

12. Mazodier, P. and A. Trognon (1978), "Heteroscedasticity and stratification in error components models", *Annales de l'INSEE*, 30–31, 451– 509.
13. Rao, C. R. (1948), "Large sample tests of statistical hypotheses concerning several parameters with applications to problems of estimation," *Proceedings of the Cambridge Philosophical Society*, 44, 50–57.
14. Silvey, S. D. (1959), "The Lagrangian multiplier test", *The Annals of Mathematical Statistics* , 30, 389-407.
15. Trognon, A. (1984), *Econométrie II*, Lecture notes, INSEE–ENSAE.

Panel Data Econometrics: Future Directions
J. Krishnakumar and E. Ronchetti (Editors)

CHAPTER 11

AGGREGATION AND UNIT ROOTS IN ECONOMIC TIME SERIES

Attila HORNOK and László MÁTYÁS

Abstract

This paper analyses the effects of aggregation on testing the null hypothesis of unit root in time series. It shows that when an economic time series is derived through the aggregations of several individual time series, the usual Dickey-Fuller and Phillips-Perron tests can be misleading. Here an alternative test is introduced which explicitly takes into account the behaviour of the individual series. We derive the theoretical distribution of the new test under quite general conditions and give some simulated critical values as well.

1. INTRODUCTION

Perron and Phillips (1987), Stock and Watson (1986) and many others asked the important question: "Does the GNP have a unit root?" No one has come up, however, with a definite answer to this, as in all empirical studies the outcome of the investigation depends on the time series and the sample periods used. Most of the analyses working with longer data sets (frequently going back to the last century) tend to reject the stochastic trend hypothesis, while studies using "shorter" time series find strong evidence for the random walk hypothesis (e.g., Nelson and Plosser (1982), Perron (1989), Zivot and Andrews (1992), Ben-David and Papell (1996), Diebold and Senhadji (1996), Nelson and Murray (1997)). The question is important though, as whether an economic shock has temporary or a lasting effect has serious theoretical (and practical) implications.

Most of the theoretical explanations of this phenomenon went along the lines of structural breaks, non-homogeneity of the data, misspecification of the models (inclusion of different types of dummies), or wrong size of the tests. In this paper we try to follow another path and get some insights into the effects of the aggregation. We extend Phillips and Perron's approach and test for a unit root in aggregate series including ARIMA models as well, and show the meanings of the nuisance parameters as far as aggregation is concerned. Although the transformations of the test statistics proposed by Phillips (1987) eliminate asymptotically the nuisance parameters these become focus parameters in our case since we can get from them important information about the aggregate process. If we ignore this information and we treat them as nuisance parameters they can cause serious size distortion as well, as we demonstrate by simulation, even in relatively large samples, which results in over-rejection of the null hypothesis of unit root.

We suggest that we should take into account the heterogeneity of the micro time series making up the GNP (GDP) before testing for unit roots. In our context, the heterogeneity means the form of the aggregate stationary and non-stationary processes which make up the aggregate process. There are several factors influencing the long run behavior of these aggregate series not considered by most of the previous studies.

Granger (1980) shows that the aggregation can lead to fractionally integrated processes, where he considers different types of heterogeneity. He assumes that the autoregressive parameters of many AR(1) processes are continuous random variables. Lippi (1988) studies how the individual microbehaviors can effect the complexity of the dynamic macromodels and the dynamic shape of aggregated Error Correction Models. For further developments in this area see Lippi and Zaffaroni (1998).

It is quite well understood that macroeconomic time series reflect the behavior of individual economic agents through an "aggregation window" (Granger (1992)). Although the problem of aggregation has been studied extensively in the literature, little is known about its effect on the nature of economic time series.

Macroeconometric modelling explicitly or implicitly assumes the homogenous behavior of individual agents in the economy (representative agent), in order to make the modelling process feasible. If we accept, however, that macro time series are produced by aggregating up a large number of individual micro series, it is foolish to believe in the homogeneity of all series. The usual argument then goes by assuming that the effect of the "outlier" time series cancel each other out, which, as we are going to show is misleading and incorrect.

In this paper we demonstrate that the heterogeneity of individual time series, that is the parameters of the aggregate stationary and non-stationary processes have a strong effect of the behavior of the aggregate series. We show how unit root tests are affected by this heterogeneity and come up with some constructive suggestions to get proper inference on the stationary/non-stationary nature of an aggregate macroeconomic data series.

In Section 2 we analyze a simple model to represent the relationships between the heterogeneity of the micro series and the nuisance parameters of the test statistics in the aggregate series. In Section 3 we provide some simulated critical values for the test statistics under different degrees of heterogeneity. In the next section we generalize our approach to more sophisticated models and in Section 5 we apply our results to the US GDP series.

2. THE PROBLEM

Conventional models treat the individual heterogeneity in the aggregate series by fitting ARMA models for the error terms. However, here we first look at the micro series and then aggregate them, so it can be analyzed what type of ARMA structure is generated.

We assume that macroeconomic series y_t is the result of an aggregation over N individuals: $y_t = \sum_{i=1}^{N} y_t^{(i)}$. Suppose that amongst the individual series there are N^* random walks and $N - N^*$ stationary AR(1) processes:

$$\begin{aligned} y_{1t} &= \rho y_{1t-1} + u_{1t} \\ y_{2t} &= \rho y_{2t-1} + u_{2t} \\ &\vdots \\ y_{N^*t} &= \rho y_{N^*t-1} + u_{N^*t} \\ y_{N^*+1,t} &= \rho^* y_{N^*+1,t-1} + u_{N^*+1,t} \\ &\vdots \\ y_{Nt} &= \rho^* y_{Nt-1} + u_{Nt} \\ \rho &= 1, \end{aligned} \tag{1}$$

where $|\rho^*| < 1$ and $0 \leq N^* \leq N$. When $N^* = 0$ all individuals are stationary, more exactly they are equivalent to stationary processes in large samples. When $N^* = N$ all individual series are integrated to order 1 (have a unit root). In any other case the individual series are a mixture of stationary and nonstationary processes.

Property 1. *When $N^* > 0$, the aggregate series y_t is integrated to order 1.* This means that the aggregate series "inherits" the unit root of even a single individual.
To start with, we assume that the following conditions are satisfied:

(a) u_{kt} ($k = 1, 2, \ldots, N,\ t = 1, 2, \ldots$) are independent random variables, and $u_{it} \sim \left(0, \sigma_{(1)}^2\right)$ for $i = 1, 2, \ldots, N^*$, $u_{jt} \sim \left(0, \sigma_{(2)}^2\right)$ for $j = N^* + 1, N^* + 2, \ldots, N$;

(b) There exists M such that $\sup_t E\left(|u_{kt}|^\beta\right) < M$ for some $\beta > 2$, for all $k = 1, \ldots, N$; and

(c) Initial conditions $y_{10}, y_{20}, \ldots, y_{N^*0}$ have distributions independent of sample size T, initial conditions of the stationary AR(1) processes $y_{N^*+1,0}, y_{N^*+2,0}, \ldots, y_{N0}$ have distributions with zero mean and finite α-th moment for some $\alpha > 2$, and $y_{N^*+1,0}, y_{N^*+2,0}, \ldots, y_{N0}$ are independent of u_{kl}.

In Section 4 we relax our assumptions allowing more realistic models.

Now, we aggregate the random walk and the stationary AR(1) processes into one random walk and one stationary AR(1) process

$$\begin{aligned} y_t^{(1)} &= y_{1t} + y_{2t} + \cdots + y_{N^*t}, \\ y_t^{(2)} &= y_{N^*+1,t} + y_{N^*+2,t} + \cdots + y_{Nt}, \end{aligned}$$

to get only two time series:

$$\begin{aligned} y_t^{(1)} &= \rho y_{t-1}^{(1)} + u_t^{(1)}, \\ y_t^{(2)} &= \rho^* y_{t-1}^{(2)} + u_t^{(2)}, \\ \rho &= 1, \end{aligned}$$

where $\left\{u_t^{(1)}\right\}$ is an independent sequence of random variables with zero mean and $N^*\sigma_{(1)}^2$ variance and $\left\{u_t^{(2)}\right\}$ is an independent sequence of random variables with zero mean and $(N-N^*)\,\sigma_{(2)}^2$ variance and both with uniformly bounded β-th moments. Let $u_0^{(1)}$, $u_0^{(2)}$ be zero. Moreover, $\left\{u_1^{(1)}, u_1^{(2)}, u_2^{(1)}, u_2^{(2)}, \ldots\right\}$ sequence of the mixed innovations is independent, the distribution of $y_0^{(1)}$ is fixed and independent of T, $y_0^{(2)}$ has a distribution with zero mean and finite variance, and $y_0^{(2)}$ and the sequence $\left\{u_1^{(1)}, u_1^{(2)}, u_2^{(1)}, u_2^{(2)}, \ldots\right\}$ are independent.

Denote y_t the aggregate time series,

$$y_t = y_t^{(1)} + y_t^{(2)}, \tag{2}$$

so that

$$\begin{aligned} y_t &= \rho y_{t-1} + (\rho^* - 1)\, y_{t-1}^{(2)} + u_t^{(1)} + u_t^{(2)} \\ \rho &= 1. \end{aligned} \tag{3}$$

Define the new residuals

$$u_t^* = (\rho^* - 1)\, y_{t-1}^{(2)} + u_t^{(1)} + u_t^{(2)}, \; t = 1, 2, \ldots$$

and $u_0^* = u_0^{(1)} + u_0^{(2)}$ is zero, so the data generating process (3) can be rewritten in the form

$$\begin{aligned} y_t &= \rho y_{t-1} + u_t^* \\ \rho &= 1. \end{aligned} \tag{4}$$

Then, u_t^* is a random variable with zero mean,

$$N^*\sigma_{(1)}^2 + (N-N^*)\,\sigma_{(2)}^2 + (N-N^*)\,\sigma_{(2)}^2 \frac{\rho^*-1}{\rho^*+1}\left[(\rho^*)^{2(t-1)} - 1\right]$$
$$+ (\rho^*-1)^2 (\rho^*)^{2(t-1)}\, Var\left(y_0^{(2)}\right),$$

variance and

$$\begin{aligned} Cov\left(u_{t+1}^*, u_t^*\right) &= (\rho^*-1)^2 \rho^* \times \left[(\rho^*)^{2(t-1)} Var\left(y_0^{(2)}\right) + (N-N^*)\,\sigma_{(2)}^2 \frac{(\rho^*)^{2(t-1)} - 1}{(\rho^*)^2 - 1}\right] \\ &\quad + (\rho^*-1)(N-N^*)\,\sigma_{(2)}^2, \\ Cov\left(u_{t+j}^*, u_t^*\right) &= \rho^* Cov\left(u_{t+j-1}^*, u_t^*\right), \text{ for } j > 1. \end{aligned}$$

autocovariances. Since the autocovariances decay exponentially after $j = 1$, the first difference process of the aggregate series, u_t^* is a zero mean ARMA(1, 1) process, that is, the aggregate series is an ARIMA(1, 1, 1) process.[1] We emphasize that following our approach we can conclude not only the well-known fact that the aggregation of ARIMA processes induces higher order ARIMA process but we will see how the heterogeneity parameters form the nuisance parameters.

The coventional unit root tests in ARIMA$(p,1,q)$ models which ignore the implied information of the aggregate series are proposed by Said and Dickey (1984,1985), by Phillips and Perron (1988) Hall (1989) and by Pantula and Hall (1991). Furthermore, in the cited papers it is assumed that the innovations are identically and, further, normally distributed and "they do not take explicitly into account the effects of the aggregation and the heterogeneity of the individual time series".

In the special case of $\rho^* = 0$, u_t^* is a zero mean invertible MA(1) process (for $N^*\sigma_{(1)}^2 > 0$). Consider the partial sums of the innovation sequence $\{u_t^*\}$,

$$S_t = u_1^* + u_2^* + \ldots + u_t^*,$$

and the conventional random element

$$X_T(r) = T^{-1/2} S_{[Tr]}$$

for $(j-1)/T \le r < j/T$ $(j = 1, \cdots, T)$, where $[Tr]$ denotes the integer part of Tr. The long-run variance is $N^*\sigma_{(1)}^2$ because

$$\lim_{T\to\infty} T^{-1} E\left(S_T^2\right) = \lim_{T\to\infty} N^*\sigma_{(1)}^2 +$$

$$\lim_{T\to\infty} T^{-1}\left[\left(N - N^*\right)\sigma_{(2)}^2 \frac{(\rho^*)^{2T} - 1}{(\rho^*)^2 - 1} + \left((\rho^*)^T - 1\right)^2 Var\left(y_0^{(2)}\right)\right].$$

Then, the first lemma is the corresponding functional central limit theorem for the process X_T.

Lemma 1 *If the innovation sequences* $\{u_{kt}\}$ $(k = 1, 2, \ldots, N)$ *satisfy conditions* $(a)-(c)$, *and* $|\rho^*| < 1$, *then* $X_T \Rightarrow \sqrt{N^*}\sigma_{(1)} W$, *as* $T \to \infty$.

Here W denotes the standard Brownian motion, which has sample paths lying in $C[0,1]$ and the symbol '$\Rightarrow$' means weak convergence of the associated probability measures. The proof of Lemma 1 is clear from the 29.7 Corrolary of Davidson (1995, p.482). Under $\rho = 1$ we have $y_t = S_t + y_0$, where $y_0 = y_0^{(1)} + y_0^{(2)}$. In the following lemma we establish the results which play central role in this paper.

[1] It can easily be seen that $(1 - \rho^* L)\Delta y_t = (1 - \rho^* L) u_t^{(1)} + (1 - L) u_t^{(2)}$, where the moving average part is the sum of two MA(1) processes, so there exists the $v_t - \theta v_{t-1}$ representation for this part. If ρ^* equals to zero, the invertible solution for θ, we have $\theta = -0.5c - 1 + \sqrt{0.25c^2 + c}$, where $c = N^*\sigma_{(1)}^2 / (N - N^*)\sigma_{(2)}^2$. The problems with the standard Phillips-Perron test occur not only in the well-known cases, when θ is close to one, but also for $\theta \sim 0.5$ as it is demonstrated later on $\left(\sigma_{(1)}^2 = \sigma_{(2)}^2,\ N^* = 0.5N\right)$.

Lemma 2 *For the aggregate time series $\{y_t\}$, defined in (4), as $T \to \infty$:*

(a) $T^{-1} \sum_{t=1}^{T} y_{t-1} u_t^* \Rightarrow \frac{1}{2} N^* \sigma_{(1)}^2 \left[(W(1))^2 - \left(1 + \frac{(N - N^*) \sigma_{(2)}^2}{N^* \sigma_{(1)}^2} \cdot \frac{2}{\rho^* + 1} \right) \right]$,

(b) $T^{-2} \sum_{t=1}^{T} y_{t-1}^2 \Rightarrow N^* \sigma_{(1)}^2 \int_0^1 [W(r)]^2 \, dr$,

(c) $T^{-3/2} \sum_{t=1}^{T} y_{t-1} \Rightarrow \sqrt{N^*} \sigma_{(1)} \int_0^1 W(r) \, dr$, *which is* $N\left(0, \frac{N^* \sigma_{(1)}^2}{3}\right)$,

(d) $T^{-5/2} \sum_{t=1}^{T} t y_{t-1} \Rightarrow \sqrt{N^*} \sigma_{(1)} \int_0^1 r W(r) \, dr$, *which is* $N\left(0, \frac{2 N^* \sigma_{(1)}^2}{15}\right)$,

(e) $T^{-3/2} \sum_{t=1}^{T} t u_t^* \Rightarrow \sqrt{N^*} \sigma_{(1)} \left(W(1) - \int_0^1 W(r) \, dr \right)$, *which is* $N\left(0, \frac{N^* \sigma_{(1)}^2}{3}\right)$.

The proof of Lemma 2 is obvious. One may think that this is a direct interpretation of Phillips and Perron (1988) results. However, innovation sequence $\{u_t^*\}$ does not satisfy conditions (*iv*) in Phillips and Perron (1988, p. 336), that is, $\{u_t^*\}$ is not necessarily a strong mixing process. It is not difficult to give an example for sequence $\{u_t^*\}$, when our conditions are satisfied but it is not a strong mixing as assumed by Phillips and Perron if we use a slightly modified version of the example given by Andrews (1984) who criticizes assumptions like Phillips and Perrons condition (*iv*) as too restrictive:

"...strong mixing condition is less general than it may appear to be."

Now, we show how the heterogeneity parameters $\left(N^*, (N - N^*), \sigma_{(1)}^2, \sigma_{(2)}^2, \rho^*\right)$ enter the asymptotic distributions of the Dickey-Fuller test statistics under different regression model.

Suppose that sample $\{y_1, y_2, \ldots, y_T\}$ is generated by process (4) under $\rho = 1$ and the AR(1) specification (4) is to be estimated by OLS. Because the true value of ρ is unity, the difference between the estimate $\hat{\rho}_T$ and its true value multiplied by T is

$$T(\hat{\rho}_T - 1) = \frac{\frac{1}{T} \sum_{t=1}^{T} y_{t-1} u_t^*}{\frac{1}{T^2} \sum_{t=1}^{T} y_{t-1}^2}. \tag{5}$$

By using the results (*a*) and (*b*) in Lemma 2, we can provide the asymptotic distribution of the OLS estimator in (5) under the null hypothesis $\rho = 1$, $N^* > 0$, $|\rho^*| < 1$, $\sigma_{(1)}^2 \neq 0$:

$$T(\hat{\rho}_T - 1) \Rightarrow \frac{\frac{1}{2} \left[(W(1))^2 - \left(1 + \frac{(N - N^*) \sigma_{(2)}^2}{N^* \sigma_{(1)}^2} \frac{2}{\rho^* + 1} \right) \right]}{\int_0^1 [W(r)]^2 \, dr}$$

and the asymptotic distribution of the t statistics is given by

$$t_T \Rightarrow \left(\frac{N^* \sigma^2_{(1)}}{N^* \sigma^2_{(1)} + (N - N^*) \sigma^2_{(2)} \dfrac{2}{\rho^* + 1}} \right)^{0.5} \frac{\frac{1}{2} \left[(W(1))^2 - \left(1 + \dfrac{(N - N^*) \sigma^2_{(2)}}{N^* \sigma^2_{(1)}} \dfrac{2}{\rho^* + 1} \right) \right]}{\left\{ \int_0^1 [W(r)]^2 \, dr \right\}^{\frac{1}{2}}}.$$

Let us consider now the following regression model:

$$y_t = \alpha + \rho y_{t-1} + u^*_t. \tag{6}$$

We derive in Lemma 3 the asymptotic distributions of the standardized OLS estimator $\widehat{\rho}_T$, as well as its t-statistics under the hypothesis that the data generating process is (4) for $\rho = 1,\ N^* > 0,\ |\rho^*| < 1,\ \sigma^2_{(1)} \neq 0$. If the data generating process includes a nonzero drift, that is, we allow nonzero intercepts in all individual series in (1) and the null hypothesis is $\alpha \neq 0,\ \rho = 1,\ N^* > 0,\ |\rho^*| < 1,\ \sigma^2_{(1)} \neq 0$ in model (6), then in a standard way we get the limiting distributions of the OLS estimators as

$$\begin{pmatrix} T^{1/2} (\widehat{\alpha}_T - \alpha) \\ T^{3/2} (\widehat{\rho}_T - 1) \end{pmatrix} \Rightarrow N \left(\begin{pmatrix} 0 \\ 0 \end{pmatrix}, \sigma^2_{(1)} \begin{pmatrix} 1 & \alpha/2 \\ \alpha/2 & \alpha^2/3 \end{pmatrix}^{-1} \right)$$

Let us turn now to the case when a time trend is also included in the regression:

$$y_t = \alpha + \beta t + \rho y_{t-1} + u^*_t. \tag{7}$$

When there is an intercept as well in the data generating process, y_{t-1} would be asymptotically equivalent to a time trend. To avoid the problem, which is caused by the collinearity of the explanatory variables in large samples, regression model (7) can be written in the following form:

$$y_t = \alpha' + \beta' t + \rho' x_{t-1} + u^*_t, \tag{8}$$

where $\alpha' = (1 - \rho)\alpha$, $\beta' = \beta + \rho\alpha$, $\rho' = \rho$, and $x_t = y_t - \alpha t$. These transformations of the regression coefficients were proposed by Sims, Stock, and Watson (1990). However, the OLS estimate of ρ' and its t statistics based on model (8) is the same as the OLS estimate of ρ and its t statistics based on (7) and it is known that the OLS estimate of ρ and its t statistics in model (7) are unchanged regardless of α. Therefore, without loss of generality, the asymptotic distributions of the OLS estimator $\widetilde{\rho}_T$, as well as its t statistics based on model (7) are given only under the null hypothesis $\alpha = \beta = 0$, $\rho = 1,\ N^* > 0,\ |\rho^*| < 1,\ \sigma^2_{(1)} \neq 0$.

Now, the following properties hold:

Lemma 3 *For the regression model (6), as* $T \to \infty$,

$$(a)\ T(\hat{\rho}_T - 1) \Rightarrow \left\{ \left(\tfrac{1}{2} \left[(W(1))^2 - 1 \right] - W(1) \cdot \int_0^1 W(r)\, dr \right) - \frac{(N - N^*) \sigma^2_{(2)}}{N^* \sigma^2_{(1)} (\rho^* + 1)} \right\} C^{-1},$$

$$(b)\ t_{\hat{\rho}} \Rightarrow A\left\{\left(\tfrac{1}{2}\left[(W(1))^2-1\right]-W(1)\cdot\int_0^1 W(r)\,dr\right)-\frac{(N-N^*)\,\sigma_{(2)}^2}{N^*\sigma_{(1)}^2\,(\rho^*+1)}\right\}C^{-1/2},$$

$$\textit{where } A=\left(\frac{N^*\sigma_{(1)}^2}{N^*\sigma_{(1)}^2+(N-N^*)\,\sigma_{(2)}^2\cdot\frac{2}{\rho^*+1}}\right)^{1/2},\ C=\int_0^1\left[W(r)\right]^2dr-\left(\int_0^1 W(r)\,dr\right)^2.$$

For the regression model (7), as $T\to\infty$,

$$(c)\ T(\hat{\rho}_T-1)\Rightarrow\left[\frac{1}{2}\left[(W(1))^2-1\right]-\frac{(N-N^*)\,\sigma_{(2)}^2}{N^*\sigma_{(1)}^2\,(\rho^*+1)}\right]/C_2$$
$$+6\int_0^1 rW(r)\,dr\left(2\int_0^1 W(r)\,dr-W(1)\right)/C_2$$
$$+2\left\{\int_0^1 W(r)\,dr\left(W(1)-3\int_0^1 W(r)\,dr\right)\right\}/C_2,$$

$$(d)\ t_{\hat{\rho}}\Rightarrow A\left\{\frac{1}{2}\left[(W(1))^2-1\right]-\frac{(N-N^*)\,\sigma_{(2)}^2}{N^*\sigma_{(1)}^2\,(\rho^*+1)}\right\}/C_2^{1/2}$$
$$+6A\int_0^1 rW(r)\,dr\left(2\int_0^1 W(r)\,dr-W(1)\right)/C_2^{1/2}$$
$$+2A\left\{\int_0^1 W(r)\,dr\left(W(1)-3\int_0^1 W(r)\,dr\right)\right\}/C_2^{1/2},$$

$$\textit{where } C_2=\int_0^1 (W(r))^2\,dr-12\left(\int_0^1 rW(r)\,dr\right)^2$$
$$+12\int_0^1 W(r)\,dr\int_0^1 rW(r)\,dr-4\left(\int_0^1 W(r)\,dr\right)^2.$$

■

The proofs of these results are straightforward from the asymptotic properties of the sample moments given in Lemma 2.

When amongst the aggregate series there is no stationary AR(1) process, that is, $(N-N^*)\,\sigma_{(2)}^2=0$, the asymptotic distributions in Lemma 2 coincide with the corresponding Dickey-Fuller type distributions, which is to be expected because in this case the aggregate time series is a random walk.

Then, we introduce the notations used by Phillips and Perron to demonstrate how the heterogeneity parameters form the nuisance parameters

$$\sigma=\sqrt{N^*}\sigma_{(1)},\ \sigma_u=\sqrt{N^*\sigma_{(1)}^2+(N-N^*)\,\sigma_{(2)}^2\cdot\frac{2}{\rho^*+1}},\ \lambda=\frac{1}{2}\left(\sigma^2-\sigma_u^2\right),$$

and we use this to rewrite Lemma 2 $(a)-(d)$; we get the same results as Phillips and Perron, but for much more general assumptions on the aggregate series.

Following Phillips and Perron we define those transformations of test statistics in Lemma 2 which eliminate the nuisance parameters asymptotically.

We can estimate consistently the parameter σ_u^2 by

$$\widehat{s}_T^2 = T^{-1}\sum_{t=1}^{T}\left(\widehat{u}_t^*\right)^2 = T^{-1}\sum_{t=1}^{T}\left(y_t - \widehat{\alpha}_T - \widehat{\rho}_T \cdot y_{t-1}\right)^2 \text{ in regression (6)}$$

under the null $\alpha = 0,\ \rho = 1,\ N^* > 0,\ |\rho^*| < 1,\ \sigma_{(1)}^2 \neq 0$ and

$$\widetilde{s}_T^2 = T^{-1}\sum_{t=1}^{T}\left(\widetilde{u}_t^*\right)^2 = T^{-1}\sum_{t=1}^{T}\left(y_t - \widetilde{\alpha}_T' - \widetilde{\beta}_T' t - \widetilde{\rho}_T \cdot y_{t-1}\right)^2 \text{ in regression (8)}$$

under the null $\alpha \neq 0,\ \rho = 1,\ N^* > 0,\ |\rho^*| < 1,\ \sigma_{(1)}^2 \neq 0$. Now we establish the consistency of the Newey-West estimator of σ^2, used by Phillips and Perron in our context.

Lemma 4

(*a*) *If innovation sequences* $\{u_{kt}\}$ $(k = 1, 2, \ldots, N)$ *satisfy conditions* (a), (c) *and there exists* M *such that* $\sup_t E\left(|u_{kt}|^{2\beta}\right) < M$ *for some* $\beta > 2$, *for all* $k = 1, \ldots, N$, *and* $l \to \infty$ *as* $T \to \infty$ *such that* $l = o\left(T^{1/3}\right)$, *then* $\widehat{s}_{Tl}^2 \to N^*\sigma_{(1)}^2$ $\left(\textit{resp. } \widetilde{s}_{Tl}^2 \to N^*\sigma_{(1)}^2\right)$ *in probability as* $T \to \infty$, *where* $\widehat{s}_{Tl}^2 = T^{-1}\sum_{t=1}^{T}\left(\widehat{u}_t^*\right)^2 + 2T^{-1}\sum_{s=1}^{l}\sum_{t=s+1}^{T}\widehat{u}_t^*\widehat{u}_{t-s}^*$, $\widetilde{s}_{Tl}^2 = T^{-1}\sum_{t=1}^{T}\left(\widetilde{u}_t^*\right)^2 + 2T^{-1}\sum_{s=1}^{l}\sum_{t=s+1}^{T}\widetilde{u}_t^*\widetilde{u}_{t-s}^*$.

(*b*) *If innovation sequences* $\{u_{kt}\}$ $(k = 1, 2, \ldots, N)$ *satisfy conditions* $(a) - (c)$, *and* $l \to \infty$ *as* $T \to \infty$ *such that* $l = o\left(T^{1/2}\right)$, *then* $\widehat{\sigma}_{Tl}^2 \to N^*\sigma_{(1)}^2$ $\left(\textit{resp. } \widetilde{\sigma}_{Tl}^2 \to N^*\sigma_{(1)}^2\right)$ *in probability as* $T \to \infty$, *where* $\widehat{\sigma}_{Tl}^2 = T^{-1}\sum_{t=1}^{T}\left(\widehat{u}_t^*\right)^2 + 2T^{-1}\sum_{s=1}^{l} w_{sl}\sum_{t=s+1}^{T}\widehat{u}_t^*\widehat{u}_{t-s}^*$, $\widetilde{\sigma}_{Tl}^2 = T^{-1}\sum_{t=1}^{T}\left(\widetilde{u}_t^*\right)^2 + 2T^{-1}\sum_{s=1}^{l} w_{sl}\sum_{l-s+1}^{T}\widetilde{u}_t^*\widetilde{u}_{t-s}^*$.

The first part of Lemma 4 is straightforward while the second part is a direct conclusion of the 2.2 Theorem of de Jong and Davidson (1997).

Next, we provide the transformations which eliminate the nuisance parameters asymptotically

$$Z\left(\widehat{\rho}_T\right) = T\left(\widehat{\rho}_T - 1\right) - \widehat{\lambda}/\overline{m}_{yy}, \quad Z\left(t_{\widehat{\rho}}\right) = \left(\widehat{s}_T/\widehat{\sigma}_{Tl}\right)t_{\widehat{\rho}} - \widehat{\lambda}'\widehat{\sigma}_{Tl}/\overline{m}_{yy}^{\frac{1}{2}}, \tag{9}$$

$$Z\left(t_{\widehat{\alpha}}\right) = \left(\widehat{s}_T/\widehat{\sigma}_{Tl}\right)t_{\widehat{\alpha}} + \widehat{\lambda}'\widehat{\sigma}_{Tl}m_y/\overline{m}_{yy}^{\frac{1}{2}}m_{yy}^{\frac{1}{2}}, \tag{10}$$

$$Z\left(\widetilde{\rho}_T\right) = T\left(\widetilde{\rho}_T - 1\right) - \widetilde{\lambda}/M, \quad Z\left(t_{\widetilde{\rho}}\right) = \left(\widetilde{s}_T/\widetilde{\sigma}_{Tl}\right)t_{\widetilde{\rho}} - \widetilde{\lambda}'\widetilde{\sigma}_{Tl}/M^{\frac{1}{2}}, \tag{11}$$

where

$$m_{yy} = T^{-2}\sum_{t=1}^{T} y_{t-1}^2,\ \overline{m}_{yy} = T^{-2}\sum_{t=1}^{T} y_{t-1}^2 - \left(T^{-3/2}\sum_{t=1}^{T} y_{t-1}\right)^2,$$

$$m_y = T^{-3/2}\sum_{t=1}^{T} y_{t-1},\ m_{ty} = T^{-5/2}\sum_{t=1}^{T} t y_{t-1},$$

$$M = \left(1 - T^{-2}\right) m_{yy} - 12 m_{ty}^2 + 12\left(1 + T^{-1}\right) m_{ty} m_y - \left(4 + 6T^{-1} + 2T^{-2}\right) m_y^2$$

$$\widehat{\lambda} = (1/2)\left(\widehat{\sigma}_{Tl}^2 - \widehat{s}_T^2\right),\quad \widehat{\lambda}' = \widehat{\lambda}/\widehat{\sigma}_{Tl}^2,\quad \widetilde{\lambda} = (1/2)\left(\widetilde{\sigma}_{Tl}^2 - \widetilde{s}_T^2\right),\quad \widetilde{\lambda}' = \widetilde{\lambda}/\widetilde{\sigma}_{Tl}^2.$$

The asymptotic distributions of these Z statistics are given in the following theorem.

Theorem 1 *(i) For model (6) the statistics $Z\left(\hat{\rho}_T\right)$ and $Z\left(t_{\hat{\rho}}\right)$ have the same limit distributions, as in Lemma 3 (a) and (b), when the null includes $\left(N - N^*\right)\sigma_{(2)}^2 = 0$.*

(ii) For model (8) the statistics of $Z\left(\widetilde{\rho}_T\right)$ and $Z\left(t_{\widetilde{\rho}_T}\right)$have the same limit distributions, as in Lemma 3 (c) and (d), when the null includes $\left(N - N^*\right)\sigma_{(2)}^2 = 0$.

Theorem 1 sums up the first main results of this paper, since it sets down the base to calculate the relevant critical values for these tests. Of course asymptotically we should get back the Dickey-Fuller critical values as shown in the lemma.

3. SIMULATED CRITICAL VALUES

Tables 1 – 4 contain the 5 % simulated critical values for the $Z(\widehat{\rho})$ and $Z(\widetilde{\rho})$ statistics, for different sample sizes. In each case the innovations are normally distributed with zero mean and variances indicated in the null. The distributions depend on four parameters: the sample size, T, the lag truncation parameter, l, the autoregressive coefficient, ρ^*, and the ratio of the variances of the aggregated random walk and stationary AR(1) processes, $N^*\sigma_{(1)}^2 /\ \left(N - N^*\right)\ \sigma_{(2)}^2$ (which means that there is a trade-off between the ratio of the number of the disaggregated random walk and stationary AR(1) processes and the ratio of their variances).

The tabulated results are based on simulations, using 20,000 Monte Carlo replications for $T = 20$, 50, 100, 400, 600, 1000, and 1000 replications for the sample size 10,000. The lag truncation parameter, l was fixed to 2 for 20, 50, 100, 400, 600 and 3 for 1000 and 10 for the sample size 10,000, since the larger l, the larger sample is required for the corresponding Dickey-Fuller critical values to be relevant.

The most striking and interesting behavior in each case is the "short-run explosion" of the distributions and critical values. In the case of the estimated model (6) (Tables 1 and 2), the detected explosion can be explained by the fact that the aggregate series can behave as a stationary AR(1) process, even in relatively large samples. This can be seen, if we re-write equation (3) in the following way

$$y_t = \rho^* y_{t-1} + u_t^{**},$$

where

$$u_t^{**} = u_t^{(2)} + u_t^{(1)} + (1-\rho^*)\sum_{i=1}^{t-1} u_i^{(1)}.$$

Now let us consider the mean, the variance of each y_t, and the covariance between y_t and $y_{t-\tau}$

$$E(y_t) = 0,$$

$$Var(y_t) = (N - N^*)\,\sigma_{(2)}^2 \frac{1-(\rho^*)^{2t}}{1-(\rho^*)^2} + tN^*\sigma_{(1)}^2 + Var\left(y_0^{(1)}\right) + (\rho^*)^{2t}\, Var\left(y_0^{(2)}\right),$$

$$Cov(y_t, y_{t-\tau}) = (\rho^*)^\tau (N - N^*)\,\sigma_{(2)}^2 \frac{1-(\rho^*)^{2(t-\tau)}}{1-(\rho^*)^2} + (t-\tau)\,N^*\sigma_{(1)}^2$$
$$+Var\left(y_0^{(1)}\right) + (\rho^*)^{2t-k}\, Var\left(y_0^{(2)}\right), \ \tau \geq 1,$$

where in every equation, the first term on the right-hand side is the asymptotically stationary bit and the second term is the corresponding random walk bit. Hence it is very reasonable that even in large samples, until the

$$(N - N^*)\,\sigma_{(2)}^2 \frac{1-(\rho^*)^{2t}}{1-(\rho^*)^2} << tN^*\sigma_{(1)}^2,$$

condition is not satisfied, the decelerating explosion goes on, since for an asymptotically stationary AR(1) process the centered OLS estimator is scaled by $\sqrt{T}$ to converge in distribution, while here it is scaled by T, due to the superconsistency. In other words, it may well happen that the random walk processes dominate the asymptotically stationary processes in the aggregate time series very slowly. On the other hand, it is easy to see that the null distribution of $Z(\widehat{\rho})$ depends on the parameters T, ρ^*, $\sigma_{(1)}^2/\,\sigma_{(2)}^2$, $N^*/\,(N-N^*)$, since

$$\widehat{\rho}_T - \frac{T^{-1}\sum_{t=1}^{T} y_t y_{t-1} - \left(T^{-1}\sum_{t=1}^{T} y_{t-1}\right)\left(T^{-1}\sum_{t=1}^{T} y_t\right)}{T^{-1}\sum_{t=1}^{T} y_{t-1}^2 - \left(T^{-1}\sum_{t=1}^{T} y_{t-1}\right)^2}.$$

Tables 1 and 2 provide the evidences that for all relevant sample sizes we reject too often the null hypothesis of unit root if we use the conventional tests and critical values. There are frequently considerable size distortions for $T = 50, 100, 400, 600$ or 1000 and somewhat smaller distortions for $T = 20$. If the ratio of the variances is 1 or it is very close to 1, the tabulated critical values are very far from the relevant Dickey-Fuller results, even if half of the aggregated processes are random walks. In the unrealistic case, when the variances of the random walks are ten times larger than the variances of the stationary processes, the size distortions are small only when the proportions of random walks is at least 50%. Closer critical values to the original Dickey-Fuller ones are obtained when the

Table 1

5% Monte Carlo Critical Values
No Drift, No Trend
($\rho^* = 0.5$)

	$T = 20$	$T = 50$	$T = 100$	$T = 400$	$T = 600$	$T = 1000$	$T = 10000$
	$\sigma^2_{(1)} = \sigma^2_{(2)} = 0.5$	$\sigma^2_{(1)} = \sigma^2_{(2)} = 0.5$	$\sigma^2_{(1)} = \sigma^2_{(2)} = 0.5$	$\sigma^2_{(1)} = \sigma^2_{(2)} = 0.5$			
$N^* = 0.05N$	−18.8	−34.5	−54.8	−127.5	−152.7	−190.6	−172.6
$N^* = 0.1N$	−18.2	−31.5	−47.8	−89.2	−97.2	−101.9	−52.9
$N^* = 0.2N$	−17.1	−27.9	−37.4	−53.3	−54.8	−48.9	−25.2
$N^* = 0.3N$	−16.2	−24.6	−31.1	−37.5	−38.7	−32.4	−19.3
$N^* = 0.5N$	−14.7	−20.0	−23.0	−25.0	−24.8	−21.0	−14.4
	$\sigma^2_{(1)} = 1, \sigma^2_{(2)} = 0.1$	$\sigma^2_{(1)} = 1, \sigma^2_{(2)} = 0.1$	$\sigma^2_{(1)} = 1, \sigma^2_{(2)} = 0.1$	$\sigma^2_{(1)} = 1, \sigma^2_{(2)} = 0.1$			
$N^* = 0.05N$	−16.0	−23.4	−29.0	−34.2	−34.4	−29.5	−17.4
$N^* = 0.1N$	−14.6	−19.6	−22.3	−23.5	−23.6	−20.8	−15.8
$N^* = 0.2N$	−13.3	−16.8	−18.1	−18.4	−18.4	−17.0	−15.1
$N^* = 0.3N$	−12.8	−15.6	−16.0	−16.6	−16.6	−15.9	−14.4
$N^* = 0.5N$	−12.4	−14.5	−15.1	−15.2	−15.2	−14.9	−14.1
	$\sigma^2_{(1)} = 10, \sigma^2_{(2)} = 0.1$	$\sigma^2_{(1)} = 10, \sigma^2_{(2)} = 0.1$	$\sigma^2_{(1)} = 10, \sigma^2_{(2)} = 0.1$	$\sigma^2_{(1)} = 10, \sigma^2_{(2)} = 0.1$			
$N^* = 0.05N$	−12.6	−15.0	−15.7	−15.9	−16.1	−15.6	−14.8
$N^* = 0.1N$	−12.3	−14.3	−14.8	−14.8	−14.9	−15.0	−14.4
$N^* = 0.2N$	−12.0	−13.9	−14.6	−14.5	−14.5	−14.6	−14.0
$N^* = 0.3N$	−11.9	−13.8	−14.2	−14.3	−14.3	−14.5	−14.3
$N^* = 0.5N$	−11.9	−13.6	−14.0	−14.0	−14.3	−14.3	−14.2

Table 2

5% Monte Carlo Critical Values
No Drift, No Trend
$(\rho^* = 0)$

	$T = 20$	$T = 50$	$T = 100$	$T = 400$
	$\sigma^2_{(1)} = \sigma^2_{(2)} = 0.5$			
$N^* = 0.05N$	−26.4	−57.1	−99.4	−251.4
$N^* = 0.1N$	−26.0	−52.2	−85.5	−141.5
$N^* = 0.2N$	−23.8	−44.8	−64.0	−70.7
$N^* = 0.3N$	−22.3	−38.3	−48.1	−45.7
$N^* = 0.5N$	−18.9	−27.5	−29.5	−28.7
	$\sigma^2_{(1)} = 1, \sigma^2_{(2)} = 0.1$			
$N^* = 0.05N$	−21.3	−35.6	43.2	−39.9
$N^* = 0.1N$	−18.5	−26.5	−27.6	−24.9
$N^* = 0.2N$	−15.2	−19.3	−20.0	−18.5
$N^* = 0.3N$	−13.8	−17.2	−17.5	−17.2
$N^* - 0.5N$	−12.7	−15.0	−15.4	−16.2
	$\sigma^2_{(1)} = 10, \sigma^2_{(2)} = 0.1$			
$N^* = 0.05N$	−13.5	−16.4	−17.1	−16.3
$N^* = 0.1N$	−12.5	−15.2	−15.3	−15.1
$N^* = 0.2N$	−12.2	−14.3	−14.7	−14.7
$N^* = 0.3N$	−12.0	−13.8	−14.4	−14.9
$N^* = 0.5N$	−11.9	−13.8	−14.3	−14.3

variance ratio is about one hundredth and the random walks make up at least 20 percent of the disaggregated processes. A very close trade-off between the ratio of the number of the disaggregate random walk and stationary AR(1) processes and the ratio of their variances can be observed, when $N^* = 50$, $N = 100$, $\sigma^2_{(1)} = 1$, $\sigma^2_{(2)} = 0.1$ and $N^* = 10$, $N = 100$, $\sigma^2_{(1)} = 10$, $\sigma^2_{(2)} = 0.1$ and another example is given for $N^* = 50$, $N = 100$, $\sigma^2_{(1)} = 1$, $\sigma^2_{(2)} = 0.1$ and $N^* = 10$, $N = 100$, $\sigma^2_{(1)} = 10$, $\sigma^2_{(2)} = 0.1$.

Very similar conclusions can be drawn from the results presented in Tables 3 and 4, when the estimated model (8) and all null hypotheses include a nonzero intercept, that is $\mu \neq 0$. The 5 percent critical values in the case of a drift parameter 1.5 are tabulated, but its value has no significant effect on the results. The analogue "short-run explosion" of the distributions can be explained by the same reasons, that is, the aggregated series behave as an (asymptotically) stationary AR(1) process, even in relatively large samples, if the proportion of the random walks is small or the variance ratio not very large.

Table 3

5% Monte Carlo Critical Values
with Drift = 1.5 and Trend
($\rho^* = 0.5$)

	$T = 20$	$T = 50$	$T = 100$	$T = 400$	$T = 600$	$T = 1000$	$T = 10000$
	$\sigma^2_{(1)} = \sigma^2_{(2)} = 0.5$	$\sigma^2_{(1)} = \sigma^2_{(2)} = 0.5$	$\sigma^2_{(1)} = \sigma^2_{(2)} = 0.5$	$\sigma^2_{(1)} = \sigma^2_{(2)} = 0.5$			
$N^* = 0.05N$	−19.0	−36.9	−60.6	−155.7	−194.5	−269.0	−380.1
$N^* = 0.1N$	−18.8	−35.1	−55.2	−116.9	−135.4	−157.8	−131.0
$N^* = 0.2N$	−18.2	−32.3	−47.1	−77.0	−82.5	−81.1	−47.1
$N^* = 0.3N$	−17.6	−30.0	−40.7	−57.3	−58.7	−53.9	−33.0
$N^* = 0.5N$	−16.7	−26.1	−32.2	−38.1	−38.3	−35.0	−24.5
	$\sigma^2_{(1)} = 1, \sigma^2_{(2)} = 0.1$	$\sigma^2_{(1)} = 1, \sigma^2_{(2)} = 0.1$	$\sigma^2_{(1)} = 1, \sigma^2_{(2)} = 0.1$	$\sigma^2_{(1)} = 1, \sigma^2_{(2)} = 0.1$			
$N^* = 0.05N$	−17.3	−29.0	−38.8	−51.1	−52.3	−47.7	−29.9
$N^* = 0.1N$	−16.5	−25.5	−31.4	−36.8	−36.5	−33.2	−25.8
$N^* = 0.2N$	−15.7	−22.9	−26.3	−28.0	−28.1	−26.8	−23.4
$N^* = 0.3N$	−15.3	−21.5	−23.9	−25.3	−25.5	−24.7	−22.5
$N^* = 0.5N$	−14.7	−20.3	−22.2	−23.2	−23.2	−23.3	−22.8
	$\sigma^2_{(1)} = 10, \sigma^2_{(2)} = 0.1$	$\sigma^2_{(1)} = 10, \sigma^2_{(2)} = 0.1$	$\sigma^2_{(1)} = 10, \sigma^2_{(2)} = 0.1$	$\sigma^2_{(1)} = 10, \sigma^2_{(2)} = 0.1$			
$N^* = 0.05N$	−15.1	−21.1	−23.5	−24.7	−25.0	−24.1	−22.9
$N^* = 0.1N$	−14.7	−20.2	−22.2	−22.8	−23.2	−22.9	−22.5
$N^* = 0.2N$	−14.5	−19.7	−21.6	−22.2	−22.4	−22.5	−22.8
$N^* = 0.3N$	−14.4	−19.5	−21.1	−22.1	−22.1	−22.2	−21.9
$N^* = 0.5N$	−14.4	−19.5	−21.1	−21.9	−21.8	−22.1	−21.2

Table 4

5% Monte Carlo Critical Values
with Drift = 1.5 and Trend
($\rho^* = 0$)

	$T = 20$ $\sigma^2_{(1)} = \sigma^2_{(2)} = 0.5$	$T = 50$	$T = 100$	$T = 400$
$N^* = 0.05N$	−26.1	−57.7	−103.3	−283.0
$N^* = 0.1N$	−25.4	−54.5	−92.4	−196.6
$N^* = 0.2N$	−24.4	−49.0	−74.8	−111.5
$N^* = 0.3N$	−23.4	−43.7	−61.3	−73.5
$N^* = 0.5N$	−20.8	−34.7	−42.5	−41.8
	$\sigma^2_{(1)} = 1, \sigma^2_{(2)} = 0.1$			
$N^* = 0.05N$	−22.4	−41.5	−56.5	−62.0
$N^* = 0.1N$	−20.8	−33.4	−39.2	−39.4
$N^* = 0.2N$	−18.1	−26.7	−29.3	−28.7
$N^* = 0.3N$	−17.0	−23.9	−25.9	−25.8
$N^* = 0.5N$	−15.7	−21.2	−22.6	−23.3
	$\sigma^2_{(1)} = 10, \sigma^2_{(2)} = 0.1$			
$N^* = 0.05N$	−16.7	−23.0	−24.8	−24.9
$N^* = 0.1N$	−15.4	−21.2	−22.9	−23.2
$N^* = 0.2N$	−14.9	−19.8	−22.0	−22.4
$N^* = 0.3N$	−14.7	−19.5	−21.3	−22.3
$N^* = 0.5N$	−14.6	−19.5	−21.1	−22.0

In all null hypotheses analyzed the value of ρ^* was 0.5 and 0. Now, if we decrease its value in the null, we get even stranger critical values, since the null distribution's special behavior means that the estimator of ρ take values with higher probability around ρ^* than its probability limit, 1, for the sample sizes used in here.

4. EXTENSIONS

In this section we generalize our results allowing for much less restrictive behavior of the stationary term in the aggregation problem. We show that as a special case of our approach we can obtain the results of Phillips and Perron (1988 p. 336), that is our conditions are weaker than the strong mixing regularity conditions or the linear process conditions of the cited papers.

Let us consider the following series

$$y_t^{(1)} = \rho y_{t-1}^{(1)} + u_t^{(1)}$$
$$y_t^{(2)} = u_t^{(2)}$$
$$\rho - 1,$$

where the first series represents the aggregate random walk whilst the second one is the corresponding stationary part.

We impose the following conditions:

(a') $\left\{u_t^{(1)}\right\}$ and $\left\{u_t^{(2)}\right\}$ are uniformly L_r-bounded zero mean sequences, $r > 2$;

(b') $\left\{u_t^{(1)}\right\}$ and $\left\{u_t^{(2)}\right\}$ are L_2-NED of size -1/2 on a strong mixing (α-mixing process) $\mathbf{V}_t$ of size $-r/(r-2)$;

(c') $\lim T^{-1}Var\left(\sum_{t=1}^{T} u_t^{(1)}\right) = \sigma^2$, $\sigma^2 > 0$;

(d') $y_0^{(1)}$ has distribution independent of sample size, $y_0^{(2)}$ L_r-bounded random variable with zero mean.

It can be seen that our assumptions allow very wide range of possible underlying errors. Namely, in the case of ARIMA(p,1,q) models (with finite fourth moments) our conditions are satisfied for $u_t^{(1)}$ and we can set up $u_t^{(2)} = 0$. While, in the case when the innovation sequence satisfies the strong mixing regularity conditions (e.g., conditions $(i) - (iv)$ of Phillips and Perron) it is clear that our conditions are implied by those ones for $u_t^{(1)}$ and we can set up $u_t^{(2)} = 0$, as above.

Then, for the aggregate process $y_t = y_t^{(1)} + y_t^{(2)}$, we have

$$y_t = \rho y_{t-1} + u_t^* \qquad (12)$$
$$\rho = 1,$$

where the new residuals are $u_t^* = u_t^{(1)} + y_t^{(2)} - y_{t-1}^{(2)}$. Therefore, it is not difficult to see that u_t^* has zero mean, uniformly L_r-bounded and L_2-NED of size -1/2 on $\mathbf{V}_t$. Furthermore,

$$\begin{aligned}
T^{-1}Var\left(\sum_{t=1}^{T} u_t^*\right) &= T^{-1}Var\left(\sum_{t=1}^{T} u_t^{(1)} + u_T^{(2)} - y_0^{(2)}\right) \\
&= T^{-1}Var\left(\sum_{t=1}^{T} u_t^{(1)} + u_T^{(2)}\right) + T^{-1}Var\left(y_0^{(2)}\right) \\
&= T^{-1}Var\left(\sum_{t=1}^{T} u_t^{(1)}\right) + T^{-1}Var\left(u_T^{(2)}\right) \\
&\quad +2T^{-1}Cov\left(\sum_{t=1}^{T} u_t^{(1)}, u_T^{(2)}\right) + T^{-1}Var\left(y_0^{(2)}\right),
\end{aligned}$$

here the second and the fourth term obviously converge to zero, as $T \to \infty$, while the third term also tends to zero, which follows directly from the Cauchy-Schwarz inequality

$$T^{-1}Cov\left(\sum_{t=1}^{T} u_t^{(1)}, u_T^{(2)}\right) \leq \left(T^{-1}Var\left(\sum_{t=1}^{T} u_t^{(1)}\right)\right)^{1/2} \left(T^{-1}Var\left(u_T^{(2)}\right)\right)^{1/2}.$$

Hence, the long run variance is given by

$$\lim_{T\to\infty} T^{-1}Var\left(\sum_{t=1}^{T} u_t^*\right) = \sigma^2.$$

Now, we provide the functional central limit theorem for the new innovation sequence under the more general assumptions on the individual time series.

Lemma 5 *If the innovation sequences* $\left\{u_t^{(k)}\right\}$ $(k=1,2)$ *satisfy conditions* $(a')-(d')$*, then* $T^{-1/2}\sum_{t=1}^{[Tr]} u_t^* \Rightarrow \sigma W$*, as* $T\to\infty$.

The proof is clear. The next lemma is the "sister" of Lemma 2.

Lemma 6 *For the aggregate time series* $\{y_t\}$*, defined in (12), as* $T\to\infty$:

(a) $T^{-1}\sum_{t=1}^{T} y_{t-1}u_t^* \Rightarrow \frac{1}{2}\sigma^2\left[(W(1))^2 - \sigma_u^2/\sigma^2\right]$,

(b) $T^{-2}\sum_{t=1}^{T} y_{t-1}^2 \Rightarrow \sigma^2\int_0^1 [W(r)]^2\,dr$,

(c) $T^{-3/2}\sum_{t=1}^{T} y_{t-1} \Rightarrow \sigma\int_0^1 W(r)\,dr$, *which is* $N\left(0,\frac{\sigma^2}{3}\right)$,

(d) $T^{-5/2}\sum_{t=1}^{T} t y_{t-1} \Rightarrow \sigma\int_0^1 rW(r)\,dr$, *which is* $N\left(0,\frac{2\sigma^2}{15}\right)$,

(e) $T^{-3/2}\sum_{t=1}^{T} t u_t^* \Rightarrow \sigma\left(W(1)-\int_0^1 W(r)\,dr\right)$, *which is* $N\left(0,\frac{\sigma^2}{3}\right)$,

where $\sigma_u^2 = \lim T^{-1}\sum_{t=1}^{T} E(u_t^*)^2$.

The proof is straightforward. The limit in the last row of the lemma exists, since u_t^* is uniformly L_r-bounded.

In the case of the aggregation model in Section 1 we allow the variances of the individual series and the autoregressive coefficients to be heterogenous, that is, the aggregation model is specified in the following way:

$$\begin{aligned}
y_{1t} &= \rho y_{1t-1} + u_{1t}\\
y_{2t} &= \rho y_{2t-1} + u_{2t}\\
&\vdots\\
y_{N^*t} &= \rho y_{N^*t-1} + u_{N^*t}\\
y_{N^*+1,t} &= \rho_1^* y_{N^*+1,t-1} + u_{N^*+1,t}\\
&\vdots\\
y_{Nt} &= \rho_{N-N^*}^* y_{Nt-1} + u_{Nt}\\
\rho &- 1,
\end{aligned} \tag{13}$$

where $|\rho_j^*| < 1$ for all j and $0 < N^* \leq N$, and $u_{kt} \sim \left(0, \sigma_{(k)}^2\right)$ for $k = 1, 2, \ldots, N$, the parameters σ^2 and σ_u^2 are given by

$$\sigma^2 = \sum_{i=1}^{N^*} \sigma_{(i)}^2, \; \sigma_u^2 = \sigma^2 + \sum_{j=N^*+1}^{N} \sigma_{(j)}^2 \frac{2}{\rho_{j-N^*}^* + 1}.$$

Moreover, when $u_t^{(1)} \sim iid\left(0, \sigma_{(1)}^2\right)$ and $y_t^{(2)}$ is an ARMA(p,q) process with $iid\left(0, \sigma_\varepsilon^2\right)$ innovations, we have

$$\sigma^2 = \sigma_{(1)}^2, \; \sigma_u^2 = \sigma_{(1)}^2 + 2\left(\gamma(0) - \gamma(1)\right),$$

where $\gamma(j)$ is the autocovariance function of $y_t^{(2)}$.

Next, following the same line as in the first section, we reconsider the regression model (6) under the null hypothesis that data is generated by process (12) for $\rho = 1$, $\sigma^2 > 0$ and regression model (7) under the null hypothesis $\alpha = \beta = 0$, $\rho = 1$, $\sigma^2 > 0$. Next, we derive the asymptotic distributions.

Lemma 7 *For the regression model (6), as $T \to \infty$,*

$$(a)\; T(\hat{\rho}_T - 1) \Rightarrow \left\{\tfrac{1}{2}\left[(W(1))^2 - 1\right] - W(1)\int_0^1 W(r)\,dr - (1/2)\left(\sigma_u^2 - \sigma^2\right)/\sigma^2\right\} C^{-1},$$

$$(b)\; t_{\hat{\rho}} \Rightarrow A\left\{\left(\tfrac{1}{2}\left[(W(1))^2 - 1\right] - W(1)\cdot\int_0^1 W(r)\,dr\right) - (1/2)\left(\sigma_u^2 - \sigma^2\right)\right\} C^{-1/2},$$

where $A = \sigma/\sigma_u, C = \int_0^1 [W(r)]^2\,dr - \left(\int_0^1 W(r)\,dr\right)^2.$

For the regression model (7), as $T \to \infty$,

$$(c)\; T(\tilde{\rho}_T - 1) \Rightarrow \left[\tfrac{1}{2}\left[(W(1))^2 - 1\right] - D_1\right]/C_2 + 6\int_0^1 rW(r)\,dr\left(2\int_0^1 W(r)\,dr - W(1)\right)/C_2 + 2\left\{\int_0^1 W(r)\,dr\left(W(1) - 3\int_0^1 W(r)\,dr\right)\right\}/C_2,$$

$$(d)\; t_{\tilde{\rho}} \Rightarrow A\left\{\tfrac{1}{2}\left[(W(1))^2 - 1\right] - D_1\right\}/C_2^{1/2} + 6A\int_0^1 rW(r)\,dr\left(2\int_0^1 W(r)\,dr - W(1)\right)/C_2^{1/2} + 2A\left\{\int_0^1 W(r)\,dr\left(W(1) - 3\int_0^1 W(r)\,dr\right)\right\}/C_2^{1/2},$$

where $C_2 = \int_0^1 (W(r))^2\,dr - 12\left(\int_0^1 rW(r)\,dr\right)^2$

$$+12\int_0^1 W(r)\,dr\int_0^1 rW(r)\,dr-4\left(\int_0^1 W(r)\,dr\right)^2,$$

$$D_1=\left((1/2)\left(\sigma_u^2-\sigma^2\right)/\sigma^2\right)\int_0^1 W(r)\,dr.$$

The proof of these results is also straightforward from the asymptotic properties of the sample moments given in Lemma 6. It is clear that when the variances of the stationary processes and their autoregressive coefficients are the same for all individuals and this is true for the individual random walk processes as well in (13), then we get back the results of Lemma 3. In order to eliminate the nuisance parameters asymptotically, we have to establish the consistency of the estimators $\widehat{\sigma}_{Tl}^2$ and $\widetilde{\sigma}_{Tl}^2$ defined in Lemma 4.

Lemma 8 *If the innovation sequences* $\left\{u_t^{(k)}\right\}$ $(k=1,2)$ *satisfy conditions* $(a')-(d')$, *and* $l\to\infty$ *as* $T\to\infty$ *such that* $l=o\left(T^{1/2}\right)$, *then* $\widehat{\sigma}_{Tl}^2\to\sigma^2$ *(resp.* $\widetilde{\sigma}_{Tl}^2\to\sigma^2$*) in probability as* $T\to\infty$.

See the proof of Lemma 4. The asymptotic distributions of the Z statistics in (9), (10), (11) under the corresponding nulls set up in this section are given below.

Theorem 2

(*i*) *For model (6) the statistics* $Z(\hat{\rho}_T)$ *and* $Z(t_{\hat{\rho}})$ *have the same limit distributions, as in Lemma 3 (a) and (b) when the null includes* $\sigma^2=\sigma_u^2$.

(*ii*) *For model (8) the statistics of* $Z(\widetilde{\rho}_T)$ *and* $Z\left(t_{\widetilde{\rho}_T}\right)$ *have the same limit distributions, as in Lemma 7 (c) and (d), when the null includes* $\sigma^2=\sigma_u^2$.

This theorem generalizes Theorem 6 for more heterogenous individual time series.

5. APPLICATION

In this section we apply our test based on model (7) to the Friedman-Schwartz series (annual, 1969-1975). After demeaning the first differences series the order of the autoregressive process was selected by the BIC criterion. The criterion picked out the ARMA(1,1) model for this series. It yields that we can consider the original series as the sum of an aggregate random walk and an aggregate stationary process

$$y_t^{(1)}=\rho y_{t-1}^{(1)}+u_t^{(1)},$$
$$y_t^{(2)}=\rho^* y_{t-1}^{(2)}+u_t^{(2)},$$
$$\rho=1,$$

so that, for the series $y_t=y_t^{(1)}+y_t^{(2)}$ we have

$$\Delta y_t=\rho^*\Delta y_{t-1}+u_t^{(1)}-\rho^* u_{t-1}^{(1)}+u_t^{(2)}-u_{t-1}^{(2)}.$$

We then produced the instrumental variable estimate of the autoregressive coefficient, $\widetilde{\rho}_{IV}^*$, by applying the instrumental variables proposed by Hall (1989). Since, we can estimate consistently the variance of the random walk by $\widetilde{s}^2_{Tl}$ (we used the truncation number 5) and the parameters $N^*\sigma^2_{(1)} + (N - N^*)\,\sigma^2_{(2)} \cdot \frac{2}{\rho^*+1}$ by $\widetilde{s}^2_T$, we get a consistent estimate of the variance of the aggregate stationary process by $(\widetilde{s}^2_T - \widetilde{s}^2_{Tl})\,(\widetilde{\rho}^*_{IV} + 1)\,/2$. Using these estimates we obtain that the ratio of the variances of the aggregated random walk and stationary AR(1) processes is about 8. Table 5 contains these results.

Table 5

Estimation Results
Friedman and Schwartz Series (1869-1975)

$\widetilde{\rho}$	$Z(\widetilde{\rho})$	$\widetilde{\rho}^*_{IV}$	$\widetilde{s}^2_{Tl}$	$\widetilde{s}^2_T$
0.82	−21.24	−0.38	2.6741 10^{-3}	3.7975 10^{-3}
$(\widetilde{s}^2_T - \widetilde{s}^2_{Tl})\,(1 + \widetilde{\rho}^*_{IV})\,/2$			estimated 5% critical value	
0.348 10^{-3}			−27.9	

According to our results we conclude that we cannot reject the null hypothesis of a unit root without trend for the Friedman-Schwartz series in contrast to result of Phillips and Perron (1987) since they can reject the null hypothesis at close to the 5% level using the conventional critical values.

If we would adopt a higher order ARMA process, our procedure could easily be carried out as well, keeping in mind that the null distribution of $Z(\widetilde{\rho})$ depends on such factors as the sample size, the ARMA parameters, the variance of the aggregate random walk and $\gamma(0) - \gamma(1)$, where $\gamma(j)$ is the autocovariance function of the aggregate stationary process.

6. CONCLUSION

In the introduction we asked the question: "Does the GNP have a unit root?" As we demonstrated it in this paper, we should get some inferences about the heterogeneity of the disaggregated processes (stationary/nonstationary behavior) from the estimates of the nuisance parameters before trying to answer the question. This information is ignored if we use the conventional approaches. It may well happen that we reject too often the null hypothesis of unit root and the size distortion can also become very serious even in relatively large samples. It is demonstrated that in the case of very long data sets going back to the middle of the last century, when the Dickey-Fuller and the Phillips-Perron tests fail to show any evidence of unit root, our testing procedure proves that this behavior was indeed dominant.

The series of the newly obtained critical values help to get some insights into the behavior of the agents making up the economy (and the GDP, GNP).

Following our approach it also helps to accommodate the usual structural break problem, as in this framework a structural break most of the time means a shift in the proportion individual agents behave in a stationary/nonstationary manner.

REFERENCES

1. Andrews, D.W.K. (1984), "Non-Strong Mixing Autoregressive Processes", *Journal of Applied Probability*, 21, 930-934.
2. Andrews, D.W.K. (1988), "Laws of Large Numbers for Dependent Non-Identically Distributed Random Variables", *Econometric Theory*, 4, 458-467.
3. Ben-David, D. and D. H. Papell (1995), "The Great Wars, the Great Crash, and Steady State Growth: Some New Evidence About an Old Stylized Fact", *Journal of Monetary Economics*, 36, 453-475.
4. Davidson, J. (1995), *Stochastic Limit Theory*. Oxford: Oxford University Press.
5. Davidson, J. and R. M. de Jong (1997), "Consistency of Kernel Estimators of Heteroscedastic and Autocorrelated Covariance Matrices", mimeo.
6. Dickey, D. A. and W. A. Fuller (1979), "Distribution of the Estimators for Autoregressive Time Series with a Unit Root", *Journal of the American Statistical Association*, 74, 427-431.
7. Diebold, F. X. and A. S. Senhadji (1996), "The Uncertain Unit Root in Real GNP: Comment", *American Economic Review*, 86, 1291-1298.
8. Granger, C. W. J. (1980), "Long Memory Relationships and the Aggregation of Dynamic Models", *Journal of Econometrics*, 14, 227-238.
9. Granger, C. W. J. (1992), "Implications of Seeing Economic Variables Through an Aggregation Window", University of California, San Diego, Department of Economics, mimeo.
10. Hall, A. (1989), "Testing for a Unit Root in the Presence of Moving Average Errors", *Biometrika*, 76, 49-56.
11. Lippi, M. (1988), "On the Dynamic Shape of Aggregated Error Correction Models", *Journal of Economic Dynamic and Control*, 12, 561-585.
12. Lippi, M. and Zaffaroni (1998), "Aggregation of Simple Linear Dynamics: Exact Asymptotic Results", University of Rome, mimeo.
13. Nelson, C. R. and C. J. Murray (1997), "The Uncertain Trend in U.S. GDP", mimeo.
14. Nelson, C. R. and C. I. Plosser (1982), "Trends and Random Walks in Macroeconomic Time Series: Some Evidence and Implications", *Journal of Monetary Economics*, 10, 139-162.
15. Newey, N. K. and K. D. West (1987), "A Simple, Positive Definite, Heteroskedasticity and Autocorrelation Consistent Covariance Matrix", *Econometrica*, 55, 703-708.
16. Pantula, S. G. and A. Hall (1991), "Testing for Unit Roots in Autoregressive Moving Average Models", *Journal of Econometrics*, 48, 325-353.
17. Perron, P. (1989), "The Great Crash, the Oil Price Shock, and the Unit Root Hypothesis", *Econometrica*, 57, 335-346.
18. Phillips, P. C. B. (1987), "Time Series Regression with a Unit Root", *Econometrica*, 55, 277-301.
19. Phillips, P. C. B. and P. Perron (1988), "Testing for a Unit Root in Time Series

Regression", *Biometrika*, 75, 335-346.
20. Phillips, P. C. B. and P. Perron (1987), "Does GNP Have a Unit Root?", *Economics Letters*, 23, 139-145.
21. Dickey, D. A. and S. E. Said (1984), "Testing for Unit Roots in Autoregressive-Moving Average Models of Unknown Order", *Biometrika*, 71, 599-607.
22. Dickey, D. A. and S. E. Said (1985), "Hypothesis Testing in ARIMA(p,1,q) Models", *Journal of the American Statistical Association*, 80, 369-374.
23. Sims, C. A., J. H. Stock and M. W. Watson (1990), "Inference in Linear Time Series Models with Some Unit Roots", *Econometrica*, 58, 113-144.
24. Stock, J. H. and M. W. Watson (1986), "Does GNP Have a Unit Root?", *Economics Letters*, 22, 147-151.
25. Zivot, E. and D. W. K. Andrews (1992), "Further Evidence on the Great Crash, the Oil-Price Shock, and the Unit Root Hypothesis", *Journal of Business and Economic Statistics*, 10, 251-270.

Panel Data Econometrics: Future Directions
J. Krishnakumar and E. Ronchetti (Editors)

CHAPTER 12

KERNEL M-ESTIMATORS AND FUNCTIONAL RESIDUAL PLOTS

Christian GOURIEROUX, Alain MONFORT and Carlos TENREIRO

Abstract

We consider kernel M-estimators defined as a solution of an optimization problem of the kind:

$$\hat{\theta}_T(s) = \arg\min_{\theta} \sum_{t=1}^{T} \frac{1}{Th_T^d} K\left[\frac{S_t - s}{h_T}\right] \psi(Y_t, \theta).$$

Such estimators will tend to the functional parameter $\theta(s)$ solution of:

$\theta(s) = \arg\min_{\theta} E(\psi(Y_t;\theta)/S_t = s)$. Local versions of such estimators may be used as functional residual plots to check the hypothesis of a constant function $\theta(\cdot)$. We explain how these functional residual plots are related with some more usual testing procedures of this hypothesis, and how they may be introduced as important tools in an upward parametric modelling strategy.

1. INTRODUCTION

Whatever the problem of interest is : behavior analysis, prediction, control... econometrics is mainly interested in conditional distribution parameters. The aim of this paper is to discuss the estimation of a functional parameter defined in an implicit way, and to explain how such functional estimators may be used in a modelling strategy searching for a well-specified parametric specification.

We introduce the notion of functional implicit parameter in the following way. Let us consider a stationary process $(y_t, x_t, t \in \mathbf{Z})$ and denote by $(I_t, t \in \mathbf{Z})$ the sequence of informations ($\sigma -$ algebra) generated by past values of y, and by the present and the past values of x. Let us also introduce a parameterized objective function:

$$\psi(y_t, y_{t-1}, x_t; \theta) = \psi(Y_t; \theta) \text{ (say)}.$$

We assume that there exists some stationary, I_t-measurable, d-dimensional, process S_t, such that the two optimization problems:

$$\min_\theta E\left[\psi(Y_t;\theta)/I_t\right] \text{ and } \min_\theta E\left[\psi(Y_t;\theta)/S_t\right],$$

provide a same unique solution $\theta(S_t)$. $\theta(\cdot)$ will be the functional parameter of interest. If (Y_t, S_t) $t = 1, \ldots, T$ are observable, an estimator of $\theta(\cdot)$ may be derived by replacing the theoretical objective function:

$$s \longrightarrow E\left[\psi(Y_t;\theta)/S_t = s\right],$$

with a kernel based approximation. It leads to the introduction of a kernel M-estimator defined by:

$$s \rightarrow \hat{\theta}_T(s) = \min_\theta \sum_{t=1}^{T} \frac{1}{Th_T^d} K\left[\frac{S_t - s}{h_T}\right] \psi(Y_t;\theta),$$

where d is the dimension of S, K is a d-variate kernel and h_T is the bandwidth.

Such kernel M-estimators have already been introduced for some particular objective function and conditioning variables. When $\psi(Y_t;\theta) = (y_t - \theta)^2$, we get the usual kernel estimator of the regression function $E(y_t/S_t = s)$ [see Härdle 1990 p9.20]. When $\psi(Y_t;\theta) = [y_t - \theta_o - \theta_1(S_t - s) \ldots - \theta_p(S_t - s)^p]^2$, we get the locally weighted least squares regression which locally fits a polynomial of degree p to the data [see Cleveland (1979)]. In these examples the corresponding kernel M-estimator has an explicit form. In some other cases an analytical form of the estimator cannot be obtained. Robinson (1984) considered the estimator of a location parameter: $\psi(Y_t;\theta) = \rho(y_t - \theta)$, Gozalo-Linton (1994) are interested in nonlinear least squares criteria. Finally some applications to log-likelihood or pseudo log-likelihood criteria have been performed by Tibshirani-Hastie (1987), Staniswalis (1989), Fan-Heckman-Wang (1992), for probit and duration models.

The asymptotic properties of the kernel M-estimator $\hat{\theta}_T(\cdot)$ are given in section 2.

In a pure parametric framework the parameters are assumed to be constant, i.e. not variate dependent. Therefore it is important to consider the hypothesis:

$$H_o = \{\theta(s) \text{ independent of } s\},$$

and to propose, either testing procedures, or residual plots to check if this hypothesis may or not be considered as valid. It is the aim of section 3. Residuals will be defined from some expansion of the estimator in a neighbourhood of the null hypothesis. It leads to the introduction of a local kernel M-estimator , whose explicit form is:

$$\tilde{\theta}_T(s) = \hat{\theta}_T^o - \left[\sum_{t=1}^{T} K\left(\frac{S_t - s}{h_T}\right) \frac{\partial^2 \psi}{\partial\theta\partial\theta'}(Y_t; \hat{\theta}_T^o)\right]^{-1} \sum_{t=1}^{T} K\left(\frac{S_t - s}{h_T}\right) \frac{\partial \psi}{\partial \theta}(Y_t; \hat{\theta}_T^o),$$

where $\hat{\theta}_T^o$ is a parametric estimator of θ:

$$\hat{\theta}_T^o = \arg\min_{\theta} \sum_{t=1}^{T} \psi(Y_t; \theta)$$

In section 3 we give the asymptotic properties of $\tilde{\theta}_T(\cdot)$ under the null hypothesis and we discuss the links with more classical testing procedures.

In section 4 we explain how the functional residual plots may be used in practice for determining some parametric models. This modelling strategy is illustrated by the determination of an implicit stochastic volatility, when the Black-Scholes modelling is misspecified. As a byproduct it leads to a better understanding of the so-called smile effect.

Some extension to the case where the S_t variable is not directly observed, but may be consistently approximated, is discussed in section 5. It is an important point for taking into account nonlinear moving average effects.

Since the aim of this paper is mainly to explain how to use nonparametric tools in a structural parametric modelling approach, and since the asymptotic theory of kernel regression estimator is now standard, we only give in the appendices some additional regularity conditions which are sufficient to derive the asymptotic properties of kernel M-estimators from those of kernel regression estimators. They are designed to cover two specificities of the problem: the fact that the parameter of interest is defined implicitly, and the possibility that the conditioning variable is not directly observed (section 5).

2. IMPLICIT FUNCTIONAL PARAMETERS AND KERNEL M-ESTIMATORS

Before studying the properties of kernel M-estimators , it is useful to give some examples of implicit functional parameters. We consider below such parameters associated with first and second order expansion of nonlinear dynamic models. Some other examples are considered in the next sections, especially in section 4 where the notion of implicit stochastic volatility is introduced.

2.1. Nonlinear dynamic models

Nonlinear autoregressive models of order one are generally specified as:

$$y_t = \varphi(y_{t-1}) + \sigma\varepsilon_t,$$

where ε_t is a strong white noise. However the introduction of an additive error term does not take into account some possible interaction between y_{t-1} and ε_t, and in particular it is not suitable for a study of stochastically disturbed deterministic chaotic models. A better formulation has to be jointly nonlinear in y_{t-1} and ε_t:

$$y_t = F(y_{t-1}, \sigma\varepsilon_t), \tag{1}$$

where ε_t is a strong white noise and $\sigma > 0$. In such a formulation F and the distribution of ε_t are not identifiable, but if the distribution of the error is continuous, it is possible to introduce an identifying constraint by imposing that ε_t has a standard gaussian distribution.

Let us now consider the first and second order expansions of model (1), when σ is small.

$$\begin{aligned} y_t &= F(y_{t-1}, 0) + \frac{\partial F}{\partial \varepsilon}(y_{t-1}, 0)\, \sigma\varepsilon_t, \\ y_t &= a_o(y_{t-1}) + a_1(y_{t-1})\, \varepsilon_t, \qquad \text{(say)}, \end{aligned} \tag{2}$$

and:

$$\begin{aligned} y_t &= F(y_{t-1}, 0) + \frac{\partial F}{\partial \varepsilon}(y_{t-1}, 0)\, \sigma\varepsilon_t + \frac{\partial^2 F}{\partial \varepsilon^2}(y_{t-1}, 0)\, \frac{\sigma^2\varepsilon_t^2}{2}, \\ y_t &= a_o(y_{t-1}) + a_1(y_{t-1})\, \varepsilon_t + a_2(y_{t-1})\, \frac{\varepsilon_t^2 - 1}{\sqrt{2}}. \qquad \text{(say)} \end{aligned} \tag{3}$$

Model (2) is an ARCH formulation, where the two functional parameters a_o, a_1 corresponding to the trend and to the volatility depend on the lagged value of y [see Pagan-Ullah (1988), Masry-Tjostheim (1995)].

Model (3) contains an additional term, and, since $\frac{\varepsilon_t^2 - 1}{\sqrt{2}}$ has a chi-square type distribution, it may capture asymmetry and leptokurticity for the conditional distribution of y_t given y_{t-1}. More precisely, it is easily seen that the conditional moments of y_t are given by:

$$E(y_t/y_{t-1}) = a_o(y_{t-1}),$$

$$V(y_t/y_{t-1}) = a_1(y_{t-1})^2 + a_2(y_{t-1})^2,$$

$$E([y_t - E(y_t/y_{t-1})]^3/y_{t-1}) = \sqrt{2}a_2(3a_1^2 + 2a_2^2),$$

$$E([y_t - E(y_t/y_{t-1})]^4/y_{t-1}) = 3(a_1^2 + a_2^2)^2 + 4a_2^2[11a_1^2 + 10a_2^2]$$

From these formulae, the conditional distribution of y_t is skewed and leptokurtic as soon as a_2 is different from zero.

In both cases the functional parameters of interest a_o, a_1, a_2 may be defined by taking the ψ function equal to the conditional log-likelihood function.

For model (2), this function is given by:

$$\ell(y_t/y_{t-1};a) = -\frac{1}{2}\log 2\pi - \log a_1(y_{t-1}) - \frac{1}{2}\frac{[y_t - a_o(y_{t-1})]^2}{a_1(y_{t-1})},$$

and the corresponding kernel M-estimator will be:

$$\begin{bmatrix} \hat{a}_{oT}(y) \\ \hat{a}_{1T}(y) \end{bmatrix} = \underset{a_o,\, a_1}{\arg\max} \sum_{t=1}^{T} \frac{1}{Th_T} K\left[\frac{y_{t-1} - y}{h_T}\right] \ell(y_t/y_{t-1};a). \tag{4}$$

The same kind of kernel maximum likelihood approach may be applied to the second order model (3) with the corresponding form of the log-likelihood function:

$$\begin{aligned}\ell(y_t/y_{t-1};a) = & -\log(a_2\sqrt{2}) - \frac{1}{2}\log\left[\frac{\sqrt{2}}{a_2}(y_t - a_o) + 1 + \frac{a_1^2}{2a_2}\right] \\ & + \log\left\{\varphi\left[\frac{-a_1}{a_2\sqrt{2}} + \left(\frac{\sqrt{2}}{a_2}(y_t - a_o) + 1 + \frac{a_1^2}{2a_2}\right)^{1/2}\right]\right. \\ & \left. + \varphi\left[\frac{-a_1}{a_2\sqrt{2}} - \left(\frac{\sqrt{2}}{a_2}(y_t - a_o) + 1 + \frac{a_1^2}{2a_2}\right)^{1/2}\right]\right\},\end{aligned}$$

where a_o, a_1, a_2 stand for $a_o(y_{t-1}), a_1(y_{t-1}), a_2(y_{t-1})$, and φ is the pdf of the standard normal distribution.

2.2. Kernel M-estimators

Let us consider the functional parameter:

$$\theta(s) = \underset{\theta}{\arg\min}\; E[\psi(Y_t;\theta)/S_t = s].$$

The kernel M-estimators of $\theta(\cdot)$ are defined as solutions of an optimization problem:

$$\begin{aligned}\hat{\theta}_T(s) &= \underset{\theta}{\arg\min} \sum_{t=1}^{T} \frac{1}{Th_T^d} K\left[\frac{S_t - s}{h_T}\right] \psi(Y_t;\theta) \\ &= \underset{\theta}{\arg\min}\; L_T(s,\theta), \qquad \text{(say)}\end{aligned} \tag{5}$$

where $Y_t, S_t,\ t = 1, \ldots, T$ are observable variables, S_t is of dimension d, K is a kernel and ψ the theoretical objective function.

The asymptotic properties of such kernel M-estimators can be deduced from the asymptotic properties of kernel regression estimators applied to the conditional objective function $E[\psi(Y_t;\theta)/S_t = s]$. We just sketch the proof whose specific aspects are discussed in appendices 1 and 2.

Indeed, under standard regularity conditions [see e.g. Nadaraya (1964), Watson (1964), Bosq (1996), Doukhan-Ghindes (1980), Robinson (1983), Collomb (1982), Mack-Silverman (1982)], we know that $L_T(s;\theta)$ converges a.s. to:

$$L_T(s;\theta) \to L_\infty(s;\theta) = E[\psi(Y;\theta)/S = s] f_S(s),$$

where f_S is the marginal pdf of S_t. If we assume that θ belongs to some compact set Θ, that $L_T(s;\theta)$ is continuous w.r.t θ, and that the previous convergence is uniform in $\theta \in \Theta$, we deduce the pointwise a.s. convergence of $\hat{\theta}_T(s)$ to its theoretical analogue $\theta(s)$. Some additional conditions (see appendix 1) may allow for such an a.s. convergence uniformly in s.

The derivation of the asymptotic distribution of $\hat{\theta}_T(s)$ (see appendix 2) is deduced from an expansion of the first order conditions around $\theta(s)$. We get:

$$\sqrt{Th_T^d}[\hat{\theta}_T(s) - \theta(s)] = \left\{ f_S(s) E\left[\frac{\partial^2 \psi}{\partial\theta\partial\theta'}[Y;\theta(s)]/S = s\right]\right\}^{-1} \sqrt{Th_T^d}\frac{\partial}{\partial\theta}L_T(s;\theta) + o_p(1),$$

where: $\sqrt{Th_T^d}\dfrac{\partial}{\partial\theta}L_T(s;\theta)$ is asymptotically normal, zero mean and with a covariance matrix given by:

$$\Omega(s) = f_S(s) I(s) \int K^2(v)dv,$$

where: $I(s) = E\left[\dfrac{\partial\psi}{\partial\theta}[Y;\theta(s)]\dfrac{\partial\psi}{\partial\theta'}[Y;\theta(s)]/S = s\right]$.

Therefore we get the following property, where only the main regularity conditions are given [see appendices 1 and 2 for details].

Property 1: Let us assume:

i. $h_T \to 0, Th_T^d \to +\infty$, when $T \to \infty$;

ii. the kernel K is continuous, with bounded support, assigns mass one to $I\!R^d$, $\int K(u)du = 1$;

iii. (Y_t, S_t) is a strictly stationary process satisfying geometric mixing conditions;

iv. there exists a unique solution $\theta(s)$ to the optimization problem

$$\min_{\theta} E[\psi(Y;\theta)/S = s];$$

and some additional technical conditions, then:

a. $\hat{\theta}_T(s)$ is a.s. consistent for $\theta(s)$,

b. $\sqrt{Th_T^d}[\hat{\theta}_T(s) - \theta(s) - f_S^{-1}(s)J^{-1}(s)B_T(s)] \xrightarrow{d} N(0, \sum(s))$;

where:

$$B_T(s) = \int_{\mathbb{R}^d} K(u)\frac{\partial L_\infty}{\partial \theta}(s - uh_T; \theta(s))du,$$

$$\Sigma(s) = \frac{J(s)^{-1}I(s)J(s)^{-1}}{f_S(s)} \int K^2(v)dv,$$

$$J(s) = E\left[-\frac{\partial^2 \psi}{\partial\theta\partial\theta'}(Y, \theta(s))/S = s\right]$$

$$I(s) = E\left[\frac{\partial \psi}{\partial \theta}(Y;\theta(s))\frac{\partial \psi}{\partial \theta'}(Y;\theta(s))/S = s\right].$$

As expected we obtain the classical expression $J(s)^{-1}I(s)J(s)^{-1}$ corresponding to a parametric M-estimator [see White (1982)], but in which each matrix is evaluated conditionally to $S = s$. It has also to be noted that the matrix $I(s)$ contains no term of the form $E\left[\frac{\partial \psi}{\partial \theta}(Y_t;\theta(s))\frac{\partial \psi}{\partial \theta'}(Y_{t-k};\theta(s))/S = s\right]$, $k \neq 0$ which are negligible with respect to the diagonal term corresponding to $k = 0$, even if some correlation exists in the process (Y_t, S_t) [see also Robinson (1984)]. The other factors appearing in $\Sigma(s)$ are standard in kernel regression.

The asymptotic variance-covariance matrix may be consistently estimated by:

$$\hat{\Sigma}(s) = Th_T^d \left\{\sum_{t=1}^{T} K\left(\frac{S_t - s}{h_T}\right)\frac{\partial^2\psi(Y_t;\hat{\theta}_T(s))}{\partial\theta\partial\theta'}\right\}^{-1}$$

$$\sum_{t=1}^{T} K^2\left(\frac{S_t - s}{h_T}\right)\frac{\partial\psi}{\partial\theta}(Y_t;\hat{\theta}_T(s))\frac{\partial\psi}{\partial\theta'}(Y_t;\hat{\theta}_T(s))$$

$$\left\{\sum_{t=1}^{T} K\left(\frac{S_t - s}{h_T}\right)\frac{\partial^2\psi}{\partial\theta\partial\theta'}(Y_t;\hat{\theta}_T(s))\right\}^{-1}$$

As usual there is a bias term in the asymptotic distribution of the estimator. Because of the asymptotic first order condition, this term is equivalent to:

$$\sqrt{Th_T^d}B_T(s) \simeq \sqrt{Th_T^d}h_T \int_{\mathbb{R}^d} uK(u)du \, \frac{\partial^2 L_\infty}{\partial\theta\partial s'} (s; \theta(s))$$
$$+\frac{1}{2}\sqrt{Th_T^d h_T^2} \sum_i \int_{\mathbb{R}^2} u_i u K(u) du \frac{\partial^3 L_\infty[s; \theta(s)]}{\partial\theta\partial s'\partial s_i}.$$

It is for instance negligible if $Th_T^{d+4} \to 0$ and the kernel is of order 1: $\int_{\mathbb{R}^d} uK(u)du = 0$. But, contrary to the usual practice, we are not really interested in considering the limit case where $Th_T^{d+4} = 0(1)$ and in considering cross-validation aspects [see Härdle (1990), Theorem 7.11]. Indeed the estimator $\hat{\theta}(\cdot)$ is essentially used for some intermediate diagnostics of the constancy hypothesis and, as noted at the beginning of the next section, the bias is identically zero under the null hypothesis.

Similarly, we may expect an improvement of the asymptotic precision of the estimator under the alternative by introducing a local correction of the criterion function. Following Cleveland's approach [see Fan-Heckman-Wang (1992), Gozalo-Linton (1994)], we may consider the modified criterion function:

$$L_T(s; \theta, \alpha) = \sum_{t=1}^{T} \frac{1}{Th_T^d} K\left[\frac{S_t - s}{h_T}\right] \psi[Y_t; \theta + g(S_t, s)'\alpha],$$

where g is a given function such that $g(s, s) = 0$, we may optimize this criterion with respect to both θ, α, and take as the functional estimator the result associated with the subparameter θ. In such a framework similar asymptotic results may be derived as soon as the strict identifiability condition iv) applied to (θ, α) has been replaced by a local identifiable uniqueness condition [see e.g. Gozalo-Linton (1994)]. However it is easily seen that such a correction may also induce a non zero bias term under the null hypothesis, and require additional constraints on the rate of the bandwidth.

3. LOCAL KERNEL M-ESTIMATOR AND THE CONSTANCY HYPOTHESIS

3.1. Definition

Let us consider the hypothesis:

$$H_o = \{\theta(s) \text{ independent of s}\}, \tag{6}$$

and let us introduce the constrained parametric estimator of θ defined by:

$$\hat{\theta}_T^o = \underset{\theta}{\arg\min} \sum_{t=1}^{T} \psi(Y_t; \theta)$$

Under the null hypothesis and denoting by θ_o the value of $\theta(s)$, we deduce from the asymptotic first order condition: $\frac{\partial L_\infty}{\partial \theta}(s;\theta_o) = 0, \forall s$, that the bias term is zero since:

$$B_T(s) = \int_{\mathbb{R}^d} K(u) \frac{\partial L_\infty}{\partial \theta}(s - uh_T;\theta)du = 0.$$

Therefore under the null hypothesis, $\hat{\theta}_T^o$ and $\hat{\theta}_T(s)$ both converge to the true constant value θ_o, but at different rates: $\sqrt{T}$ and $\sqrt{Th_T^d}$ respectively. Therefore under H_o, it is possible to perform an expansion of the first order conditions giving $\hat{\theta}_T(s)$ around $\hat{\theta}_T^o$:

$$\hat{\theta}_T(s) \sim \hat{\theta}_T^o - \left\{ \sum_{t=1}^T K\left[\frac{S_t - s}{h_T}\right] \frac{\partial^2 \psi}{\partial\theta\partial\theta'}(Y_t;\hat{\theta}_T^o)\right\}^{-1} \sum_{t=1}^T K\left[\frac{S_t - s}{h_T}\right] \frac{\partial \psi}{\partial \theta}(Y_t;\hat{\theta}_T^o)$$

Definition 2: The local kernel estimator of $\theta(\cdot)$ in a neighbourhood of H_o is:

$$\tilde{\theta}_T(s) = \hat{\theta}_T^o - \left[\sum_{t=1}^T K\left[\frac{S_t - s}{h_T}\right] \frac{\partial^2 \psi}{\partial\theta\partial\theta'}(Y_t;\hat{\theta}_T^o)\right]^{-1} \sum_{t=1}^T K\left[\frac{S_t - s}{h_T}\right] \frac{\partial \psi}{\partial \theta}(Y_t;\hat{\theta}_T^o).$$

In general $\hat{\theta}_T(s)$ does not admit an explicit expression, but its approximation $\tilde{\theta}_T(s)$ does, as soon as $\hat{\theta}_T^o$ has been computed. Therefore the determination of $\tilde{\theta}_T(\cdot)$ only requires one optimization, the one corresponding to the parametric estimator, whereas the determination of $\hat{\theta}_T(\cdot)$ requires as many optimizations as the number of points in a grid of values for s. In fact the previous expression for $\tilde{\theta}_T(s)$ is nothing else than the first step iteration of a Newton-Raphson algorithm starting from the constant function $\hat{\theta}_T^o$. With additional iterations, we get an approximation of the kernel estimator $\hat{\theta}_T(s)$.

The discrepancy between the local kernel M-estimator and the constrained parametric one has a direct interpretation in terms of residuals. More precisely we have:

$$\tilde{\theta}_T(s) = \hat{\theta}_T^o - \left[\sum_{t=1}^T K\left[\frac{S_t - s}{h_T}\right] \frac{\partial^2 \psi}{\partial\theta\partial\theta'}(Y_t;\hat{\theta}_T^o)\right]^{-1} \sum_{t=1}^T K\left[\frac{S_t - s}{h_T}\right] \frac{\partial^2 \psi}{\partial\theta\partial\theta'}(Y_t;\hat{\theta}_T^o)\hat{v}_{t,T}, \quad (7)$$

where:

$$\hat{v}_{t,T} = \left[\frac{\partial^2 \psi}{\partial\theta\partial\theta'}(Y_t;\hat{\theta}_T^o)\right]^{-1} \frac{\partial \psi}{\partial \theta}(Y_t;\hat{\theta}_T^o),$$

are normalized scores or generalized residuals [see Gourieroux-Monfort-Renault-Trognon (1987), Chesher-Irish (1987)]. Therefore $\hat{v}_T(\cdot) = \tilde{\theta}_T(\cdot) - \hat{\theta}_T^o$ is simply obtained by a kernel regression of these generalized residuals with respect to the variable S. In some sense: $\hat{v}_T(\cdot) = \tilde{\theta}_T(\cdot) - \hat{\theta}_T^o$ provides a residual function with respect to a specific parameter of interest θ, and a potentially omitted variable S ; it will provide some functional residual plots.

Definition 3: The functional residual associated with θ and S is:

$$\hat{v}_T(\cdot) = \tilde{\theta}_T(\cdot) - \hat{\theta}_T^o$$

3.2. Asymptotic properties of local kernel M-estimators under the null hypothesis

Because of the interpretation of $\tilde{\theta}_T(\cdot) - \hat{\theta}_T^o$ as a kernel regression, and of the differences between the rate of convergence of parametric and kernel estimators, we have under the null:

$$\tilde{\theta}_T(s) \sim \theta_o - \left\{ \sum_{t=1}^T K\left[\frac{S_t - s}{h_T}\right] \frac{\partial^2 \psi}{\partial\theta\partial\theta'}(Y_t;\theta^o) \right\}^{-1} \sum_{t=1}^T K\left[\frac{S_t - s}{h_T}\right] \frac{\partial \psi}{\partial\theta}(Y_t;\theta^o)$$

This is the same expansion as for $\hat{\theta}_T(s)$ under H_o (see appendix 2). Therefore the asymptotic distribution described in property 1, where $B_T(s) = 0$ and $\Sigma(s)$ is evaluated under the null, may be used to derive pointwise confidence intervals for $\tilde{\theta}_T(s) - \hat{\theta}_T^o$. As usual for residual plots, pointwise confidence intervals seem more interesting in practice than uniform ones ; essentially they allow to detect a potential nonconstancy on a subset of the S-values, if H_o is not satisfied.

3.3. Testing procedures of the constancy hypothesis

Two kinds of testing procedures of the hypothesis H_o may be considered depending if they are directly based on the functional residual or on parametric estimators.

i) Test based on the functional residual

The idea is to define a uniform confidence interval for the functional residual by using classical results on kernel regression [Härdle (1990), Horowitz (1993)]. Indeed we have seen in subsection 3.2 that:

$$\left\{ \sum_{t=1}^T \frac{1}{Th_T^d} K\left[\frac{S_t - s}{h_T}\right] \frac{\partial^2 \psi}{\partial\theta\partial\theta'}(Y_t,\hat{\theta}_T^o) \right\} \sqrt{Th_T^d}\,\hat{v}_T(s) =$$

$$\sum_{t=1}^T \frac{1}{\sqrt{Th_T^d}} K\left[\frac{S_t - s}{h_T}\right] \frac{\partial \psi}{\partial\theta}(Y_t;\theta_o) + o_p(1)$$

Let us for convenience consider the case of a single parameter. The RHS term is a kernel regression estimator of $\frac{\partial\psi}{\partial\theta}(Y_t;\theta_o)$ on S_t. Therefore as soon as we have a uniform band $[-c_T(s), +c_T(s)]$, such that:

$$\left| \sum_{t=1}^T \frac{1}{\sqrt{Th_T^d}} K\left[\frac{S_t - s}{h_T}\right] \frac{\partial \psi}{\partial\theta}(Y_t;\theta_o) \right| < c_T(s), \forall s,$$

with an asymptotic probability of 95 % under the null, we deduce an asymptotic uniform band for $\hat{v}_T(\cdot)$ by considering $[-\gamma_T(s), +\gamma_T(s)]$, where:

$$\gamma_T(s) = \left[\sum_{t=1}^T \frac{1}{\sqrt{Th_T^d}} K\left[\frac{S_t - s}{h_T}\right] \frac{\partial^2 \psi}{\partial\theta^2}(Y_t;\hat{\theta}_T^o) \right]^{-1} c_T(s)$$

The determination of such a uniform band for the Nadaraya-Watson estimator has been obtained in the i.i.d. case by [Konakov-Piterborg (1984), Härdle (1989)], but similar results for time series do not seem to have been derived. It is due to a lack of a functional limit theorem and of a precise bound for the approximation error between the empirical process and the brownian motion valid for general α-mixing processes [a question out of the scope of this paper]. This uniform bound is likely to be asymptotically infinitely wider than the pointwise one as in the i.i.d case.

As seen below when comparing parametric specification tests with tests based on functional residual plots, the choice between pointwise, and uniform confidence intervals depends on the sequence of alternatives that we have in mind [see part iii)].

ii) Tests based on parametric estimators

Under the constancy hypothesis $\theta(s) = \theta_o, \theta_o$ is the solution of an infinite number of optimization problems:

$$\theta_o = \arg\min_{\theta} E(\psi(Y_t;\theta)/S_t = s), s \text{ varying.}$$

Therefore θ_o is also the solution of the optimisation problems:

$$\theta_o = \arg\min_{\theta} E[\omega(S_t)\psi(Y_t;\theta)],$$

where ω is some positive weighting function. Under the null, this value may be estimated using various parametric M-estimators defined by:

$$\hat{\theta}^o_T(\omega) = \arg\min_{\theta} \sum_{t=1}^{T} \omega(S_t)\psi(Y_t;\theta). \tag{8}$$

All these estimators (including $\hat{\theta}^o_T$ which corresponds to $\omega(\cdot) = 1$) are consistent estimators of θ_o under the null, but generally tends to different limits, when H_o is not satisfied. They may be used as a basis for some specification tests. For such a purpose we have to introduce two different weighting functions ω_1, ω_2 and to consider the joint behaviour of $\hat{\theta}^o_T(\omega_1), \hat{\theta}^o_T(\omega_2)$ under the null. The following property is immediately deduced from the classical properties of parametric M-estimators [see e.g White (1982), Gallant (1987), Gourieroux-Monfort (1995) for the discussion of sufficient sets of regularity conditions).

Property 4: Under standard regularity conditions, we have under the null hypothesis:

$$\sqrt{T}\begin{pmatrix} \hat{\theta}^o_T(\omega_1) - \theta_o \\ \hat{\theta}^o_T(\omega_2) - \theta_o \end{pmatrix} \xrightarrow{d} N\left[\begin{pmatrix} 0 \\ 0 \end{pmatrix}, J(\omega)^{-1}I(\omega)J(\omega)^{-1}\right]$$

where:

$$J(\omega) = \begin{pmatrix} J_1(\omega) & 0 \\ 0 & J_2(\omega) \end{pmatrix},$$

$$J_i(\omega) = E\left[-\omega_i(S_t)\frac{\partial^2 \psi}{\partial\theta\partial\theta'}(Y_t;\theta_o)\right], \quad i = 1, 2,$$

$$I(\omega) = \begin{pmatrix} I_{11}(\omega) & I_{12}(\omega) \\ I_{21}(\omega) & I_{22}(\omega) \end{pmatrix},$$

$$I_{ij}(\omega) = \lim \text{Cov}\left[\frac{1}{\sqrt{T}}\sum_{t=1}^{T}\omega_i(S_t)\frac{\partial\psi}{\partial\theta}(Y_t;\theta_o), \frac{1}{\sqrt{T}}\sum_{t=1}^{T}\omega_j(S_t)\frac{\partial\psi}{\partial\theta}(Y_t;\theta_o)\right]$$

$$= \sum_{h=-\infty}^{+\infty}\Gamma_{ij}(h,\omega), \quad i, j = 1, 2,$$

$$\Gamma_{i,j}(h,\omega) = E\left[\omega_i(S_t)\frac{\partial\psi}{\partial\theta}(Y_t;\theta_o)\omega_j(S_{t-h})\frac{\partial\psi}{\partial\theta'}(Y_{t-h},\theta_o)\right].$$

Then we can introduce a Wald test statistic based on the discrepancy between the two estimators.

Corollary 5: Under the constancy hypothesis, the statistic:

$$\xi_T(\omega_1,\omega_2) = T[\hat{\theta}_T^o(\omega_1) - \hat{\theta}_T^o(\omega_2)]'\hat{Q}^-[\hat{\theta}_T^o(\omega_1) - \hat{\theta}_T^o(\omega_2)]$$

where $\hat{Q}^-$ is a consistent estimator of a generalized inverse of:

$$Q(\omega) = [J_1(\omega)^{-1} - J_2(\omega)^{-1}]I(\omega)\begin{bmatrix} J_1(\omega)^{-1} \\ -J_2(\omega)^{-1} \end{bmatrix}$$

is asymptotically distributed as a chi-square with a number of degrees of freedom equal to the rank of Q. The critical region of this specification test is defined by: $\xi_T(\omega_1,\omega_2) > \chi^2_{95\%}(rk\ Q)$, for a type I error of 5 %.

iii) Lagrange multiplier test against a parameterized alternative

Another approach for analyzing the constancy of θ consists in selecting a parameterized alternative:

$$H_1(g) = \{\theta(S_t) = \theta^* + \alpha g(S_t)\}, \tag{9}$$

and in performing a Lagrange multiplier test of $\{\alpha = 0\}$ based on the parametric criterion:

$$L_T(\theta^*, \alpha) = \sum_{t=1}^{T} \omega_1(S_t)\psi(Y_t; \theta(S_t)).$$

For the discussion below we consider the case of a unidimensional α parameter. The first order derivative used for the LM test is:

$$\frac{\partial L_T}{\partial \alpha}\left[\hat{\theta}_T^*(\omega_1), 0\right] = \sum_{t=1}^{T} \omega_1(S_t)g(S_t)\frac{\partial \psi}{\partial \theta}\left[Y_t, \hat{\theta}_T^*(\omega_1)\right]. \tag{10}$$

Let us denote: $\omega_2(\cdot) = \omega_1(\cdot)g(\cdot)$. Asymptotically, we get:

$$\begin{aligned}
\frac{1}{\sqrt{T}}\frac{\partial L_T}{\partial \alpha}\left[\hat{\theta}_T^*(\omega_1), 0\right] &= \frac{1}{\sqrt{T}}\sum_{t=1}^{T} \omega_2(S_t)\frac{\partial \psi}{\partial \theta}\left[Y_t; \hat{\theta}_T^*(\omega_1)\right] \\
&= \frac{1}{\sqrt{T}}\sum_{t=1}^{T} \omega_2(S_t)\frac{\partial \psi}{\partial \theta}(Y_t; \theta_o) \\
&\quad + \frac{1}{T}\sum_{t=1}^{T} \omega_2(S_t)\frac{\partial^2 \psi}{\partial \theta \partial \theta'}(Y_t; \theta)\sqrt{T}(\hat{\theta}_T^*(\omega_1) - \theta_o) + o_p(1) \\
&= J_2(\omega)\sqrt{T}\left[\hat{\theta}_T^*(\omega_2) - \hat{\theta}_T^*(\omega_1)\right] + o_p(1)
\end{aligned}$$

Therefore we directly deduce the following property.

Property 6: The Lagrange multiplier test for testing H_o against $H_1(g)$ is asymptotically equivalent under H_o to the specification test based on the weighted criteria if: $\omega_2(\cdot) = \omega_1(\cdot)g(\cdot)$.

This property means that in the specification test introduced in the previous subsection the ratio of the weighting functions gives the direction of the implicit alternative.

A similar interpretation exists for the analysis based on the functional residuals. When we consider the residual $\hat{v}_T(s)$ corresponding to a given value of s, and compare it with the bounds of the pointwise confidence interval, the procedure is equivalent to a Lagrange multiplier test corresponding to the sequence of alternatives:

$$H_{1T}(s) = \left\{\theta(S_t) = \theta_o + \alpha K\left(\frac{S_t - s}{h_T}\right)\right\},$$

associated with the same s. To summarize the choice between pointwise or uniform confidence intervals depends on the local, or global form of the alternative.

4. INCLUDING FUNCTIONAL RESIDUAL PLOTS IN A PARAMETRIC MODELLING STRATEGY

4.1. An upward approach

As usual residual plots are informative, when we try to enlarge a too constrained structural model, i.e. in the case of an upward modelling strategy.

Let us consider a parametric problem characterized by a criterion function $\psi_1(Y_t;\theta_1)$.

In a first step, θ_1 is considered as a constant parameter and estimated by:

$$\hat{\theta}^o_{1T} = \arg\min_{\theta_1} \sum_{t=1}^{T} \psi_1(Y_t;\theta_1).$$

Then we can use the functional residual plots associated with θ_1 and various potentially omitted variables $S_j,\ j=1,\dots,J$ to check if the constancy hypothesis is or not satisfied. Let us assume that one variable S_{j_1} may seem to have an effect on θ_1. The form of the functional residual may give an idea for a parametric specification of θ_1 as a function of S_{j_1} :

$$\theta_1(s_{j_1}) = g_1(s_{j_1};\theta_2),$$

where θ_2 are second step parameters.

In the second step, we have now to consider the new criterion function:

$$\psi_2(Y_t;\theta_2) = \psi_1[Y_t; g_1(S_{j_{1,t}},\theta_2)],$$

and so on.

4.2. Implicit stochastic volatility

The previous approach seems particularly important for financial applications as soon as a convenient criterion function is retained (other illustrations are given in appendix 3). We give some ideas of this kind of applications by starting from the usual Black-Scholes modelling [Black-Scholes (1973)].

i) Black-Scholes modelling

The basis is a dynamic model giving the joint evolution of the price of a risky asset, denoted by y_t, and of the short term interest rate r_t. The price is assumed to follow a geometric brownian motion:

$$dy_t/y_t = \mu_o dt + \sigma_o dW_t, \tag{11}$$

where the parameters are the drift μ_o, the volatility σ_o, and where (W_t) is a standard brownian motion. The short term interest rate is assumed to be deterministic and constant:

$$r_t = r \tag{12}$$

To answer questions concerning pricing (a prediction problem) or hedging (a control problem), additional assumptions are usually introduced. Let us consider the pricing of an european call. (An application to an hedging problem may be found in Gourieroux-Laurent (1995), see also: Bossaerts-Hillion (1995)). Such a contingent claim backed on the asset y_t, maturing at time T, with strike K, is characterized by the cash-flow $(y_t - K)^+$, which is delivered at T. This option has a price $P[t, T, K]$ at time t.

If we introduce the following additional assumptions:

i. the price $P(t, T, K)$ is a function of past and current values of (y_t) ;

ii. it is possible to have continuous trading, without transaction costs, without liquidity constraints ;

iii. there is no arbitrage opportunity,

we derive a unique price for the option given by:

$$\begin{aligned} P[T,t,K] &= S_t \left\{ \Phi \left[\frac{1}{\sigma_o \sqrt{T-t}} \log \frac{y_t}{K \exp -r(T-t)} + \sigma_0 \frac{\sqrt{T-t}}{2} \right] \right. \\ &\quad \left. - \frac{K \exp -r(T-t)}{S_t} \Phi \left[\frac{1}{\sigma_o \sqrt{T-t}} \log \frac{y_t}{K \exp -r(T-t)} - \sigma_0 \frac{\sqrt{T-t}}{2} \right] \right\} \\ &= g_{BS}(y_t, \tau, K, r, \sigma_o), \qquad \text{(say)} \end{aligned} \tag{13}$$

where Φ is the cdf of the standard normal distribution, and $\tau = T - t$ is the residual maturity.

ii) Some misspecifications

In practice such a complete structural modelling is often misspecified either because of a too simplified evolution model, or because of unrealistic additional assumptions. For instance in the Black-Scholes modelling, the interest rates are not constant, the price evolution presents some conditional heteroscedasticity, the price of the option depends on some other factors (such as the prices of some other assets, the traded volumes...), there exists some transaction cost...

What can we do ? A first solution is to look for a new well specified complete modelling and to try to theoretically deduce an answer to the problem of interest (i.e. the pricing of an european call). For instance we might introduce a stochastic volatility model for y_t, an Ornstein-Uhlenbeck process for the instantaneous interest rate. But first the search for a correct specification of the evolution model may be cumbersome, second we are now in an incomplete market framework where the prices of derivative assets are not unique, and third the Black-Scholes formula (13) remains a kind of benchmark for a number of practitioners.

In this section we defend a second approach directly based on an extension of the Black-Scholes formula, by replacing the constants r, K and/or σ by some functions of the past $I_t = \{y_{t-1}, r_{t-1}, P_{t-1}, y_{t-2}, r_{t-2}, P_{t-2}\}$, where P_t are option prices. We are essentially looking for prediction models of the option price of the form:

$$E\left(P[t, t+\tau, K]/I_t\right) = g_{BS}\left[y_t, \tau, K(I_t), r_t + s(I_t), \sigma(I_t)\right], \tag{14}$$

where $K(I_t), s(I_t), \sigma(I_t)$ are interpretable as a stochastic implicit strike, a stochastic implicit spread on interest rate and a stochastic implicit volatility respectively.

Of course the previous formula may be introduced for a subclass of options, such as those with given maturity..., and the $K(\cdot), s(\cdot), \sigma(\cdot)$ functions are then indexed by this subclass.

It is also worth noting that the use of functional residual plots in such a framework is not direct, since the price (y_t) is nonstationary under Black-Scholes modelling. Therefore it is necessary to choose a suitable subclass of derivative assets, and a suitable criterion ψ in order to stationarize the problem, i.e. to get the ψ process stationary (even if (y_t) is not). For instance we may consider the subclass of options indexed by t, with a given maturity τ_0, a cash-flow at $t + \tau_0$ given by:

$$\left(\frac{y_{t+\tau_o}}{y_t} - K_o\right)^+ = \frac{1}{y_t}(y_{t+\tau_o} - K_o\, y_t)^+, K_o \text{ given,} \tag{15}$$

and a price P_t at date t. For such options, K_o is the strike expressed in the numeraire of date t, if this numeraire is assimilated to the underlying asset. In particular for $K_o = 1$, we price at the money options. The Black-Scholes price has to be normalized accordingly. It is given by:

$$\frac{1}{y_t} g_{BS}(y_t, \tau, K y_t, r, \sigma) = P_t^{BS}(\tau, K, r, \sigma), \text{(say)}$$

and it no longer depends on the current values y_t. Then a possible stationarized criterion function is based either on

$$\left(P_t - P_t^{BS}(\tau, K, r, \sigma)\right)^2, \theta = (K, r, \sigma),$$

or

$$\left(P_t - P_t^{BS}(\tau, K, r_t + s, \sigma)\right)^2, \theta = (K, s, \sigma)$$

The corresponding implicit functional parameters will depend on τ_o and K_o. Therefore "this approach will address what is often mentioned as the most important defect of the BS formula for equity option: the non constancy of the implicit volatility across moneyness, i.e. across different values of K_o", i.e the so-called smile effect. The same remark holds for the dependence on the maturity τ_0.

4.3. Application

i) The data

We now illustrate the determination of implicit stochastic volatility corresponding to a set of artificial data, on the three different prices, i.e. the short term interest rate r_t, the price of the underlying asset, and the price P_t of the option. They will be generated with an evolution model extending the Black-Scholes one. We first introduce some conditional heteroscedasticity in the evolution of the asset price:

$$\begin{cases} dy_t/y_t &= \mu + \sigma_t \, dW_{ot}, \\ d\log\sigma_t &= c_o(c_1 - \log\sigma_t)dt + c_2 \, dW_{1t}, \end{cases} \tag{16}$$

where the two brownian motions are assumed to be independent. The interest rate follows an Ornstein-Uhlenbeck model:

$$dr_t = a_o(a_1 - r_t)dt + a_2 dW_{2t}, \tag{17}$$

where (W_{2t}) is a brownian motion independent of $(W_{ot}), (W_{1t})$. Finally the price of the option is computed through the Hull-White formula [Hull-White (1987)], with the constant interest rate replaced by its value at t. It is given by:

$$\begin{aligned} P_t = E_t \Big\{ \Phi \left[-\frac{1}{\bar{\sigma}_{t,\tau}} \log(K \exp -r_t\tau) + \frac{1}{2}\bar{\sigma}_{t,\tau} \right] \\ -K \exp -r_t\tau \; \Phi \left[-\frac{1}{\bar{\sigma}_{t,\tau}} \log(K \exp -r_t\tau) - \frac{1}{2}\bar{\sigma}_{t,\tau} \right] \Big\}. \end{aligned} \tag{18}$$

where: $\bar{\sigma}^2_{t,\tau} = \int_t^{t+\tau} \sigma_u^2 \, du$. This formula is simply the conditional expectation of the stationarized Black-Scholes formula (13), in which r is replaced by r_t and σ_o^2 by the time average stochastic volatilities. All the simulations of these data are performed through some discretizations with a small time unit, equal to 1/10, for the stochastic differential equations, for the computation of $\bar{\sigma}^2_{t,\tau}$ and of the conditional expectation. Then we only retain the values (y_t, r_t, P_t) corresponding to the discrete dates $t = 1, \ldots, T$.

In figure 1, we give some simulated paths for y, σ, r, P corresponding to the following values of the parameters:

$$\mu = 4.10^{-4}, \qquad c_o = -\log 0.9, \quad c_1 = \log[20\ 10^{-4}], \quad c_2 = c_1/15,$$

$$a_1 = -\log 0.9, \quad a_1 = 2.10^{-4}, \qquad a_2 = 10^{-5},$$

and to a European call with strike $K_o = 1$ and maturity $\tau_o = 25$. The number of observations is: $T = 250$.

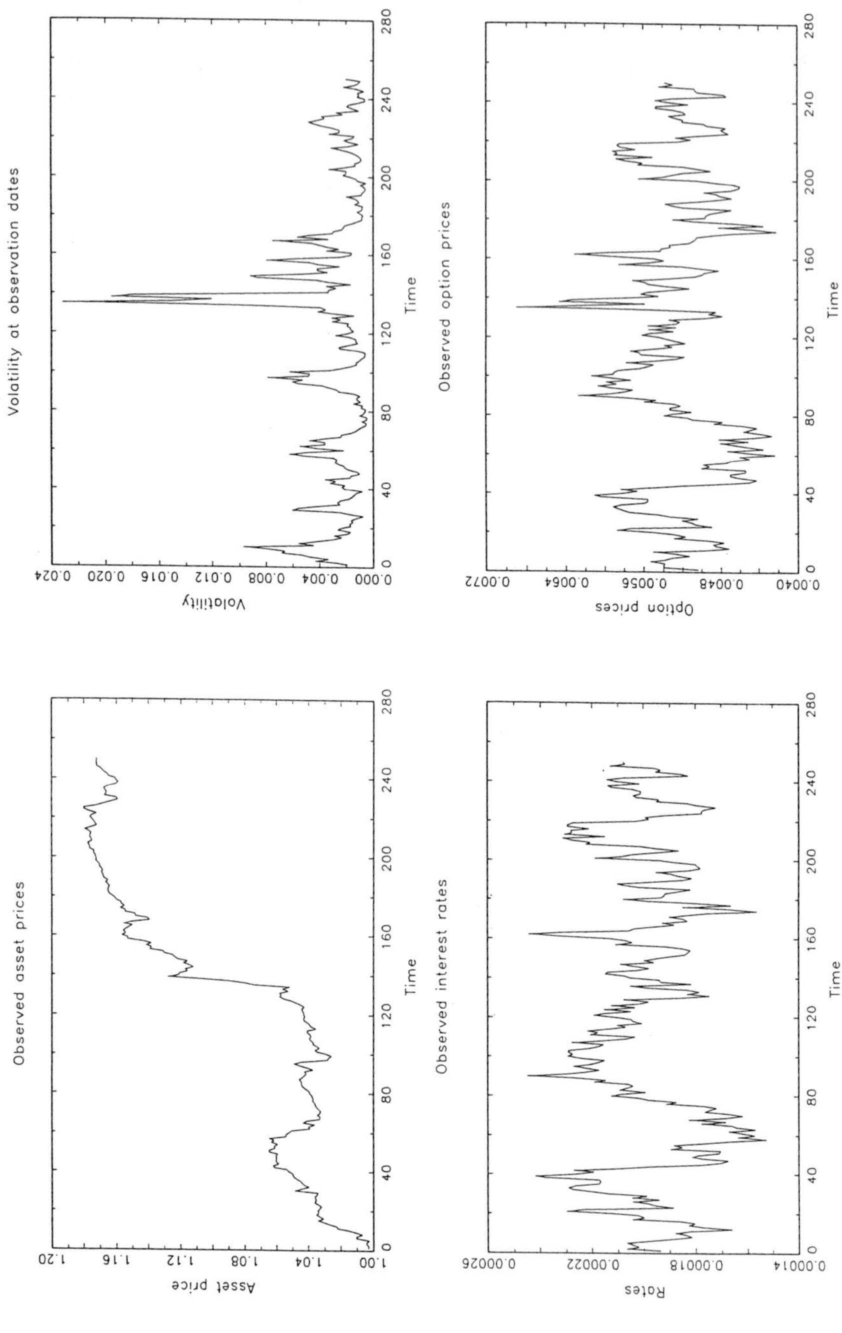

Figure 1. Simulated Paths

ii) Empirical determination of an implicit stochastic volatility

We first focus on the volatility parameter constraining $K(\cdot)$ to the nominal strike K_o, and $s(\cdot)$ to zero.

(*) In a first step we compute from the previous set of artificial data the parametric estimation of the constant implicit volatility:

$$\hat{\sigma}_T^o(K_o) = \arg\min_{\sigma} \sum_{t=1}^{T} \left[P_t - P_t^{BS}(\tau_o, K_o, r_t, \sigma)\right]^2$$

It is given by: $\hat{\sigma}_T^o = 0.00085$, for $K_o = 1$, i.e. for at the money options.

(**) In a second step, we determine the functional residual plots associated with the different lagged variable $\Delta \log y_{t-1}$ (return on the underlying asset), r_{t-1} (instantaneous interest rate), $\Delta \log P_{t-1}$ (return on the option). They are computed with a gaussian kernel with a bandwidth adjusted on the empirical standard error of the conditioning variable. The functional residual plot corresponding to $\Delta \log y_{t-1}$ is given in the top of figure 2 for $K_o = 1$. We have also considered the functional residual plots associated with the two other variables $r_{t-1}, \Delta \log P_{t-1}$. It was not possible to reject the constancy hypothesis for these variables. Figure 2 suggests the following parametric specification for the implicit stochastic volatility:

$$\sigma_{t,K_o}^2(\theta) = a_{K_o} + b_{K_o} \left(\Delta \log y_{t-1}\right)^2$$

A direct parametric estimation provides the following values:

$$\hat{a}_{K_o} = 0.00084, \hat{b}_{K_o} = 1.53,$$

for $K_o = 1$.

(***) In a third step, we compute the functional residual plot:

$$\sigma_{t,K_o}^2(\theta) = \hat{a}_{K_o} + \hat{b}_{K_o} \left(\Delta \log y_{t-1}\right)^2 + \theta,$$

for the parameter θ the omitted variable ($\Delta \log y_{t-1}$, with $K_o = 1$).

It is seen [bottom of figure 2] that the quadratic specification of the implicit stochastic volatility cannot be rejected .

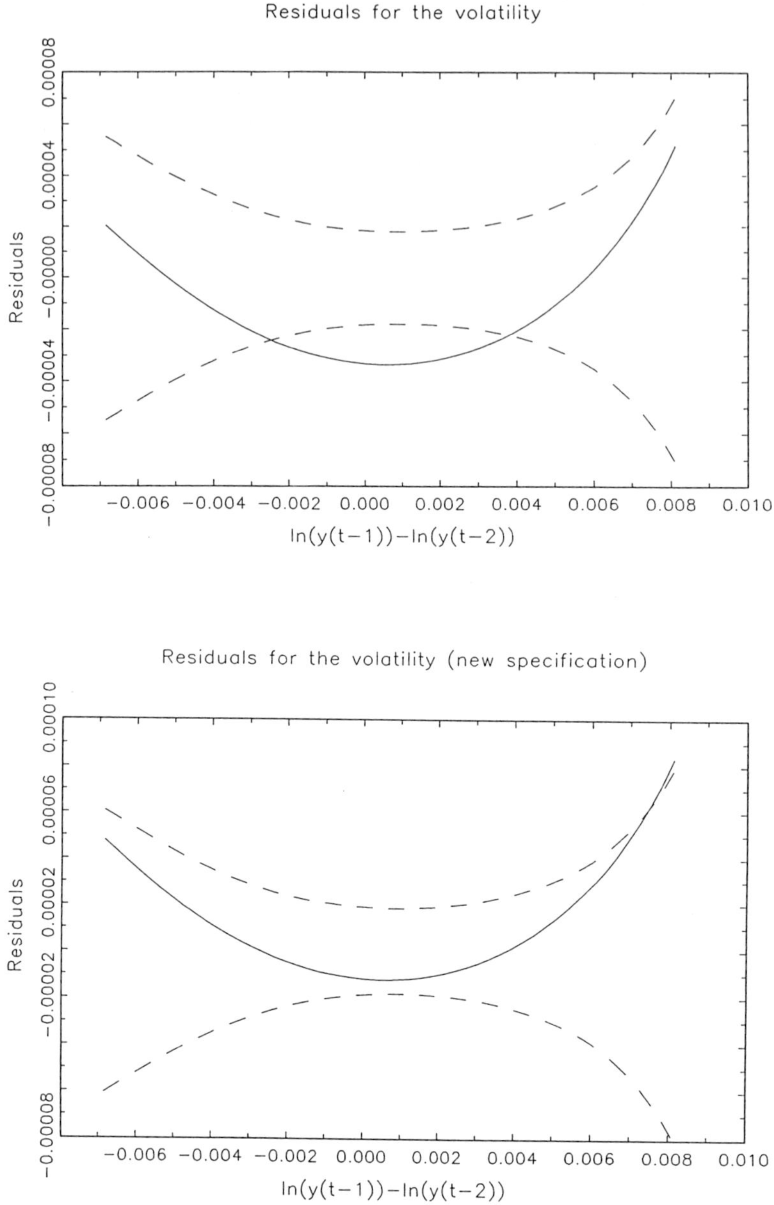

Figure 2. Functional Residual Plots

iii) The smile effect

The previous approach has been applied for different values of the strike K_o. For all these values a quadratic specification is finally accepted. We give in figures 3 and 4 the values of the estimated parameters a_{K_o}, b_{K_o} as functions of K_o for the values 0.97, 0.98,..., 1.02, 1.03. The classical smile effect is directly observed on the constant parameter, but an inverse smile effect appears for the path-dependent effect parameter b [see also Gourieroux-Laurent (1995)].

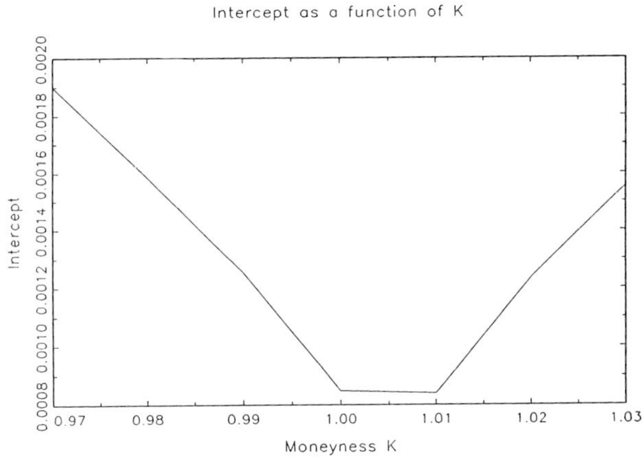

Figure 3. The Smile Effect on a.

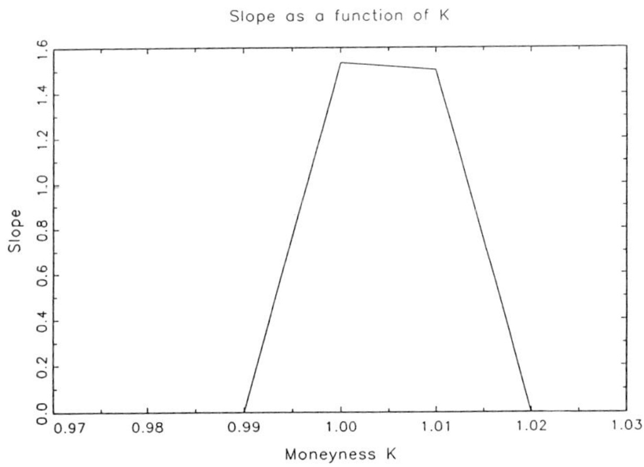

Figure 4. The Sad Smile Effect on b.

iv) Comparison of the underlying and implicit stochastic volatilities

It is also possible to compare the paths of the underlying volatility σ_t^2 and of the quadratic implicit stochastic volatility $\sigma_{t,K}^2 = a_K + b_K (\Delta \log y_{t-1})^2$. In presence of stochastic volatilities, the implicit Black-Scholes volatilities are heavily biased when they are interpreted as predictors of the underlying volatilities ; they are given in figure 5. For this reason we first regress linearly σ_t^2 on $\sigma_{t,K}^2$, and compute the corresponding linear predictor $\tilde{\sigma}_{t,K}^2$ in this regression. It gives the best affine approximation of σ_t^2 through the implicit volatility. The paths of σ_t^2 and $\tilde{\sigma}_{t,K_o}^2$ are given in figure 6 for an at the money option $K_o = 1$.

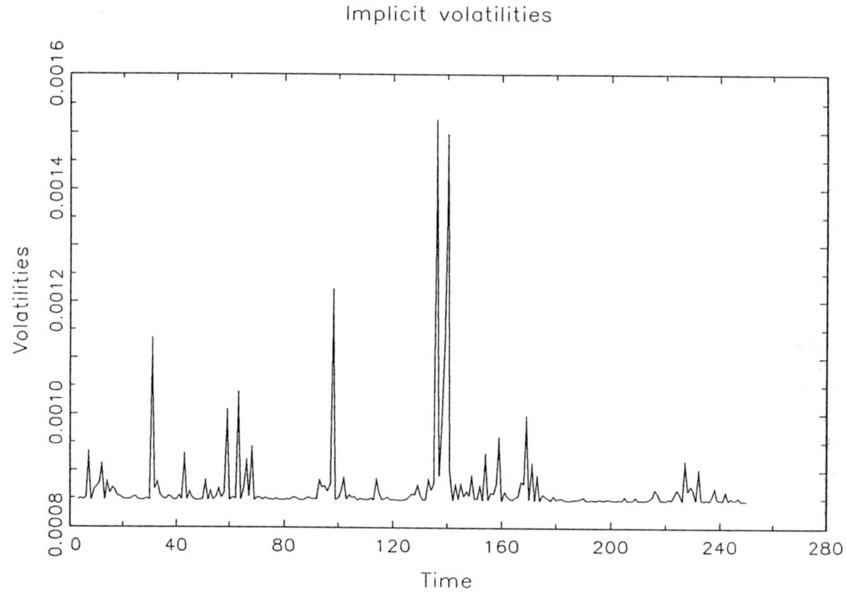

Figure 5. Implicit Volatilities

The path dependent stochastic volatility is able to detect the large peaks in the underlying volatility, but not the small ones. The Black-Scholes formula seems to oversmooth the stochastic volatility.

v) Implicit spread of interest rate

We finally study if it is useful to introduce a path dependent correction on the short term interest rate used in the Black-Scholes formula. We first consider a constant implicit

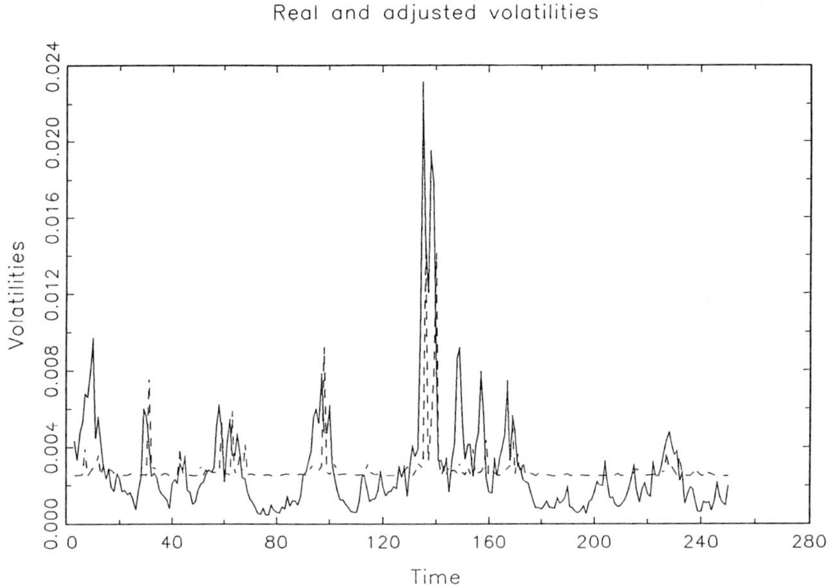

Figure 6. Underlying Volatilities and Prediction Based on the Implicit Volatilities

volatility. We give in the top of figure 7 the functional residual plot corresponding to this spread and to the omitted variable $\Delta \log y_{t-1}$, for $K_o = 1$. It is seen that the local constancy hypothesis is rejected. But the same conclusion does not hold for the other potentially omitted variables such as $r_{t-1}, \Delta P_{t-1}$. When the correction on the spread is applied after the correction on the implicit volatility derived in the previous subsection, the constancy hypothesis cannot be rejected for all the potentially omitted variables [see the bottom of figure 7].

5. LAGGED ERRORS AS CONDITIONING VARIABLES

Let us now discuss the case where the conditioning variable is a lagged error, and, since it is unobservable, has to be replaced by some residual.

5.1. An example

We consider an AR(1) model with ARCH (1) errors:

$$y_t = ay_{t-1} + b + \varepsilon_t,$$

where: $V(y_t/y_{t-1}) = k_t = c_0 + c_1\varepsilon_{t-1}^2$.

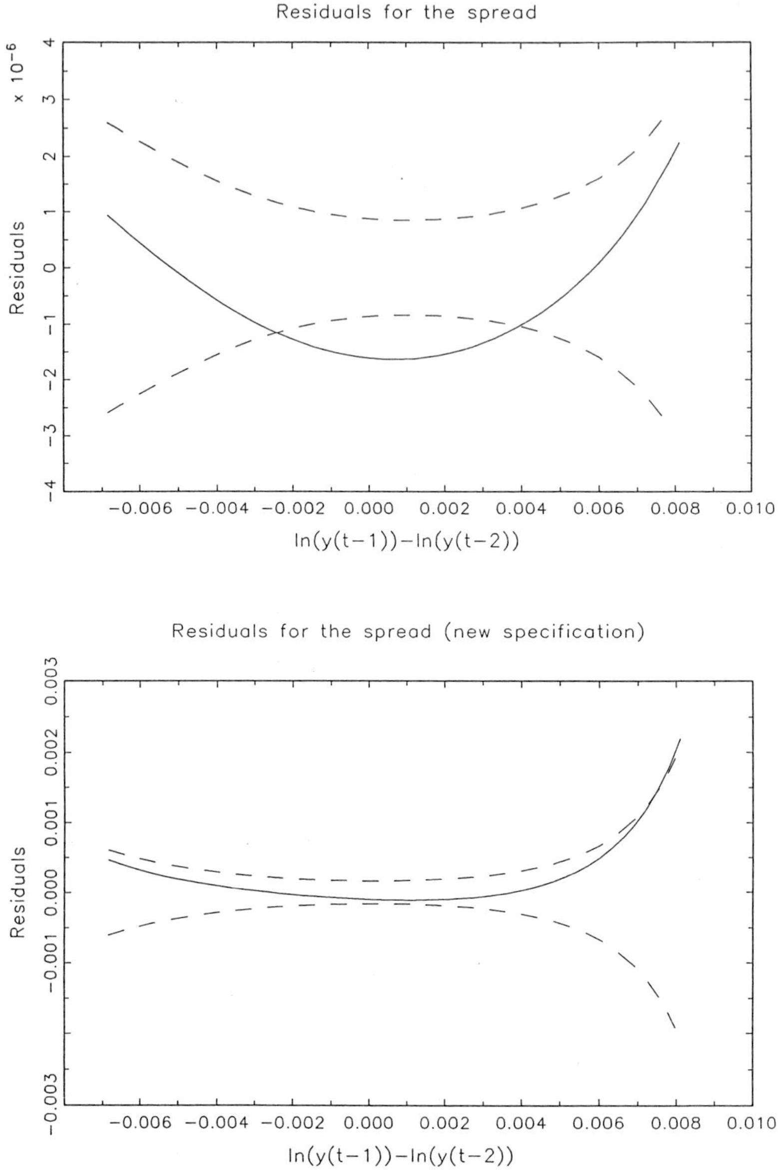

Figure 7. Functional Residual Plots for the Spread of Interest Rate

The different parameters can be estimated by the pseudo-maximum likelihood method. These estimators are denoted by $\hat{a}_T, \hat{b}_T, \hat{c}_{0T}, \hat{c}_{1T}$ respectively, and the corresponding residuals by:

$$\hat{\varepsilon}_t^o = y_t - \hat{a}_T\, y_{t-1} - \hat{b}_T.$$

But it is known that financial series often show a leverage effect, i.e. an asymmetric reaction of the volatility to positive or negative values of the ε_{t-1} [Black (1976), Gourieroux-Monfort (1992), Engle-Ng (1993), Härdle-Tsybakov (1995)]. Therefore it is interesting to compare the initial model: $H_o = \{k_t = c_o + c_1\varepsilon_{t-1}^2\}$ with the more general one: $H_1 = [k_t = k(\varepsilon_{t-1})]$.

For such a diagnostic we may consider the optimization problem:

$$\min_v \sum_{t=1}^{T} K\left(\frac{\hat{\varepsilon}_{t-1}^o - \varepsilon}{h_T}\right)\left\{-\frac{1}{2}\log(\hat{c}_{0T} + \hat{c}_{1T}\,\hat{\varepsilon}_{t-1}^{o2} + v) - \frac{1}{2}\left(\frac{\hat{\varepsilon}_t^{o2}}{\hat{c}_{0T} + \hat{c}_{1T}\,\hat{\varepsilon}_{t-1}^{o2} + v}\right)\right\},$$

or better its second order expansion with respect to v, which provides the functional residual plot:

$$\hat{v}_T(\varepsilon) = \left\{\sum_{t=1}^{T} K\left(\frac{\hat{\varepsilon}_{t-1}^o - \varepsilon}{h_T}\right)\left[\frac{1}{2}\frac{1}{\left(\hat{c}_{0T} + \hat{c}_{1T}\,\hat{\varepsilon}_{t-1}^{02}\right)^2} - \frac{\hat{\varepsilon}_t^{02}}{\left(\hat{c}_{0T} + \hat{c}_{1T}\,\hat{\varepsilon}_{t-1}^{02}\right)^3}\right]\right\}^{-1}$$
$$\sum_{t=1}^{T} K\left(\frac{\hat{\varepsilon}_{t-1}^o - \varepsilon}{h_T}\right)\left[-\frac{1}{2}\frac{1}{\left(\hat{c}_{0T} + \hat{c}_{1T}\,\hat{\varepsilon}_{t-1}^{02}\right)} + \frac{\hat{\varepsilon}_t^{02}}{2\left(\hat{c}_{0T} + \hat{c}_{1T}\hat{\varepsilon}_{t-1}^{02}\right)^2}\right]$$

5.2. Study of the functional residual plots

In such a framework the functional residual plots have a form of the type [see definition 3]:

$$\tilde{\theta}_T(s) - \hat{\theta}_T^o = -\left[\sum_{t=1}^{T} K\left[\frac{S[Z_t;\hat{\theta}_T^o] - s}{h_T}\right]\frac{\partial^2\psi}{\partial\theta\partial\theta'}(Y_t;\hat{\theta}_T^o)\right]^{-1}\sum_{t=1}^{T} K\left(\frac{S[Z_t;\hat{\theta}_T^o] - s}{h_T}\right)\frac{\partial\psi}{\partial\theta}(Y_t;\hat{\theta}_T^o)$$

where Z_t is some observable process, such that (Z_t, Y_t) satisfies the geometric mixing condition.

Under some additional regularity conditions concerning the differentiability of S with respect to θ, and the differentiability of K, it is easily checked that this functional residual has under the null hypothesis the same asymptotic distribution as:

$$-\left[\sum_{t=1}^{T} K\left[\frac{S(Z_t;\theta_o) - s}{h_T}\right]\frac{\partial^2\psi}{\partial\theta\partial\theta'}(Y_t;\hat{\theta}_T^o)\right]^{-1}\sum_{t=1}^{T} K\left[\frac{S(Z_t;\theta_o) - s}{h_T}\right]\frac{\partial\psi}{\partial\theta}(Y_t;\hat{\theta}_T^o).$$

Therefore we may apply property 1 with $S_t = S(Z_t;\theta_o)$.

Appendix 1: Consistency of the kernel M-estimator

Contrary to the case of kernel M-estimators a la Huber (1981) introduced for robustness purpose, it is not possible in our framework to assume the convexity of the criterion function with respect to the parameter θ [see Robinson (1984)].

We shall prove the uniform a.s. convergence of the objective function:

$$\sup_{s \in C} \sup_{\theta \in \Theta} \|L_T(s;\theta) - L_\infty(s;\theta)\| \underset{T \to +\infty}{\longrightarrow} 0 \ a.s., \tag{19}$$

which implies the asymptotic existence and the strong uniform convergence of the associated M-estimator:

$$\sup_{s \in C} \left\|\hat{\theta}_T(s) - \theta(s)\right\| \underset{T \to +\infty}{\longrightarrow} 0 \ a.s.,$$

as soon as the limit objective function is continuous, the parameter space and the set $C \subset I\!R^d$ are compact, and $\theta(s)$ is the unique solution of the optimisation problem:

$$\max_{\theta \in \Theta} L_\infty(s;\theta), \text{ for } s \in C.$$

[see a classical argument introduced by Wald and used for instance by Jennrich (1969)].

To establish (1), we decompose the objective function into two parts:

$$L_T(s;\theta) = [L_T(s;\theta) - EL_T(s;\theta)] + EL_T(s;\theta),$$

where: $L_T(s;\theta) = \sum_{t=1}^{T} \frac{1}{Th_T^d} K\left(\frac{S_t - s}{h_T}\right) \Phi(Y_t;\theta).$

Then we prove that:

i. $EL_T(s;\theta)$ converges uniformly to $L_\infty(s;\theta)$.

ii. $L_T(s;\theta) - EL_T(s;\theta)$ converges a.s. to zero.

iii. $L_T(s;\theta) - EL_T(s;\theta)$ satisfies some equicontinuity property, which with ii), implies the uniform a.s convergence of $L_T(s;\theta) - EL_T(s;\theta)$ to zero.

A. The set of assumptions

A sufficient set of assumptions is the following one.

Conditions on the kernel

i. K is a function with a bounded support and satisfies $\int_{I\!R^d} K(u)du = 1$.

ii. It satisfies the Lipschitz condition:

$$\exists c_o > 0, \forall u, u' \in I\!R^d : |K(u) - K(u')| \leq c_o \|u - u'\|.$$

Condition on the parameter set

Θ is a compact set.

Conditions on the subset C

C is a compact subset of $I\!R^d$.

Conditions on the bandwidth

i. $h_T \to 0$, when $T \to +\infty$.

ii. There exists $\beta \in]0,1[$ such that:

$$\frac{T^{(1-\beta)/2} h_T^d}{\log T} \to +\infty, \text{ when } T \to +\infty.$$

Conditions on the observable process

i. $(Y_t, S_t, t \in \mathbf{Z})$ is a strictly stationary process.

ii. It satisfies the geometric mixing condition:

$$\sup_{A \in F^o_{-\infty}, B \in F_k^{+\infty}} [P(A \cap B) - P(A)P(B)] < a\rho^K, \forall K \in \mathbf{N}^*,$$

where $a \geq 0, 1 > \rho \geq 0, F^o_{-\infty} = \sigma(Y_\tau, S_\tau, \tau \leq 0), F_K^{+\infty} = \sigma(Y_\tau, S_\tau, \tau \geq K)$.

iii. S_t has a continuous distribution with a continuous strictly positive p.d.f. f_S on C.

Conditions on the criterion function

i. $\theta \to \Psi(y; \theta)$ is continuous on $\Theta, \forall y$.

ii. $y \to \Psi(y; \theta)$ is measurable, $\forall \theta$.

iii. Ψ satisfies the Lipschitz conditions:
there exists $c_1(y)$ with $E[c_1(Y_t)] < +\infty$ such that:

$$\forall y, \forall \theta, \theta' \in \Theta : |\psi(y; \theta) - \psi(y; \theta')| \leq c_1(y) \|\theta - \theta'\|.$$

iv. $\exists \delta > 0 : E\left[\sup_{\theta \in \Theta} |\Psi(Y_t;\theta)|^{\frac{2}{\beta}+\delta}\right] < +\infty$, where β is the parameter appearing in condition ii. on the bandwidth.

Conditions on the objective function

i. L_∞ satisfies the uniform equicontinuity condition [see Collomb-Härdle (1986)]:

$$\forall \varepsilon > 0, \exists \delta > 0 : \sup_{s \in C} \sup_{u : \|u-s\| < \delta} \sup_{\theta \in \Theta} |L_\infty(s;\theta) - L_\infty(u;\theta)| < \varepsilon$$

ii. There exists a unique solution $\theta(s)$ to the optimization problem:

$$\max_{\theta \in \Theta} L_\infty(s;\theta), \text{ for any } s \in C$$

(Note that the continuity of L_∞ follows from condition iii. on the criterion function and from the previous conditions i.)

B. **Uniform consistency of $EL_T(s;\theta)$**

Since $h_T \to 0, K$ sums to one and has a compact support, we know that for any $\delta > 0$, there exists T_o such that for $T \geq T_o$:

$$\begin{aligned}
&\sup_{s \in C} \sup_{\theta \in \Theta} |EL_T(s;\theta) - L_\infty(s;\theta)| \\
&\leq \sup_{s \in C} \sup_{\theta \in \Theta} \int_{\mathbb{R}^d} |K(u)||L_\infty(s - uh_T;\theta) - L_\infty(s;\theta)|du \\
&\leq \sup_{s \in C} \sup_{v : \|v-s\| < \delta} \sup_{\theta \in \Theta} |L_\infty(v;\theta) - L_\infty(s;\theta)| \int_{\mathbb{R}^d} |K(u)|du.
\end{aligned}$$

Therefore the uniform consistency results from assumption i) on the limit objective function L_∞.

C. **Almost sure convergence of $L_T(s;\theta) - EL_T(s;\theta)$** to zero

We first consider the following decomposition of L_T:

$$L_T(s;\theta) = L'_T(s;\theta) + L''_T(s;\theta)$$

$$= \sum_{t=1}^{T} \frac{1}{Th_T^d} K\left(\frac{S_t - s}{h_T}\right) \psi(Y_t;\theta) \mathbb{1}_{|\psi(Y_t;\theta)| \le M_T}$$

$$+ \sum_{t=1}^{T} \frac{1}{Th_T^d} K\left(\frac{S_t - s}{h_T}\right) \psi(Y_t;\theta) \mathbb{1}_{|\psi(Y_t;\theta)| > M_T},$$

where $M_T = T^\gamma$ with $\gamma \in \left]\left(\frac{2}{\beta}+\delta\right)^{-1}, \left(\frac{2}{\beta}\right)^{-1}\right[$, $\beta \in]0,1[$ is the value given in condition ii) on the bandwidth, and δ the value appearing in condition iv) on the criterion function.

i. Following the idea of the proof of proposition 1 given in Mack-Silverman (1982) [see also the proof of proposition 3.1 in Roussas (1990)], we conclude from condition iv) on the criterion function and from the choice of γ, that, for each ω outside a null set, there exists $T_o(\omega)$ such that $L"_T(s;\theta) = 0$ for $T \geq T_o(\omega), s \in C$ and $\theta \in \Theta$. Then we have:

$$\sup_{s \in C} \sup_{\theta \subset \Theta} |L_T"(s;\theta) - EL"_T(s;\theta)| = 0 \ a.s.$$

for T large enough.

ii. Following standard arguments and using a Bernstein type inequality for partial sums of geometrically mixing processes given in Bosq (1996), we have for all $s \in C, \theta \in \Theta$ and $\varepsilon > 0$:

$$P(|L'_T(s;\theta) - EL'_T(s;\theta)| > \varepsilon) \leq 3\exp\left[-\frac{\varepsilon}{28}\frac{T^{(1-\beta)/2}h_T^d}{\sup_{u \in I\!R^d} |K(u)|}\right]$$

The result follows.

D. **Equicontinuity of $L_T(s;\theta) - EL_T(s;\theta)$**

Let us consider $s_1, s_2 \in C$ and $\theta_1, \theta_2 \in \Theta$. We have:

$$|L_T(s_1;\theta_1) - L_T(s_2;\theta_2)| \leq \sum_{t=1}^{T} \frac{1}{Th_T^d}\left|K\left(\frac{S_t - s_1}{h_T}\right) - K\left(\frac{S_t - s_2}{h_T}\right)\right| |\Psi(Y_t;\theta_1)|$$

$$+ \sum_{t=1}^{T} \frac{1}{Th_T^d}\left|K\left(\frac{S_t - s_2}{h_T}\right)\right| |\Psi(Y_t;\theta_1) - \Psi(Y_t;\theta_2)|$$

$$\leq \sum_{t=1}^{T} \frac{1}{Th_T^d} c_o \frac{\|s_1 - s_2\|}{h_T} |\Psi(Y_t;\theta_1)|$$

$$+ \sum_{t=1}^{T} \frac{1}{Th_T^d} \sup_{u \in IR^d} |K(u)| \, c_1(Y_t) \|\theta_1 - \theta_2\|,$$

from conditions ii. on the kernel and iii. on the criterion function. Finally from the ergodic theorem, we have:

$$|L_T(s_1;\theta_1) - L_T(s_2;\theta_2)| = 0 \left[\frac{\|s_1 - s_2\|}{h_T^{d+1}} + \frac{\|\theta_1 - \theta_2\|}{h_T^d} \right].$$

E. **Uniform consistency of $L_T(s;\theta) - EL_T(s;\theta)$**

Now we may introduce a finite covering of the compact set $C \times \Theta : C_\ell \times \Theta_{\ell'}, \ell = 1,\ldots,N, \ell' = 1,\ldots,N'$ (say), where C_ℓ is of size smaller than $\frac{h_T}{T}$ and $\Theta_{\ell'}$ is of size smaller than $\frac{1}{T}$. This covering may be chosen in such a way that: $N < \left(\frac{T}{h_T} \text{ diam } C + 1\right)^d$, and $N' < (T \text{ diam } \Theta + 1)^p$.

From section C we have for T large enough:

$$\sup_{s \in C} \sup_{\theta \in \Theta} |L_T(s;\theta) - EL_T(s;\theta)|$$

$$\leq \max_{\ell,\ell'} \sup_{\substack{s \in C_\ell \\ \theta \in \Theta_{\ell'}}} |L_T(s;\theta) - EL_T(s;\theta)|$$

$$\leq \max_{\ell,\ell'} \sup_{\substack{s \in C_\ell \\ \theta \in \Theta_{\ell'}}} |L_T(s;\theta) - L_T(s_\ell;\theta_{\ell'}) - E[L_T(s;\theta) - L_T(s_\ell;\theta_{\ell'})]|$$

$$+ \max_{\ell,\ell'} |L'_T(s_\ell;\theta_{\ell'}) - EL'_T(s_\ell;\theta_{\ell'})|,$$

where: $(s_\ell, \theta_{\ell'}) \in C_\ell \times \Theta_{\ell'}, \ell = 1,\ldots,N, \ell' = 1,\ldots,N'$.

Therefore from section D:

$$\sup_{s \in C} \sup_{\theta \in \Theta} |L_T(s;\theta) - EL_T(s;\theta)|$$

$$\leq \max_{\ell,\ell'} \sup_{\substack{s\in C_\ell \\ \theta \in \Theta_{\ell'}}} 0\left(\frac{\|s - s_\ell\|}{h_T^{d+1}} + \frac{\|\theta - \theta_{\ell'}\|}{h_T^d}\right)$$

$$+ \max_{\ell,\ell'} |L'_T(s_\ell;\theta_{\ell'}) - EL'_T(s_\ell;\theta_{\ell'})|$$

$$\leq 0\left(\frac{1}{Th_T^d}\right) + \max_{\ell,\ell'} |L'_T(s_\ell;\theta_{\ell'}) - EL'_T(s_\ell;\theta_{\ell'})|.$$

Since $Th_T^d \to +\infty$, when $T \to \infty$, we have just to establish the a.s. convergence to zero of the second term. From section C and for all $\varepsilon > 0$, we have:

$$P\left[\max_{\ell,\ell'} |L'_T(s_\ell;\theta_{\ell'}) - EL'_T(s_\ell;\theta_{\ell'})| > \varepsilon\right] \leq 3NN' \exp\left[-\frac{\varepsilon}{28}\frac{T^{(1-\beta)/2}h_T^d}{\sup_{u \in I\!R^d} |K(u)|}\right]$$

Since: $NN' = 0(T^{p+d+1})$, we deduce from the condition:

$$\lim_{T \to +\infty} \frac{T^{(1-\beta)/2}h_T^d}{\log T} = +\infty, \text{ that:}$$

$$\sum_{T=1}^{\infty} P\left(\max_{\ell,\ell'} |L'_T(s_\ell;\theta_{\ell'}) - EL'_T(s_\ell;\theta_{\ell'})| > \varepsilon\right) < +\infty,$$

which implies the a.s. convergence.

Appendix 2: Asymptotic normality of the kernel M-estimator

A. The expansion

The asymptotic normality is derived in a standard way. If the mapping $\theta \to \psi(y;\theta)$ is differentiable, if the kernel M-estimator asymptotically exists and if the estimator is consistent (see appendix 1), the estimator satisfies for T large enough the first order conditions:

$$\sum_{t=1}^{T} \frac{1}{\sqrt{Th_T^d}} K\left(\frac{S_t - s}{h_T}\right) \frac{\partial \Psi}{\partial \theta}(Y_t; \hat{\theta}_T(s)) = 0.$$

Then we may expand these equations around $\theta(s)$, which provides:

$$\sum_{t=1}^{T} \frac{1}{\sqrt{Th_T^d}} \left\{ K\left(\frac{S_t - s}{h_T}\right) \frac{\partial \Psi}{\partial \theta}(Y_t; \theta(s)) - E\left[K\left(\frac{S_t - s}{h_T}\right) \frac{\partial \Psi}{\partial \theta}(Y_t; \theta(s))\right]\right\}$$

$$+\sum_{t=1}^{T} \frac{1}{\sqrt{Th_T^d}} K\left(\frac{S_t - s}{h_T}\right) \frac{\partial^2 \Psi}{\partial \theta \partial \theta'}(Y_t; \theta(s)) \sqrt{Th_T^d}[\hat{\theta}_T(s) - \theta(s)]$$

$$+\sum_{t=1}^{T} \frac{1}{\sqrt{Th_T^d}} E\left[K\left(\frac{S_t - s}{h_T}\right) \frac{\partial \Psi}{\partial \theta}(Y_t; \theta(s))\right] + R_T(S_t, Y_t; s) = 0$$

Then we only have to introduce some additional sufficient conditions to ensure that the first term is asymptotically normal with the right asymptotic variance [assumptions B2 and B3], that the sum on t in the second term converges in probability to $f_S(s)J(s)$ [assumption B2 and B4], and the last term is negligible with respect to the two first ones (assumption B1). For the two first convergences we use properties 2 ans 3 (and remark 3) given in Tenreiro (1994) [see also Robinson (1983)].

B. The set of assumptions

This set contains all the assumptions of appendix 1, where we consider $C = \{s\}$ and $s \in I\!R^d$ is fixed, plus some other ones.

Additional condition on the criterion function

iv. The mapping $\theta \to \Psi(y;\theta)$ is differentiable.

Assumptions for the asymptotic expansion of the first order conditions.

B.1 There exists a neighbourhood $V[\theta(s)]$ of $\theta(s)$ such that:

$$\forall y, \forall \theta \in V[\theta(s)] :$$
$$\left\| \frac{\partial \Psi}{\partial \theta}(y;\theta) - \frac{\partial \Psi}{\partial \theta}(y;\theta(s)) - \frac{\partial^2 \Psi}{\partial \theta \partial \theta'}(y;\theta(s))(\theta - \theta(s)) \right\| \leq \|\theta - \theta(s)\|^2 Q(y;\theta(s)),$$

where: $E|Q(Y_t;\theta(s))| < +\infty$ and $E[Q(Y_t;\theta(s))/S_t = \cdot] f_S(\cdot)$ is bounded in a neighbourhood of s.

B.2 For $t \geq 1$, (S_t, S_o) has a continuous distribution whose density function $f_{S_t,S_o}(\cdot,\cdot)$ is uniformly bounded in a neighbourhood of (s,s).

B.3 i. $E\left\{ \left\| \frac{\partial \Psi}{\partial \theta}(Y_t;\theta(s)) \right\|^{2+\delta} \right\} < \infty$, for some $\delta > 0$;

ii. $E\left[\frac{\partial \Psi}{\partial \theta}(Y_t;\theta(s)) \frac{\partial \Psi}{\partial \theta'}(Y_t;\theta(s)) \Big/ S_t = \cdot \right]$ is continuous in s ;

iii. $E\left\{ \left\| \frac{\partial \Psi}{\partial \theta}(Y_t;\theta(s)) \right\|^{2+\delta} \Big/ S_t = \cdot \right\} f_{s_t}(\cdot)$ is bounded in a neighbourhood of s.

B.4 i. $E\left\{ \left\| \frac{\partial^2 \Psi}{\partial \theta \partial \theta'}(Y_t;\theta(s)) \right\|^{2+\delta} \right\} < +\infty$ for some $\delta > 0$;

ii. $E\left[\frac{\partial^2 \Psi}{\partial \theta \partial \theta'}(Y_t;\theta(s)) \Big/ S_t = \cdot \right] f_{S_t}(\cdot)$ is continuous in s ;

iii. $E\left\{ \left\| \frac{\partial^2 \Psi}{\partial \theta \partial \theta'}(Y_t;\theta(s)) \right\|^{2+\delta} \Big/ S_t = \cdot \right\} f_{S_t}(\cdot)$ is bounded in a neighbourhood of s.

C. Analysis of the bias term

From the conditions iii. and iv. on the criterion function, we have:

$$E\left[\frac{1}{h_T^d} K\left(\frac{S_t - s}{h_T} \right) \frac{\partial \Psi}{\partial \theta}(Y_t;\theta(s)) \right]$$
$$= \int_{\mathbb{R}^d} K(u) E\left[\frac{\partial \Psi}{\partial \theta}(Y_t;\theta(s))/S_t = s - uh_T \right] f_S(s - uh_T) du$$
$$= \int_{\mathbb{R}^d} K(u) \frac{\partial L_\infty}{\partial \theta}(s - uh_T;\theta(s)) du = B_T(s).$$

Appendix 3: Other illustrations

The implementation of the approach proposed in the paper may be illustrated by a regression model with cross effects.

The data generating process. The data are generated in the following way:

$$y_t = a_o(S_t)x_t + b_o + u_t, \tag{20}$$

x_t, S_t, u_t are independent standard gaussian white noise processes, $a_o(\cdot)$ is a function and b_o a scalar.

In the Monte Carlo study we use two data generating processes:

DGP I: $a_o(S_t) = S_t, b_o = 1,$

DGP II: $a_o(S_t) = S_t^2, b_o = 1$

Linear regression

Suppose now that we estimate a linear model of the form:

$$y_t = ax_t + b + u_t. \tag{21}$$

A straightforward computation shows that the OLS estimators $\hat{a}_T, \hat{b}_T$ converge respectively to the pseudo-true values $Ea_o(S_t)$ and b_o. In the Monte-Carlo studies these values are:

DGP I: $ES_t = 0, b_o = 1,$

DGP II: $E(S_t^2) = 1, b_o = 1.$

The linear residuals $\hat{u}_{tT} = y_t - \hat{a}_T x_t$ converge to $u_t^o = [a_o(S_t) - Ea_o(S_t)]x_t + u_t$; this implies that $E[u_t^o S_t] = E[S_t a_o(S_t) - ES_t Ea_o(S_t)]Ex_t = 0$, since $Ex_t = 0$ and, therefore, a usual test on a possible omission of S_t as an exogenous variable is likely to reject this omission. Moreover since u_t^o is a white noise and since $E[u_t^o/S_t]$ is equal to zero, a residual plot of $\hat{u}_{tT}$ against t or against S_t will probably not detect any anomaly.

These predictions are confirmed by finite sample experiments ; for instance we give below (see figure 8) the residual plots against t and S_t, for DGP I and II, and for T = 50 and T = 200.

Note that, if $Ex_t = c \neq 0$, we have, in the case of DGP II for instance, $E[u_t^o S_t] = 0$ and $E(u_t^o/S_t) = c[S_t^2 - 1]$; therefore a residual plot of $\hat{u}_{tT}$ against S_t could lead to the introduction of S_t^2 as explanatory variable but, in this new model, the OLS residuals would not detect any anomaly even though the model is still misspecified.

Functional residuals

The functional residuals associated with the two parameters are simply given by the solutions of:

$$\min_{v_1, v_2} \sum_{t=1}^{T} K\left(\frac{S_t - s}{h_T}\right) [y_t - \hat{a}_T x_t - \hat{b}_T - v_1 X_t - v_2]^2,$$

i.e.

$$[\hat{v}_{1T}(s), \hat{v}_{2T}(s)]' = \left\{ \sum_{t=1}^{T} K\left(\frac{S_t - s}{h_T}\right) \begin{pmatrix} x_t^2 & x_t \\ x_t & 1 \end{pmatrix} \right\}^{-1} \sum_{t=1}^{T} K\left(\frac{S_t - s}{h_T}\right) \begin{pmatrix} x_t \hat{u}_{tT} \\ \hat{u}_{tT} \end{pmatrix},$$

whose limit is:

$$[v_{1\infty}(s), v_{2\infty}]' = [a_o(s) - E a_o(S_t), 0]'. \tag{22}$$

The values of the residuals $\hat{v}_{1T}(s), \hat{v}_{2T}(s)$ depend on the kernel K, on the bandwidth h_T and on the number of observations T. We have considered three kernels : the Epanechnikov kernel $[K(u) = 3/4(1-u^2)\mathbb{1}_{\{|u|<1\}}]$, the quartic kernel $[K(u) = 15/16(1-u^2)^2\mathbb{1}_{\{|u|<1\}}]$ and the Gaussian kernel $[K(u) = (2\pi)^{-1/2}\exp(-u^2/2)]$; these kernels provide fairly similar results and in the sequel we retain the Epanechnikov kernel.

Moreover, we are interested in the null hypothesis $H_o = \{a(s), b(s) \text{ constant } \}$ and, under H_o, the asymptotic covariance matrix of $\sqrt{Th_T}\ \hat{v}_T(s)$ is:

$$\Sigma(s) = \frac{J^{-1}(s) I(s) J^{-1}(s)}{f_S(s)} \int K^2(v) dv$$

It is easily seen that $J(s)$ and $I(s)$ are consistently estimated by $2\dfrac{X'X}{T}$ and $4\hat{\sigma}_T^2\left(\dfrac{X'X}{T}\right)$ respectively, where X is the matrix whose rows are $(x_t, 1)$ and $\hat{\sigma}_T^2$ is the usual OLS estimator of the error variance. Moreover, $\int K^2(v)dv = 3/5$ for the Epanechnikov kernel, and $f_S(s)$, the pdf of S, can be estimated by using the same kernel and the same bandwith as in the estimation of $\hat{v}_T(s)$. Finally, under H_o, the distribution of $\hat{v}_T(s)$ is approximated by:

$$N\left[0, \frac{3\hat{\sigma}_T^2}{5\hat{f}_S(s) h_T}(X'X)^{-1}\right]. \tag{23}$$

This provides for any s, asymptotic confidence intervals under H_o for the residuals corresponding to the slope and the intercept. Figures 9 and 10 provide the graphs of the functional residuals as well as their 95 % asymptotic pointwise confidence intervals under H_o, for DGPI and DGPII respectively. For each DGP we consider two values of h_T : 0.5 and 1, and two values of T: 50 and 200. From these figures it is seen that all the intercept functional residuals are inside the confidence intervals, whereas some slope residuals are outside the intervals for all the values of h_T and T. It is also seen that, as expected, the curves are much smoother for $h_T = 1$ than for $h_T = 5$. The smoothness is also increasing with T.

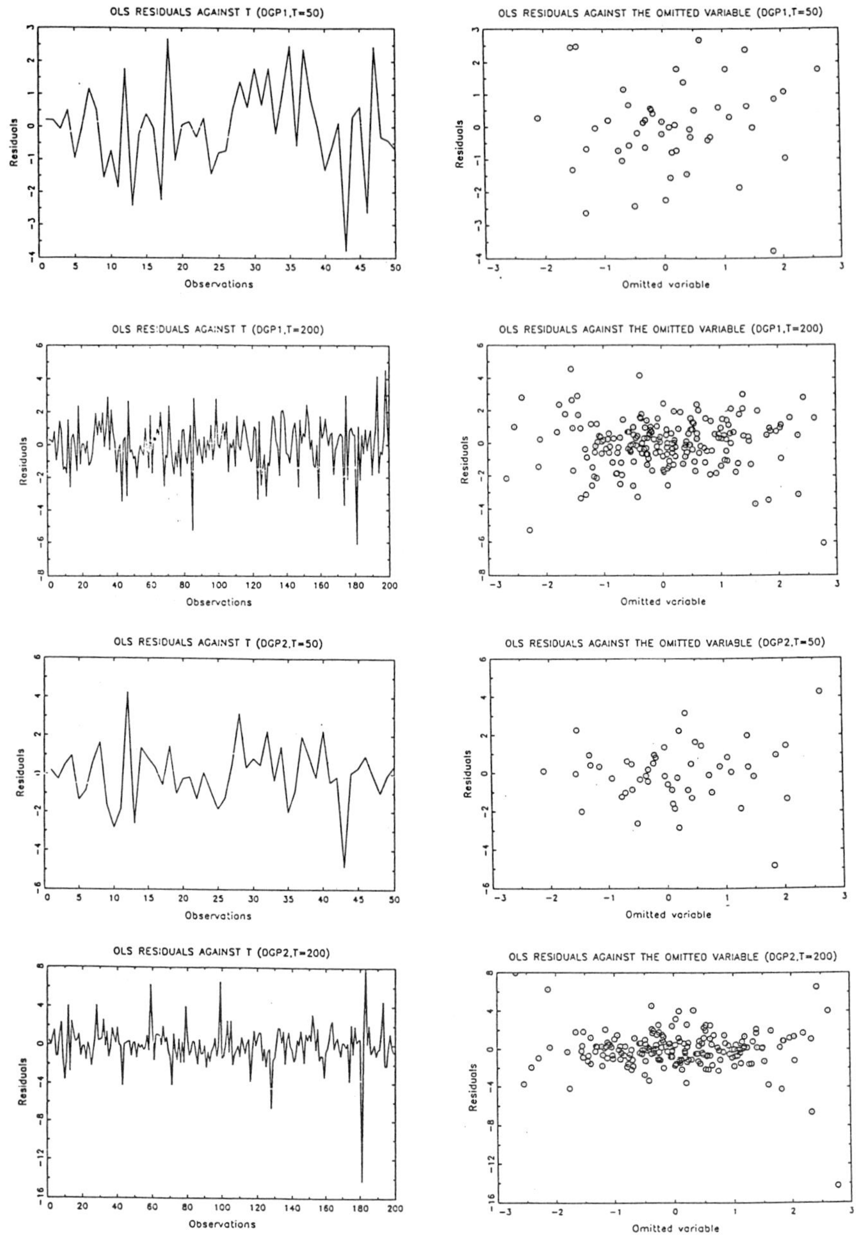

Figure 8. Linear Residual Plots

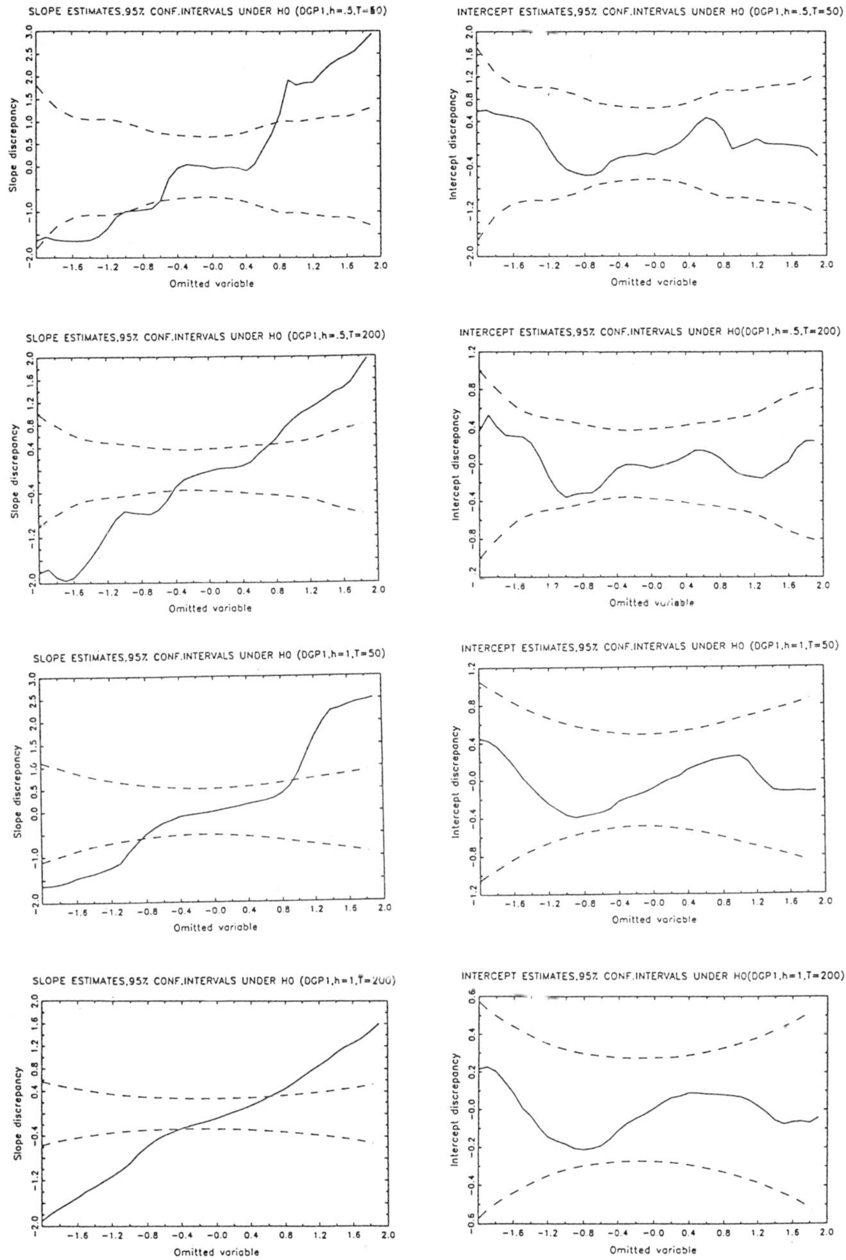

Figure 9. Slope and Intercept Functional Residuals (DGPI)

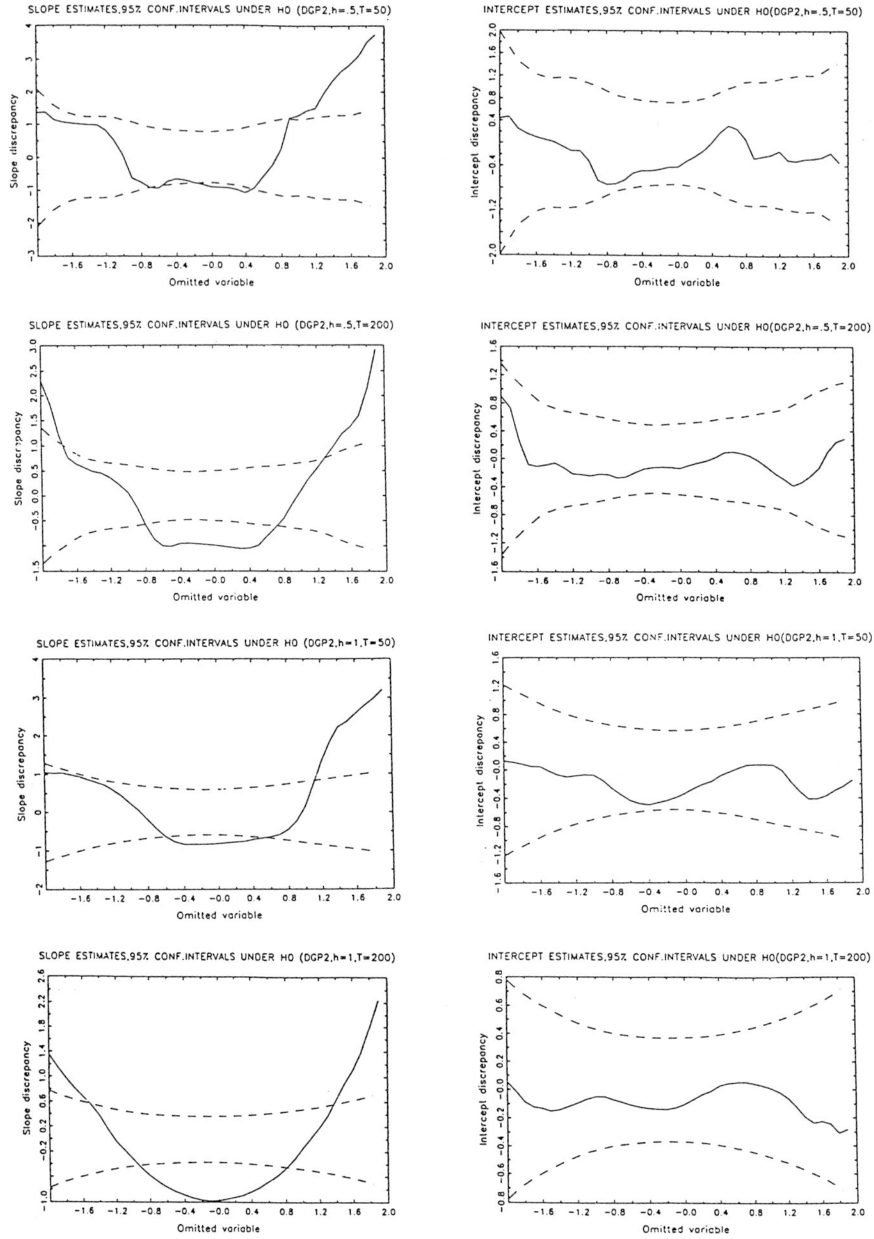

Figure 10. Slope and Intercept Functional Residuals (DGPII)

REFERENCES

1. Ait Sahalia, Y., P. Bickel and T. Stocker (1994), "Goodness of Fit Tests for Regression Using Kernel Methods", Univ. of Chicago DP.
2. Ait Sahalia, Y. and A. Lo (1995), "Nonparametric Estimation of State Price Densities Implicit In Financial Asset Prices", Univ of Chicago DP.
3. Andrews, D (1993), "Nonparametric Kernel Estimation for Semiparametric Models", *Econometric Theory*, 11, 560-596.
4. Azzalini, A., A. Bowman and W. Härdle (1989), "On the Use of Non Parametric Regression for Model Checking", *Biometrika*, 76, 1-12.
5. Bierens, H.J (1987), "Kernel Estimators of Regression Functions", in *Advances in Econometrics: Fifth World Congress*, Vol 1, Ed.Bewley, Cambridge Univ. Press.
6. Bierens, H.J (1983), "Uniform Consistency of Kernel Estimators of a Regression Function Under Generalized Conditions", *Journal of the American Statistical Association*, 77, 699-707.
7. Black, F. (1976), "Studies in Stock Price Volatility Changes", Proceedings of the 1976 Business Meeting of the Business and Economics Statistics Section, American Statistical Association, 177-181.
8. Black, F. and M. Scholes (1973), "The Pricing of Options and Corporate Liabilities", *Journal of Political Economy*, 81, 637-659.
9. Bollerslev, T., R. Engle and D. Nelson (1993), "ARCH Models", *Handbook of Econometrics*, Vol 4.
10. Bosq, D. (1980), "Une Méthode Non Paramétrique de Prédiction d'un Processus Stationnaire. Prédictions d'une Mesure Aléatoire", C.R. Acad. Sci, Paris, 290, 711-713.
11. Bosq, D. (1996), *Nonparametric Statistics for Stochastic Processes*, Springer Verlag.
12. Bosq, D. and J.P. Lecoutre (1987), *Théorie de l'Estimation Fonctionnelle*, Economica.
13. Bossaerts, P. and P. Hillion (1995), "Local Parametric Analysis of Hedging in Discrete Time", *Journal of Econometrics*, (forthcoming).
14. Burguete, J., R. Gallant and G. Souza (1982), "On Unification of the Asymptotic Theory of Nonlinear Econometric Methods", *Econometric Review*, 1, 151-190.
15. Cheng, K.F. and R.L. Taylor (1980), "On the Uniform Complete Convergence of Estimates of Multivariate Density Functions and Regression Curves", *Ann. Inst. Math.*, 32, 187-199.
16. Chesher, A. and M. Irish (1987), "Numerical and Graphical Residual Analysis in the Grouped and Censored Normal Linear Model", *Journal of Econometrics*, 34, 33-62.
17. Cleveland, W. (1979), "Robust Locally Weighted Regression and Smoothing Scatterplots", *Journal of the American Statistical Association*, 74, 823-836.
18. Collomb, G. (1982), "Estimation Nonparamétrique de la Régression par la Méthode du Noyau", Ph. D. thesis, Toulouse Univ.
19. Collomb, G. and W. Härdle (1986), "Strong Uniform Convergence Rates in Robust Nonparametric Time Series Analysis and Prediction Kernel Regression Estimation From Dependent Observations", *Stochastic Processes and their Applications*, 23, 77-89.
20. Devroye, L.P (1979), "The Uniform Convergence of the Nadaraya-Watson Regression Function Estimate," *Canad. J. Statist.*, 6, 179-191.

21. Doukhan, P. and M. Ghindes (1980), "Estimations dans le Processus : $X_{n+1} = f(X_n) + \varepsilon_n$", C.R. Acad. Sci, Paris, 291, 61-64.
22. Engle, R. and V.K. Ng (1993), "Measuring the Impact of News on Volatility", *Journal of Finance*, 48(5), 1749-1778.
23. Fan, J., N. Heckman and H. Wang (1992), "Local Polynomial Kernel Regression for Generalized Linear Models and Quasi-Likelihood Functions", Univ. British Columbia, WP 92-028.
24. Gallant, R.A. (1987), *Nonlinear Statistical Models*, New York, Wiley.
25. Gourieroux, C. and J.P. Laurent (1995), "Estimation of a Dynamic Hedge", *Mathematical Finance*, (forthcoming).
26. Gourieroux, C. and A. Monfort (1992), "Qualitative Threshold ARCH Models", *Journal of Econometrics*, 52, 159-199.
27. Gourieroux, C. and A. Monfort (1995) *Statistics and Econometric Models*, Cambridge University Press.
28. Gourieroux, C., A. Monfort, E. Renault and A. Trognon (1987), "Generalized Residuals", *Journal of Econometrics*, 34, 5-32.
29. Gourieroux, C., A. Monfort and A. Tenreiro (1994), "Kernel M-Estimators: Nonparametric Diagnostics for Structural Models", CEPREMAP DP.
30. Gozalo, P. and O. Linton (1994), "Local Nonlinear Least Squares Estimation : Using Parametric Information Nonparametrically", Cowles Foundation DP 1075.
31. Guorfi, L., W. Härdle, P. Sarda and P. Vien (1989), *Nonparametric Curve Estimation from Time Series*, Lecture Notes in Statistics, 60, Springer Verlag.
32. Härdle, W. (1989), " Asymptotic Maximal Deviation of M-smoothers", *Journal of Multivariate Analysis*, 29, 163-179.
33. Härdle, W. (1990), *Applied Nonparametric Regression*, Cambridge Univ. Press.
34. Härdle, W. and A. Tsybakov (1995), "Local Polynomial Estimators of the Volatility Function", Humboldt Univ., DP.
35. Horowitz, J.L (1993), "Semi-parametric Estimation of a Work-Trip Mode Choice Model ", *Journal of Econometrics*, 58, 49-70.
36. Huber, P.J. (1981), *Robust Statistics*, New York, Wiley.
37. Hull, J. and A. White (1987), "The Pricing of Options on Assets with Stochastic Volatilities", *the Journal of Finance*, 3, 281-300 .
38. Jennrich, R (1969), "Asymptotic Properties of Nonlinear Least Squares Estimators," *Annals of Mathematical Statistics*, 40, 633-643.
39. Konakov, V. D. and V. Piterborg (1984), "On the Convergence Rate of Maximal Deviation Distribution for Kernel Regression Estimator", *J. Multivariate Analysis*, 15, 297-294.
40. Mack, Y.P. and B. Silvermann (1982), "Weak and Strong Uniform Consistency of Kernel Regression Estimates", *Z. Wahrscheinlichkeitstheorie. Verw. Gebiete*, 61, 405-415.
41. Masry, E. and D. Tjostheim (1995), "Nonparametric Estimation and Identification of Nonlinear ARCH Time Series", *Econometric Theory*, 11, 258-289.
42. Nadaraya, E (1964), "On Estimating Regression", *Theory Prob. Appl.*, 10, 186-190.
43. Newey, W.K. and J.L Powell (1988), "Instrumental Variables Estimation for Nonparametric Models", Princeton Univ. DP.

44. Pagan, A. and A. Ullah (1988), "The Econometric Analysis of Models with Risk Terms," *Journal of Applied Econometrics*, 5, 87-1050
45. Robinson, P. (1983), "Nonparametric Estimators For Time Series", *Journal of Time Series Analysis*, 4, 185-207.
46. Robinson, P. (1984), "Robust Nonparametric Autoregression", in *Robust and Nonlinear Time Series Analysis*, J. Franck *et al.* eds, Lecture Notes in Statistics, Vol 26, 247-255, Springer Verlag.
47. Roussas, G. (1969), "Nonparametric Estimation in Markov Processes", *Ann. Inst. Statist. Math*, 21, 73-87.
48. Roussas, G.G. (1990), "Nonparametric Regression Estimation Under Mixing Conditions", *Stoch. Processes and Their Applic.*, 36, 107-116.
49. Staniswalis, J (1989), "The Kernel Estimate of a Regression Function in Likelihood-Based Models", *Journal of the American Statistical Association*, 84, 276-283.
50. Staniswalis, J. and T. Severini (1991), "Diagnostics for Assessing Regression Models", *Journal of the American Statistical Association*, 86, 684-691.
51. Stone, C.J. (1977), "Consistent Nonparametric Regression", *Ann. Statist.*, 5, 595-620.
52. Tenreiro, C. (1994), "Estimation Non Paramétrique d'une Fonction de Moments Conditionnels sous des Conditions Locales", C.R. Acad. Sci, Paris, 318, 1149-1152.
53. Tibshirani, R. and T. Hastie (1987), "Local Likelihood Estimation", *Journal of the American Statistical Association*, 82, 559-567.
54. Watson, G.S (1964), "Smooth Regression Analysis", *Sankhya, Series A*, 26, 359-372.
55. White, H. (1982), "Maximum Likelihood Estimation of Misspecified Models, *Econometrica*, 50, 1-25.
56. Wiggins, J (1987), "Option Values Under Stochastic Volatility", *Journal of Financial Economics*, 19, 351-372.

PART III

Elaborating on Balestra's work

Panel Data Econometrics: Future Directions
J. Krishnakumar and E. Ronchetti (Editors)

CHAPTER 13

FURTHER EVIDENCE ON THE EFFICIENCY OF LEAST SQUARES IN REGRESSION MODELS

Badi H. BALTAGI

Abstract

Balestra (1970) studied the efficiency of least squares in regression models. This paper reconsiders this problem and surveys the econometrics literature for examples where OLS is efficient. These examples cover various areas in econometrics including panel data, grouped or aggregated data, seemingly unrelated regressions, simultaneous equation models, two-step estimators, experimental design and random coefficient models. These examples are important for students of econometrics and are collected here in the tradition of the pioneering contribution by Balestra.

1. INTRODUCTION

Balestra (1970) generalized a necessary and sufficient condition for OLS to be BLUE derived by McElroy (1967) and illustrated its usefulness using five examples. This paper reconsiders the question of efficiency of least squares in regression problems and surveys the econometric literature for useful examples. Necessary and sufficient conditions for OLS to be BLUE have been derived by Rao (1967), Zyskind (1967), McElroy (1967), Kruskal (1968), Balestra (1970) and Milliken and Albohali (1984) to mention a few. A historical as well as a more complete survey of the necessary and sufficient conditions (NSC) derived in the statistical literature is given by Puntanen and Styan (1989). It is the purpose of this paper to illustrate the usefulness of these conditions by focusing on several examples from economics. The first example considers a set of Zellner's (1962) seemingly unrelated regressions (SUR) and the two textbook cases (under which the Zellner GLS estimator reduces to OLS) are shown to satisfy the above NSC. A simple NSC for OLS on the SUR model to be BLUE is given by Gourieroux and Monfort (1980) and Baltagi (1988). An earlier, more complicated NSC for the SUR model was derived by

Dwivedi and Srivastava (1978). This result is also applied to the simultaneous equation model to derive a necessary and sufficient condition for 2SLS to be equivalent to 3SLS, see Srivastava and Tiwari (1978), Gourieroux and Monfort (1980), Kapteyn and Fiebig (1981) and Baltagi (1989a). Next, the random coefficient model considered by Rao (1965) is shown to satisfy the above NSC, see also McAleer (1992). The third example considers a pooled time-series of cross-sections regression where the disturbances have an error components structure, see Balestra and Nerlove (1966) and the within or fixed effects regression is shown to satisfy the above NSC. This example turns out to be a special case of the partitioned regression model considered by Balestra (1970) and McAleer (1992). It is important to note that Kruskal (1968) also considered an unbalanced fixed effects model with heteroscedastic variances. For this simple model it is shown that OLS is BLUE. The fourth example considers McElroy's (1967) regression with equi-correlated disturbances and the extension by Balestra (1970) to the partitioned regression case. An important application of these results is the regression with grouped data considered by Kloek (1981). Again, it is shown that such a model satisfies the above NSC. In fact, this result extends to any two-way error component model where the microvariable is explained by a constant and aggregate variables that are invariant over time or across cross-sections, see Baltagi (1989b). Another important application of these results to a study of the optimal experimental design for error components models is considered by Aigner and Balestra (1988). Finally, we consider several extensions of the above results given by Fiebig, Bartels and Krämer (1996), Baltagi and Krämer (1995, 1997) and McAleer and McKenzie (1991).

2. MODEL AND RESULTS

Consider the general linear model

$$y = X\beta + u \tag{1}$$

where X is an $n \times k$ matrix of rank k. $E(u) = 0$ and $\text{var}(u) = \sigma^2\Omega$, where Ω is non-singular. It is well known that Ordinary Least Squares (OLS) is inefficient relative to Generalized Least Squares (GLS). The latter estimator is best linear unbiased (BLU) for β. Several necessary and sufficient conditions for OLS to be BLUE are given by Rao (1967), Zyskind (1967), McElroy (1967), Kruskal (1968), Balestra (1970), Milliken and Albohali (1984) and Puntanen and Styan (1989) to mention a few. For the case of integrated regressors, see Phillips and Park (1988). One of the easy conditions to check in practice is given by Zyskind (1967). This states that $\hat{\beta}_{ols} = (X'X)^{-1}X'y$ is BLUE for β if and only if

$$P_X\Omega = \Omega P_X \qquad \text{where} \qquad P_X = X(X'X)^{-1}X' \tag{2}$$

Let us illustrate with examples:

Example 1: Consider a seemingly unrelated regression (SUR) model consisting of M equations. In this case, $X = \text{Diag}[X_i]$ where X_i is $n \times k_i$ and is of full column rank k_i for $i = 1, 2, .., M$. $\text{Var}(u) = \Sigma \otimes I_n$ where $\Sigma = [\sigma_{ij}]$ is $M \times M$, and I_n is an identity matrix of dimension n. Also, $P_X = \text{Diag}[P_{X_i}]$. It is well known, see Zellner (1962), that if either $X_1 = X_2 = .. = X_M$ or Σ is diagonal, then $\hat{\beta}_{ols}$ is BLUE. Let us examine if these two cases satisfy the Zyskind condition given in (2).

Case 1: $X_1 = X_2 = .. = X_M = X^*$ where X^* is $n \times k^*$, and $k_i = k^*$ for all i. In this case $X = \text{Diag}[X^*] = I_M \otimes X^*$, and $P_X = \text{Diag}[P_{X^*}] = I_M \otimes P_{X^*}$. Substituting in (2), we get

$$P_X\Omega \equiv [I_M \otimes P_{X^*}][\Sigma \otimes I_T] = \Sigma \otimes P_{X^*} = [\Sigma \otimes I_T][I_M \otimes P_{X^*}] \equiv \Omega P_X.$$

Case 2: Σ is diagonal, *i.e.*, $\Sigma = \text{Diag}[\sigma_{ii}]$. In this case

$$P_X\Omega \equiv \text{Diag}[P_{X_i}]\,\text{Diag}[\sigma_{ii}] = \text{Diag}[\sigma_{ii}P_{X_i}] = \text{Diag}[\sigma_{ii}]\,\text{Diag}[P_{X_i}] \equiv \Omega P_X.$$

In a problem for *Econometric Theory*, Baltagi (1988) used the Milliken and Albohali (1984) NSC to show that, in general, for the SUR model, OLS is BLUE if and only if $\sigma^{ij}X_i'\bar{P}_{X_j} = 0$ for all $i, j, = 1, 2, .., M$. Here $\bar{P}_{X_j} = I_n - P_{X_j}$ and σ^{ij} is the *(i,j)-th* element of Σ^{-1}. Therefore, OLS is BLUE for SUR if for every $i \neq j$; either (i) $\sigma_{ij} = 0$ or (ii) X_i and X_j span the same column space for $i, j = 1, 2, .., M$. See also the solution by Baksalary and Trenkler (1989). This simple result was also derived by Gourieroux and Monfort (1980). An earlier necessary and sufficient condition based on Rao (1967) was derived for the SUR model by Dwivedi and Srivastava (1978). However, this latter condition does not readily yield the simple condition given in (ii).

If the number of regressors are different across equations, one can group equations by the same number of regressors. In this case, the covariance across the different groups of equations must be zero, *i.e.*, Σ must be block diagonal, and each block must satisfy either (i) or (ii), see Baltagi (1989b). Bartels and Fiebig (1991) group equations into a number of equivalence classes where by definition equations i and j belong to the same equivalence class when X_i and X_j span the same column space. Since condition (ii) is satisfied within each class, OLS is BLUE if and only if Σ is block diagonal across different equivalence classes. An important application is the transcendental logarithmic (translog) model commonly used in economic studies of the cost of production. In this case, one estimates the cost equation along with the share equations for each factor of production. One factor share equation is excluded since these share equations have to sum to one. From Shephard's lemma, the share equations have the same regressors. Therefore condition (ii) is satisfied and the share equations form an equivalence class. For OLS on this translog system to be BLUE, the cost equation has to have zero covariance with each share equation. However, the share equations can have any arbitrary variance-covariance matrix among themselves This condition means that the cost disturbances should be uncorrelated with factors of production, or that these cost disturbances are factor-neutral.

The results derived for the seemingly unrelated regression model can also be applied to the simultaneous equation model to derive a necessary and sufficient condition for 2SLS to be equivalent to 3SLS, see Srivastava and Tiwari (1978), Gourieroux and Monfort (1980), Kapteyn and Fiebig (1981) and Baltagi (1989a). In fact, Baltagi (1989a) showed that 2SLS on each equation is equivalent to 3SLS on a system of M identified equations if and only if $\sigma^{ij}\widehat{X}_i'\bar{P}_{\widehat{X}_j} = 0$ for $i, j, = 1, 2, .., M$. Here X_i denotes the regressors of the *i-th* equation. $\widehat{X}_i = P_W X_i$ with W being the matrix of instruments. Therefore $\widehat{X}_i$ is the matrix of second stage regressors of 2SLS for the *i-th* equation. $\bar{P}_{\widehat{X}_j} = I_n - P_{\widehat{X}_j}$ and

$P_{\widehat{X}_j} = \widehat{X}_j(\widehat{X}_j'\widehat{X}_j)^{-1}\widehat{X}_j'$. Therefore, 2SLS is equivalent to 3SLS if for every $i \neq j$; either (i) $\sigma_{ij} = 0$ or (ii) the set of second stage regressors of 2SLS of the *i-th* equation span the same column space as those for the *j-th* equation for $i, j = 1, 2, .., M$. Note that the two well known sufficient conditions for 2SLS to be equivalent to 3SLS are that $\sigma_{ij} = 0$ for $i \neq j$ or that each equation is just identified. It is easy to verify that the latter condition is a special case of (ii). If every equation is identified, then every set of second stage regressors is of full column rank and condition (ii) can only hold when the *i-th* and *j-th* equations have the same number of right hand side variables. In practice, different structural equations contain a different number of right hand side variables. One can group structural equations by the same number of right hand side variables. In this case, for 2SLS to be equivalent to 3SLS, the covariance across the different groups of equations must be zero, *i.e.*, Σ must be block diagonal. But, 3SLS on the whole system is equivalent to 3SLS on each block taken separately. Hence, 2SLS is equivalent to 3SLS if and only if each block satisfies either (i) or (ii), see Baltagi (1989a). One can define equivalence classes for the set of second stage regressors just like the SUR case. By definition, equations i and j belong to the same equivalence class when the set of second stage regressors of the *i-th* and *j-th* equation span the same column space. Since condition (ii) is satisfied within each class, 2SLS is equivalent to 3SLS if Σ is block diagonal across different equivalence classes.

Example 2: Consider a random coefficient regression model where β in (1) is no longer a set of k unknown parameters, but rather a $k \times 1$ vector of random coefficients with mean β_o and variance Λ, *i.e.*, $\beta = \beta_o + v$ where $v \sim (0, \Lambda)$. Substituting this in (1) we get

$$y = X\beta_o + Xv + u = X\beta_o + \epsilon \tag{3}$$

where $\epsilon = Xv + u$. If $u \sim (0, \sigma^2 I_n)$ and u and v are independent, then ϵ has mean 0 and variance

$$\Omega = X\Lambda X' + \sigma^2 I_n \tag{4}$$

For this random coefficient regression model OLS is BLUE, see Rao (1965). In this case it is easy to verify Zyskind's condition by substituting (4) in (2) to get

$$P_X\Omega = P_X(X\Lambda X' + \sigma^2 I_n) = X\Lambda X' + \sigma^2 P_X = (X\Lambda X' + \sigma^2 I_n)P_X = \Omega P_X \tag{5}$$

since $P_X X = X$.

Example 3: Consider the panel data regression where y is an $NT \times 1$ vector with a typical element y_{it} denoting the observation for the *i-th* individual in the *t-th* time period, for $i = 1, 2, .., N$, and $t = 1, 2, .., T$. The disturbances are assumed to have the following two-way error components structure, see Balestra and Nerlove (1966):

$$u_{it} = \mu_i + \lambda_t + \nu_{it} \qquad i = 1, 2, .., N; \qquad t = 1, 2, .., T \tag{6}$$

where μ_i denotes the individual (time-invariant) effect, λ_t denotes the time-period (cross-section-invariant) effect, and ν_{it} denotes the remainder disturbance which is $IID(0, \sigma_\nu^2)$. We can rewrite (6) in matrix form as

$$u = Z_\mu \mu + Z_\lambda \lambda + \nu \tag{7}$$

where $Z_\mu = I_N \otimes \iota_T$, $Z_\lambda = \iota_N \otimes I_T$, with ι_N and ι_T denoting vectors of ones of dimensions N and T, respectively. These are the matrices of dummy variables for cross-sections and time periods. Substituting (7) in (1) we get

$$y = X\beta + Z_\mu \mu + Z_\lambda \lambda + \nu \tag{8}$$

where $\nu \sim (0, \sigma_\nu^2 I_{NT})$, y is $NT\times 1$ and X is $NT\times k$. If the μ_i's and λ_t's are fixed parameters to be estimated then OLS on (8) is BLUE. However, N can be large for typical labor or consumer panels, and brute force OLS on (8) may not be feasible. From the Frisch-Waugh-Lovell (FWL) Theorem, see Davidson and MacKinnon (1993), one can premultiply (8) by the orthogonal projection of $[Z_\mu, Z_\lambda]$ and perform OLS on the transformed model. This will yield the same OLS estimates of β as those obtained from (8). This orthogonal projection is given by the matrix $Q = E_N \otimes E_T$ where $E_N = I_N - \bar{J}_N$, $\bar{J}_N = J_N/N$ and $J_N = \iota_N \iota_N'$ is a matrix of ones of dimension N. $\bar{J}_N$ is the averaging matrix over cross-sections and E_N is the deviation from these averages. E_T can be similarly defined as the deviations from time period averages. A typical element of Qy is $(y_{it} - \bar{y}_{i.} - \bar{y}_{.t} + \bar{y}_{..})$ with the dot and the bar denoting the sum and average over that index, respectively. Q is known as the within transformation, see Wallace and Hussain (1969), since it generates the within variation usually reported in an analysis of variance table. This Q transformation when applied to (8) sweeps away the μ and λ effects leaving

$$Qy = QX\beta + Q\nu \tag{9}$$

since $QZ_\mu = QZ_\lambda = 0$. Of course, if there is a constant in X, or any time-invariant or cross-section invariant variables in the regression model, these will all be swept away by Q. The transformed model in (9) can also be written as

$$\widetilde{y} = \widetilde{X}\beta + \widetilde{\nu} \tag{10}$$

where $\widetilde{y} = Qy$, $\widetilde{X} = QX$ and $\widetilde{\nu} \sim (0, \sigma_\nu^2 Q)$. The FWL Theorem guarantees that the OLS estimator of β from (10) is identical to the OLS estimator of β from (8). This is given by

$$\widetilde{\beta} = (\widetilde{X}'\widetilde{X})^{-1}\widetilde{X}'\widetilde{y} = (X'QX)^{-1}X'Qy \tag{11}$$

and is called the within (or fixed effects) estimator. Note that the transformed disturbance in (10) $\widetilde{\nu}$ does not have a scalar times identity variance-covariance matrix. In fact, $\widetilde{\nu} \sim (0, \sigma_\nu^2 Q)$ where Q is symmetric, idempotent and of rank $(N-1)(T-1)$. Hence the variance-covariance matrix of $\widetilde{\nu}$ is positive semi-definite and not positive definite. But positive definiteness is not required, see Zyskind (1967) or Puntanen and Styan (1989). To show that OLS on (10) is BLUE we verify Zyskind's condition (2) as follows:

$$P_X\Omega \equiv P_{\widetilde{X}}(\sigma_\nu^2 Q) = \sigma_\nu^2 P_{\widetilde{X}} = (\sigma_\nu^2 Q)P_{\widetilde{X}} \equiv \Omega P_X$$

since $\widetilde{X}'Q = (QX)'Q = X'QQ = X'Q = \widetilde{X}'$.

Similarly, for the one-way error component model with $\lambda_t = 0$ in (6) for all $t = 1, 2, .., T$, one can wipe out the μ_i's by premultiplying by the orthogonal transformation of Z_μ given by $Q_\mu = I_N \otimes E_T$. This is the one-way within transformation with the typical element of

$Q_\mu y$ given by $(y_{it} - \bar{y}_{i.})$. The transformed disturbances will have zero mean and variance-covariance given by $\sigma_\nu^2 Q_\mu$. Once again it is easy to verify Zyskind's condition given in (2) and OLS on this transformed model is BLUE.

The results of this example apply to more general partitioned models of the form

$$y = X_1\beta_1 + X_2\beta_2 + u \tag{12}$$

where X_1 is $n \times k_1$ and X_2 is $n \times k_2$ both of full column rank and linearly independent of each other. Also, $u \sim (0, \sigma^2 I_n)$, see Balestra (1970) and McAleer (1992). Premultiplying (12) by $\bar{P}_{X_1}$ we get

$$\bar{P}_{X_1} y = \bar{P}_{X_1} X_2\beta_2 + \bar{P}_{X_1} u \tag{13}$$

since $\bar{P}_{X_1} X_1 = 0$. But $\bar{P}_{X_1} u \sim (0, \sigma^2 \bar{P}_{X_1})$ and $\bar{P}_{X_1}$ is of rank $(n - k_1)$ so that the variance-covariance matrix of the transformed disturbances is singular. The Frisch-Waugh-Lovell Theorem states that the OLS estimator of β_2 obtained from (12) or (13) are identical. But why do we apply OLS rather than GLS on (13)? The answer is that OLS on (13) is BLUE. Zyskind's condition (2) can be easily verified for (13) as follows:

$$\begin{aligned} P_X\Omega \equiv\ & [\bar{P}_{X_1} X_2 (X_2' \bar{P}_{X_1} X_2)^{-1} X_2' \bar{P}_{X_1}](\sigma^2 \bar{P}_{X_1}) \\ =\ & \sigma^2 \bar{P}_{X_1} X_2 (X_2' \bar{P}_{X_1} X_2)^{-1} X_2' \bar{P}_{X_1} \equiv \Omega P_X \end{aligned}$$

using the fact that $\bar{P}_{X_1}$ is idempotent. For the special case of the panel data regression given in (8), $X_1 = [Z_\mu, Z_\lambda]$ and $X_2 \equiv X$, so that $Q = \bar{P}_{X_1}$. Regression (13) becomes regression (9) and OLS for either regression is BLUE.

In case the disturbance in (12) has a general variance covariance matrix Ω, Aigner and Balestra (1988) provide a simpler necessary and sufficient condition for OLS to be BLUE. This is given by $\Omega \bar{P}_{X_1} = \lambda \bar{P}_{X_1}$ for some positive scalar λ. This can be easily verified for some of the partitioned regression examples given above. Aigner and Balestra (1988) utilized this condition in their study of the optimal experimental design for error components models.

In a problem for *Econometric Theory*, Baltagi and Krämer (1995) considered the mixed error component model where $\mu_i \sim IID(0, \sigma_\mu^2)$ is random but λ_t denote a set of fixed effects parameters to be estimated. In this case one can show that applying the within-time-effects transformation to wipe out the matrix of time dummies and then performing the usual one-way GLS is equivalent to performing GLS on the original model with the time dummies included, see the solution by Xiong (1996). This is a special case of a more general result on partitioned models with a general variance-covariance matrix considered by Fiebig, Bartels and Krämer (1996). The latter study is an extension of the Frisch-Waugh-Lovell Theorem to the case where $u \sim (0, \sigma^2\Omega)$. In this case, the regression in (13) has a variance-covariance matrix $\sigma^2 \bar{P}_{X_1} \Omega \bar{P}_{X_1}$. Fiebig, *et al.* (1996) show that GLS on the original model (12) is equivalent to GLS on (13) using $\sigma^2 \bar{P}_{X_1} \Omega \bar{P}_{X_1}$ as the variance-covariance matrix. They also show that, applying GLS on (13) using Ω (named pseudo-GLS) rather than $\sigma^2 \bar{P}_{X_1} \Omega \bar{P}_{X_1}$ (true GLS) does not necessarily yield the same estimator. They also derive a necessary and sufficient condition for pseudo-GLS on (13) to be BLUE. This condition is given by $X_2'\bar{P}_{X_1}\Omega^{-1}X_1 = 0$. It is satisfied for the mixed error component model considered by Baltagi and Krämer (1995) as well as the simple linear trend model with AR(1) disturbances considered by Krämer (1982) and the fixed effects model with arbitrary interpersonal covariance considered by Schmidt (1983). For the Krämer(1982) model, this allows us to obtain the GLS estimate of the linear trend coefficient as pseudo-GLS after wiping out the constant. For the Schmidt (1983) model, this allows SUR estimation of the original model with individual dummies to be equivalent to SUR estimation of the reduced model using within-transformed data. It is important to emphasize that in general pseudo-GLS is not necessarily equivalent to GLS. However, we have an easy NSC to check it.

Finally, it is important to point out that Kruskal (1968) considered a simple fixed effects model with no explanatory variables, *i.e.*,

$$y_{it} = \alpha_i + u_{it} \qquad i = 1, 2, .., N \qquad \text{and} \qquad t = 1, 2, .., T_i$$

In this case, the fixed effects are given by α_i and the disturbances u_{it} are assumed to be independent with zero mean and heteroscedastic variances σ_i^2. This differs from the above model in that the disturbances are heteroscedastic and the panel is unbalanced, *i.e.*, with different number of observations on each individual. Kruskal (1968) showed that OLS is BLUE. For this model, $X = \text{Diag}(\iota_{T_i})$ with ι_{T_i} denoting a vector of ones of dimension T_i. Therefore, $P_X = \text{Diag}(\bar{J}_{T_i})$ where $\bar{J}_{T_i} = \iota_{T_i}\iota_{T_i}'/T_i$. $\text{Var}(u) \equiv \Sigma = \text{Diag}[\sigma_i^2 I_{T_i}]$ where I_{T_i} is an identity matrix of dimension T_i. Zyskind's condition given in (2) can be easily verified as follows:

$$P_X\Sigma = \text{Diag}(\bar{J}_{T_i})\text{Diag}[\sigma_i^2 I_{T_i}] = \text{Diag}[\sigma_i^2 \bar{J}_{T_i}] = \text{Diag}[\sigma_i^2 I_{T_i}]\text{Diag}(\bar{J}_{T_i}) = \Sigma P_X$$

Even though the OLS and GLS estimates of α_i are identical, the standard errors as usually computed by the OLS regression package are incorrect. See Fiebig, McAleer and Bartels (1992) for a general discussion of the bias in the computation of the variance-covariance matrix of the OLS estimator.

Example 4 : McElroy (1967) showed that if Ω is fixed and X contains an intercept and other regressors that are free to vary, then OLS is BLUE if and only if Ω has the equi-correlated structure given by:

$$\Omega = \sigma^2[(1-\rho)I_n + \rho J_n] \tag{14}$$

where $-1/(n-1) < \rho < 1$ insures that Ω is positive definite. Note that $P_X\iota_n = \iota_n$ since the intercept is one of the regressors. Hence $P_X J_n = J_n$ and from (14) it is easy to verify Zyskind's condition $P_X\Omega = \sigma^2[(1-\rho)P_X + \rho P_X J_n] = \sigma^2[(1-\rho)P_X + \rho J_n] = \Omega P_X$.

Balestra (1970) generalizes McElroy's (1967) result to the partitioned regression case given in (12) where $X = [X_1, X_2]$ with X_1 containing k_1 *known* vectors and the other set of k_2 vectors are free to vary. X_1, X_2 and X are assumed to be of full column rank. Balestra's (1970; p.1331) necessary and sufficient condition for OLS to be BLUE is (i) that there exist k_1 orthogonal eigenvectors of Ω which span the columns of X_1; and (ii) that all eigenvectors of Ω orthogonal to the vectors in this subset be associated with the same eigenvalue. Balestra illustrates this condition with five examples.

The first example shows that McElroy's (1967) result follows as a special case. In fact, $X_1 \equiv \iota_n$ is the known constant included in the regression. Ω in (14) has two distinct roots. One single root $1+(n-1)\rho$ associated with the eigenvector ι_n. The other distinct root of Ω is $(1-\rho)$ of multiplicity $(n-1)$.

The second example is all regression models containing a linear time trend. In this case OLS is BLUE if and only if

$$\begin{aligned} E(u_i u_j) &= \sigma^2[b+(a-b)dij] \qquad \text{for} \quad i=j \\ &= \sigma^2[(a-b)dij] \qquad \text{for} \quad i \neq j \end{aligned}$$

where a and b are positive arbitrary constants and where $d = 6/n(n+1)(2n+1)$. In this case, the linear time trend is the eigenvector of Ω associated with the single eigenvalue a and all other eigenvalues of Ω are equal to b.

The third example includes both a constant and a linear trend in X_1. For simplicity, n is assumed to be odd and the linear trend is centered around zero. In this case OLS is BLUE if and only if

$$\begin{aligned} E(u_i u_j) &= \sigma^2[b+(a-b)d_1+(c-b)d_2(i-(n+1)/2)(j-(n+1)/2)] \qquad \text{for} \quad i=j \\ &= \sigma^2[(a-b)d_1+(c-b)d_2(i-(n+1)/2)(j-(n+1)/2)] \qquad \text{for} \quad i \neq j \end{aligned}$$

where a, b and c are arbitrary constants. Also, $d_1 = 1/n$ and $d_2 = 12/n(n+1)(n-1)$. In this case, X_1 (the constant and the time trend) represents two orthogonal eigenvectors of Ω associated with two single roots a and c and all other roots are equal to b.

The fourth example is the *random* one-way error component model. This can be obtained from (6) by assuming that $\lambda_t = 0$ and $\mu_i \sim IID(0, \sigma_\nu^2)$ independent of $\nu_{it} \sim IID(0, \sigma_\nu^2)$. If X contains a set of N individual dummies (one for each individual), then OLS is BLUE since each dummy variable is an eigenvector of Ω associated with the eigenvalue of multiplicity N. Ω has one other distinct eigenvalue of multiplicity $N(T-1)$.

The fifth example is the random two-way error component model given in (6) with $\lambda_t \sim IID(0, \sigma_\lambda^2)$, $\mu_i \sim IID(0, \sigma_\nu^2)$ and $\nu_{it} \sim IID(0, \sigma_\nu^2)$ independent of each other and among themselves. If X contains a constant term, $N-1$ cross-section dummies and $T-1$ time dummies, then OLS is BLUE. In this case, these $N+T-1$ column vectors are spanned by the $N+T-1$ orthogonal eigenvectors of Ω associated with three of the four distinct eigenvalues of Ω, see Nerlove (1971).

It is important to emphasize that for the Balestra (1970) result, X_2 is unrestricted except for having full column rank. The relevance of this necessary and sufficient condition was demonstrated for models with a constant; a linear time trend; both a constant and a linear time trend; individual dummy variables; and both individual and time dummy variables.

An important application of the results of McElroy (1967) and Balestra (1970) is considered by Kloek (1981) to regressions with grouped data with equi-correlated disturbances. In this case, y is a microvariable and the micro-observations are grouped by such variables as geographical region or industry and are observed over time. Kloek (1981) orders the observations with time being the slower index, *i.e.*, the observations for the first time period across all industries are stacked on top of those for the second time period and so on. The X's, on the other hand, are aggregate variables that are invariant across industries and vary only over time. In fact

$$y' = (y_1', y_2', .., y_T'),\ X' = [x_1, x_2, .., x_T] \otimes \iota_N' , \qquad \text{and} \qquad u' = (u_1', u_2', .., u_T'),$$

where y_t and u_t are $(N \times 1)$ vectors for $t = 1, 2, .., T$. x_t is a $(k \times 1)$ vector representing the *t-th* observation on all k explanatory variables. ι_N is a column vector of ones of dimension N, showing that the observations on X have been replicated over each grouping, and vary only over time. The disturbances are assumed to be homoskedastic, equi-correlated within time periods, and uncorrelated across time periods. So that Ω is block diagonal

$$\Omega = \sigma^2 \{ I_T \otimes [(1-\rho) I_N + \rho J_N] \} \tag{15}$$

If X varies across groupings, or the data are unbalanced (different number of observations for each group) then OLS on this model is not necessarily BLUE. However, because the data is balanced and the X's are invariant across groupings, Kloek (1981) shows that OLS is BLUE. In fact

$$X'\Omega = \sigma^2 \{ [x_1, x_2, .., x_T] \otimes [1 + (N-1)\rho] \iota_N' \} = \sigma^2 \tau X' \tag{16}$$

where $\tau = 1 + (N-1)\rho$. Premultiplying both sides of (16) by $X(X'X)^{-1}$ yields $P_X\Omega = \sigma^2 \tau P_X$. Similarly, by transposing (16) we get $\Omega X = \sigma^2 \tau X$ and postmultiplying both sides by $(X'X)^{-1}X'$ yields $\Omega P_X = \sigma^2 \tau P_X$. Hence, we conclude that $P_X \Omega = \Omega P_X$ and OLS is BLUE. Note that

$$\text{var}(\hat{\beta}_{OLS}) = (X'X)^{-1} X' \Omega X (X'X)^{-1} = \sigma^2 \tau (X'X)^{-1} \tag{17}$$

and this is different from $\sigma^2 (X'X)^{-1}$ the usual variance covariance matrix of OLS which is reported by any regression package. Kloek (1981) warned about the bias in the OLS standard errors that could result from ignoring this fact, and Moulton (1986) gave three empirical illustrations showing the extent of this bias.

Baltagi (1989b) showed that Kloek's (1981) results apply to a more general model where the aggregate variables can be invariant over time or across cross-sections and the disturbances follow a two-way rather than a one-way error component structure. In this case, the micro dependent variable y is explained by a constant and aggregate variables that are invariant over time or across cross-sections. Let $X = [Z, W]$ where Z denotes the g explanatory variables that are invariant across cross-sections, and W denotes the $(k-g)$ variables that are invariant over time. Here we adopt the ordering of example 3, *i.e.*, the observations are ordered such that the faster index is that over time and the slower index is the one across groupings. In this case $Z = Z_\mu z$ and $W = Z_\lambda w$ where Z is $NT \times g$, $z' - (z_1, z_2, .., z_N)$ is $g \times N$, W is $NT \times (k-g)$, and $w' = (w_1, w_2, .., w_T)$

is $(k-g) \times T$. The constant can be either in Z or in W. The disturbances are given by the random two-way error component model given in (6) with $\mu_i \sim IID(0, \sigma_\mu^2)$ and $\lambda_t \sim IID(0, \sigma_\lambda^2)$ independent of each other and the ν_{it}'s. It is well known, see Balestra and Nerlove (1966), that the variance covariance matrix is given by

$$\Omega = \sigma_\nu^2 Q + \sigma_1^2(E_N \otimes \bar{J}_T) + \sigma_2^2(\bar{J}_N \otimes E_T) + \sigma_3^2 \bar{J}_{NT} \tag{18}$$

where $\sigma_1^2 = T\sigma_\mu^2 + \sigma_\nu^2$, $\sigma_2^2 = N\sigma_\lambda^2 + \sigma_\nu^2$ and $\sigma_3^2 = T\sigma_\mu^2 + N\sigma_\lambda^2 + \sigma_\nu^2$. This is also the spectral decomposition of Ω, see Wansbeek and Kapteyn (1982, 1983). This means that

$$\Omega^{-1} = Q/\sigma_\nu^2 + (E_N \otimes \bar{J}_T)/\sigma_1^2 + (\bar{J}_N \otimes E_T)/\sigma_2^2 + \bar{J}_{NT}/\sigma_3^2 \tag{19}$$

For this example it is simple to verify the Milliken and Albohali (1984) necessary and sufficient condition for OLS to be BLUE. This is given by $X'\Omega^{-1}\bar{P}_X = 0$ and involves Ω^{-1} rather than Ω. Using (19), we get

$$Z'\Omega^{-1} = z'Z'_\mu\Omega^{-1} = Z'(I_{NT} - \theta_1 \bar{J}_{NT})/\sigma_1^2 \tag{20}$$

where $\theta_1 = N\sigma_\lambda^2/\sigma_3^2$. Similarly,

$$W'\Omega^{-1} = w'Z'_\lambda\Omega^{-1} = W'(I_{NT} - \theta_2 \bar{J}_{NT})/\sigma_2^2 \tag{21}$$

where $\theta_2 = T\sigma_\mu^2/\sigma_3^2$. Therefore

$$X'\Omega^{-1}\bar{P}_X = \begin{bmatrix} Z'\Omega^{-1}\bar{P}_X \\ \\ W'\Omega^{-1}\bar{P}_X \end{bmatrix} = \begin{bmatrix} Z'(I_{NT} - \theta_1 \bar{J}_{NT})\bar{P}_X/\sigma_1^2 \\ \\ W'(I_{NT} + \theta_2 \bar{J}_{NT})\bar{P}_X/\sigma_2^2 \end{bmatrix} = 0 \tag{22}$$

where the last equality follows from the fact that $\bar{P}_X X = \bar{P}_X[Z \quad W] = 0$ and the fact that X contains a constant, *i.e.*, $\bar{P}_X \iota_{NT} = \bar{P}_X J_{NT} = 0$. Using (22) we conclude that OLS is BLUE. However, as in the Kloek (1981) example, $\text{var}(\hat{\beta}_{OLS}) = \sigma^2(X'X)^{-1}X'\Omega X(X'X)^{-1} = (X'\Omega^{-1}X)^{-1}$ and not $\sigma^2(X'X)^{-1}$, otherwise the standard errors of the OLS estimator would be seriously biased.

Other examples include (i) the linear regression model with stationary AR(1) disturbances, see Chipman (1979) and Krämer (1980, 1982) to mention a few. (ii) McAleer and McKenzie (1991) who use Kruskal's condition to provide an alternative derivation of the efficiency of some two-step estimators for models containing anticipated and unanticipated variables. Also, (iii) Baltagi and Krämer (1997) who consider a simple linear trend model with one-way error component disturbances and no regressors:

$$y_{it} = \alpha + \beta t + \mu_i + \nu_{it} \qquad i = 1, 2, .., N \qquad \text{and} \qquad t = 1, 2, .., T \tag{23}$$

In this case $\mu_i \sim IID(0, \sigma_\mu^2)$ and $\nu_{it} \sim IID(0, \sigma_\nu^2)$ independent of each other and among themselves. Baltagi and Krämer (1997) show that the OLS, GLS and the fixed effects (within) estimators of β in (23) are all identical.

3. CONCLUSION

In the tradition of Balestra (1970), this paper considered several examples from the econometric literature where OLS is BLUE. This was verified using simple necessary and sufficient conditions based on Zyskind (1967), Kruskal (1968), Balestra (1970) and Milliken and Albohali (1984). Several extensions were discussed covering seemingly unrelated regressions, simultaneous equations, panel data, grouped or aggregated data, random coefficient models, two-step estimators and experimental design.

REFERENCES

1. Aigner, D.J. and P. Balestra (1988), "Optimal experimental design for error components models", *Econometrica*, 56, 955-972.
2. Baksalary, J.K. and G. Trenkler (1989), "The efficiency of OLS in a seemingly unrelated regressions model", Solution 88.3.4, *Econometric Theory*, 5, 463-465.
3. Balestra, P. (1970), "On the efficiency of ordinary least squares in regression models", *Journal of the American Statistical Association*, 65, 1330-1337.
4. Balestra, P. and M. Nerlove (1966), "Pooling cross-section and time-series data in the estimation of a dynamic model: the demand for natural gas", *Econometrica*, 34, 585-612.
5. Baltagi, B.H. (1988), "The efficiency of OLS in a seemingly unrelated regressions model", Problem 88.3.4, *Econometric Theory*, 4, 536-537.
6. Baltagi, B.H. (1989a), "On the efficiency of two-stage and three-stage least squares estimators", *Econometric Reviews*, 7, 165-169.
7. Baltagi, B.H. (1989b), "Applications of a necessary and sufficient condition for OLS to be BLUE", *Statistics and Probability Letters*, 8, 457-461.
8. Baltagi, B.H. and W. Krämer (1995), "A mixed error component model", Problem 95.1.4, *Econometric Theory*, 11, 192-193.
9. Baltagi, B.H. and W. Krämer (1997), "A simple linear trend model with error components", Problem 97.2.1, *Econometric Theory*, 13, 463.
10. Bartels, R. and D.G. Fiebig (1991), "A simple characterization of seemingly unrelated regressions models in which OLS is BLUE", *The American Statistician*, 45, 137-140.
11. Chipman, J.S. (1979), "Efficiency of least-squares estimation of linear trend when residuals are autocorrelated", *Econometrica*, 47, 115-128.
12. Davidson, R. and J. MacKinnon (1993), *Estimation and inference in econometrics*, Oxford: Oxford University Press.
13. Dwivedi, T.D. and V.K. Srivastava (1978), "Optimality of least squares in the seemingly unrelated regression equation model", *Journal of Econometrics*, 7, 391-395.
14. Fiebig, D.G., R. Bartels and W. Krämer (1996), "The Frisch-Waugh theorem and generalized least squares", *Econometric Reviews*, 15, 431-443.
15. Fiebig, D.G., M. McAleer and R. Bartels (1992), "Properties of ordinary least squares estimators in regression models with nonspherical disturbances", *Journal of Econometrics*, 54, 321-334.
16. Gourieroux, C. and A. Monfort (1980), "Sufficient linear structures: econometric applications", *Econometrica*, 48, 1083-1097.

17. Kapteyn, A. and D. G. Fiebig (1981), "When are two-stage and three-stage least squares estimators identical?", *Economics Letters*, 8, 53-57.
18. Kloek, T. (1981), "OLS estimation in a model where a microvariable is explained by aggregates and contemporaneous disturbances are equicorrelated", *Econometrica*, 49, 205-207.
19. Krämer, W. (1980), "Finite sample efficiency of ordinary least squares in the linear regression model with autocorrelated errors", *Journal of the American Statistical Association*, 75, 1005-1009.
20. Krämer, W. (1982), "Note on estimating linear trend when residuals are autocorrelated", *Econometrica*, 50, 1065-1067.
21. Kruskal, W. (1968), "When are Gauss-Markov and least squares estimators identical: A coordinate-free approach", *Annals of Mathematical Statistics*, 39, 70-75.
22. McAleer, M. (1992), "Efficient Estimation: The Rao-Zyskind condition, Kruskal's theorem and ordinary least squares, *Economic Record*, 68, 65-72.
23. McAleer, M. and C.R. McKenzie (1991), "When are two step estimators efficient?", *Econometric Reviews*, 10, 235-252.
24. McElroy, F. (1967), "A necessary and sufficient condition that ordinary least squares estimators be best linear unbiased", *Journal of the American Statistical Association*, 62, 1302-1304.
25. Milliken, G.A. and M. Albohali (1984), "On necessary and sufficient conditions for ordinary least squares estimators to be best linear unbiased estimators", *The American Statistician*, 38, 298-299.
26. Moulton, B.R. (1986), "Random group effects and the precision of regression estimates", *Journal of Econometrics*, 32, 385-397.
27. Nerlove, M. (1971), "A note on error components models", *Econometrica*, 39, 383-396.
28. Phillips, P.C.B. and J. Y. Park (1988), "Asymptotic equivalence of ordinary least squares and generalized least squares in regressions with integrated regressors", *Journal of the American Statistical Association*, 83, 111-115.
29. Puntanen, S. and G.P.H. Styan (1989), "The equality of the ordinary least squares estimator and the best linear unbiased estimator", *The American Statistician*, 43, 153-164.
30. Rao, C.R. (1965), "The theory of least squares when the parameters are stochastic and its application to the analysis of growth curves", *Biometrika*, 52, 447-458.
31. Rao, C.R. (1967), "Least squares theory using an estimated dispersion matrix and its application to measurement of signals", *Proceedings of the Fifth Berkeley Symposium on Mathematical Statistics and Probability*, 1, 355-372.
32. Schmidt, P. (1983), "A note on a fixed effect model with arbitrary interpersonal covariance", *Journal of Econometrics*, 22, 391-393.
33. Srivastava, V.K. and R. Tiwari (1978), Efficiency of two-stage and three-stage least squares estimators", *Econometrica*, 46, 1495-1498.
34. Wallace, T.D. and A. Hussain (1969), "The use of error components models in combining cross-section with time-series data", *Econometrica*, 37, 55-72.
35. Wansbeek, T. and A. Kapteyn (1982), "A simple way to obtain the spectral decomposition of variance components models for balanced data", *Communications in Statistics*, A11, 2105-2112.

36. Wansbeek, T. and A. Kapteyn (1983), "A note on spectral decomposition and maximum likelihood estimation in ANOVA models with balanced data", *Statistics and Probability Letters*, 1, 213-215.
37. Xiong, W. (1996), "A mixed-error component model", Solution 95.1.4, *Econometric Theory*, 12, 401.
38. Zellner, A. (1962), "An efficient method of estimating seemingly unrelated regressions and tests for aggregation bias", *Journal of the American Statistical Association*, 57, 348-368.
39. Zyskind, G. (1967), "On canonical forms, non-negative covariance matrices and best and simple least squares linear estimators in linear models", *Annals of Mathematical Statistics*, 38, 1092-1109.

Panel Data Econometrics: Future Directions
J. Krishnakumar and E. Ronchetti (Editors)

Chapter 14

BALESTRA'S CONTRIBUTION IN THE FIELD OF ECONOMIC GROWTH, INCOME DISTRIBUTION AND CAPITAL ACCUMULATION*

Mauro L. BARANZINI

Abstract

In this paper we want to assess the relevance of Pietro Balestra's contribution in the field of economic theory, in particular income distribution, profit determination and long term development. The area covered ranges from classical, to neo-classical and post-Keynesian economics. In a paper presented at CORE, Louvain-La Neuve, in the early Seventies, and subsequently published in *Kyklos*, Balestra considers, within a neo-classical framework, the significance and implications of the relaxation of the equality between rate of profits and rate of interest in the Keynes-Kaldor-Pasinetti model of income distribution and profit determination. Under this condition, new results apply, which enrich the traditional Cambridge equation P/K=n/s(c). Looking at optimal growth, which was and still is a widely explored field of research, his model develops two distinct arguments. First, in a traditional manner, it establishes the conditions under which there exists an interest rate on workers' life-cycle savings which maximises per capita consumption. Second, in a more original way, the usual criterion of optimal growth is replaced by the criterion of maximum workers' consumption, not an unreasonable criterion in a two- or multi-class economy. It turns out that workers' consumption is maximised when the interest rate is equal to the profits rate; but here equality appears as an optimality condition, while in the Kaldor-Pasinetti's model it is an assumption. Balestra's model has generated quite a large body of literature (e.g. Baranzini, 1991b), and has opened up new frontiers for the study of income distribution. For instance, the division between life-cycle savings and inter-generational capital may be analysed more efficiently by postulating a different rate of return; this, too, has given rise to a wide and far-reaching literature in these last 25 years.

*I am grateful to Simona Cain for her invaluable assistance and encouragement at various stages of this essay.

Another important contribution by Balestra, yet to be published, concerns the long-term trend distribution of income in Ricardo's model, and the way in which global or local disturbances ensure convergence, or indeed divergence, from the solutions put forward, among others, by Pasinetti and Samuelson. In more general terms Balestra's contribution to economic analysis, although less renowned than his work in econometrics, has been seminal for the ever-raging controversy on income distribution and profit determination between the two Cambridges (U.K. *vs.* Mass., USA).

1. INTRODUCTION

1.1. A personal note, or how Balestra helped me to breach into the Citadel of Oxford

The episode takes place in a rather spartan, spacious Fellow's room, full of books, at Nuffield College, Oxford, in early October 1971, week 0 of Michaelmas Term. Behind a desk surprisingly free from all the clutter that usually occupies an Oxbridge don's working space, sits a severe figure, Professor James Alexander Mirrlees. Exactly a quarter of a century later, he was to become Sir James, Nobel Laureate, and again, fellow of Trinity College, Cambridge, where he got his Ph.D. in economics and where he had been a research fellow. I had just been admitted as a research student at The Queen's College, the holder of a Lord Florey's European Studentship which (similarly to the Rhodes Scholarships for the U.S. and Australia) was designed to attract to Oxford promising research students from Continental universities. But I needed to gain admission to the sub-faculty of economics, and for that reason, before the beginning of Term, I had to be interviewed by the Chairman of the Admissions Committee. Mirrlees had a reputation for being extremely tough, especially with candidates coming from 'Latin' countries, where non-mainstream economics was strong. "So, you studied at the University of Fribourg, didn't you?"... and there was a long pause, during which he went on browsing through my doctoral dissertation, which I had just submitted to that University. ('Here we go, I said to myself, remembering Bernard Schmitt's remark when he heard that I had been offered a scholarship to Oxford: "Fribourg? Where is Fribourg?', they will ask you as soon as you get to Oxford".) And then he suddenly spoke: "So. I see you were supervised by Balestra, the author (with Marc Nerlove) of that article in *Econometrica* on the demand for natural gas in the United States, back in 1966..." and he went on to mention other works by Balestra (for example, the paper "On the Efficiency of Ordinary Least Squares in Regression Models", published in *Journal of the American Statistical Association* in September 1970).

That was the beginning of a long scientific relationship with James Mirrlees. If nothing else, his acquaintance with Balestra, and possibly the impression he gained from reading my Fribourg thesis, written under Balestra's supervision, led him to exempt me from sitting the D. Phil. qualifying examinations, a great advantage indeed since these exams were reputed to be tough, especially when Mirrlees himself sat on the Exams Committee.

1.2. The aim of the paper

In this paper I want to assess the relevance of Pietro Balestra's contribution in the field of economic theory, in particular income distribution, profit determination and long term development. Generally speaking, the area covered ranges from classical[1], to neo-classical and post-Keynesian economics. In a paper published (jointly with the present author) in 1971 in *Kyklos*, Balestra considers, within a neo-classical framework, the significance and implications of the relaxation of the equality between rate of profits and rate of interest in the Keynes-Kaldor-Pasinetti model of income distribution and profit determination. Under this condition, new results apply, which enrich the traditional Cambridge or Kaldor-Pasinetti equation on income distribution $P/K = n/s(c)$, where P/K is the equilibrium rate of profits, n the equilibrium rate of growth of the system and $s(c)$ the constant (average equal to marginal) propensity to save of the entrepreneurs' class. Looking at optimal growth, which was and still is a widely explored field of research, his model develops two distinct arguments. First, in a traditional manner, it establishes the conditions under which there exists an interest rate on workers' life-cycle savings which maximises per capita consumption. Second, in a more original way, the usual criterion of optimal growth is replaced by the criterion of maximum workers' consumption, not an unreasonable criterion in a two- or multi-class economy (where most of private consumption is generated by families). It turns out that workers' consumption is maximised when the interest rate is equal to the profits rate, but here equality appears as an optimality condition, while in the Kaldor-Pasinetti's model it is an assumption.

Balestra's seminal model has generated quite a large body of literature (see, for instance, Pasinetti, 1974, Ch. VI; and Baranzini, 1991b), and has opened up new frontiers for the study of income distribution. For instance, the division between life-cycle savings and inter-generational capital may be analysed more efficiently by postulating a different rate of return; this, too, has given rise to a wide and far-reaching literature in these last 25 years. In more general terms Balestra's contribution to economic analysis, although less renowned than his work in econometrics, has been seminal for the ever-raging controversy on income distribution and profit determination between the two Cambridges (U.K. *vs.* Mass., USA).

2. THE HYPOTHESIS OF A DIFFERENTIATED INTEREST RATE IN A MODEL OF GROWTH AND DISTRIBUTION

Balestra's superb set of lectures held at the University of Fribourg starting from the academic year 1966/7, with a sabbatical at the Université de Louvain in 1967/8, expounded, among other things, the state of the Cambridge controversy on growth, income distribution and profit determination, which had just broken out between James E. Meade, Paul A. Samuelson and Franco Modigliani on the one hand, and Luigi L. Pasinetti, Nicholas Kaldor and Joan Robinson on the other. After discussing the most recent literature in the field (let us recall that the *Review of Economic Studies* had just devoted, in 1966, a

[1] He has recently written a paper where he considers the long-term properties of Ricardo's model of income distribution subject to external once-for-all shocks.

special issue to this topic), Balestra drew our attention to the fact that the most common criticism of the post-Keynesian and neo-classical models generally reflects the main differences dividing the various streams of economic thought in this vast field of research. These critiques, Balestra said, concentrate mainly on:

- The constancy of the propensities to save of the classes, exogenously given and hence independent of other variables such as the rate of return on capital and the rate of growth of population;
- The assumption and identification of individuals who retain their class identity forever, i.e. of classes which are inter-generationally stable;
- The assumption of equality, in the long-run, between the rate of profits which capitalists get from their investments and the rate of interest received by workers on their accumulated savings (and hence lent indirectly to the active capitalists);
- The assumption of classes which are almost entirely identified with given factors of production.

During the Winter Semester 1967/8, half-way through my economics degree at Fribourg, I had to choose a topic for my degree dissertation; and while a friend of mine chose Kaldor's theory on technical change, I chose Pasinetti's Theorem on income distribution and profit determination (originally published in 1962). I went immediately to work, and after a few months I sent Balestra – who was then teaching at the Centre for Operations Research and Econometrics, Louvain – a first draft. In this dissertation (*mémoire de licence*), I attempted to introduce into Pasinetti's original model the hypothesis of a lower rate of return on workers' savings, with respect to the overall rate of profit of the system. I was, however, unable to obtain explicit values for the overall rate of profit of the system; nonetheless, from the preliminary results, it seemed clear that the equilibrium solutions of the model would become a function of *all* propensities to save, not only of capitalists', as was the case in Pasinetti. Balestra wrote me a long letter (I still keep it among my private papers) on January 2nd, 1969, which he began by conveying his sympathy on my father's sudden and premature death, and then went on to provide me with numerous, very helpful suggestions (more came, in a second letter, in April of the same year) as to how to obtain an explicit solution for the distributive variables of the model in the case of a differentiated interest rate. It goes without saying that his help and encouragement were crucial for the preparation of the final draft of the *mémoire*, which I submitted in Spring 1969, shortly before my final exams.

Balestra's outstanding analytical skills, combined with a sound understanding of the mechanisms that support the modern economic systems, as well as his wide knowledge of the most recent literature, were to sustain me long and at various moments in my scientific career. They were to prove particularly useful as I worked on my Oxford D. Phil., and as I prepared my reply to Paul A. Samuelson's virulent attack on my 1975 *Oxford Economic Papers* article, a reply published as part of the debate to be found in the April 1991 issue of the same journal (see Baranzini, 1975 and 1991a). It must also be said that Balestra continued to be a valuable source of help and encouragement even when, after long scientific clashes with John S. Flemming (then at Nuffield College), James A. Mirrlees and many other neo-classical economists, I became increasingly disenchanted with marginalist economics, took up post-Keynesian lines (for both *object and method*) and came under the influence of the Cambridge School of economic thought and of Luigi Pasinetti in particular, with whom I had corresponded since 1972. Such a shift in interest never bothered Balestra. For one thing, you can always tell a truly good teacher by the fact that he will grant maximum freedom to his pupils. Secondly, it should be acknowledged that, although *objects and methods* may differ, the final answers will generally coincide (which is what, not surprisingly, Pasinetti claims).

During the Summer Semester of 1969, at the CORE of the University of Louvain, where he was staying as a visiting professor, Balestra presented a much revised and expanded version of the analysis of the case of a differentiated interest rate within the Kaldor-Pasinetti model of profit determination and income distribution. Later on, a written version of this conference was submitted to *Kyklos*, and was accepted without revisions for publication in Vol. XXIV, June 1971. The title of the paper was 'Some Optimal Aspects in A Two-Class Growth Model With a Differentiated Interest Rate'. Balestra was exceedingly (and characteristically) generous in deciding to publish it jointly with me. As one may expect, the paper (henceforward referred to as 'B-B') first explores the consequences of rejecting the hypothesis of the equality between the profit rate and the interest rate in a two-class model of economic growth à la Kaldor-Pasinetti and Meade-Samuelson & Modigliani. As we shall see below, with a differentiated interest rate, the well-known (Kaldor-Pasinetti's) independence of the equilibrium profit rate with respect to the propensity to save of the workers is no longer valid. The paper provides the general solutions of the model for this case. Additionally, looking at optimal growth, it develops two distinct arguments. First, in a traditional manner, the author establishes the conditions under which there exists an interest rate which maximises *per capita* consumption. Second, in a much more original way (and this goes wholly to Balestra's credit) the author replaces the usual criterion of optimal growth with the criterion of maximum workers' consumption, not unreasonably in a two-class economy. Finally, the author derives the maximising conditions for this special case[2].

The assumption that the rate of interest received by workers is equal to the rate of profits generated by the system (and perceived by capitalists) is, we know, obvious in a neo-classical world, where individuals may differ because of their initial endowments, but where equilibrating mechanisms are always at work: in this case, the differences between the various rates of return may be explained only in terms of risk differences, bound to disappear in the long-run in the perfect information context.

As already anticipated above, there are far-reaching implications in the assumption of a different rate of return for the accumulated savings of the various classes. First

[2]It should be underlined that the joint publication of this paper was instrumental in persuading the special Committee of The Queen's College, Oxford, to award me a very generous two-year Florey European Scholarship for carrying out post-graduate research in Oxford. After a first encouraging spell of research under the guidance of Balestra, this constituted a unique opportunity for me to pursue my academic training and career in a prestigious and highly stimulating setting.

of all, this assumption affects directly the distribution of income among classes, and subsequently, the overall saving ratio and the patterns of wealth accumulation. In this way the steady-state solutions of the model are profoundly modified, and at least two new research programmes have been launched along these lines (for an exhaustive agenda, see, for instance, Baranzini, 1991a, Ch. 2).

3. AT THE ROOT OF THE PROBLEM

But what are the reasons behind the hypothesis of a different rate of return on investment for the two or more classes? Several reasons may be put forward in support of a differentiated interest rate in a two- or multi-class model.

Property rights are fundamental determinants of distribution in post-Keynesian, as well as classical and neo-Ricardian, theories where the production process implicitly or explicitly requires some form of co-operation from individuals empowered to 'withdraw' (or at least 'condition') certain essential inputs. As in most classical theories, social classes remain crucial for post-Keynesian theories, and their distinctive feature is given by saving-, consumption-, and investment-behaviour. In more sophisticated theories (such as Pasinetti's, but also of a number of other recent authors) the assumption of 'separate appropriation' of each production factor is no longer as drastic as in other models, although it hovers in the background, even if the income – or indeed wealth – of certain classes is made up by different types of income, or respectively, by accumulated wealth. For instance, in Pasinetti's (1962, 1974, 1989b) models of growth and distribution – which consider a multitude of aspects related to these issues – workers' income is made up of wages and interests on accumulated savings. [On the nature of savings one may distinguish between life-cycle and inter-generational; forced (pension funds for instance) and free; real and financial; liquid and less liquid; households and non-households, and so on; the literature has already considered a number of cases.] Back to our argument, one might argue that accumulated savings may be linked only indirectly to the profits rate, as in the case of deposit and savings accounts, which have a predetermined rate of interest (not necessarily linked to the overall rate of profits of the economy).

Of course, in a general sense in post-Keynesian theories different rate of savings are associated with different economic and social classes. And the distribution of savings among classes will be such as to yield an overall saving equal to the desired level of full employment. In this way, a differentiated interest rate may further redistribute income among the classes of the system: for this reason its analysis represents a key element in the determination of the overall equilibrium interest rate.

Considering specific points we might say that the differential between the rate of interest and the rate of profits may be justified as follows :

i. First, from an historical point of view, the interest rate has been considerably lower than the average profit rate (both in nominal and in real terms), except for some periods coinciding with the initial phase of depression or high inflation periods. In general a ratio of 2:3 is more likely to reflect the world's realities than a ratio of

1:1. This observation implies one of two things: either the economy is not on an equilibrium growth path and there is no evident hope of ever achieving such a path, or it becomes necessary to incorporate a different hypothesis into the model. Such a hypothesis will have to take into account the observed difference between the rate of interest on normal life-cycle savings and the overall profit rate.

ii. Secondly, one might argue that the act of saving and the act of investing are two distinct operations. They refer, in fact, to two distinct 'acts of appropriation' : one is closely connected with labour-income, i.e. a wage-rate, and hence only indirectly with the average profit rate of the economy. (Workers, in particular, will make their consumption and savings plans, inter alia, by taking into account the level of their actual labour income and the expectations relative to the evolution of their wages in the years to come; which has very little to do with the tendencies of the profits.) The act of investing, on the other hand, is directly related to the average profit rate of the economy and its tendency over the medium term : here the business cycle of aggregate demand, investment and profits share is crucial. One might also say that the act of saving is passive (what remains after consumption has been provided for) and that the act of investing is active (it usually requires a sound knowledge of the economic and financial environment).

iii. Thirdly, a different way of looking at the same phenomenon is to postulate that there is a risk associated with the act of investing. This risk should be reflected in the differential between rate of interest on risk-free savings and overall profit rate.

iv. Finally, it may be said that to be profitable investment must be larger than a certain minimum. Wage-earners, taken individually, may not be able to exploit the profit opportunities of large investments. Accordingly, their savings are likely to carry a smaller reward. This, of course, does not mean that we would have to introduce the argument of increasing returns to scale on savings. One might simply maintain that the rate of interest is not necessarily identical to the profits rate. It should however be stressed that in this context by interest rate we mean the rate at which the workers place their savings in the hands of the entrepreneurial class (or in the hands of the state in a socialist society - but this observation was more pertinent in the early Seventies than it is now at the end of the century).

The introduction of a differentiated interest rate was initially criticised by Pasinetti, since, according to him "... in order to say anything about the share and rate of profits, one needs first a *theory of the rate of interest.* In a long-run equilibrium model, the obvious hypothesis to make is that of a rate of interest equal to the rate of profits" (Pasinetti, 1962, pp. 271-2). In a first draft of Chapter VI of his *Growth and Income Distribution,* in fact, he inserted a special paragraph in which he maintained that the assumption of a differentiated interest rate was out of touch with the philosophy underlying the whole macro-economic distributive model. I recall that in a letter he sent me at The Queen's College in October 1973 (I remember collecting it from the old pigeon-hole in Back Quad 5), Pasinetti had not yet decided whether to write a strong attack to our joint paper, or to confine himself to a straightforward quotation (see Pasinetti, 1974, p. 144n). (This should come as no surprise knowing that Pasinetti used to rewrite his early scientific papers up to eight times, with a nearly maniacal obsession with the tiniest detail.)

The assumption that the rate of interest earned by workers is equal to the overall rate of profits generated by the system (and earned by capitalists) may of course be more obvious in a neo-classical or marginalist world, where individuals may be considered different because of their initial endowments, but where equilibrating or balancing mechanisms are always at work: in this case the differences between the various rates of return may be explained only in terms of risk differences bound to disappear in the long-run if the perfect information context remains. But if complete foresight exists as to all possible events in the neo-classical model, as Eichner and Kregel (1975, p. 1309) point out, in post-Keynesian theory 'only the past is known, the future is uncertain'. In other words, if we abandon the neo-classical approach, it may not be clear which particular mechanisms make the interest rate equal to the rate of profit, even if Pasinetti initially thought, as quoted above, that in the long-run the obvious hypothesis is that of a rate of interest equal to the rate of profit.

Gupta (1976) has proved that this particular case can be examined with post-Keynesian tools as well. It is worth quoting the initial part of Gupta's paper (which, incidentally, Balestra himself refereed) published in *Kyklos* :

> *In a recent article in this Journal, Balestra and Baranzini (1971), assuming that workers and capitalists receive different rates of return on their capital, established two important modifications to Pasinetti's analysis (1962). First, that the equilibrium rate of profit was not independent of workers' propensity to save as claimed by Pasinetti, and second, that the equilibrium rate of profit was lower than in Pasinetti's case. They established these conclusions from a model which used a neo-classical production function and the marginal productivity theory. However, it is well-known that one of Pasinetti's major claims was to have demonstrated that his theorems could be established without any recourse to these neoclassical devices. Therefore, their paper might lead to the conclusion that their results are dependent on their use of the neoclassical tools of analysis and may not be valid in their absence. One of the aims of this paper is to show that this is not the case and that their two basic conclusions can be shown to follow from Pasinetti's own analysis. In the second part of the paper we shall suggest two other applications of their analysis, more particularly, of their notion of a differentiated interest rate.* (Gupta, 1976, p. 310)

It must finally be said that Pasinetti (1974, pp. 139-41) developed a post-Keynesian model of growth and distribution in which the assumption of equality, in the long-run, between the rate of profits which capitalists get from their investments and the rate of interest earned by the workers is dropped. In truth, such a digression was advanced in order to show that in the long-run the propensity to save of the workers does not determine the equilibrium value of the rate of return $P(c)/K(c) = n/s(c)$ on capitalists' assets, nor the distribution of income between wages and profits. According to Pasinetti:

> *[...] The assumption, kept so far, of a rate of interest exactly equal to the rate of profit is in fact not necessary. [...] Suppose that the workers lend their savings to the capitalists and receive interest $i = P(w)/K(w)$, which is lower than the rate of profit the capitalists obtain. [...] such relation holds independently of whether the rates of profit and of interest are uniform or differentiated. And since, in equilibrium, $I = S$ and $(I/K) = g(n)$, it follows immediately [...] that : $P(c)/K(c) = s(c)/g(n)$. (VI.12.1) This expression represents in fact a more general version of the "Cambridge equation". It shows that the natural rate of growth and the capitalists propensity to save determine the rate of profit on capitalists' capital first of all, independently of anything else, and therefore also independently of the rate of interest.* (Pasinetti, 1974, pp. 139-40)

At the end of his analysis, Pasinetti (1974b, p. 141) obtains the following value of the equilibrium rate of profits $P/K = g(n)/j.s(c)$, where $j = f[g(n), K/Y^*, s(c), s(w), \text{and } i]$, which leads him to conclude that:

> *The interest of (VI.12.6) is that it shows that j comes to reinforce $s(c)$. A rate of interest lower than the rate of profit has the same effect as a higher propensity to save of the capitalists, as it redistributes income in favour of the class that owns the physical capital stock.* (Pasinetti, 1974, p. 141)

One may argue that in post-Keynesian models, as in most classical models, to begin with, individuals belong to different classes, with a different function and 'withdrawal power', as pointed out above. Even the nature of their income is different, since for workers wages are of a residual nature. From this standpoint, consumers and entrepreneurs (or workers and capitalists) have a completely different socio-economic profile, and the difference between profits and rate of interest may not be imputed solely to the risk factor, but it takes on a much wider significance, as will become clearer later on.

4. FROM 'THE OLD PROPOSITION OF THE EQUALITY OF THE INTEREST RATE AND THE PROFIT RATE' TO THE ANALYSIS OF THE OPTIMALITY CONDITIONS

The introduction of the hypothesis of a different interest rate earned (directly or indirectly) on the savings by the classes of the model of growth and distribution does of course lead to the conclusion that the well-known (Kaldor-Pasinetti's) independence of the equilibrium profit rate with respect to the propensity to save of the non-capitalists classes is no longer valid. This is true as long as the rate of interest on capitalists' savings is plotted as a function of the overall rate of interest (or profits as post-Keynesians prefer to write) of the economic system.

Having explored the equilibrium properties of the model in this particular case, and of the reactions expressed in the early literature, Balestra asked himself whether an interest rate (or profits rate in equilibrium) exists which maximises consumption *per capita*. This question is particularly relevant whenever the interest rate is considered as a control variable. If such a rate exists, it may be called the *Golden Rule Interest Rate* (see B-B,

1971, p. 250). To answer this question one might use the established (neo-classical as well as post-Keynesian, in particular Robinsonian) theorem, which states that consumption per capita is maximised in a state of steady-state (balanced) growth when the profit rate $[(P/K)^* = r^*]$ is equal to the exogenously given rate of growth. In a two-class model characterised by a different rate of interest, where r is the rate earned on workers' savings and $f(k)$ the overall rate of profits of the system [with $r = jf(k)$] total consumption is maximised when $j^* = f(\text{all parameters}; P/Y, K/Y)$. As pointed out:

> *It will come as no surprise that the Golden Rule Interest Rate does not exist for all possible configurations of the two propensities to save, since it is well known that on the consumption maximising path the over-all saving ratio must be equal to the profit share. What is remarkable, however, is that, if the proper conditions are met, the interest rate may be used to achieve such equality. Furthermore, this equality may be obtained for different constellations of the propensities to save.* (B-B, 1971, p. 251)

Alternatively, by assuming a constant risk-factor (j), a fixed (not alterable) propensity to save of the workers $s(w)$ and a given technology (P/Y^*), one wonders what value of the propensity to save of the capitalists (or of the State) will maximise consumption per capita:

> *[...] In the presence of risk (or, alternatively, in the presence of a differentiated interest rate), there always exists a propensity to save of the capitalists of less than unity which maximises consumption per capita in balanced growth. Hence the stringent condition* $[s(c) = 1]$ *of Pasinetti's two class model is removed.* (B-B, 1971, p. 252)

5. MAXIMISING WORKERS' CONSUMPTION

In a two- or many-class growth model the criterion underlying optimal growth may be questioned. In fact the class of workers, who earn labour income as well as interest income on their accumulated savings, may be assumed to represent families or the consumers' class, while capitalists (who earn a profit rate on their capital as well as the difference between the overall profit rate and the interest rate earned by other classes) may well represent firms in a modern industrialised society. Therefore, instead of finding the path which maximises total consumption, one may be more interested in the path which maximises the consumption of workers, i.e. 'non-capitalists' or families :

> *It is absolutely clear that workers' consumption is maximised when total consumption is maximised and at the same time the consumption of the capitalists is zero. This obviously implies* $s(c) = 1$ *and* $r^* = m$ *(or* $r^* = 1$*)*[3]. *If we were free to choose the values of the propensities to save in addition to the interest rate, there would*

[3]Where $s(c)$, the average and marginal propensity to save of the capitalists' class, is equal to unity; and the equilibrium rate of interest earned by the workers (r^*) is equal to the rate of growth of the system (m); or in other words where r^* is equal to unity, which means that the rate of interest earned by workers on their savings is equal to the overall rate of profits of the system.

> *be nothing more to be said. This case, however, is rather uninteresting for at least two reasons. First, it assumes that by appropriate policy measures we can effectively act on the saving propensities so as to reach the optimal growth path. Second, even if policy measures are effective, the requirement that the propensity to save of the capitalists be equal to unity seems to be a rather stringent assumption.* (B-B, 1971, p. 252)

It is at this point that the question is set. Given the values of the propensities to save, and a given capital/output ratio (which is a very post-Keynesian assumption to make at this stage) what value of the interest rate maximises workers' consumption? This question may be especially relevant in a socialist society in which the State spends (or perhaps better: spent) a given proportion of its revenue on investment (and hence in this case $s(c)$ may be considered as a constant) and where the natural instrument of economic policy used to be the rate of interest.

> *An increase in the interest rate has two distinct effects on workers' consumption. First, the total remuneration perceived by the workers [on their accumulated savings, both generational and inter-generational if it is the case] is automatically increased, since their return on their accumulated savings increases. They will have a positive effect on their consumption. Second, given that* $s(c) > s(w)$*, an increase in the interest rate means a decrease in over-all savings. Hence investment is reduced and consequently income will fall. They will tend to reduce the income received by the workers and therefore their consumption is likely to fall. Since these two effects play in opposite directions, presumably they will offset each other at some point. At this point a maximum obtains.* (B-B, 1971, pp. 252-3)

The analysis of this specific case shows that workers' consumption is maximized when the rate of interest is equal to the profit rate:

> *Thus, at the end of our journey, we rejoin Pasinetti's old proposition of the equality of the interest rate and the profit rate. But there is one important difference: here the equality appears as an* <u>*optimality condition,*</u> *whereas in Pasinetti's model it is an assumption. In this connection, a parallel may be drawn with respect to the neo-classical Golden Rule, which implies the equality between savings and profits. Here again we are back to the old Ricardian proposition, but the perspective is completely different.* (B-B, 1971, p. 254)

It was these results which led a number of authors (see the list below) seriously to consider the hypothesis that individuals, dynasties or classes, maximise the utility derived from the discounted flow of their life-cycle consumption, which might also include a bequest motive.

6. THE LINES OF EXTENSION OF THE MODEL

The introduction of the above hypotheses concerning on the one hand a different rate of return on savings, and on the other the rule of optimality, into the two-class growth model (both of the post-Keynesian or marginalist type, as the analysis in Gupta, 1976, has proved) has sparked off two distinct lines of research. We consider them in some detail.

6.1. The direct implications of the hypothesis of a differentiated interest rate

The implications of the assumption of a different rate of return for the accumulated savings of the various classes are far-reaching. First of all, as it has been explained above, it affects directly the distribution of income among classes, the overall saving ratio and the process of capital accumulation of the classes. The number of contributions and comments, starting from classical, marginalist, post-Keynesian or neo-Ricardian frameworks, is still growing, and chronologically includes Harcourt (1972), Sheng Cheng Hu (1973), Moore (1974), Pasinetti (1974, pp. 139-41), Campa (1975) and Pasinetti's reply (1975), Baranzini (1975, 1982, 1991a, 1991b), Gupta (1976), Fazi and Salvadori (1981) and Pasinetti's Reply (1983), Miyazaki (1991), Ewijk, C. Van (1991), Dutt and Amadeo (1994). Other authors, as Ramanathan (1976), Marglin (1980), Craven (1979), and Panico (1984, 1985) although not developing a straightforward model, enquire into the significance and implications of the long-run equality between the rate of return and the rate of interest earned on accumulated savings, both life-cycle and inter-generationally.

The results obtained within this context vary according to the assumptions made and to the framework of analysis adopted, although the basic results may be obtained in both post-Keynesian and neoclassical cases, as expounded above. Perhaps the most interesting results are to be found in the implications relative to the process of capital accumulation. In fact, a lower than average rate of return on savings, in order to ensure a steady-state growth of the system, requires, all other things being equal, either a higher propensity to save or a larger share of income of the class under consideration, which has a strong influence on income distribution (which would have to be reallocated in order to maintain such steady growth). The implications of this assumption outside the balanced growth path would be even more far-reaching, since it would, ceteris paribus, lead to a lower rate of capital accumulation by those classes that benefit from a lower rate of return. In other words this would lead, in the long-run, to a polarisation of the socio-economic classes of the system, except in the case in which such a disparity is counterbalanced by an increase in other kinds of income, like wages or rent.

My paper in the *Oxford Economic Papers*, December 1995, with the title 'The Pasinetti and Anti-Pasinetti Theorems: A Reconciliation', is a by-product of the B-B (1971) paper, since the Pasinetti and Meade-Samuelson and Modigliani's Dual Theorems are obtained as the roots of a single quadratic equation, which is exactly the quadratic equation (16) of the B-B's paper (1971, p. 246) in the case in which the rate of profits is set equal to the rate of interest. Hence it is clear that an analysis of the hypothesis of a differentiated interest rate has proved fruitful also for the generalisation of the basic model. In fact, this stirred up afresh the controversy on profit determination and income distribution which then erupted in 1991, exactly a quarter of a century after the special issue of the *Review of Economic Studies* (with contributions by Paul A. Samuelson, Franco Modigliani, Luigi L. Pasinetti, Joan Robinson, Nicholas Kaldor, and K. Sato).

The March 1991 issue of the *Oxford Economic Papers* contains three articles (by Koichi Miyazaki, Paul A. Samuelson, and myself), in which the applicability of the Meade and Samuelson & Modigliani's Dual Theorem is discussed at length and where, at the end of the mini-debate, I stated that :

> *I would like however to stress the validity of the fundamental outcome of my (1975) paper – i.e. the formulation of both Theorems as roots of a single quadratic equation – which provides a kind of symmetry between the Pasinetti and Meade-Samuelson-Modigliani Theorems, so far undiscovered in the literature, and which has led to the use of the term 'reconciliation'. In order to prove this – and in order to answer the various points raised by Miyazaki and Samuelson, especially concerning the tendency of the capital stocks of the two classes outside the steady state of growth of all variables – I shall reconsider the main issue by focusing on the rates of growth of the two capital stocks.* (Baranzini, 1991b, p. 195)

At the end of the journey (which, as indicated above, was based on the B-B approach) we reach the following conclusions:

> *The above arguments have expounded the difference between steady states of growth of the totals and the (unique) steady state of all variables (i.e. including $K(c)$ and $K(w)$), and we have considered the equilibrating mechanisms of the system, quite independently of the well-behaved production function. The analysis has additionally confirmed the validity of the 'quadratic equation' reached without dividing or multiplying by $K(c)/K$ and thus avoiding the much feared '$0 = 0$ minefields'.* (Baranzini, 1991b, p. 198)

It should also be said that the B-B paper has been reprinted on several occasions, as for instance in Kurz and Salvadori (1998).

6.2. The micro-economic foundations of the model

The second research programme sparked off by the hypothesis of a different rate of return on savings concerns the introduction of micro-economic elements into the model. In fact, if it is feasible to differentiate classes according to their rate of return on savings, why not differentiate them even further, by considering small socio-economic groups or even dynasties of individuals with a common behaviour.

In spite of its division of the system into classes, the post-Keynesian distribution model has essentially macro-economic foundations. This absence of micro-foundations has attracted the attention of those, like Samuelson, Modigliani and Kregel, who believe it to be one of the weakest points in post-Keynesian theory. According to the MIT economists the Kaldor-Pasinetti model

> *completely disregards the life-cycle and its effects on saving and worker behaviour. In the first part with a large portion of saving known to occur in some phases of the life-cycle in order to finance dissaving in other phases, it is unrealistic to posit values for $s(c)$ and $s(w)$ [the propensities to save of the two classes] which are independent of n (the rate of growth of the system).* (Samuelson and Modigliani, 1966a, p. 297)

Samuelson and Modigliani (1966a, p. 297) conclude their analysis by stating that 'this shortcoming is probably not too serious and could be handled without changing our results drastically'. The literature which followed shows that such a conclusion is not necessarily true, and that the results obtained are much more complicated and ambiguous than it would seem at first sight.

Pasinetti however, in a lecture given in 1997 to an Italian-Soviet conference at the Catholic University of Milan, stressed that there is no necessary incompatibility between a macro- and a micro-economic framework, as long as the macro-economic framework is given priority:

> *Once the conditions of satisfactory growth (structural efficiency) have been fulfilled, a second stage follows in which the way becomes open to the investigation and solution of so to speak local problems of efficiency at the level of the single production units and of the single individuals. To these local problems the procedure and methods of maximization under constraints may well be appropriate in many circumstances; even though never in an exclusive way. We may talk in this respect of local or micro-economic efficiency.* (Pasinetti, 1987, pp. 991)

This means that, if the distributive macro-economic framework is preserved in its entirety (with its chains of causality and, in certain cases, sub-systems of inter-dependencies, as pointed out in Baranzini and Scazzieri, 1987), the model may be extended to include a certain micro-structure. For example, it may be extended in order to provide a more exhaustive explanation of the propensities to save and consume of socio-economic classes or groups (or even dynasties) and of the mechanisms responsible for the inter-generational transmission of capital.

The first moves in this direction came from the neo-classical and marginalist economists, who were probably inspired by the above-quoted passage from Samuelson and Modigliani. In the case of the marginalists this is not surprising, since they see distribution primarily in micro-economic terms. However, several non-neoclassical economists, too, entered the field; several of them spurred on by the Balestra-Baranzini paper of 1971, to which a number of works make direct reference. We might mention, here, published work by Britto (1972), Bevan (1974, 1979), and others referred to in Baranzini (1991b) and Targetti (1993).

The essential contributions the life-cycle theory can make to the analysis of a society characterised by the presence of socio-economic classes with different income structures and different consumption and saving attitudes, are the following (an exhaustive analysis of the significance of this approach is given in Baranzini, 1991b, Ch. 4) :

i. More insight into the determination of the distribution of income among classes (at least when they all own a positive share of the capital stock) and the determination of the equilibrium variables of the model;

ii. An understanding of the sorts of reasons that may lead to historical class differences, to a different accumulation of capital (both life-cycle and inter-generational), and to the particular conditions under which a class may start accumulating inter-generational assets;

iii. An elucidation of the applicability of the Meade-Samuelson and Modigliani condition (following which the capitalists' capital share vanishes in the long run) or of the opposite condition (following which the workers' inter-generational capital share tends to zero). This would allow to determine when the equilibrium (i.e. optimal) interest rate is the same for all classes of the system and when there exists the possibility of a multiple equilibrium. (The discussion which took place in the 1991 April issue of the *Oxford Economic Papers* has been in part made possible by this framework, and by the precious suggestions Balestra passed on to me.)

iv. An assessment of the relative strength of the life-cycle versus the inter-national capital stock and the conditions which favour one or the other of the capital stocks.

These are, briefly, the main issues which the introduction of a modified version of the life-cycle theory tackles. To these we may add the following questions:

5. What are, in this context, the consequences of the introduction (both in a deterministic and stochastic context) of the hypothesis of an imperfect capital market, which is rather appealing in a two-class or multi-class context, and which of course represents one of the links between the two research lines which we are considering here, i.e. of a differentiated interest rate and of the introduction of the life-cycle into the post-Keynesian framework?

6. What are the consequences of the introduction of uncertainty (relative to the rate of return on accumulated savings) on the optimal consumption and accumulation rates of the two classes; and how relevant is uncertainty in generating differences among classes, i.e. classes with a high propensity to save (or to accumulate) than average? Additionally, in what way will classes react, according to their risk-aversion, to the existence of different investment possibilities, with different rates of return and different expectations?

By and large the results achieved by these models show (as it will be partly expounded below), that the system's rate of interest is in all cases positively correlated with its rate of growth - a result which is in line with the Cambridge Equation - and, in most cases, inversely related to the propensities to save of the various classes of the system. Other important components emerge, however, such as mechanisms related to legacies to the future generations or the proportion of inter-generational assets in the overall capital of the classes. More complicated results are obtained in the case where all classes in the system hold not only life-cycle savings, but also a part of the inter-generational capital stock.

In the next Section we shall try to develop the argument relative to the concept and behaviour of classes, which are normally exogenously given. It is to be noted that the above arguments inevitably lead to the consideration of endogenously determined classes.

7. THE RELEVANCE AND GENERALISATION OF CLASS DIFFERENCES IN A STEADY-STATE GROWTH MODEL *À LA* CAMBRIDGE

The above argument about a different rate of capital growth of the two classes, or about a different rate of return on their savings, may indeed open up new horizons in the field of steady-state growth analysis. In particular, the idea of a different endowment of classes may be put forward: the entrepreneurial class, which owns mainly inter-generational (as well as human) capital, and the workers' class which owns mainly life-cycle savings (as well as human capital). Alternatively, one might consider the case in which both classes own inter-generational capital, but are characterised by a different propensity to endow the next generation. This is not a completely new assumption. We know, in fact, that the entrepreneurial class has a higher propensity to save than the other classes (in particular the workers' class). We know, on the other hand, that one of the motives behind the savings is to endow the next generation with a physical or financial capital stock. (cf. Horioka and Watanabe, 1997). Hence a higher propensity to save will almost inevitably imply a higher willingness to transmit physical or financial capital to the next generation.

The point about these various working hypotheses is that in a steady-state situation the capital stock of all classes present in the system must grow at the same overall rate. Secondly, the assumption of a long-term horizon may be associated with the presence in the model of different generations, either overlapping or clearly separated from one another. Meade often took this position; while Sir John Hicks was never explicit on this point, though in many of his works the indirect reference to various generations is obvious.

A model of wealth distribution and accumulation is considered in Baranzini (1991b, chapters 5-7), which includes all the elements quoted above. The results obtained are interesting since, within an original framework, the micro-economic pure exchange model (or utility-maximisation model, also following Hicks, 1965, Ch. 21) is in turn encompassed by the post-Keynesian framework to define a more flexible approach to income and wealth distribution. An analysis of this kind elicits two main conclusions :

i. In a life-cycle model where the transmission of inter-generational financial assets is a prerogative of the entrepreneurial class, the equilibrium rate of interest depends on the behavioural parameters of the capitalist class; it doesn't depend on those of other classes or on technology. The fact that the equilibrium rate of interest is independent of technological factors (i.e. of the capital/output ratio) is particularly relevant, and seems to reinforce the solution which was put forward by the Cambridge School as well as by Sir John Hicks (1965).

ii. When both classes are allowed to pass on inter-generational assets (excluding education) to their children, then, in order to have a steady-state path, capitalists must have a much stronger will to bequeath capital to their children than the other classes. It is only in such a situation that all classes will hold a positive share of the total capital stock. The results obtained lead us to ask the following question : 'Can this analytical result be reconciled with economic reality and common sense?' To a certain extent the answer is yes, since (a) the workers' class, by definition, derives a high proportion of its income from human capital stock, so that it may be inclined to discount its inter-generational bequest at a rate lower than the average (on this point see Flemming, 1979); and (b) it is not unrealistic to posit a situation where, in general, low-income families give high priority to life-cycle consumption and consequently a lower one to the inter-generational capital stock. On the other hand, those classes that derive a high proportion of their income from inter-generational wealth (and the remaining part from life-cycle savings) in the long-term are bound to give weight to the accumulation of such wealth, by discounting it at a rate higher than average. This different approach to the inter-generational bequest notwithstanding, as we have shown in this chapter, there exists a real possibility of a balanced growth of the system, where each class maintains a constant relative economic strength and a constant share of the capital stock. Clearly, the system may well leave such a path: this would happen if the capitalists were to show too low a propensity to pass on bequests to their children, thereby diminishing their strength. Similarly a much stronger desire on the part of the workers to transmit inter-generational wealth would eventually achieve the same result.

8. THE GENESIS OF SOCIO-ECONOMIC CLASSES

The arguments developed above lead us to another important issue which is to be found in the background of long-run analysis, i.e. that of the formation, persistence, and dispersion of socio-economic classes at large. This issue is present in a number of studies which have appeared in the last two decades; it is also present in most of Sir John Hicks's works on economic growth, especially in his *Capital and Growth*, but it has not been directly taken up. There exist a number of elements that are continuously at work in the determination of the progressive concentration or dispersion of wealth, which is at the very basis of the strength of a socio-economic class in the long run.

Various factors account for the dispersion of wealth. Some of them tend to level off life-cycle savings; while others may reduce the relevance of inter-generational assets in total wealth. Their impact on the formation or dispersion of classes, however, is the same, and may even be hard to identify once the process has been set in motion. Among these factors we may quote: (1) the fiscal policies of redistribution ; (2) a decline, for whatever reason, in the value of holdings; (3) the handing down of savings; (4) transfers in the donor's lifetime; and (5) dispersion at death. Among the factors contributing to the process of wealth concentration, we might mention instead: (1) a differentiated propensity to save, according to the level of income; (2) different age-cohorts, which account for a different value of life-cycle savings; (3) a higher return for large capital stocks; (4) a small number of children inheriting the inter-generational capital stock; (5) an unequal distribution of bequests and (6) *assorted mating* which tends to concentrate wealth in the hands of a given socio-economic class.

Let us hold on to one single point, here, namely that of the fiscal policies of redistribution (see, for a recent development in this area, Teixeira, Sugahara, and Baranzini, 1998). This is an instrument of economic policy which has become increasingly used in recent decades. Atkinson and Stiglitz (1980, p. 63) indicate a variety of taxes on capital and/or return on capital which may be considered in this context: (a) taxes on interest income, either at the same rate as other income – like labour – or at a differential rate (for instance the U.K. investment income surcharge); (b) taxes on (short-term or long-term) capital gains; (c) wealth taxes on the net value of assets owned (with special provisions that reduce the effective rate - like special treatment of housing, or life insurance and pensions, as well as certain tax-exempt bonds); and (d) special taxes, for example those on houses, land, etc. The latter are labelled as 'property taxes' in the US, 'rates' and later 'council tax' in the U.K., and 'house tax' ("*tassa sulla casa*") in Italy. In certain cases, the policies on redistribution and/or taxation have been successful in stopping or slowing down the progressive concentration of wealth. Such was the explicit goal of the Labour Manifesto drafted in the U.K. in the late Sixties and early Seventies, which was aimed at limiting to about half a million pounds the personal wealth a single individual may inherit or accumulate.

Many economists have paid particular attention to the relevance of all direct and indirect taxes for the process of wealth accumulation, and their conclusions have often been ambiguous. Nonetheless it seems clear that wealth taxes and estate duties have led to a lower concentration of wealth than one would otherwise have experienced.

We may say that the conditions in which a class is born, consolidates itself or even vanishes, are multiple, and can only be studied in the framework of a fairly complicated model. The traverse successfully studied by Sir John Hicks is surely a good starting point; however, more work is needed in this direction. Some recent work in the field of institutional change and structural analysis may also be of help in clearing the ground for the whole issue.

9. CONCLUSION

I hope that this paper has demonstrated the direct and indirect relevance of Pietro Balestra's work in the wide field of economic theory, in particular of income distribution, profit determination and long-term development. Through his original and stimulating lectures on *Questions Spéciales d'Economie Politique*, held over more than a decade at the University of Fribourg, and later at Dijon and Geneva, he has inspired a number of pupils to write seminar papers, *mémoires de licence* as well as doctoral theses on economic theory topics. He has also directly furthered research in this field by publishing a seminal paper on a modified version of the Kaldor-Pasinetti as well as Meade-Samuelson & Modigliani's Theorems on income distribution and profit determination. Over the last quarter of a century, his analyses and findings have sparked off at least two research programmes with dozens of papers published in learned journals or volumes. Indirectly, too, Pietro Balestra's contribution has been valuable in that he has helped and encouraged promising young students to pursue their studies in the best British and American Universities, an effort which has often paid off for the academic community at large.

REFERENCES

1. Ahmad, S. (1986), "A Pasinetti Theory of Relative Profit Share for the Anti-Pasinetti Case", *Journal of Post-Keynesian Economics*, 149-58.
2. Arestis, P., G. Palma and M. Sawyer (eds.) (1997), *Capital Controversy, Post-Keynesian Economics and the History of Economic Thought: Essays in Honour of Geoff C. Harcourt*, London and New York: Routledge.
3. Ando, A. and F. Modigliani (1963, 1964) "The Life-Cycle Hypothesis of Saving: Aggregate Implications and Tests", *American Economic Review*, 53, 55-84; 54, Part I, 111-13.
4. Atkinson, A. B. (1997) "Bringing Income Distribution in From the Cold", *The Economic Journal*, 107, 297-321.
5. Atkinson, A. B. and J.E. Stiglitz (1980), *Lectures on Public Economics*, London and New York: McGraw-Hill.
6. Atsumi, H. (1960), "Mr. Kaldor's Theory of Income Distribution", *The Review of Economic Studies*, 109-18.
7. Balestra, P. (1967), *The Demand for Natural Gas in the United States (A Dynamic Approach for the Residential and Commercial Market)*, Amsterdam and New York: North-Holland.
8. Balestra, P. (1967-9), "Questions Spéciales d'Economie Politique", mimeo, University of Fribourg, Switzerland.
9. Balestra, P. (1977), *Calcul Matriciel pour Economistes*, Albeuve (Switzerland): Castella
10. Balestra, P. (1982), "Dummy Variables in Regression Analysis", in M. Baranzini (ed.) *Advances in Economic Theory*, Oxford: Basil Blackewell, 273-92.
11. Balestra, P. (1985), "Commentaire à la conférence du Professeur Luigi Pasinetti: Technical Progress and the Wealth of Nations", in H. Bortis, and L. Bosshart (eds.) *Technologischer Wandel in Wirtschaft und Gesellschaft*, (Festschrift in honour of Florian Fleck), Freiburg (i.ü.): Universitätsverlag, 67-74.
12. Balestra, P. (1989), "La science économique des années nonante", *Revue Suisse d'Economie Politique et de Statistique*, 125.3, 239-48.
13. Balestra, P. (1994), "Statistique et analyse économique: quel mariage?", *Revue Suisse d'Economie Politique et de Statistique*, 130.3, 363-76.
14. Balestra, P. and M. Baranzini (1971), "Some optimal Aspects in a Two Class Growth Model With a Differentiated Interest Rate", 24.2, *Kyklos*, 240-56.
15. Balestra, P. and M. Nerlove (1966), "Pooling Cross-Section and Time Series Data in the Estimation of Dynamic Models: The Demand for Natural Gas", *Econometrica*, 34, 585-612.
16. Baranzini, M. (1975), "The Pasinetti and The Anti-Pasinetti Theorems: A Reconciliation", *Oxford Economic Papers*, 27.3, 470-3.
17. Baranzini, M. (1976), "On the Distribution of Income in Two-Class Growth Models", D. Phil. thesis, The Queen's College, University of Oxford.
18. Baranzini, M., (ed.) (1982), *Advances in Economic Theory*, Oxford: Basil Blackwell; New York: St. Martin's Press.
19. Baranzini, M. (1991a), "The Pasinetti and Anti-Pasinetti Theorems: A Reply to K.

Miyazaki and P.A. Samuelson", *Oxford Economic Papers*, 43.2, 195-8.
20. Baranzini, M. (1991b), *A Theory of Wealth Distribution and Accumulation*, Oxford: Clarendon Press.
21. Baranzini, M. (1992), "The Debate on Kaldor's Theory of Distribution", in F. Targetti, *Nicholas Kaldor (The Economics and Politics of Capitalism as a Dynamic System)*, Oxford: Clarendon Press, 143-59.
22. Baranzini, M. (1995), "Distribution, Accumulation and Institutions", in A. Heertje (ed.) *The Makers of Modern Economics*, Vol. II, Aldershot, U.K. and Brookfield, U. S.: E. Elgar, 1-28.
23. Baranzini, M. and G.C. Harcourt (eds.) (1994), *The Dynamics of the Wealth of Nations (Growth, Distribution and Structural Change), Essays in Honour of Luigi L. Pasinetti*, London: Macmillan.
24. Baranzini, M. and R. Scazzieri (eds.) (1986), *Foundations of Economics. Structures of Inquiry and Economic Theory*, Oxford and New York: Basil Blackwell.
25. Bertaux, D. and P. Thompson (eds.) (1997), *Pathways to Social Class (A Qualitative Approach to Social Mobility)*, Oxford: Clarendon Press.
26. Bevan, D. L. (1974), "Savings, Inheritance and Economic Growth in the Presence of Earning Inequality", mimeo, St. John's College, University of Oxford.
27. Bevan, D. L. (1979), "Inheritance and the Distribution of Wealth", *Economica*, 381-402.
28. Bortis, H. (1976), "On the Determination of the Level of Employment in a Growing Economy", *Revue Suisse d'Economie Politique et de Statistique*, 112, 67-93.
29. Bortis, H. (1997), *Institutions, Behaviour and Economic Theory*, Cambridge: Cambridge University Press.
30. Britto, R. (1969), "The Life-Cycle Savings in a Two-Class Growth Model", paper presented at the December meeting of the Econometric Society, New York.
31. Britto, R. (1972), "On Differential Savings Propensities in Two-Class Growth Models", *The Review of Economic Studies*, 40, 491-4.
32. Britto, R. (1973), "Some Recent Development in the Theory of Economic Growth: An Interpretation", *Journal of Economic Literature*, 1343-66.
33. Campa, G. (1975) "Indeterminatezza del saggio di profitto nel paradosso di Pasinetti", *Giornale degli Economisti e Annali di Economia*, 16-55.
34. Chiang, A. C. (1973), "A Simple Generalisation of the Kaldor-Pasinetti Theory of the Profit Rate and Income Distribution", *Economica*, 40, 311-13.
35. Craven, J. (1979), *The Distribution of the Product*, London: Allen & Unwin.
36. Dalziel, P. C. (1989), "Cambridge (UK) versus Cambridge (Mass.): A Keynesian Solution of the Pasinetti Paradox", *Journal of Post-Keynesian Economics*, 11, 648-53.
37. Dalziel, P. C. (1991), "A Generalisation and Simplification of the Cambridge Theorem with Budget Deficits", *Cambridge Journal of Economics*, 15.3, 288-300.
38. Denicolò, V and M. Matteuzzi (1990), "Public Debt and the Pasinetti Paradox", *Cambridge Journal of Economics*, 14, 339-44.
39. Domenghino, C.-M. (1982), *Die Weiterentwicklung der postkeynesianischen Verteilungstheorie*, Berne and Frankfurt: Peter Lang.
40. Dow, S. C. (1985), *Macroeconomic Thought. A Methodological Approach*, Oxford and

New York: Basil Blackwell.
41. Dutt, A. K. and E.J. Amadeo (1994), "A Post-Keynesian Theory of Growth, Interest and Money", in M. Baranzini and G. C. Harcourt (eds.) *The Dynamics of the Wealth of Nations (Growth, Distribution and Structural Change) Essays in Honour of Luigi L. Pasinetti*, London: Macmillan, 181-205.
42. Eichner, A. S. and J.A. Kregel (1975), "An Essay on Post-Keynesian Theory: A New Paradigm in Economics", *Journal of Economic Literature*, 1293-314.
43. Ewijk, C. van ,(1991), *On the Dynamics of Growth and Debt*, Oxford: Clarendon Press.
44. Fazi, E. and N. Salvadori (1981), "The Existence of a Two-Class Economy in the Kaldor Model of Growth and Distribution", *Kyklos*, 34, 582-92.
45. Fleck, F. H. and C.-M. Domenghino (1987), "Cambridge (UK) versus Cambridge (Mass.): A Keynesian Solution of the "Pasinetti Paradox" ", *Journal of Post-Keynesian Economics*, 22-36.
46. Flemming, J. S. (1979), "The Effects of Earnings Inequality, Imperfect Capital Markets, and Dynastic Altruism on the Distribution of Wealth in Life-Cycle Models", *Economica*, 363-80.
47. Gupta, K. L. (1976), "Differentiated Interest Rate and Kaldor-Pasinetti Paradoxes", *Kyklos*, 29.2, 310-14.
48. Hahn, F. H. and R.C.O. Matthews (1964), "The Theory of Economic Growth: A Survey", *The Economic Journal*, 74, 779-902.
49. Harcourt, G. C. (1972), *Some Cambridge Controversies in the Theory of Capital*, Cambridge: Cambridge University Press.
50. Hattori, Y. (1975), "A Note on Pasinetti's Theorem", *Bulletin of University of Osaka Prefecture*, 13-15.
51. Hicks, J. (1965), *Capital and Growth*, Oxford: Oxford University Press.
52. Horioka, C. Y. and W. Watanabe (1997), "Why do People Save? A Micro-Analysis of Motives for Household Saving in Japan?", *The Economic Journal*, 107, 537-52.
53. Kaldor, N. (1956), "Alternative Theories of Distribution", *The Review of Economic Studies*, 83-100.
54. Kaldor N. (1960), "A Rejoinder of Mr. Atsumi and Professor Tobin", *The Review of Economic Studies*, 28, 121-3.
55. Kaldor, N. (1966), "Marginal Productivity and the Macro-Economic Theories of Distribution", *The Review of Economic Studies*, 33, 309-19.
56. Kessler, D. and A. Masson (eds.) (1988), *Modelling the Accumulation and Distribution of Wealth*, Oxford: Oxford University Press.
57. Kotlikoff, L. J. and L.H. Summers (1980), "The Role of Intergenerational Transfers in Aggregate Capital Accumulation", (Working Paper No. 445), Washington, DC: National Bureau of Economic Research.
58. Kubota, K. (1968), "A Re-Examination of the Existence and Stability Propositions in Kaldor's Growth Models", *The Review of Economic Studies*, 353-60.
59. Kurz, H. and N. Salvadori (eds.) (1998), *Growth and Distribution*, Aldershot: E. Elgar.
60. Maneschi, A. (1974), "The Existence of a Two-Class Economy in the Kaldor and Pasinetti Models of Growth and Distribution", *The Review of Economic Studies*, 42,

149-50.
61. Meade, J. E. (1963), "The Rate of Profits in a Growing Economy", *The Economic Journal*, 73, 665-74.
62. Meade, J. E. (1966), "The Outcome of the Pasinetti Process: A Note", *The Review of Economic Studies*, 34, 61-78.
63. Miyazaki, K. (1991), "On the Neo-Keynesian Interpretation of the Anti-Pasinetti Theory", *Oxford Economic Papers*, 43.2, 187-94.
64. Modigliani, F. (1970), "The Life-Cycle Hypothesis of Saving and Intercountry Differences in the Saving Ratio", in W. A. Eltis, M. FG. Scott, and J. N. Wolfe, *Induction, Growth and Trade (Essays in Honour of Sir Roy Harrod)*, Oxford: Clarendon Press, 197-225.
65. Modigliani, F. (1988), "Measuring the Contribution of Inter-generational Transfers to Total Wealth: Conceptual Issues and Empirical Findings", in D. Kessler, and A. Masson (eds.) *Modelling the Accumulation and Distribution of Wealth*, op. cit., 21-52.
66. Moore, A. M. (1967), "A Reformulation of the Kaldor Effect', *The Economic Journal*, 77, 84-99.
67. Moore, B. J. (1974), "The Pasinetti Paradox Revisited", *The Review of Economic Studies*, 42, 297-9.
68. Morishima, M. (1997), "Pasinetti's Growth and Income Distribution Revisited", *The Journal of Economic Literature*, 56-61.
69. Panico, C. (1984), "Interest and Profit in the Theories of Value and Distribution", Ph. D. Thesis, University of Cambridge.
70. Panico, C. (1985), "Market Forces and the Relation Between the Rates of Interest and Profits", *Contributions to Political Economy*, 37-60.
71. Pasinetti, L. L. (1962), "The Rate of Profit and Income Distribution in Relation to the Rate of Economic Growth", *The Review of Economic Studies*, 29, 267-79.
72. Pasinetti, L. L. (1964), "A Comment on Professor Meade's Rate of Profit in A Growing Economy", *The Economic Journal*, 74, 488-9.
73. Pasinetti, L. L. (1966a) "The Rate of Profit in A Growing Economy: A Reply", *The Economic Journal*, 76, 158-60.
74. Pasinetti, L. L. (1966b), "New Results in an Old Framework: Comment on Samuelson and Modigliani", *The Review of Economic Studies*, 33, 303-6.
75. Pasinetti, L. L. (1974), *Growth and Income Distribution. Essays in Economic Theory*, Cambridge: Cambridge University Press.
76. Pasinetti, L. L. (1975), "Determinatezza del saggio di profitto nella teoria post-keynesiana: risposta al Professor Campa", *Giornale degli Economisti e Annali di Economia*, 34, 639-47.
77. Pasinetti, L. L. (1983), "Conditions of Existence of a Two Class Economy in the Kaldor and More General Models of Growth and Income Distribution", *Kyklos*, 34, 91-102.
78. Pasinetti, L. L. (1987), " "Satisfactory" versus Optimal Economic Growth", *Rivista Internazionale di Scienze Economiche e Commerciali*, 34, 989-1000.
79. Pasinetti, L. L. (1989a), "Ricardian Debt/Taxation Equivalence in the Kaldor Theory of Profits and Income Distribution", *Cambridge Journal of Economics*, 13, 25-36.
80. Pasinetti, L. L. (1989b), "Government Deficit Spending is not Incompatible with

the Cambridge Theorem of the Rate of Profit: A Reply to Fleck and Domenghino", *Journal of Post-Keynesian Economics*, 11.3, 641-7.
81. Ramanathan, R. (1976), "The Pasinetti Paradox in a Two-Class Monetary Growth Model", *Journal of Monetary Economics*, 389-97.
82. Rau, N. (1972), "Two-Class Neoclassical Growth: A Conjecture Proved", *Quarterly Journal of Economics*, 344-5.
83. Robinson, J. V. (1966), "Comment on Samuelson and Modigliani", *The Review of Economic Studies*, 33.4, 307-8.
84. Samuelson, P. A. and F. Modigliani (1966a), "The Pasinetti Paradox in Neoclassical and More General Models", *The Review of Economic Studies*, 33, 269-302.
85. Samuelson, P. A. and F. Modigliani (1966b), "Reply to Pasinetti and Robinson", *The Review of Economic Studies*, 33.4, 321-30.
86. Samuelson, P. A. (1991), "Extirpating Error Contamination Concerning the Post-Keynesian Anti-Pasinetti Equilibrium", *Oxford Economic Papers*, 43.2, 177-86.
87. Sato, K. (1966), "The Neoclassical Theorem and Distribution of Income and Wealth", *The Review of Economic Studies*, 33, 331-6.
88. Sheng Cheng Hu (1973), "On Optimal Capital Accumulation in a Two Class Model of Economic Growth", *Metroeconomica*, 229-49.
89. Steedman, I. (1972), "The State and the Outcome of the Pasinetti Process", *The Economic Journal*, 82, 1387-95.
90. Targetti, F. (1992), *Nicholas Kaldor: The Economics and Politics of Capitalism as a Dynamic System*, Oxford: Clarendon Press.
91. Targetti, F. (1993), "Vecchie e nuove teorie della crescita: una rassegna", *Economia politica*, 10.2, 261-349.
92. Teixeira, J. R. (1991), "The Kaldor-Pasinetti Process Reconsidered", *Metroeconomica*, 42.3, 257-67.
93. Teixeira, J. R. and J.T. Araùjo (1991), "A Note on Dalziel's Model of Long-Run Distributive Equilibrium", *Journal of Post-Keynesian Economics*, 14.1, 117-20.
94. Teixeira, J. R., R.N. Sugahara and M. Baranzini (1998), "The Micro-Foundations of the Kaldor-Pasinetti Growth Model with Taxation on Inter-Generational Bequest", mimeo, University of Southern Switzerland, Lugano.
95. Tobin, J. (1960), "Towards A General Kaldorian Theory of Distribution", *The Review of Economic Studies*, 27, 11-20.
96. Vaughan, R. N (1971), "The Pasinetti Paradox in Neoclassical and More General Models: A Correction", *The Review of Economic Studies*, 38, 271.
97. Vaughan, R. N. (1979), "Class Behaviour and the Distribution of Wealth', *The Review of Economic Studies*, 46, 447-65.

Panel Data Econometrics: Future Directions
J. Krishnakumar and E. Ronchetti (Editors)

CHAPTER 15

PUBLIC DEBT IN THE EUROPEAN UNION COUNTRIES: Two Ways of Facing the Problem*

Luigi L. PASINETTI

Abstract

The author, after briefly reviewing previous contributions of his on sustainability, resumes a relation involving 3 magnitudes (deficit/GDP ratio, debt/GDP ratio, and rate of growth). He defines - algebraically and graphically - the boundary to the area of sustainability of public finance. He shows how the parameters given in the famous Annex to the Maastricht Treaty only represent one particular point on such boundary. Then, the author concentrates on the burden of public debt for the community as a whole (in

****A personal note**: I am pleased to be a contributor to the *Papers in Honour of Pietro Balestra*, by now a leading econonometrician both in Western Europe and in the United States. A number of threads link me personally to him. Our acquaintance goes back to the mid-Sixties, when he had just been appointed to the Chair of Econometrics at the University of Fribourg. I happened to be attracted to Fribourg for personal reasons. I thus came across Pietro Balestra, who from 1965, among other things, taught a special degree course, *Questions spéciales d'économie politique*, centred on classical, neo-classical and post-Keynesian distribution theories. Many of his students (let me mention in particular: Henrich Bortis and Mauro Baranzini) later contributed substantially to the development of Keynesian economics. More recently, Pietro Balestra and I have been involved, with a small number of senior economists, in the project for the creation of a Faculty of Economics, at the newly-established Università della Svizzera italiana in Lugano. By becoming its first Dean, Pietro Balestra is providing the Faculty with strong academic and scientific leadership.

The topic I have chosen for my essay is meant to link up with the spirit of Pietro Balestra's Fribourg lectures on *Questions spéciales d'économie politique*. At a time when the newly-founded European Union is in need of an imaginative economic and monetary policy, Keynesian economics seems to be crying out for a thorough re-visitation.

This paper incorporates arguments and proposals that were made at a meeting on Public Debt held at the Accademia dei Lincei, Rome, on April 24, 1998 (see *Rendiconti Classe Scienze Morali, Accademia Nazionale dei Lincei*, serie IX, vol. IX, pp. 509-525).

I am grateful to Simona Cain for translation work and secretarial help. Financial support from the Italian Ministry for University and Research (MURST 40%) is also acknowledged.

terms of extra taxation necessary to service the debt) . He introduces the concept of iso-social-burden curve, which represents all combinations of debt/GDP and $(i-g)$ that entail the same social burden. He concludes that the usual way of aiming at decreasing the social burden, by cutting down public debt, is not the only way to pursue such aim. Another, much neglected but very important, way is to aim at decreasing $(i-g)$, that is at decreasing the difference between rate of interest and rate of growth. If such a difference were to be reduced to zero, the burden of public debt would also be reduced to zero, whatever the magnitude of the debt/GDP ratio may be.

1. INTRODUCTION

The problem of public debt has of late attracted increasing attention, especially as a consequence of the Maastricht Treaty, which - among other things - has required E.U. countries not to exceed a public debt/GDP ratio of 60% and a deficit/GDP ratio of 3%. Whereas the majority of E.U. countries are in fact satisfying these requirements, two countries (Belgium and Italy) happen to be conspicuously far from the mark, with a public debt/GDP ratio exceeding 120%, though they have managed to cut their deficits to the required level.

2. SUSTAINABILITY OF PUBLIC FINANCE AND RELATIVE POSITIONS OF E.U. COUNTRIES AT THE END OF 1997

It is reasonable to wonder seriously how any country is to face a high level of public debt. This is a problem that arises *regardless* of the causes of that debt. The obvious question is: at what point does public debt become unsustainable?

To answer this question correctly, one needs to distinguish between two quite separate issues: that of the level of the public debt and that of its rate of change in time.

A positive rate of change of the debt/GDP ratio, especially if it is persistent and not merely temporary, is a *prima facie* indication of fiscal disorder, and should immediately ring alarm bells. It is rather frightening to notice that this has been the case for several governments' budgets since the early Sixties, and that no country ever did much about it. But things have changed lately. Since 1993, we have witnessed a general, across-the-board, drop of debt figures, expressed as a percentage of GDP.

The other issue, that of the *level* of public debt, is a rather different matter. When the public debt level, however high, is *stable* and - more importantly - when it decreases with time, it implies a surplus of the primary public budget (that is of the public budget *excluding* interests) sufficient to cover entirely the payment of interests and also to repay at least part of the outstanding debt. This is precisely what has been happening in the last few years.

If we take such a situation as one that defines a sustainable financial position, it is easy to notice how the two 'reference figures', already mentioned and specified in the *Additional Protocol* of the Maastricth Treaty (namely, 3% for the total deficit/GDP ratio, and 60% for the public debt/GDP ratio), are but one of *many* pairs of 'values' which satisfy the 'sustainability of public expenditure' criterion defined above. (On this point the reader may be referred back to three previous articles of mine: Pasinetti, 1997a, 1998a, 1998b.) The picture presented in these publications shows that the sustainability area in the case of public debt may be represented by a relation between surplus (or deficit) and public debt for any given growth rate of GDP. There are two alternative versions of this relation, according to whether it is referred to the total surplus (or deficit) or to the primary surplus (or deficit).

Following the above-mentioned references, I shall use the symbols:

$D > 0$	: end-of-year public debt;
Y	: annual Gross Domestic Product (GDP), in nominal terms;
g	: (annual) nominal growth rate of GDP
$S^{(p)}$	: (annual) primary public surplus (or deficit, if negative);
$S = -\Delta D$	: (annual) total public unbalance (surplus or deficit);
i	: (annual) nominal rate of interest.

By using the first of the two versions just mentioned, the boundary relation between total surplus (or deficit) and public debt is:

$$\frac{S}{Y} = -g\frac{D}{Y} \quad , \tag{1}$$

while the sustainability area of the debt (and of the overall deficit) may be expressed algebraically as follows:

$$\frac{S}{Y} \geq -g\frac{D}{Y} \quad , \tag{1-bis}$$

and graphically by Figure 1.

In the second version, the boundary relation between primary deficit (or surplus) and public debt is:

$$\frac{S^{(p)}}{Y} = (i - g)\frac{D}{Y} \quad , \tag{2}$$

while the sustainability area of the debt (and of the primary deficit or surplus) may be expressed algebraically as:

$$\frac{S^{(p)}}{Y} \geq (i - g)\frac{D}{Y} \quad , \tag{2-bis}$$

and graphically by Figure 2.

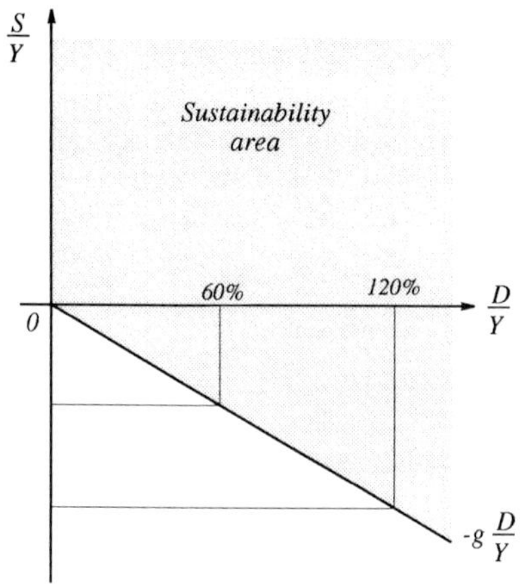

Figure 1. Sustainability Area with Regard to the Total Deficit/GDP Ratio (for $g > 0$).

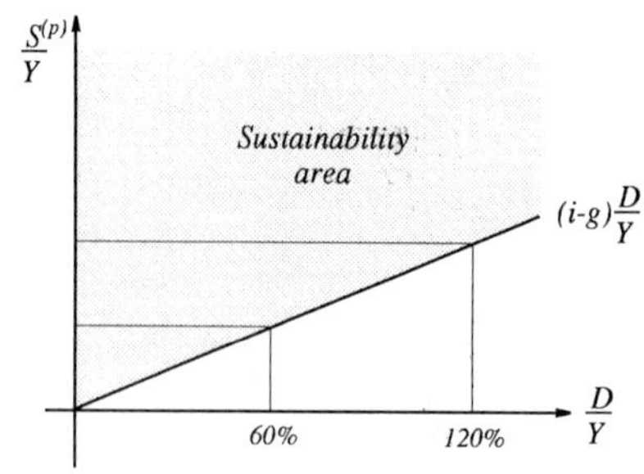

Figure 2. Sustainability Area with Regard to Primary Surplus (Deficit)/GDP Ratio (for $i > g$).

Tables 1 and 2 (which update those included in Pasinetti, 1998b) have been constructed by applying formulae (1) and (2). These Tables avail themselves of official end-of-1997 figures published by OECD (1997) and by EMI (1998).

In Table 1, columns 1, 2, and 3 show the three relevant magnitudes (debt/GDP ratio, nominal rate of growth, and deficit/GDP ratio), at end of 1997, concerning the 15 E.U. member countries, including those countries (Denmark, Sweden and Great Britain) that have decided *not* to join the single currency in its first stage.

Column 4 shows the computation of relation (1), as applied to each country. Each figure represents the maximum budget deficit each country can sustain; more precisely, it indicates the maximum hypothetical ratio between deficit and GDP that each country can afford, while keeping a non-increasing public debt/GDP ratio, whatever this ratio may have been at the beginning of the year. It represents, so to speak, each country's watershed between sustainability and divergence.

Column 5 shows the gap between the corresponding magnitudes in columns 3 and 4. Each figure in column 5 expresses the *distance* in number of percentage points, of the actual debt/GDP ratio from the hypothetical borderline ratio – a positive distance if the country lies within the sustainability area, a negative distance if it is outside. Since each year's deficit goes to increase the outstanding debt, the higher the figures – that is, the wider the gap between actual budget deficit and hypothetical deficit which would nevertheless keep the debt/GDP ratio constant, the higher the speed at which the debt decreases. That is why the figures (in percentage points) in column 5 may be seen as *indices of the speed of convergence* when positive (or of divergence when negative).

Table 1
Situation of the E.U. Countries with Regard to the Relation between the Total Deficit and Public Debt (as % of GDP) at end 1997.

	(1)	(2)	(3)	(4)	(5)
	D/Y	g	S/Y	$-gD/Y$	$S/Y - gD/Y$
Italy	121.6	4.0	-2.7	-4.86	2.16
Germany	61.3	3.3	-2.7	-2.02	-0.68
France	58.0	3.3	-3.0	-1.91	-1.09
United Kingdom	53.4	5.8	-1.9	-3.10	1.20
Spain	68.8	5.2	-2.6	-3.58	0.98
Belgium	122.2	4.2	-2.1	-5.13	3.03
The Netherlands	72.1	5.8	-1.4	-4.18	2.78
Ireland	66.3	8.1	-0.9	-5.37	4.47
Greece	108.7	10.1	-4.0	-10.98	6.98
Finland	55.8	5.8	-0.9	-3.24	2.34
Luxemburg	6.7	5.5	1.7	-0.37	2.07
Austria	66.1	3.7	-2.5	-2.45	-0.05
Portugal	62.0	6.5	-2.5	-4.03	1.53
Denmark	65.1	5.9	0.7	-3.84	4.54
Sweden	76.6	3.6	-0.8	-2.76	1.96

Source: adapted from OECD and EMI data.

Table 2, because of its similarity to Table 1, does not need to be illustrated in detail. It refers to relation (2), i.e. to the *primary* version of the deficit-debt relation. Column 7 provides us with an alternative version of the distance of the actual position of each country from the borderline of the sustainability area. Here, too, the distance may be considered as an index of the speed of convergence (if positive) or of divergence (if negative).

One may notice that, at the end of 1997, all E.U. countries lie inside the sustainability area, when this is expressed in terms of relation (1), except for France, Germany and Austria (which runs counter to what is commonly taken for granted in current debate). When the sustainability area is defined in terms of relation (2), two further countries (the United Kingdom and Sweden, who in any case have decided not to take part in the first stage of the single currency experiment) end up outside it, though by very little. The discrepancy, however, is not significant[1].

Needless to say, all E.U. countries have hastened to apply drastic measures to force their public budgets into the sustainability zone.

Table 2

Situation of the E.U. Countries with Regard to the Relation between Primary Deficit (or Surplus) and Public Debt (as % of GDP) at end 1997

	(1)	(2)	(3)	(4)	(5)	(6)	(7)
	D/Y	i	g	$(i-g)$	$S^{(p)}/Y$	$(i-g)D/Y$	$S^{(p)}/Y-$ $(i-g)D/Y$
Italy	121.6	6.8	4.0	2.8	5.2	3.40	1.80
Germany	61.3	5.7	3.3	2.4	0.2	1.47	-1.27
France	58.0	5.7	3.3	2.4	0.4	1.39	-0.99
United Kingdom	53.4	7.0	5.8	1.2	0.4	0.64	-0.24
Spain	68.8	6.5	5.2	1.3	1.5	0.89	0.61
Belgium	122.2	5.8	4.2	1.6	5.1	1.96	3.14
The Netherlands	72.1	5.7	5.8	-0.1	2.3	-0.07	2.37
Ireland	66.3	6.5	8.1	-1.6	3.7	-1.06	4.76
Greece	108.7	10.3	10.1	0.2	5.0	0.22	4.78
Finland	55.8	4.8	5.8	-1.0	0.6	-0.56	1.16
Luxemburg	6.7		5.5				
Austria	66.1	5.8	3.7	2.1	0.6	1.39	-0.79
Portugal	62.0	6.5	6.5	0.0	1.7	0.00	1.70
Denmark	65.1	6.4	5.9	0.5	2.7	0.33	2.37
Sweden	76.6	6.7	3.6	3.1	1.9	2.37	-0.47

Source: adapted from OECD and EMI data. (Where data were not available, cells have been left blank)

[1] Tables 1 and 2 use the same OECD data. The explanation of the small discrepancies is that the rate of interest that appears in Table 2 is the current rate of interest. In Table 1, on the other hand, the rate of interest enters indirectly the total amount of the government deficit. It refers to the interest actually paid on the outstanding debt. Since the debt was contracted at different dates in the past, the rate of interest actually paid may be different from the current one.

3. THE QUESTION OF A HIGH LEVEL OF PUBLIC DEBT

Having ascertained that at present all E.U. countries' public budgets lie either within the sustainability area, or not far off, there remains for us to consider the position of those countries where the level of public debt is much higher than average (specifically, Belgium and Italy). Their present positions raise certain questions. Is it justifiable or realistic to request that their public debt should be reduced? And if so, by how much? And how fast? We should stress that the official answer to these questions is already contained in the Maastricht Treaty, namely that the higher public debts must decrease. The 60% 'reference value' for the debt/GDP ratio is not simply considered as one of the many figures on the boundary line; it is given as a precise figure towards which the public debts of all countries should converge. How rapidly they should converge has not been clearly defined. Rather vaguely, the Treaty states that the debt must decrease "sufficiently and ... [in such a way as to] move closer to the reference value (60%) at an adequate pace" (art.104c).

Moreover, it must be added that an agreement, known as the 'stability and growth pact', has recently been underwritten by E.U. representatives that goes even further than demanding a straightforward reduction of public debt. It confirms the 3% figure for the overall deficit/GDP ratio, independently of the level of the debt/GDP ratio. Hence, this dictates that the debt is to be reduced at a pace which is the faster the higher the original level of the debt/GDP ratio. One may well accept that this generates financial stability. It is however doubtful that it may bring about 'growth'. What is more, some representatives of the E.U. countries have openly declared that in future they intend to go much further than the Maastricht Treaty, and aim at a zero public debt.

On these problems I should like to introduce a discordant view.

Obviously it is important to grasp what underlies the widespread preoccupations with a high public debt. Two of these preoccupations appear the most relevant.

(i) It is said that we do not want to burden our children (and grandchildren) with a high level of public debt. Yet this argument should be stretched further, at least to take into the account also the private sector's indebtedness. Now, no sooner one does this, then one realises that the total private debt (in relation to GDP) is lower in those industrialised countries (such as Belgium and Italy) that show high public indebtedness, while total indebtedness (public plus private) turns out to be roughly of the same order of magnitude relatively to GDP. I have shown this in Pasinetti, 1998a, 1998b. This means that the difference between high publicly indebted and low publicly indebted industrialised countries boils down to different *proportions* between public and private debts, while *total* indebtedness appears to be roughly at the same level. It seems therefore that in some countries the accumulation of public debt has crowded out private debt. If this is so, one legitimately wonders: is it really important – now that sustainability has been achieved – to request high primary surpluses, merely so that the proportion between public and private indebtedness may change fast? One must not forget that the process of privatization of public companies, now under way everywhere, and the efforts made to extend private financial markets are in any case leading in this direction. (In other words, granted that the sustainability zone will not be abandoned, public debt will of necessity decrease.)

(ii) It is also said that, when financial markets go through turbulent periods, a rise in interest rates may render the countries with high public debts particularly vulnerable. And yet the same turbulence of international financial markets may equally render vulnerable the financial structures of the private sector. Suffice it to think of recent events in the Asian financial markets, which if nothing else show how the public sector is severely affected by bankruptcies in the private sector.

To conclude, it seems to me that there is no good reason for the concern mentioned above, whereas it is no doubt essential that public debt should be kept within sustainable boundaries.

Something else needs to be said. In all discussions that have been carried out on the subject, no convincing theoretical basis has been found for fixing a satisfactory 'optimum' level of the public debt (expressed in % of GDP). In the economic literature on the sustainability of public debt (for a comprehensive overview, see Blanchard *et al.*, 1990) the ideal level of the public debt/GDP ratio is taken as given from outside, i.e. as a subject for exogeneous decisions, with respect to economic investigation.

What truly matters at this stage, it seems to me, is to move on to an objective assessment of what a high level of public debt entails, compared to any alternative. More concretely, we should seriously enquire on what additional social burden is materializing in any country where the level of public debt is higher than that of its neighbours. All other things being equal, such a social burden is represented by the higher fiscal pressure which is necessary in order to cope with interest payments. But how much higher is this fiscal pressure going to be? This is the point that needs clarification.

4. THE 'SOCIAL BURDEN' OF PUBLIC DEBT

Let us turn the problem upside down and begin to ask what social burden – in the sense specified above – derives, in high public debt countries, from a hypothetical stand to keep the public debt at its present level, whatever this level may be. Evidently, a public debt involves interest payments. Nevertheless, the burden for the community does not necessarily coincide with such payments. To be more precise, a certain expenditure turns out to be a 'burden' for the community concerned only insofar as, provided that the public debt is kept within sustainable limits, the State is obliged to set up corresponding taxes and duties. If no such taxes and duties need to be imposed, then there is no social burden.

From this point of view, interest payments become a 'social burden' solely for that part that corresponds to the taxes that are necessary in order to achieve that primary surplus which is required to maintain the budget within the sustainability area. The remainder of interest payments can be added to the total public debt without increasing the debt/

GDP ratio, because GDP has meanwhile increased. This part of interest expenditure does not entail any 'social burden'.

This means that total interest payments and 'social burden' coincide only in the case of a stationary economy. By contrast, when the GDP is growing, there is a part of interest payments which (by being added to the debt, while keeping the debt/GDP ratio constant) requires no taxation and therefore entails no 'social burden'.

In formal terms, the 'social burden' of public debt may be denoted by t, defined as the tax rate (as a percentage of GDP) that needs to be imposed additionally, with respect to the case in which the public debt is zero. Such tax precisely coincides with the primary surplus (expressed as a percentage of GDP) which in figure 2 above stands on the very boundary line between the sustainability area and the non-sustainability area, and which is represented by algebraic relation (2).

By re-interpreting such relation (2), we may therefore say that the social burden of public debt is expressed by:

$$t = (i - g)\frac{D}{Y} \quad . \tag{3}$$

Rate t stands for the 'excess' of fiscal pressure that is necessary in a country with public debt, as against in a country without any public debt.

A careful look to relation (3) shows that the 'social burden' of public debt, t, would of course decrease any time that D/Y is reduced (provided $i - g > 0$). However, this is not the only way to reducing t. Another way is afforded by those economic policies that bring about a reduction of the interest rate, i. A third way is afforded by those economic policies that lead to an increase of the growth rate of GDP, g.

In sum, the 'social burden' of public debt, as relation (3) clearly shows, depends both on the D/Y ratio and on the algebraic difference $(i - g)$, all of these magnitudes being expressed in nominal terms.

5. THE IMPORTANCE OF THE ALGEBRAIC DIFFERENCE BETWEEN RATE OF INTEREST AND RATE OF GROWTH

The elaborations of the previous section elicits a few further remarks that seem relevant. If we fix a pre-determined t (the tax rate with regard to GDP), that represents the top limit for the 'social burden' of interest payments that a community does not want to exceed; formula (3) describes a curve which, as can be seen, is an equilateral hyperbola, asymptotically approaching the two axes in the two variables $(i - g)$ and D/Y. Such equilateral hyperbola stands for what may be termed an 'iso-cost' curve or an 'iso-social burden' curve. It shows all the infinite possible combinations of the (stabilised) D/Y ratio and the percentage points of the $(i - g)$ algebraic difference, which entail exactly the same social burden, t, fixed in advance.

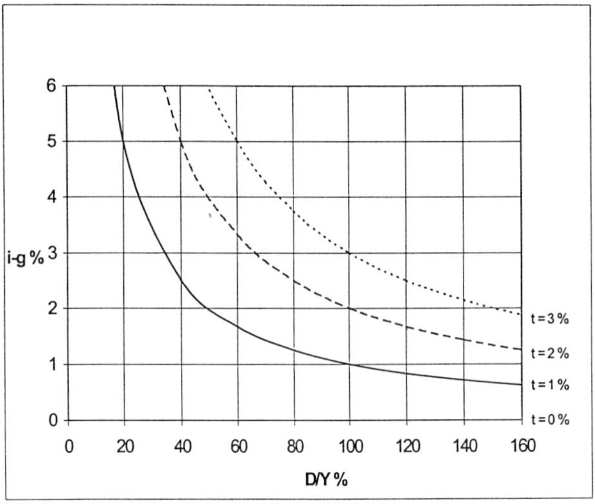

Figure 3. 'Iso-social Burden' Curves.

Figure 3 shows three of such iso-curves, for $t = 3\%$, $t = 2\%$ and $t = 1\%$. We may even consider the two asymptotes, i.e. the two cartesian axes, as a fourth case; namely the extreme case where the curve itself has been flattened to the point of adhering asymptotically to the cartesian axes and to yield $t = 0$, i.e. a zero social burden.

Looking carefully at the shape of these curves, we may compare the two numerical cases empirically relevant to our purpose, namely $(D/Y) = 120\%$ and $(D/Y) = 60\%$.

In order not to exceed a pre-determined 'social burden' of 3% of GDP, when ratio $(D/Y) = 120\%$ one must obtain a difference $(i - g) < 2.5$ percentage points; whereas if ratio $(D/Y) = 60\%$, the same result is reached with a difference that may be as high as $(i - g) < 5$ percentage points. Similarly, in order not to exceed a pre-determined 'social burden' of 2% of GDP, the same comparison yields $(i-g) < 1.66$ percentage points, when ratio $(D/Y) = 120\%$ and $(i - g) < 3.33$ percentage points, when ratio $(D/Y) = 60\%$. Finally, for $t = 1\%$, we get $(i - g) < 0.8$ percentage points when ratio $(D/Y) = 120\%$, and $(i - g) < 1.66$ percentage points when ratio $(D/Y) = 60\%$.

As may be seen, for each pre-determinate rate t fixed in advance, the smaller the difference between interest rate and growth rate, the less relevant the consequences of different alternative levels of the public debt.

These comparisons rather strikingly show how crucial the algebraic difference $(i - g)$ is for the social burden of public debt. When such difference is small, the social burden of public debt boils down to precious little. The last and extreme case, which is referred to above as the 'fourth case' , is an eye-opener. When $(i - g)$ is reduced to zero, the social burden of interest payment is nil (i.e. $t = 0$) , whatever the (stabilised) level of the D/Y ratio may be!

6. TWO DIFFERENT WAYS OF REDUCING TO ZERO THE 'SOCIAL BURDEN' OF THE PUBLIC DEBT

The conclusions that follow from the analysis of the previous sections may sound surprising. Yet they are simple and clear.

There are two distinct ways of achieving $t = 0$, and thus of reducing to zero the social burden of public debt.

The first way is the obvious one: to achieve $D/Y = 0$, i.e. to eliminate the public debt altogether, whatever the level of interest rates may be. The second way is less obvious but equally effective: to achieve $(i - g) = 0$, i.e. to bring interest rate and growth rate into equality. This result holds, whatever the level of the (stabilised) D/Y ratio may be.

7. LOOKING AHEAD

The general trend of discussions and concern with the 'social burden' of public debt that has so far prevailed in the literature – and even more in official reports – has focused exclusively on an undertaking to reduce the level of the public debt. This is the first way stated above of dealing with the problem. It is the more obvious way, but it must be stressed that it is also the more costly way. It entails not only a social burden corresponding to the tax rate, t, of formula (3), but also an extra fiscal burden, each year, aimed at a reduction of D/Y. Our analysis shows that this extra fiscal burden can be avoided.

A reduction of the social burden of the public debt can be obtained in pursuing the second way indicated above, through internationally co-ordinated efforts – within a stable context! – designed to drive interest rates down and growth rates up, thereby producing a stunning triple benefit: to reduce fiscal pressure, to boost GDP growth and to curb unemployment.

One may wonder why this second way is, almost entirely, ignored.

An answer may perhaps be found in the events of the past few decades, which have often witnessed wild financial instability. In the face of strong volatility of exchange rates, nominal interest rates have tended to fluctuate sharply. Given such conditions, countries with a high public debt/GDP ratio have felt the pressure of financial markets requiring higher interest rates and shorter debt maturities. This may have engendered a sort of 'fear of the public debt', a conviction that high public debt/GDP ratios breed financial fragility.

But this conviction is no longer justified, after the introduction of a European single currency. What has happened in the past two decades becomes impossible now, since exchange rates are going to be abolished inside the E.U., and financial stability is to be achieved on a European scale.

The very period we are now entering appears to be ideal for facing the question of public debt in the second way shown above. This means pursuing a reduction (and ideally even an elimination) of the social burden of public debt, not through extra taxation, but through internationally co-ordinated efforts to achieve lower interest rates and higher growth rates.

REFERENCES

1. Blanchard, O., J.C. Chouraqui, R.P. Hagemann and N. Sartor (1990), "The sustainability of fiscal policy: new answers to an old question", *OECD Economic Studies*, no. 15, 7-36.
2. E.M.I. (European Monetary Institute), (1998), "Report on Convergence", Frankfurt: March, 1.
3. OECD (1997), "Perspectives Economiques de l'OCSE", no. 62, Paris.
4. Pasinetti, L.L. (1996), "L'onere sociale degli alti tassi di interesse", in Terenzio Cozzi, Pier CarloNicola, Luigi Pasinetti, Alberto Quadrio Curzio (eds), *Benessere, equilibrio e sviluppo. Studi in onore di Siro Lombardini*, vol. III, Vita e Pensiero, Milano, 191-202.
5. Pasinetti, L.L. (1997), "Macroeconomia dopo Keynes (e i vincoli dei parametri di Maastricht)", in *Rendiconti Classe Scienze Morali, Accademia Nazionale Lincei*, serie IX, vol. VIII, 763-807.
6. Pasinetti, L.L. (1998a), "The myth (or folly) of the 3% deficit/GDP Maastricht 'parameter' ", *Cambridge Journal of Economics*, 22, 103-16.
7. Pasinetti, L.L. (1998b), "European Union at the End of 1997: Who is Within the Public Finance 'Sustainability' Zone?", *BNL Quarterly Review*, no. 204, 17-36.

Index